Of the Nation Born

Of the Nation Born

The Bangladesh Papers

Edited by

HAMEEDA HOSSAIN
and
AMENA MOHSIN

With an Introduction by

MEGHNA GUHATHAKURTA

ZUBAAN SERIES ON SEXUAL VIOLENCE AND IMPUNITY IN SOUTH ASIA

Zubaan
128 B Shahpur Jat, 1st floor
NEW DELHI 110 049
Email: contact@zubaanbooks.com
Website: www.zubaanbooks.com

First published by Zubaan 2016

This project was undertaken with financial support provided by the International Development Research Centre, Canada

10 9 8 7 6 5 4 3 2 1

ISBN 978 93 84757 79 3

Zubaan is an independent feminist publishing house based in New Delhi with a strong academic and general list. It was set up as an imprint of India's first feminist publishing house, Kali for Women, and carries forward Kali's tradition of publishing world quality books to high editorial and production standards. *Zubaan* means tongue, voice, language, speech in Hindustani. Zubaan publishes in the areas of the humanities, social sciences, as well as in fiction, general non-fiction, and books for children and young adults under its Young Zubaan imprint.

Typeset in Adobe Arabic 14.5/14.5 by Jojy Philip, New Delhi 110 015
Printed and bound at Raj Press, R-3 Inderpuri, New Delhi 110 012

Contents

Interviews, Case Studies and Narratives

Zubaan Series on Sexual Violence and Impunity in South Asia

An Introduction

URVASHI BUTALIA, LAXMI MURTHY AND NAVSHARAN SINGH

The Sexual Violence and Impunity project (SVI) is a three-year research project, supported by the International Development Research Centre (IDRC), Canada, and coordinated by Zubaan. Led by a group of nine advisors from five countries (Bangladesh, India, Nepal, Pakistan, Sri Lanka), and supported by groups and individuals on the ground, the SVI project started with the objectives of developing and deepening understanding on sexual violence and impunity in South Asia through workshops, discussions, interviews and commissioned research papers on the prevalence of sexual violence, and the structures that provide impunity to perpetrators in all five countries.

The project began with some key questions and concerns. We noted that recent histories and contemporary political developments in South Asia had shown an exponential increase in sexual violence, particularly mass violence. And yet, even as such violence had increased across the region, so had the ever-deepening silence around it.

Why, for example, had the end of 25 years of violent conflict in Sri Lanka in May 2009 not resulted in an open and frank discussion about sexual violence as a weapon of war? Why had the International Crimes Tribunal (Bangladesh) of 2009 set up to investigate and prosecute suspects for the genocide committed in 1971 by the Pakistan Army and their local collaborators, paid such little attention to the question of mass rape, despite it being widely acknowledged that it had happened and many women having spoken out about it. Why did discussions on Kashmir in India or Swat in Pakistan, simply ignore the question of sexual violence? Why was caste violence, violence against sex workers and men and transgender persons barely spoken about?

Nor was silence the only issue here. Crucial to maintaining the silence was—and is—the active collusion of States in providing impunity to perpetrators, sometimes under the guise of protective laws and special powers to the armed forces, at others under the guise of nationalism. So heavily were the odds stacked against women that, until recently, very few had dared to speak out. Backed by culture, and strengthened by the State, and often with the active collusion of non-state actors, impunity then, remained largely unchallenged.

We asked ourselves if these conditions were specific to the South Asian region. Elsewhere in many parts of the world, we noted, rape was increasingly being discussed and accepted, not only as a weapon of war, but also as a crime against humanity and as an instrument of genocide. The 1998 Akeyesu judgment by the International Criminal Tribunal for Rwanda (ICTR) provided a clear definition of rape and delineated its elements as a crime against humanity and as an instrument of genocide. In the International Criminal Tribunal for the former Yugoslavia (ICTY) jurisprudence pioneered the approach that used acts of rape and other forms of sexual violence to include elements of other international crimes such as torture, enslavement, and persecution, which previously had not been litigated in the context of gender violence.

The Special Court for Sierra Leone (SCSL) brought into

jurisprudence on violations of international humanitarian law a particular form of sexual violence prevalent in the conflict in Sierra Leone – forced marriages. In this case, forced marriage was distinguished from sexual slavery or sexual crimes and argued as a crime against humanity. Building on the progressive development of the case law for sexual and gender-based violence under ICTR, ICTY and SCSL, the Rome Statute of the International Criminal Court (ICC) includes rape and forms of sexual violence as part of the crimes of Genocide, Crimes against Humanity, and War Crimes, and specifically enumerates rape, forced prostitution, sexual slavery, forced pregnancy, enforced sterilization and prosecution on account of gender as specific crimes punishable under the statute.

The progressive thinking developed in the course of these trials brought sexual violence into the mainstream of international jurisprudence (something that was largely invisible until the 1990s) such that it became part of the collective knowledge to which women's movements worldwide have contributed enormously. In South Asia a comprehensive and critical analysis of existing jurisprudence on sexual violence is a newly emerging area of scholarship, and a solid community of practice is still to emerge in this field. There are many dimensions of sexual violence – ranging from conceptual clarity on definitions of sexual violence, to legal, medical and forensic understandings of evidence gathering and monitoring and more - that remain inadequately explored.

South Asia has much to learn from advancements elsewhere. How do our countries expect a 'return' to peace (and we need to question the composition of such a peace) without addressing the question of the large-scale and calculated attack by perpetrators on women and the systematic violation of their right to bodily integrity and autonomy? How can this question be addressed without including rape and sexual violation squarely within definitions of crimes against humanity? What are the glaring silences of our domestic laws and policies? What do they have to say about the endemic sexual violence and rape driven by caste, ethnicity and religion? How can we think creatively about questions of reparation beyond the ways States in the region have done by ghettoizing women in rehabilitation camps where they remain stigmatized and marked as raped women to be separated from others, as we saw in India following the partition of 1947 and post-1971 relief measures in Bangladesh.

As feminist activists and academics we were—and continue to be—concerned about the growing violence and the serious and continuing lack of accountability on the part of States and governments, the failure to address the impunity enjoyed by perpetrators, the absence of effective mechanisms to provide justice and reparations, and the virtual indifference to the psychological damage suffered by victims, survivors and their families and communities. We feel that our collective inability and unwillingness to address the profound impact of such violence is a serious impediment to peace and justice in our region.

Our discussions began in January 2012, when a group of women from South Asia came together in a meeting facilitated by a small IDRC grant, to begin the process of thinking about these issues. We were concerned not only at the legal silences around the question of sexual violence and impunity, but also how deeply the 'normalization' of sexual violence and the acceptance of impunity, had taken root in our societies.

It became clear to us that women's movements across South Asia had made important contributions in bringing the issue of sexual violence and impunity to public attention. And yet, there were significant knowledge gaps, as we have pointed out earlier. However, an absence of adequate literature on the subject did not mean that there was nothing available. South Asia has a rich literary and scholarly tradition and indeed there is a fair amount of writing on sexual violence, and while impunity is not necessarily directly addressed in these writings, concern about it is implicit in most of them. We felt it was important to systematically understand the nature of impunity, and what legal, social and cultural norms States draw upon to enable and allow impunity for the perpetrators and to silence the demands for accountability. We thought, too, that it was important to document the lesser known ways in which women, and sometimes communities, create structures to deal with the trauma and dislocation caused by sexual violence. These stories had remained largely unknown. In much of caste violence in India for example, or in cases of feudal or tribal instances of retribution and punishment, the violation of women's bodies is an accepted way of establishing male superiority. And because these hierarchies of caste and tribe are so embedded even in the 'minds' of our secular, modern States, the victims/survivors often find solutions of their own, creating ways of ensuring some sense of justice.

It was out of these concerns that the SVI project grew. Over a period of time, we contacted scholars and researchers, conducted research, held several country meetings and a series of methodology workshops and, step by step, the project brought together a community of young researchers (we had consciously planned to stay away from established and overstretched scholars), more than 85 per cent of whom are, we are proud to say, under the age of 40. Our workshops focused on unpeeling the layers of impunity for sexual violence, on writing skills, on questions of ethics in researching subjects as sensitive as sexual violence, on the nature of evidence, on working with States and more.

During the time that the project has been under way, the region witnessed many changes—in the public domain, a changed public discourse, as well as legal reform as a result of feminist and human rights' activism. These critical moments found resonance in the ongoing research—and indeed many of our researchers were centrally involved in working for these changes—and pointed to directions for future work.

The gang-rape and subsequent death of a young student in Delhi in December 2012 culminated in mass public anger, and generated public debate and feminist interventions. The testimonies of feminist activists to the Justice Verma Committee, constituted to recommend amendments to the criminal law for sexual assault against women, were an outcome of decades of intense engagement of the women's movement in India. The occasion provided a moment of deep reflection on the questions which activists were already grappling with. It also led to serious questioning within the movement: why, for example, did caste rape, or rape by the army, not result in the same kind of outrage, the same explosion of anger as the incident of 16 December 2012 had done? In the open discussion with the Verma Committee, feminist activists' testimonies did not remain confined to amendments in the law but demonstrated a remarkable understanding as they presented the continuum of violence against women from home to communities to the frontiers of the nation states where women's safety and bodily integrity were threatened in the name of protection of the borders.

In a small but significant step towards challenging impunity, on 6 September 2015, an army court martial awarded life sentence to six of its personnel found guilty in the 'fake encounter' case of April 2010 when the army killed three youths in the Machil sector of Kupwara district of Indian Kashmir on the grounds that they were foreign militants. Even though the accused were not tried in a civil court, and the appeal process is ongoing, this conviction is significant since this is the first time army personnel in Kashmir have been handed life-terms on these charges.

Over in Sri Lanka, a significant judgment was the Jaffna High Court sentencing, on 7 October 2015, of four soldiers to 25 years rigorous imprisonment, compensation and reimbursement of legal fees for the 2010 gang-rape of a woman at a resettlement camp in Viswamadhu, Kilinochchi. Assigning culpability and ensuring strict punishment of the security personnel involved has been possible only with the sustained intervention of activists.

Undoubtedly, accountability has been a fraught issue across South Asia, especially when it comes to war crimes. December 2012 saw vehement protests in Bangladesh by the right-wing Jamaat-e-Islami supporters and their student wing, Bangladesh

Islami Chhatra Shibir, demanding the disbanding of the ICT of Bangladesh set up three years earlier to investigate and prosecute suspects for the genocide committed in 1971 during the Bangladesh Liberation War by the Pakistani Army and their local collaborators, Razakars, Al-Badr and Al-Shams. (https://en.wikipedia.org/wiki/International_Crimes_Tribunal_(Bangladesh)-cite_note-Wierda-1.) The vigorous counter protests, of those pressing for accountability and an end to impunity culminated in the 'Shahbag movement' – a popular students' movement for justice for war time crimes. The gazette notification recognition, on 12 October 2015, recognizing 41 Birangonas (war heroines) as freedom fighters for their contribution in the country's Liberation War in 1971 has been more than 40 years in the coming, but an official recognition that can be viewed as reparation for the stigma and suffering these women were made to face in addition to the sexual violence perpetrated on them.

In Sri Lanka, still staggering under the history ethnic conflict and the Eelam war that ended in 2009, the report of the Office of the High Commissioner for Human Rights (OHCHR) released in September 2015 concluded that there were reasonable grounds to believe that war crimes and/or crimes against humanity had been committed with regard to a variety of abuses, including sexual violence and other forms of torture; unlawful killings by all sides; forced recruitment of adults and recruitment of children as fighters by the LTTE and enforced disappearances. The report recommended several legal, justice and security sector reforms and establishment of an ad hoc hybrid justice mechanism integrating international judges, prosecutors, lawyers and investigators. In a move demonstrating the political will of the new regime to redress war-time human rights violations, a consensus resolution co-sponsored by Sri Lanka was passed on 1 October 2015 by the UN Human Rights Council encouraging the Government of Sri Lanka to implement its recommendations.

Following the end of Nepal's 10-year insurgency in 2006, while the Truth and Reconciliation Commission (TRC) made rape a crime for which amnesty cannot be granted, the 35-day statute of limitations for reporting of rape makes it virtually impossible for war-time rapes to go to court. Additionally, the TRC gave effective amnesty to those alleged to have been responsible for gross human rights violations and gives broad powers of reconciliation to the TRC, with the result that victims will be forced to give up their right to justice as part of the reconciliation process with the commission empowered to undertake mediation between victims and perpetrators even in the case of rape.

Over the three-year period since this project began, there have been amendments in the criminal law in India and the definition of sexual assault has expanded, we have gained considerable grounds in our understanding on impunity for sexual violence and consequently are better able to speak about it and to fight for justice. It is noteworthy that during the recent targeted violence in Muzzafarnagar in India in 2013, seven Muslim women who were brutally gang raped and sexually assaulted by men belonging to the other communities, filed writ petitions for protecting their right to life under Article 21. In a landmark judgment in March 2014, recognizing the rehabilitation needs of the survivors of targeted mass rape, the Supreme Court of India ordered that a compensation of INR 500,000 each for rehabilitation be paid to the women by the state government.

The 'Occupy Baluwatar' movement of December 2012 which some see as the ripple effects of the Delhi protests against sexual violence and demands for justice, had sexual violence and impunity at its centre. One of the major outcomes of the movement was the 27 November 2015 amendment broadening the definition of rape, bringing same-sex rape and marital rape into the ambit of law.

In Pakistan too, small steps forward were taken in the shape of a parliamentary panel approval in February 2015 of amendments in the anti-rape laws, supporting DNA profiling as evidence during the investigation and a prohibition on character assassination of rape victims during the trial. (http://tribune.com.pk/story/824931/on-the-anvil-senate-panel-approves-changes-in-anti-rape-laws/)

The eight volumes (one each on Bangladesh, Nepal, Pakistan and Sri Lanka, two on India, and two standalone books on impunity and on an incident of mass rape in Kunan Poshpora in Indian Kashmir) that comprise this series, are one of the many outcomes of this project. The collective knowledge built on the subject through workshops, discussion fora, testimonies and interviews is part of our collective repository and we are committed to making it available to be used by activists, students and scholars. Of the 50 papers that were commissioned, nearly all came in. Along the way, we tragically lost two of our co-travellers, our advisor, Sharmila Rege and our young Sri Lankan researcher, Priya Thangarajah. Both Sharmila and Priya had been central to this project, bringing their considerable knowledge, their activism, their commitment, to the work in hand. True to the feminist spirit of collectivity, their friends and colleagues rallied round to complete the work they had begun.

It is our hope that these volumes will begin the process of opening up the question of sexual violence and impunity in South Asia. The papers in these volumes, as well as the two standalone volumes, address many of the issues we have raised above, and yet, significant gaps remain. We have not been able to adequately address questions of sexual violence and caste, the question of male and transgender sexual violence, or violence on queer communities. We need to gather more evidence about sexual violence on sex workers, on agricultural workers, in urban workspaces and more. We can only say with some satisfaction that through this collective endeavour, through putting our heads together, a fairly solid beginning has been made, layers have started to be uncovered and speech is beginning to replace silence. This systematic effort has allowed us to give this critical issue the focused attention that it deserves.

Creating a community of researchers and activists, building a common understanding resting on a shared history but not guided by national interests of the countries can make a significant move towards peace building in a region fractured by political, religious and ethnic divides. The series of books and other resources are being launched with the hope they will inspire the next generation of scholars and activists to build on this knowledge, and broaden and deepen it to end impunity for sexual violence.

Kalpana Chakma

KABITA CHAKMA, 21 May 2015

How can we further our police investigation?
'Unless, a disappeared can appear
as a witness to her own disappearance,'
concludes the police-super's investigation report
of the 'Kalpana Chakma disappearance' case.

Kalpana is just a woman, belonging to an 'upa-jati', a 'sub-nation'.
The term 'upa-jati' is engraved in the grand narratives of the state.
It was an abduction from her home at gunpoint
in the bleak blackness of the early hours of 12 June 1996.
Dark Lallyaghona,
a village on the edge of the Kaptai lake.
The lake was created for electricity, for light.
It engulfed Kalpana's ancestral home.
Kalpana was abducted in front of widow Baduni,
her old, shrivelled, almost blind, loving mother,
and Charubala, her ever-amusing, lovely sister-in-law.
She was abducted with her two caring brothers,
Kalindi and Khudiram.
Their hands were tied behind their backs.
They were blindfolded.
And marched out of their home.

Khudiram was directed to walk
into the knee-deep lake water.
'Shoot him!' they ordered.
He jumped into the lake.
As the shot rang out, Kalindi ran for his life.
Over the deafening sound of the bullets
they heard Kalpana's last cry, 'Dada, Dada'.
The accused are from a 'jati', a 'nation'.
From and allied with a powerful institution.
The witnesses are her brothers,
who recognized some of the voices,
and some of the faces,
including Lieutenant Ferdous Khan
and Nurul Haq, a settler.
The report does not count the brothers as witnesses,
But names Kalpana, the disappeared, as the main witness.
Why worry about it?
This is the 21st century.
1996 is in the distant past.
Fuck your words,
fuck your sense of justice,
fuck your morality,
fuck your humanity,
fuck you, editors,
fuck you, writers,
fuck you, poets,
fuck you, journalists,
fuck you, protesters,
fuck you, justice seekers,
Fuck you, fuck you all.
Now, think of Kalpana.
A mighty woman.
No, no, it is a lie.
She is not a woman.

She is not human.
She is inhuman.
A super being,
or a sub-being.
She holds the possibility of appearing
from disappearance, slamming the guns.
She, perhaps, holds the possibility of returning
from the dead, if ever she was killed.
A 21-year-old.
An unassuming young woman.
A student.
A friend.
A revolutionary.
An ordinary, listed disappeared.
But, cracking the cruellest joke,
howling a mad demonic laugh,
she nourishes the jums of the Chittagong Hills with fire,
and floods the plains of Bangladesh in alluvial soil,
year after year …

How dare you, bitch, you smash our hearts.
How dare you, bitch, you question the satire of power.
How dare you, bitch, you shatter our sense of integrity.
How dare you, bitch, you shame our pride for humanity.
How dare you, bitch, you ignite our struggle for justice.

Kalpana Chakma, we love you.
You are the greatest bitch,
their greatest fear against injustice.

Preface

HAMEEDA HOSSAIN AND AMENA MOHSIN

This volume is a conversation of 'selves' with the 'self'. The journey began as a conversation among a group of women in South Asia. Violence against women, and a culture of silence and impunity surrounding this violence, has been a recurrent conversation amongst women across political boundaries. The beginning of war crimes trials in Bangladesh, post-conflict Sri Lanka and Nepal, and a marked and visible increase in violence against women in India and Pakistan provided a raw landscape where the issues could be memorialized, interpreted and debated.

Memory and forgetting are intimate partners. People have competing memories and competing amnesias. Whether these are conscious or dwell in the realm of the sub-conscious is also part of our constructed social reality, which has a dominant bearing on the political reality and state politics. One of the major objectives of this endeavour was to start a conversation with memory and memorialization while travelling through the difficult and varied terrains that women's struggles and movements have taken in different junctures of time and history.

While gender-based violence has formed an important dimension in women's struggles for autonomy, feminist interrogations into the prevalence of sexual violence in conflicts between states in South Asia and within communities have led us to a questioning of the sources of political and social impunity.

The studies of sexual violence in this volume have explored the feminist consciousness of how wars affect women and the course of their resistance. This is why our concerns go beyond the nationalistic discourse of the aggressor and victim, to a deeper awareness of how the violence continues to haunt women's lives even after the end of a conflict. The contributors to this volume have drawn upon their experiences, both as researchers and as participants in the women's movements, to historicize the course of women's struggles for justice. It is the perseverance of these women's movements, with the support of other groups in Bangladesh, that women survivors of sexual violence in militarized conflicts or in community strife have eventually found some space to voice their claims for justice. Earlier individual accounts by survivors, which appeared sporadically in print in a few publications that documented women's experiences of war and as victims and activists in the struggle for freedom, have been a source of strength for the women's movements. It is due to the large number of women who spoke out on how their lives were changed because they suffered rape and other forms of sexual violence that these issues were placed on the legal map of Bangladesh. Despite the stigma they faced because they were subjected to wartime rape or peacetime fatwa-instigated violence, many women have stood up to defy social humiliation and political neglect and demand legal accountability for the crimes. Survivors and women freedom fighters have spoken out from different platforms; some have testified on camera at the International Crimes Tribunal, while others have taken up legal cases against fatwa-givers. Finally, in 2015, the women survivors of wartime rape have received official recognition by the government. They resisted the military and continue to resist militarization.

This volume has been three years in the making. It began to take shape through discussions and dialogues sponsored by Zubaan and supported by the IDRC with researchers in five countries of

South Asia.[1] We must acknowledge the perseverance of Urvashi Butalia, Laxmi Murthy and their colleagues at Zubaan, which enabled us to share our perspectives across the region at several meetings: in Kathmandu in 2012 and Bangkok in 2013, followed by further reviews of ongoing research in Sri Lanka 2014. The papers included in this volume were also refined based on discussions with academics and activists in Dhaka in 2013. In these endeavours, Navsharan Singh's suggestions have moved forward our theorizing of the issues and methodologies. An understanding of how the dynamics of South Asian political and social conflicts underscore impunity for sexual violence has been deepened by analytical comments from Kumari Jayawardena, Shireen Huq, Firdaus Azim, Maheen Sultan, Sultana Kamal, Ainoon Nahar, Prashanta Tripura, Shuchi Karim and Sara Hossain.

Ain o Salish Kendra accepted the task of managing the project, which included organizing workshops, auditing and logistics because it was a step in pursuit of justice. This volume is a follow-up of its previous publication on oral histories of women survivors of the 1971 war. We would particularly like to record our thanks to Sultana Kamal, Fatema Mahmud, Shirin Akhter and other members and staff of ASK, who helped us administer the project.

Our responsibility for coordinating and editing the studies has been intellectually invigorating and emotionally rich, because these studies unravel complex pages in the history of women's resistance to sexual violence and their challenge of impunity.

Dhaka
28 December 2015

---

[1] Bangladesh, India, Nepal, Pakistan and Sri Lanka.

Introduction

Locating Sexual Violence and Impunity

MEGHNA GUHATHAKURTA

The concept of patriarchy and patriarchal structures have been central in guiding feminist scholarship and practice since its early years, helping us understand how social institutions and structures with gendered norms informed sexual discrimination and resultant violence. However, contemporary realities and scholarship have made it imperative to recognize that recent trends of violence are a result not of static social structures but of the way that these structures themselves get constructed or reconstructed in the battlefield of politics. That the nature of such politics can be woven around notions of sexuality (cultural notions of masculinity and femininity, for example, 'boys will be boys') or that sexuality can inform the nature of violence itself (such as sex trafficking or honour killing) has become an important theoretical touchstone for second-wave feminism (Millet 1970).

Feminists have moved on further to look at the issue of sexual violence in a more multilayered and complex way. Third-world or post-structuralist feminists have contested and interrogated the 'originary status' of Western feminism and located the sites of sexual politics in postcolonial diversity, as well as foregrounded and centrally located texts by women of colour in feminist scholarship

(Alexander and Mohanty 1997). The collection of essays in this anthology falls within this latter genre.

Additionally, the narrative of sexual violence in this volume is viewed through the lens of feminist notions of justice (or at least components of it), and hence raises questions of impunity that is also perceived as being multilayered and complex. Impunity is not only conceived at the systemic or institutional level of laws and jurisprudence through which a particular crime or violation goes unpunished, but also located at the individual, community and societal level, where the very nature and conditions of sexual violence lend themselves to a silencing process, or at the minimum, a reluctance to address them head on. At the more familial and pedagogic level, impunity is also moulded through the systematic privileging of the male child and the normalization of domestic violence.

Sexual violence and impunity are integral to the history of Bangladesh as a nation born out of a nine-month war in 1971 and a struggle that spans decades. In the course of its emergence as a new sovereign state, Bangladesh had inherited structures from both the British colonial and Pakistani state, some of which, like the military and the bureaucracy, had created a privileged middle class within Bengali society. In many cases, the structures themselves had contributed towards sustaining violence. In other cases, violence had resulted due to processes of structural transformation, such as modernization, globalization and the consequent disarticulation of a traditional peasant society. A small but burgeoning literature exists on the gendered analyses of the state that reveals how both violence against women as well as sexual violence are embedded in the very same state structures (Ahmed 1985; Hossain, Guhathakurta and Sur 2008). The distinct characteristics of the process of nation building in Bangladesh, on the other hand, are movements for democracy and struggles of resistance, which stem from the Language Movement from 1952, the Autonomy Movement throughout the 1960s and 1970s, the Bangladesh Liberation War of 1971, and even after its independence, the Anti-Autocracy Movement against the

Ershad regime.[1] Whereas these movements occurred at the national level, others have been sustained by socio-political forces as anti-fundamentalist movements, the movement to bring war criminals to justice, and bring to an end their impunity at different historical junctures. The women's movement has engaged in them, albeit in ways that articulate the dualities and tensions of these movements as perceived through a gendered lens. On the one hand, it cannot be denied that the struggles of democratic institutions and practices have strengthened the backbone of a women's movement in Bangladesh and especially given it strength to work within a frame of a civic discourse. On the other hand, the generic and gender-neutral orientation, and indeed, in some cases misogyny, in the content and claims of the nationalist movements have led to a sustained critique from women themselves. This has resulted in a field of feminist practice that time and again has surfaced to resist and challenge impunities embedded in the patriarchal structures of Bangladeshi society. The essays in this volume bear witness to this field of feminist practice in Bangladesh, and uphold both its promises and challenges.

The essays seek to address the structural dynamics of impunity at the individual and societal level, looking at the conditions that go into the creation of impunity and also the elements that fuel it, and to enquire as to what helps it become so embedded that it is almost invisible. Impunity has human costs, ecological costs, global and national costs. In cases of sexual violence, impunity prolongs the suffering of victims by creating obstructions to justice. In failing to address environmental justice, it incurs irreparable damage and cost in both the national and global arena. When we fail to recognize rape as a form of torture in one conflict area, it can lead to it being adopted by perpetrators in another conflict area, globally as well as nationally, located within the same body politic. Thus, in Bangladesh, the failure to redress rape victims in 1971 can often be said to lead to rape as military strategy in the Chittagong Hill Tracts (CHT).[2] It is said that usually when the oppressed cannot find justice, they often turn into oppressors themselves. Bengalis who have suffered atrocity at the hands of Pakistani soldiers during the Liberation War of 1971 but did not get redress from them turned into perpetrators of such crimes when conducting a state-sanctioned 'counter-insurgency' warfare led by the Bangladeshi military against indigenous peoples in the CHT, who were demanding autonomy of the region (Guhathakurta 1996). Sexual violence, in turn, may form part of a greater cycle of impunity. Rape or even the rumour of rape is used by establishment forces to counter resistance since it creates panic among the resisting community. Targeting 'innocents' (militarily defined as women, dependants and children) and causing them to flee their homes and shelter destroys the last vestiges of civil society in a conflict zone. During the post-partition communal riots and even in present-day Bangladesh, actual incidents or even rumours of sexual harassment of minority women have caused communities to migrate across borders, often instantaneously, and sometimes at the cost of having to sell their lands at dirt-cheap prices. Such a situation has also taken place in the CHT (Guhathakurta 2001b, 2008). Systemic structures such as politico-legal administrative units often fail to deal with sexual violence effectively because they themselves have imbibed this structure in which impunity is strengthened and victims suffer it at the existential level because there is no option.

SITES OF SEXUAL VIOLENCE

Two distinct sites of sexual violence may be characterized: one in the public sphere and one in the private or domestic sphere. The first may be further distinguished as: (*a*) that occurring during wartime or conflict (such as intra- or interethnic or caste based); and (*b*) that occurring in public spaces during peacetime or during the everyday conduct of people's lives.

Conflict-related sexual violence is perpetrated by combatants, including rebels, militias and government forces. Various forms of sexual violence can be used systematically in conflicts to torture, injure, extract information, degrade, threaten, intimidate or punish. Sexual violence can in such cases amount to being a weapon of war. Such characteristics of war can also be 'normalized' in everyday life as outward manifestations of gendered, racial, ethnic and caste-based discrimination. *Domestic sexual violence* is that which is perpetrated by intimate partners and by other family/household members, and is often termed *intimate partner violence.* This kind of sexual violence is widespread both during conflict and in peacetime. It is commonly believed that incidences of domestic sexual violence increase in wartime and in post-conflict environments.

It must be reiterated that grey areas persist between and within areas of violence, gender-based violence and sexual violence. Patriarchal structures that permeate each society both help to trigger and institutionalize values that legitimize sexual violence. Sexual violence, in turn, may form an act that helps strengthen gender discrimination as is pervasive in the transmission of media images. Further, there may be terrains skirting patriarchy, where violence occurs and they may be sexual but not gendered in any heteronormative sense, for example, prison rapes. Given the multifaceted nature of the query that is embedded in the title itself, the authors of the essays in this volume have also found different points of entry into the subject and have, therefore, adopted their own focus, sometimes exploratory, sometimes incisive.

In the Bangladesh context, all the aforementioned sites appear with questions of impunity interlocked in their narratives. The two most cited conflict situations in the literature on sexual violence are the 1971 Liberation War and the CHT movement for autonomy and its aftermath. Dina Siddiqi, in her chapter, reviews the literature that has helped to create a discursive practice in Bangladesh.

The 1971 Liberation War was somewhat foundational in shaping the subsequent discourse on sexual violence in Bangladesh. Women activists and scholars had a two-pronged struggle to wage when addressing issues of rape and sexual violence. The first was to inscribe women's proactive role in the war into a male-dominant nationalist paradigm of history, as well as to redefine rape and sexual violence as visible crimes against humanity from a feminist perspective. The literature and activism on this aspect of the struggle remain vibrant in Bangladesh. This is evident in the chapters written by Amena Mohsin and in her interviews of Maleka Khan, who led a women's rehabilitation centre after the war, as well as in the case studies of women victims by Keya Chowdhury. It is also evident in many of the activities of women's organizations that have sought to recognize women as freedom fighters equal in status to men, regardless of whether they fought in battle alongside men or gave support in numerous ways, such as taking part in reconnaissance activities, hiding and supplying arms, cooking meals for them or tending to them as nurses.

The second struggle is a more subtle one and one that exists in an embryonic form. It is the one where feminist notions contest nationalist paradigms and seek solutions that are not to be found within nationalist symbols or parameters. The trials and tribulations that women experienced during the war often could not be understood through the lens of nationalism. For example, why did women who were raped and imprisoned by Pakistani soldiers opt to flee with them to Pakistan and not stay at home and face the shame and guilt thrown upon them by friends, family and society? Such questions lead us to explore gendered notions of sexuality in Bengali society and how they reproduce feelings of shame and guilt for the rape victims of the war. Neither the analysis nor the solutions are to be found in nationalist discourses. Hence, we see that the term *birangona* (war heroine), which was declared by A.H.M. Kamruzzaman, the home minister in the post-independence period with the intent to give dignity to the women who were raped, was easily subverted by the 'man in the street' through a simple pun: '*Era ki birangona na barangona?*' (Are they war heroines or prostitutes?).[3] This was something that was related to me by Nilima Ibrahim, author of *Ami Birangona Bolchi*

(This Is a Birangona Speaking) (1998), and a family friend. The very punning of the term in this manner bespoke of the simple lack of dignity that existing societal values offered women. It was also interesting to note that most post-war films that talked about rape portrayed women in pitiful circumstances who either had to be given respectability through marriage or ended up committing suicide. For a few years, film directors continued to speak in this genre of shame and guilt with respect to rape, and then suddenly there was a silence that lasted till the 1990s. Silences too were part of this discourse, where sexual violence against other communities, such as Bihari or ethnic women, were not discussed and hence remained invisible. Some effort has been made to address the gaps in the chapters written by Dina Siddiqi, Bina D'Costa and Amena Mohsin. The book *Rising from the Ashes* (Akhter et al. 2012), first published in Bangla as *Narir Ekattor* by the Ain o Salish Kendra (ASK) (2001), marks the beginning of such an approach.

In brief, we can say that the search for finding a feminist perspective of sexual violence in the Liberation War has barely begun. The underlying conditions of breaking silences may be varied for different societies as much of what is cultural is factored in the process. There is, however, a common strand evident in the retelling of any history and that is brilliantly articulated in Maya Angelou's poem, 'On the Pulse of Morning':

> History, despite its wrenching pain,
> Cannot be unlived, and if faced with courage,
> Need not be lived again. (1993)

In other words, history cannot be told or retold without confronting pain or courage, the pain of confronting known truths with new realities and the courage to break that silence. Individual memories through an intricate process of storytelling and legend building may fit in organically with collective memories (or mainstream thinking or official histories), or again, they may not. We witness such individual reminiscences of victims and fighters periodically during national day celebrations. But in the play of power (that is, those who control the media, education or, broadly speaking, production of culture), some stories get valorized over others, thus influencing the direction of history. Aspects of partition history in South Asia or the Liberation War in Bangladesh too bear this resemblance.

However, individual memories also have a potential for playing the *subversive* role of deconstructing some of the collective legends through creative translation. Artists in general facilitate the translation of memory or recall of events even decades after that event is over. Masterpieces of films on the world wars even a hundred years on still hold us spellbound not so much as a documentation of the events or an informed retelling of history, but as an emotional reconnection with events based on principles that transcend time and space—principles such as humanity or a rediscovery of truths, which the conscious mind had so far denied or not previously acknowledged.

Collective memories are all too often conflated with national memories or national consciousness. The reasons are obvious. The emergence of the nation-state came with all the power of the state, which was deemed to control a unifying process of bringing a nation together, ideally under the aegis of one single, broader identity. Whosoever is in control of state power uses the same marker, albeit with their own constructed legends and polemics. But on the other hand, if you ask a Dalit in India, a Buddhist in Bangladesh or a Sindhi in Pakistan what her or his markers of consciousness are, they can be very different from their respective national polemics. When doing research in the CHT in Bangladesh, I came across the same question about what the markers of national consciousness were and they had responded with a variety of markers that we Bengalis would not relate to: the Kaptai Dam eviction, the entrenchment of the army, when the Bengali 'refugees'/settlers first came in, the declaration of a stable ceasefire. Exploring further, if you asked women of *any* community in Bangladesh, or India or Pakistan, what their markers of consciousness were, the responses vary even more. More than grand-scale political events, they would relate stories of when they could wear a bindi on their foreheads without fear or when schools stopped becoming concentration camps, or perhaps for a future generation of garments factory workers in Bangladesh, it would be the Great Disaster of Rana Plaza. Their responses could also tell you about the nearness and the distance of the state from their own daily lives. The long and short of it is that collective memory may be very different from the state-sponsored national discourses and debates on memories. They, in fact, may be broader, more complex and run parallel to or in opposition to national discourses and hence failed to get integrated into it. But that is not to say they do not exist. They manifest themselves in the movements and uprisings that surface at different periods, often demanding recognition both of the memories as well as the realities that they represent.

GENDER AND ETHNICITY: INTERSECTIONAL APPROACH TO SEXUAL VIOLENCE AND IMPUNITY

Much of the literature on the 1971 Liberation War can be read and reread in the context of conflicts that have occurred globally in recent years: Serbia, Bosnia, Kashmir and subsequent developments in Bangladesh, as in the CHT. The militarized conflict in this region manifested itself as a movement for autonomy from the perspectives of ethnic groups who identified themselves as Jummas and from the perspective of the state that identified it as counter-insurgency warfare.[4] Even when a peace accord was signed (1997), the aftermath was described in military terms as a low-intensity conflict, whilst ethnic people in the CHT called it a non-implementation of the promises made.

Raja Devasish Roy (2003), Shapan Adnan and Ranajit Dastidar (2011), and Amena Mohsin (2002) have produced seminal works where they critically engage with the Bangladeshi state on the notion of indigenous concepts of landownership, self-administration and cultural hegemony. Guhathakurta (1996, 2001b) brings in the gendered dimension of the conflict and critiques the mainstream women's movement based on perceptions of peace building by intertwining class, ethnicity and gender in identity politics. After this, many others have started writing on ethnicity and gender (Chakravarty and Ali 2009; Haque 2011).

Women's writings have foregrounded questions of justice and peace drawn from the analysis of the 1971 war and explored the CHT crises in the same vein (Guhathakurta 1996; Mohsin 2003). The essays in this book not only relate the new markers of intersectional analysis to issues of sexual violence in post-conflict situations, but also look at some illustrative case studies derived from a report published by the Chittagong Hill Tracts Commission (D'Costa 2014), where sexual violence continues to occur amidst the backdrop of a system that enjoys impunity from the state in military, political and socio-economic terms. The changing connotation of sexual violence in the Hills in a new landscape where Bengali settlers and indigenous peoples live as uneasy neighbours has also been analysed and discussed (Guhathakurta 2010). In addition, women's movements both in the Bangladeshi mainstream rights movement as well as among indigenous organizations have focused attention on the growth of gender-based violence against indigenous women, and thus argued for looking at issues such as land grabbing, militarization and ethno-politics from a gendered perspective. Current research in conflict and post-conflict situations in Bangladesh, therefore, have come to influence studies of rape, assault, abduction and other forms of violence against women in mainstream society in both public and domestic spaces.

PUBLIC AND DOMESTIC SPACE

Sexual violence as a criminal offence intersperses the public and the private, the personal and the political. This is very well illustrated in the essays written by Faustina Pereira, Ishita Dutta and Hameeda Hossain. Pereira, in her piece, writes about the impunity that manifests itself in both the broader cultural and social norms of society as well as in social institutions such as kinship or local power structures, and legal institutions and practices. She also analyses in depth the implications of such systemic inadequacies or problems, and critically engages with approaches taken by legal aid practitioners against the backdrop of the contemporary rights regime, both globally and nationally. Ishita Dutta, on the other hand, explores the systemic gaps evident from the micro standpoint of seeking medico-legal evidence that is crucial for a victim of rape who tries to seek justice for the crime committed. This work opens up new areas of research into impunity, which interrogates the very architecture of a legal system that bases its credibility on seemingly neutral, scientific characteristics of medical examination or the collection of forensic evidence. Hameeda Hossain's piece is by far the one that probes most deeply into the private–public divide in the social and legal terrain as she deals with fatwas against women in rural areas. Fatwas are specialist opinions of competent jurisconsults on any legal or religious matter where the rules of law are not clear, or because the issue or situation is novel, the existing rules do not provide an answer. The person who gives a fatwa is a mufti, who must be of an unimpeachable character, have a deep insight into Islamic theology, be well versed in the original sources of law, have mastery over the languages of the original works and be competent to form an informed independent judgement. Fatwas are not legal tender in Bangladesh, but are observed in rural society as guides to religious rituals. The essay, therefore, interrogates the plural judicial systems that exist in the country on issues of 'personal law', which have had an impact on women in Bangladesh through the decades.

The findings are quite telling in that they are a narration of how cultural and social norms permeate both social and legal systems so much that these are almost always tilted in favour of the perpetrators rather than the victims, although in Hameeda Hossain's piece some positive decisions and overtures by the judicial system and legal aid organizations are mentioned. Furthermore, the mechanisms that are needed to support the victim psychologically and help her transcend and transform victimhood into survival mode are insufficient and barely evident. Such works, as mentioned earlier, indeed break new ground in the hitherto legalistic literature that analyses sexual violence and impunities.

What this kind of literature illustrates is that sexual violence encompasses violations and offences that are considered deeply personal, intimate and, hence, fall outside the public space. Thus, it becomes doubly difficult to gain clarity and objectivity when these are being brought out into the open. This is to be seen especially in local-level village arbitrations, where women have traditionally been left out, although in some areas this is slowly changing. In a nationwide empirical study conducted by Research Initiatives, Bangladesh (Guhathakurta et al. 2012), on the importance and necessity of the Hindu Marriage Law, it was seen that most women who were interviewed preferred to have problems relating to domestic abuse, neglect or violence settled within the family. Most said that when they took their complaints to the local arbitration councils, they would be defeated because being married women, the council would be headed by elders of their in-laws' village and, naturally, their husbands' side of the story would be more privileged than theirs. A woman would only be seen to have an edge in the process if she had a father or brother (in short, a male guardian) who was either well off or embedded in the village power structure. On the other hand, while legal aid organizations, where they existed, were of some assistance, very few women could avail of such facilities due to their marginalization in terms of wealth and education.

The prevalence of fatwas, issued by and large for transgressions of a 'personal' nature usually relating to women (for example, adultery, mixed marriage, elopement, etc.), makes the biases of power structures even more noticeable. Although by the rule of the court, such fatwas may only be issued by those who are properly informed of the Sharia and the law of the land at large, this is hardly followed in remote rural areas. The case of Nurjahan in Sylhet was one such instance that raised awareness among women's organizations nationwide, as noted in Hameeda Hossain's essay.

But the situation is evolving. In recent years, women have been seen to be more vocal about domestic violence than before. In a nationwide survey of Hindu women on questions of linking gender violence with compulsory registration of marriage (Guhathakurta et al. 2012), over 50 per cent admitted to having been physically abused by their husbands or close family members. This could have been the result of years of mobilization by grassroots organizations or the increased exposure to education and media. The enactment of the new Domestic Violence Act has also come as a result of proactive mobilization by women's and legal aid organizations. It is a strong Act that brings in many innovative dimensions to the arena of legal redress for sexual violence in domestic spheres. At the same time, it is a new Act that still needs to be understood, internalized and used by most practitioners as well as by victims.

MOVEMENTS, POLEMICS, AND A BIT OF SOUL SEARCHING

The women's movement in Bangladesh has followed more or less a civic discourse, that is, the polemics of women's rights has followed the discourse of civil liberties rather than that of interpretation within religious principles. This has differentiated Bangladesh from many other Muslim countries, especially where the Sharia law prevails, where women have had to claim their rights through the reinterpretation of religious texts. There has been some debate within the country as to whether one could have taken that path as well and whether that would have been a more effective weapon to fight fundamentalism, but the matter is far from resolved and, as of now, the dominant trend is still the civic discourse, as portrayed in the chapter by Hameeda Hossain.

The women's movement in Bangladesh has taken issue with sexual violence and impunity in different periods of its history. Some of them have been mentioned earlier, as in the case of fatwas and domestic violence. Diverse interpretations of impunity stemmed from different organizations, often in the same movement. In the movement against violence against women in the late 1980s, mainstream organizations chose to analyse gender-based violence in terms of inequality and discrimination of the sexes, whereas organizations with feminist visions interpreted it from the viewpoint of patriarchal values and structures of masculinities. But one of the striking things about debates of this kind in Bangladesh is that they remain contained within the development sphere and hardly ever navigate political terrains such as party politics. During the students' movement against sexual harassment in Dhaka University, there were disagreements between students on using the word 'sexual' in the banner, which said: 'Stop sexual harassment' (in Bengali, *Jouno hoyrani*). Some students, mostly male and belonging to student wings of political parties who were 'supportive' of the cause, objected to the use of the word and wanted to use just '*Nari nirjaton*' (Violence against women). The students had to have a close consultation with their fellow comrades inside the Madhur Canteen (a place where all political parties meet at the university) before they could use the banner in the rally with the word 'sexual' written on it. Such kinds of polemics that traverse the political terrain are much needed in taking the movement to the next level; in other words, making it a movement that is informed by a feminist discursive practice, whatever the issues or sites that it navigates.

Feminist thought and movement, however embryonic or peripheral to mainstream thinking in Bangladesh, nevertheless has had moments of critical intervention in social and political movements as in the anti-Ershad demonstration of the 1980s (Ahmed 1985). The more recent Shahbagh movement of 2013, where a post-war generation of bloggers and youth activists spontaneously came together to demand justice for war criminals and seek an end to impunity, at first drew forth criticisms for not taking on board issues of sexual violence such as rape as a war crime or participation of indigenous communities. But voices for their inclusion were heard in the later phases of the movement, when International Women's Day was celebrated, from the Gonojagoron Moncho (the platform for mass awakening as it was called in the Shahbagh junction), and slogans were changed to make it more inclusive of indigenous communities.[5] Although much of this critique took place on social media, a branch from the Shahbagh movement, the Bikhubbdo Nari Shomaj, was instrumental in constructing a direct line of communication on the ground between leaders of the Gonojagoron Moncho and other women activists in the peripheries of the movement. They also demonstrated this liaison by staging parallel events on the occasion of International Women's Day in the vicinity of the Gonojagoron Moncho.

Bina D'Costa talks of the trajectories taken by indigenous women's movements in the CHT in her paper, and develops a model that demonstrates how, in the absence or incapacity of state's support to meaningful justice, civil society networks could involve women and girls in developing their own gender justice framework. Eva Gerharz (2014) talks about how recent attempts to institutionalize the concept of indigenous people at the global level relate to local claims. Although Gerharz's article is not exclusively focused on indigenous women, she points out contradictions within the movement (essentialist connotations of identity politics to more porous definitions accepted at the global level), which may have grave implications for future trajectories relevant to indigenous women's movements in particular.

Juxtaposed with these notions, one may try to understand how indigenous women themselves may perceive such trajectories. A women lawyer of the Khagrachari court was of the opinion that sexual violence was previously considered to be a community affair and the victim's welfare was taken care of by the community, but now, through a modernist understanding perpetuated by the state and rights discourse, it is personalized and made individual, and the burden has to be borne by the victim herself. The notion of shame, therefore, becomes more individualized. Hence, the networks extrapolated in D'Costa and Gerharz's papers come in to fill the space of the traditional community. Some soul searching needs to be undertaken by both indigenous and Bengali feminists to understand the limits that are placed by tradition and modernity, and to try to gauge how indigenous women feel about it. Linked with this predicament is also the role of development aid and to what extent it is changing society and values, and in accordance with whose agenda. People in conflict areas do not often feel very easy about having to take on strategies from stakeholders who are outsiders to the region, especially during peak conflict. Yet, some kind of mechanism needs to be put in place where cognizance of the violence is taken and a space is created where grievances can be aired in a safe manner. This is a challenging and daunting task, but one that needs to be done, preferably in close consultation with internal stakeholders.

Focusing only on the individual is problematic. When individuals enter the public space, the transition is not easy. We have seen from experiences of village arbitration that a battered woman has a tough time defending herself in a village court that is located in her in-laws' village and where her natal family members are not there to protect her (Guhathakurta et al. 2012). How much does the victim have to depend on her family networks, and how much access to police stations and courts can she have on her own or through support of women's organizations and legal institutions? In a state where thirty-two out of three hundred MPs are garment factory owners, how can a woman's labour rights be upheld? Structural issues seem to get sidelined while taking the firefighting approach, that is, moving from case to case. It becomes a different feminist project from fighting structural impunity. These questions are posed so that women's organizations as well as justice systems in Bangladesh can engage in some soul searching.

The discourse on sexual violence has often been accused of having heteronormative underpinnings, implying that it is dominated by heterosexual perceptions of sexual politics which invisibilizes and excludes considerations of homosexuality. LGBT groups are only just coming up in Bangladesh, with huge challenges facing them from social and religious structures. From this, we can deduce that notions of the body politic merit a deeper discussion than has been had so far. It refers to the practices and policies through which the powers of society regulate the human body, as well as the struggle over the degree of individual and social control over it. It is interesting to note that most notions of sexuality in Bengali tradition and culture have been expressed through literature. The nature of literary expression has also changed with the advent of modernity and the rise of middle-class values that inform the cultural codes of propriety. In medieval Bengali literature, the body was more explicitly alluded to than in modern times. Rabeya Moyeen (1989) studied the different ways in which a woman's breasts have been portrayed in Bengali literature through the ages. The more explicit descriptions by writers of an earlier period such as Krittibas, and Bijoy Gupta contrast with the more demure expressions of sexuality of the modern-day poets such as Rabindranath Tagore and Jasimuddin, influenced by colonial middle-class values of the bhadralok culture. In non-Bengali indigenous cultures, it has changed even more. For example, in Chakma society, women were freely smoking tobacco in their daily lives, but the hegemonic cultural discourse of Bengali middle-class propriety has led more and more women to discard the habit. In Bengali society in particular, issues of purdah (segregation) have entered the discourse on sexuality and the body in a big way in both international and national scholarship as well as ideologies. The institutionalization of segregation often leads one to argue that victims get attacked because they do not observe the rules of segregation. This kind of thinking exacerbates levels of impunity against the assaulter. They also bring into focus ethical issues of the body and its dignity, for example, whether only female doctors can examine female bodies or if there is some kind of ethics that everyone should observe in preserving the dignity of the person.

WAYS FORWARD

After all the analyses, can we come to a consensus on actionable points on how women's movements can address issues of impunity of sexual violence?

One of the first steps is to address the deep silence that surrounds sexual violence at both the individual and societal level. Sensitive research and fact finding through innovative methods should be undertaken, and with that goes building capacity among the younger generation on using such methods. The current volume is a step in this direction. The writings in this volume not only enable us to look at sexual violence in a multifaceted way, but to read questions of impunity as structures of the powers that prevail at familial, community, local and national levels, and need to be resisted.

The fact that there is major state collusion in questions of impunity is almost self-evident, and certainly from the evidence-based chapters that follow. Feminists as well as political analysts in general need to engage in a more structural analysis of such collusion, in areas of conflict as well as at the level of policymaking and the day-to-day implementation of such policies. This should lead to a clear directive to policy advocates on how and where to tackle issues of impunity in their lobbying activities.

Even without state collusion, impunity is often granted to perpetrators by way of patriarchal kinship patterns, which, in turn, are frequently embedded in judicial norms and regulations. Hence, there is a need to strategize how longstanding legal, social and moral impunity embedded in society can be questioned and upturned through a series of well-thought-out actions, resulting in polemical debate and discursive practice.

We now turn to questions of justice. There is no one understanding of justice among the stakeholders that seeks an end to sexual violence. Many existing notions of justice are debated, for example, the death penalty. Before one goes into arguments on this, it is important to first understand from survivors' perspectives what they mean by justice and what their notion of reparation is. Is it financial or psychological? Is it a mere acknowledgement of the crimes committed or is it the direction to live in dignity without denial of the pain that they had to suffer? There has been no self-sustained research on this in Bangladesh, and without such research, it is not possible to make any effective impact on future policies.

How do we learn from both individual and collective memories of sexual violence? How do we create a knowledge base so that people can learn from it? How do we go about this in the absence of a common code through which to communicate it to others? Women's organizations must adopt a concerted strategy to take the subject from research to a more actionable platform through which a social practice can be formed that is at the same time grounded and visionary. There is much to learn from exemplars in the regional and international arena, for example, Nepal, Sri Lanka, Rwanda, Sierra Leone and Yugoslavia, where there has been acknowledgement of rape as a crime against society. At the same time, there is a need to dissect why we have not been able to harness this in our country. Thus, when both the desire and challenge for change come, we should be ready to offer homegrown solutions and strategies that are evidence based and not simply offered in toto from systems outside our own. If we look to the success of the Beijing Conference in declaring rape as a war crime, we are actually looking at the years of hard work that feminists (researchers, lawyers and scholars) have put into this notion. We hope that the anthology of work represented here will constitute, at least in embryonic form, the beginnings of such an enterprise within the context of Bangladesh.

NOTES

1. The Bengali Language Movement, also known as the Bhasha Andolon in Bengali, was a political movement in former East Bengal advocating the recognition of Bengali as an official language of what was then the Dominion of Pakistan (see https://en.wikipedia.org/wiki/Bengali_Language_Movement [accessed 16 September 2015]). The Six Point Movement or the Autonomy Movement was a Bengali nationalist movement in East Pakistan spearheaded by Sheikh Mujibur Rahman, which eventually led to the liberation of Bangladesh. Its main agenda was to realize the six demands put forward by a coalition of Bengali nationalist political parties in 1966 to end the perceived exploitation of East Pakistan by the West Pakistani rulers (see https://en.wikipedia.org/wiki/Six_point_movement [accessed 16 September 2015]). The Anti-Autocracy Movement, led by a coalition of party alliances, student leaders and civil society, subsequently led to the fall of the nine-year military rule of H.M. Ershad on 6 December 1990.
2. The numbers of those raped and, indeed, even killed have been debated in the literature around 1971 and is still something that is fraught with tensions in the polemical battleground. Susan Brownmiller, in her book *Against Our Will: Men, Women and Rape* (1975), had mentioned the figure 200,000, which had been accepted and later projected by both national and international media without query or question. Analysts in Bangladesh had tried to look beyond numbers and more into the grievous nature of the crimes committed. Jalal Alamgir and Bina D'Costa, in their well-researched article (2011: 38), had argued thus: 'A proper estimate of rape must exceed those reported, given the stigma attached to not just rape in general but rape by the enemy.' They further said:

   > Numbers are critical in delineating a traumatized society's experience of war and the magnitude of loss. But precision is notoriously difficult: lack of demographic analysis, methodological concerns to count pre- and post-genocide populations and gaps in record-keeping pose challenges to quantify large-scale conflict. Debates still exist about the numbers of people killed or women raped in Darfur, Rwanda and Cambodia. (ibid.)

It may also be mentioned that the failure to centralize the issue of rape as a war crime in the immediate post-war situation may have been responsible for the social denial of using sexual violence in revengeful acts of freedom fighters against non-Bengali communities.

3. The declaration was published in *Purbodesh*, 23 December 1971, as cited in Mookherjee (2015).
4. The Chittagong Hill Tracts occupies a physical area of 13,191 km^2 in south-eastern Bangladesh, bordering Myanmar, and the Mizoram and Tripura borders of India. It is inhabited by about fourteen ethnic groups among whom the Chakmas, Tripuras and Marmas constitute the majority. According to the 1991 Census, 49 per cent are reported to be Bengalis from the plains. Over the last quarter of a century, the indigenous people of the CHT have been involved in a struggle for autonomy from the Bangladeshi state, the main roots of the conflict being the land issue, the transfer of population from the plains to the hills and the control of administration by non-Hill people. In 1997, an accord was reached between government representatives and the armed wing of the resistance, the Shanti Bahini, which brought an end to the armed struggle. In subsequent years, however, the non-implementation of the peace accord, especially related to the devolution of power to Hill people, has failed to address the root causes of the conflict, thereby perpetrating continued violence in the region
5. The movement first popularized slogans that valorized the Bengali identity vis-à-vis an Islamic one—for example, *Tumi key, ami key? Bangali Bangali*' (Who are you, who am I? Bengali Bengali)—but was met with protest from indigenous communities as well as Bengalis within the movement on its exclusionary nature. A modified slogan was suggested and then accepted: '*Tumi key, ami key? Pahari Bangali*'(Who are you, who am I? Pahari [Hill people] Bangali). Slogans carrying women's icons as well as indigenous women's icons too were introduced into the movement, such as '*Amader dhomonitey Kalpana Chakmar rokto*' (The blood of Kalpana Chakma [a Chakma woman leader reportedly abducted by the Bangladesh military official] runs in our veins).

REFERENCES

Adnan, Shapan and Ranajit Dastidar. 2011. *Alienation of the Lands of Indigenous Peoples in the Chittagong Hill Tracts of Bangladesh*. Dhaka: Chittagong Hill Tracts Commission and International Work Group for Indigenous Affairs.

Ahmed, R. 1985. 'Women's Movement in Bangladesh and the Left's Understanding of the Woman Question', *Journal of Social Studies*, 30 (October): 41–56.

Ain o Salish Kendra (ASK). 2001. *Narir Ekattor: Juddhoporoborti Kothhokahini* (Women's '71: Post-War Voices/Stories). Dhaka: Ain o Salish Kendra.

Akhter, Shaheen, Suraiya Begum, Meghna Guhathakurta, Hameeda Hossain and Sultana Kamal (eds). 2012. *Rising from the Ashes: Women's Narratives of 1971*. Dhaka: UPL.

Alamgir, J. and Bina D'Costa. 2011. 'The 1971 Genocide: War Crimes and Political Crimes', *Economic and Political Weekly*, 46(13): 38–41.

Alexander, M.J. and Chandra T. Mohanty. 1997. *Feminist Genealogies: Colonial Legacies, Democratic Futures*. New York: Routledge.

Angelou, M. 1993. 'On the Pulse of Morning'. http://www.poemhunter.com/poem/on-the-pulse-of-morning-2/ (accessed 18 July 2015).

Brownmiller, Susan. 1975. *Against Our Will: Men, Women and Rape*. Harmondsworth: Penguin.

Chakravarty, Ehsani and Ayoob Ali. 2009. *The Hidden Matrix: Women's Position and Gender Relations in Adibashi Societies*. Dhaka: Pathok Shomabesh.

D'Costa, B. 2014. *Marginalization and Impunity: Violence among Women and Girls in the Chittagong Hill Tracts*. Dhaka: Chittagong Hill Tracts Commission.

Gerharz, Eva. 2014. 'Indigenous Activism in Bangladesh: Translocal Spaces and Shifting Constellations of Belonging', *Asian Ethnicity*, 15(4): 552–70.

Guhathakurta, M. 1996. 'The Bangladesh Liberation War: A Summon to Memory', in Abul Kalam (ed.), *Bangladesh: Internal Dynamics and External Linkages*, pp. 20–31. Dhaka: University Press Limited.

———. 2001a. 'Families, Displacement' (bilingual), in *Transeuropeenns: Divided Countries, Separated Cities*, 19/20: International Journal of Critical Thought, Paris, Fondation Maison des Sciences de l'Homm.

————. 2001b. 'Women's Narratives from the Chittagong Hill Tracts', in Rita Manchanda (ed.), *Women, War and Peace in South Asia: Beyond Victimhood to Agency*, pp. 254–93. New Delhi: Sage.

————. 2008. 'The Chittagong Hill Tracts (CHT) Accord and After: Gendered Dimensions of Peace', in Donna Pankhurst (ed.), *Gendered Peace: Women's Struggles for Post-War Justice and Reconciliation*, Chapter 7. London: Routledge.

————. 2010. 'Cartographic Anxieties, Identity Politics and the Imperatives of Bangladesh Foreign Policy', *Peace Prints: South Asian Journal of Peacebuilding*, 3(2): 41–53.

Guhathakurta, M., Korban Ali, Sipra Goswami, Md Saidur Rahman, Babul Chandra Sutradhar, Manasi Chakma, Sabita Rani Haldar, Beuti Haldar, Rakhi Saha, Purnima Modak, Jharna Bepary, Israfil Bepary, Nusrat Jahan Chowdhury and Biplob Das. 2012. 'Study on the Necessity and Importance of Hindu Marriage Law'. Unpublished report, Dhaka, Research Initiatives, Bangladesh.

Hameeda Hossain, Meghna Guhathakurta and Malini Sur. 2008. *Freedom from Fear, Freedom from Want? Rethinking Security in Bangladesh* (mimeo). New Delhi: Rupa.

Haque, Tania. 2011. 'Militarization and the Fate of Women's Body: A Case Study of the Chittagong Hill Tracts', in A. Mohsin and Imtiaz Ahmed (ed.), *Women and_Militancy: South Asian Complexities*, pp. 41–59. Dhaka: University Press Limited.

Ibrahim, Nilima. 1998. *Ami Birangona Bolchi*. Dhaka: Jagriti Prokashoni.

Millet, K. 1970. *Sexual Politics*. Champaign: University of Illinois at Urbana-Champaign Press.

Mohsin, A. 2002. *The Politics of Nationalism: The Case of the Chittagong Hill Tracts*. Dhaka: University Press Limited.

————. 2003. 'Women, Peace and Justice: A Chronology of Denials', *Journal of Social Studies*, 100 (April–June): 55–71.

Mookherjee, Nayanika. 2015. *The Spectral Wound: Sexual Violence, Public Memories and the Bangladesh War of 1971*. Durham, NC: Duke University Press (forthcoming).

Moyeen, R. 1989. *Bakkha Bandana* (In Praise of Women's Breasts). Dhaka: Rahman.

Roy, Raja Devasish. 2003. 'The Discordant Accord: Challenges Towards the Implementation of the Chittagong Hill Tracts Accord of 1997', *Journal of Social Studies*, 6 (April–June, 100th Issue: 'Perspectives on Peace: Visions and Realities'): 4–57.

1

Gendered States

A Review of the Literature on Sexual Violence and Impunity

DINA M. SIDDIQI

INTRODUCTION

In this essay, I trace (an approximate) genealogy of sexual violence and impunity in Bangladesh as conceptualized over the past four decades. Although I focus primarily on academic literature, where possible, I connect the concerns and contours of academic scholarship to the activities of NGOs, state and non-state development actors, and the women's movement. The latter constitute three distinct but overlapping environments that are critical sites of knowledge production about Bangladeshi women.

The essay does not provide an exhaustive catalogue of the literature. It is not possible to review the entire corpus of writing produced over the course of forty years in any meaningful way in a chapter of this size. Instead, I focus on two or three major themes and historical signposts around which much of the available material clusters. In that context, I flag silences and erasures that mark particular historical junctures. I have tried to avoid falling into a methodological nationalism and use a transnational framework of analysis throughout.

Scholarship on sexual violence in Bangladesh is of fairly recent origin and coalesces around two recurring themes. The emergence of both topics can be traced to the priorities of feminist-inflected political activism in the post-military period of the 1990s. The first, and more prolific, concerns the long-ignored war of 1971 and the strategic use of mass rape during that time. Remarkably little scholarship exists on the war itself; the academic silence was broken primarily by feminist scholars in the last decade or so. As I note, although official nationalist narratives excluded women's voices, sexual violence in 1971 was memorialized, albeit selectively, in a variety of public discourses. The emerging literature on 1971, much of which centres on bringing silenced women's voices to the fore, raises a series of questions that call for further exploration. What is the relationship between quotidian forms of violence and the more spectacular manifestations during times of crisis? What is the work of unearthing testimonies of violence? Are thick descriptions of intimate sexual violence inherently powerful as narrative and necessary for challenging impunity and seeking reparations? What does it mean to give consent under conditions of extreme social and economic asymmetry?

Second, there is a small but growing corpus of work on the gendered techniques and consequences of militarization of the CHT, and the implications for majoritarian Bengali feminist ideologies. Transnational attention and the rise of a human rights discourse inside Bangladesh have also spurred interest in the CHT.

Before proceeding, a word on definitions. What is meant by sexual violence is context specific and can vary greatly. Even the lines between forms of sexual harassment (for example, verbal intimidation) and sexual violence are open to contestation. The question of sexual violence inscribed on male bodies also arises. In Bangladesh, sexual violence is rarely named as such but subsumed under the rubric of violence against women (VAW), which, by the

1980s, was well established both as a category of analysis and an object of activism in the international arena as well as domestically.[1]

Sexual violence in relation to *impunity*—exemption from punishment often in the form of political protection for injurious acts—necessarily invokes questions of state accountability and responsibility. For the purposes of this paper, I take a more capacious view of impunity. Extending notions of accountability beyond the state and its functionaries, I have tried to reflect seriously on the implications of the cultures of impunity imbricated in the (re)production of violence in everyday life.

STRATEGIC SILENCES, GENDERED COMPLICITIES

Today, it is widely accepted that sexual violence not only accompanies war but can also be fundamental to the construction and perpetuation of conflict. Feminist scholars from a variety of disciplines have established the centrality of women's bodies in boundary-making projects, in marking the 'purity' of ethnic or religious bloodlines, and in the constitution of national/community honour. In this respect, the mid-1990s proved to be a critical moment. The bloody conflagration accompanying the break-up of Yugoslavia as well as conflicts in the Congo and Rwanda left little doubt of the ways rape could be used as a tool of terror and mode of ethnic cleansing. The Yugoslav Wars in particular galvanized feminist activists working on the global arena to successfully push for the recognition of systematic wartime rape as a crime against humanity (Copelon 1994).

This turn of events brought renewed attention to 1971 that, remarkably enough, was for long a forgotten war in the global imaginary. In the interim, the systemic rape of Bengali women by the Pakistani army and its local collaborators received correspondingly little attention. For many years, the US feminist Susan Brownmiller's well-meaning but tremendously essentialist tome on rape as an instrument of male power remained the only source for official figures on the number of women raped in 1971

(Brownmiller 1975). This neglect is curious, given that *as many as* 200,000 women were raped, many held in sex camps and *up to* 25,000 women forcefully impregnated (D'Costa 2004: 227).[2]

Within Bangladesh, until recently, feminist scholars and activists had been hesitant about broaching the subject. Possible reasons for this reticence include a genuine concern to avoid doubly stigmatizing rape survivors, the realization that political accommodations made the trial of perpetrators unlikely, and a focus on nation building through development activities. I deal with the eventual rupture of this silence in a later section of the paper. Significantly, a robust state discourse on rape survivors emerged just days after independence. In a gesture of incorporation into the newly formed nation, on 22 December 1971, the first independent government of Bangladesh declared that rape survivors would be awarded the title of *birangona* or war heroine (Islam 2012: 2133). Evidently, the men who formed the new government did not feel they could ignore either the fact of wartime rapes or the individual women who had 'sacrificed' their bodies for the sake of independence. Presumably, they also felt a sense of urgency, perhaps because the scale at which girls and women were freed from 'rape camps' exceeded initial assessments. Pregnant survivors presented an especially vexing issue.

Mujib's gesture of embracing *birangona* as daughters and sisters—irretrievably patriarchal and steeped in the language of war as it was—could be read as a 'progressive' move for the times, not appreciated fully, perhaps because of the ensuing burdens of the *birangona* designation. In this connection, literary scholar Poulomi Saha writes:

> The translation of sexual violence against non-combatants into a military idiom of expected sacrifice proleptically attempted to make sense of the seemingly unthinkable and to offer it a recuperative future. These daughters of the nation were to be hallowed alongside their mukti bahini brethren as having made possible, through their noble suffering, Bangladesh's freedom. (2012: 450)

As one step towards securing this recuperative future, the new government also set in motion a series of programmes aimed at the 'rehabilitation' and reintegration of the *birangona* into mainstream society. These included standard vocational skills training along with more unusual financial and other incentives for 'patriotic' men to marry *birangonas* and restore their 'honour'. Using its international connections, the state hurriedly commissioned a programme to provide abortions for women and girls who were pregnant as a result of rape. Where abortion was not viable, social workers were under strict instructions to put 'war babies' up for international adoption.

The futures of *birangonas* were complicated by the inability or unwillingness of the nation-state to come to terms with the past. From the outset, the position of the *birangona* was, at best, a double-edged privilege under cultural conditions that stigmatized rather than celebrated women willing to go public with their experience of wartime rape. Indeed, without a corresponding effort by the state to bring the perpetrators to justice, the designation of *birangona* could not but embody stigma. Failure to confront the past meaningfully rendered the honour of the title into a visible badge of dishonour for its bearer (see D'Costa 2011). In the circumstances, it is no surprise that the lines between *birangona* and *barangona* ('fallen' woman) were wilfully blurred at times.

In a detailed analysis of media representations of the *birangona* in the immediate post-war period, Kajalie Shehreen Islam (2012: 2142) observes that, 'Despite being at the center of the discourse the *birangona* was absent from it, as if she were best kept hidden'.[3] Islam's research shows that newspapers at the time rarely used the word *birangona*, instead referring to individual women as *lanchita* (stained, soiled, disgraced, harassed), *nirjatita* (tortured), *biddhosto* (ruined, annihilated, fallen to pieces) and *bibhranto* (confused, bewildered, misguided, mistaken). Her research gives the impression that women were reduced to statistics, a list of interchangeable nameless, faceless and voiceless victims. The media was equally silent on the mothers of 'war babies', children born of rape by Pakistani soldiers and therefore considered to have polluted and polluting blood. This silence, Islam remarks, made the media complicit in enforcing state policy on abortion and adoption.

Islam also found that news stories related to *birangonas* rarely made any mention of perpetrators. This striking absence had serious consequences not only for future attempts at reparations, but on contemporary meanings of *being birangona*. The erasure of perpetrators rips the female body out of the context of wartime violence so that the 'dishonour' or shame of the body appears to be under scrutiny, not the crime of rape. The systematic erasure of women's voices and agency not only reinforced problematic state policy, but also, as Islam observes, prevented women from building a platform on which to identify perpetrators and seek justice. In-depth interviews with and profiles of women could have been a valuable source of documented evidence (ibid.).

Why did the victims/survivors not speak out, especially if they had little to lose in terms of public claims to chastity? Following Foucault, Islam suggests that the *birangona* discourse was a means of exercising bio-power, both disciplinary and regulatory. At one level, the discourse imposed certain expectations on individual women, leading to monitoring and self-policing (including silence on certain matters). Such expectations were institutionalized and reproduced in policy measures that subjected women's reproductive and productive functions to the state's regulatory apparatus (ibid.: 2139). Islam hints at, then rejects, the possibility of the *birangona* exercising agency through silence. Theirs, she insists, was a forced silence, compelled through the active national forgetting of the state. She concurs with the historian Yasmin Saikia that the subject of rape became 'unspeakable' and 'unthinkable' *for the women themselves*. Passive and dishonoured, in this view, the women served invisibly to re-establish the honour, dignity and power of men, and more broadly of the state (ibid.: 2143).

Once the abortion and adoption programmes had been completed, the identity of *birangonas* was literally erased from the nationalist record, ostensibly as protection from future stigma. State functionaries determined at some point that it would be in everyone's best interest to destroy all bureaucratic traces of the government's 'rehabilitation' efforts. The destruction of these records—names, addresses, ages, locations where the women and girls had been held—permanently 'disappeared' rape survivors from official historical archives.

THE AMBIVALENT PLACE OF *BIRANGONAS* IN PUBLIC MEMORY

From the outset, women's personal narratives that *directly* speak to their experience of war crimes have been excluded from official nationalist histories of Bangladesh (D'Costa 2004). Bina D'Costa suggests that it was critical to silence women's lived experience of the war for the new government to promote a patriotic space juggling the potentially opposing identities of Bengali and Muslim (D'Costa 2011). The selective valorization of some narratives and silencing of others in order to construct an acceptable storyline is not limited to Bangladesh, of course. Nor is it unusual for difficult matters to be confronted in national scholarship only when they are 'safely' in the past. The extraordinary silence around the gendered violence of the 1947 partition, for instance, was broken only after a distance of several decades by a small group of courageous, trail-blazing feminist scholars (see, especially, Bhasin and Menon 1998; Butalia 2000).

Until recently, Naila Kabeer's influential *New Left Review* essay of 1988 was an exception to the absence of scholarship on/of Bangladesh on sexual violence during the war. Kabeer documented the patriarchal nature of state benevolence towards the 1971 rape survivors and made the important observation that mass rapes—irrespective of class and privilege—left an indelible effect on the emergent middle-class feminist movement.

It is important to note, for our purposes, that silence in the academic realm, or among survivors themselves, did not imply invisibility in public memory and nationalist discourse. This is in contrast to silence in state and society around the gendered violence of the 1947 partition, which appears to have been of a different nature. Until 1992 and the *gana adalat* or people's court convened by Jahanara Imam, the *birangona* was largely a *non-contested* issue in public culture and politics. By non-contested, I mean that rape survivors were neither entirely invisible nor absent in popular discourse, although they could be spoken of only within a set of fixed parameters. In other words, rather than complete cultural silence, selective forgetting marked the *birangona* story. 'Her' existence was to be acknowledged, but along very specific registers and controlled patriarchal framing:

> In the collective memory of the nation, the figure of the raped Bengali woman is a powerful symbol of Pakistani lust and barbarism yet it is a figure riven by ambiguity and irresolution. In popular plays on the theme of independence, for instance, the violation of individual women is often portrayed as a sacrifice, for the family as well as for the nation.[4] A standard plot revolves around the woman whose husband has been incarcerated by the military, who surrenders her body to the depredations of army personnel in order to secure her partner's freedom. Yet this sacrifice of her body can be redeemed only by the woman's subsequent exit from the plot, for her act signifies betrayal and shame, as well as sacrifice. The choice of rejoining family and community is rarely exercised; ideally she encounters death through suicide or accident. In other words, in this nationalist discourse, women can only exercise agency within terms set by existing patriarchal structures. (Siddiqi 1998: 209)

As evident in the foregoing passage, I contend that the consequent slippage between consent and coercion obviates the need to either confront the Bengali males' inability to protect 'their' women from 'dishonour' *or* address the double standards and socio-economic/

cultural rejection the *birangona* faced after the war. Put differently, the body of the *birangona* was neither subject nor object, but the ground on which other struggles were played out (Mani 1987). *Birangona* stories were useful as representational tropes that reinforced narratives of Bengali victimization and Pakistani/Punjabi brutality.

Along these lines, the anthropologist Nayanika Mookherjee writes that during the course of her fieldwork in Bangladesh she realized that:

> Unlike the common presumption that sexual violence during wartime is consigned to oblivion there is no silence of the history of rape within the metanarrative of the war of 1971. To the contrary, I found evidence of the constant invocation of the history of rape in state speeches and policies which eulogized the women raped as 'war heroines', in documents dated 1972–1973 after the war and, in the 1990s, as exhibits in museum and as narratives of 'real' 'war-heroines' in newspapers. (2011: 7)

Mookherjee complicates any simple notion of silence around wartime rape. In a fascinating analysis of the discrepancy between raped women's national position as icons of 'honour' and their local reception through sanctions and constant *khota* (scorn), she writes how the memory of rape is often articulated as a public secret, one that is invoked at specific moments through the act of shunning or scorn (Mookherjee 2006).

INTERRUPTING PUBLIC MEMORY/RUPTURING NATIONALIST SILENCES

The (short-lived) jubilance over the restoration of formal democracy provided space and momentum to recast/contest collective public memories of the war.[5] The movement for democracy in the 1980s that eventually toppled the military dictatorship of G.M. Ershad in December 1990 had included a demand for the trial of Bengali wartime collaborators. Initially barred from politics, the latter had re-entered public life under the military rule ushered in by the murderous coup of 1975. For the next fifteen years, official narratives of the 1971 war hewed closely to a script that eschewed Pakistani culpability for war crimes, valorized the army and promoted Muslim majoritarian identity.

The *gana adalat*, or people's tribunal, convened on 26 March 1992, held a mock trial of wartime collaborators. Noted public figures such as Ghulam Azam, the leader of the Jamaat-e-Islami, a party that actively colluded with Pakistani forces, were 'tried' in absentia. The objective was to put pressure on the Bangladesh Nationalist Party (BNP) government into setting up war crimes trials. The mock court also brought up the issue of wartime rapes—inadvertently highlighting the difficulty of addressing questions of sexual violence and impunity without any corresponding groundwork. The conveners located three rape survivors from a village in western Bangladesh and persuaded them to testify at the mock trial. Unfortunately, this critical symbolic intervention failed to consider the risks entailed in public exposure for the women themselves. From complete obscurity, three unlettered, impoverished village women found themselves catapulted to national attention, not all of which was positive or supportive. Once the news reached their village, they and their families were subjected to scorn, stigma and ostracism. Nayanika Mookherjee (2004, 2006) has written extensively about the predicament of these three women, who became objects of spectacle and derision. The complicated ethics produced by the collision of urban elite nationalist interests with feminist and subaltern ones awaits further elaboration within the nationalist sphere (D'Costa 2011; Mookherjee 2008).

Within the decade, a small group of explicitly feminist activists began to rupture the selective representation of the *birangona* issue. Nilima Ibrahim broke a long public silence on her experience of working with rape survivors in the landmark 1998 publication, *Ami Birangona Bolchi* (This is the *Birangona* Speaking). The book recounted the stories of individual women Ibrahim had known, and the loss and pain that followed mostly failed efforts at re-entry into family, community and nation. ASK 2001 volume *Narir Ekattor: Juddhoporoborti Kothhokahini* (Women's '71: Post-War Voices/ Stories) went a step further. A research collective gathered the oral testimony of twenty-two women who recounted their lives during and after the war. Not all of the testimonies involved wartime rape, a decision made by the collective to offset any potential stigma from being associated with the project. Identities were kept confidential unless otherwise requested.

The explicit objective of *Narir Ekattor* was to create a record of war crimes. The foreword by Dr Hameeda Hossain and the preface by the research collective both mention the inspiration and lessons provided by exposure to the Vienna and Beijing Conferences and the international tribunals on Bosnia and Rwanda set up by the UN.[6] It is important to note that the volume is not simply a record of war crimes. It was an explicit intervention into the male-dominated space of nationalism and an effort to transform that space. The simple but powerful title makes clear that the aim is not merely to inscribe women's stories into the nationalist narrative (the 'add women and stir' approach). By underscoring the myriad ways women's struggles did not end with the attainment of nationhood, the volume forces the reader to confront the continuities in patriarchal structures before and after 1971. The volume also rejects the language of honour and shame.

It took another decade for feminist scholarship to catch up. In the intervening years, postcolonial theorization of the constitutive role of violence in community formation and the centrality of gender and sexuality to such processes forged new research agendas (see, for instance, McClintock 1995; Pandey 2001). Along with an interrogation of the highly sexualized and violent moral economies that underpin identity formation, scholars turned their attention to the relationship between spectacular and everyday forms of violence (Das et al. 2001). A new generation of scholars in Bangladesh began to challenge uncomfortable nationalist silences and elisions around sexual violence in 1971. As a result, several books and essays, some coinciding with the fortieth anniversary of Bangladesh's independence, have been published in the last few years.

Bina D'Costa's *Nationbuilding, Gender and War Crimes in South Asia*, published in 2011, broke new ground by directly addressing the question of war babies and forced abortions. The analysis is situated in a comparative analysis of 1971 and the partition of 1947, which the author calls the 'original cartographic trauma'. As mentioned earlier, D'Costa argues that reconstructions of the nation-state, in their present form in South Asia, centrally involve the silencing of women's experiences and narratives. Her primary concern is with ensuring justice and reparations for women in conflict situations. To this end, she calls for more collaboration and networking among feminists—transnationally and within South Asia.

D'Costa's main achievement, arguably, is to unsettle public memories of the period just after the 1971 war and foreground the state's problematic treatment of pregnant women and war babies. In the course of her research, she tracked down—with considerable difficulty—a number of rape survivors. Her experience with the particular social vulnerability of survivors pushed her to confront the ethical dilemmas of researching and writing about highly personalized but politically explosive topics in real time. D'Costa implicitly raises questions that feminists have grappled with in other contexts and times. What is the work of unearthing testimonies of violence? Are thick descriptions of intimate sexual violence inherently more powerful as narrative or do they run the danger of giving voyeuristic, pornographic pleasure to the reader? As Laxmi Murthy (2012) writes in a review essay on the subject: 'What do the horror stories and personal pain, the cries of anguish and the desperation of revenge, add to our understanding of the narrative of rape or the politics of silence?' Equally important, what does it mean for non-literate women to give informed consent for the publication of interviews under conditions of extreme asymmetry and vulnerability? Ultimately, considerations of confidentiality convinced D'Costa to hold back from publishing many of her accounts.

D'Costa's research included extensive interviews with Geoffrey Davis, the Australian doctor commissioned in 1972 to carry out as many late-term abortions as possible. From the book and elsewhere, it seems that assembly-line production, rather than the considered delivery of medical services, characterized the conditions under which abortions were carried out. The speed and urgency with which Davis was dispatched speaks to the masculinist state's acute anxiety over the (potential) pollution of the body politic and the urgent need to excise impurity. D'Costa also held extensive conversations with the social workers and feminist activists charged with supervising the 'rehabilitation' process, that is, those in direct contact with the women and girls forced to submit to abortions and to give up their children. The excavation of these multiple perspectives captures the ambivalence and misgivings experienced by those entrusted with carrying out 'instructions from above', regardless of the wishes of survivors. The account brings to mind the discomfort and contradictions experienced by social workers involved in the 'recovery' of abducted women in 1947 (Bhasin and Menon 1998; Das 1995).

COMPLICATING VICTIMHOOD

Postcolonial feminist scholars investigating the gendered nature of violence have interrogated received notions of agency, subjectivity and victimhood (Bacchetta 2004; Banerjee et al. 2004; Butalia and Sarkar 1995; Ivekovic and Mostov 2006). How do particular events shift subjectivities and create new forms of agency? What is the range of subject positions produced through war/conflict for different categories of women? Alternatively, what difference does structural location make to the availability of specific subject positions? Finally, how do we theorize the lines between consent and coercion without falling back on tropes of duplicity or passive victimhood?

Many of these questions were prefigured in ASK's *Narir Ekattor* volume and are of critical importance in understanding the experience and aftermath of sexual violence in 1971. Bina D'Costa, Nayanika Mookherjee and Yasmin Saikia—each from distinct disciplinary backgrounds and with different intellectual stakes—explore what the 1971 war meant for specific groups of women and so broach many of these questions. In the process, they rupture any absolute line between consent and coercion, victim and perpetrators. They also impel us to consider whether silence—the refusal to speak and bear testimony—can also be a form of agency/resistance.

Mookherjee, in her research on public memories of sexual violence in 1971, pushes the reader to think beyond the immediate moment, to a longer colonial history of racialized and gendered discourses that allow *male* as well as female bodies to be violently inscribed during the war (Mookherjee 2011). Drawing on Judith Butler's idea of performativity, she shows how, as a citational practice, performativity reiterates past colonial discourses within new colonial contexts and contributes to processes of gendering. In this backdrop, she interrogates the silence around male sexual violations during the war, a taboo topic, unlike the 'public secret' of women's rapes. It is striking that when Mookherjee's male interviewees did acknowledge rape, they attributed such acts to the implicitly *unnatural* 'culture of the frontiers' (ibid.: 13). Here, historically established discourses are redeployed to establish a naturalized 'depravity' of the perpetrators. Further, as Mookherjee underlines, the representation of such violence as 'unnatural' by extension naturalizes heterosexual rape. As a result, 'the "natural" act of raping a woman becomes an expression of masculinity' (ibid.: 14).

Yasmin Saikia's *Women, War and the Making of Bangladesh: Remembering 1971*, also published in 2011, tackles the issue of memory from a different perspective. In collecting oral testimonies of rape survivors as well as of perpetrators, her objective was to tell the story of the war as a human event, of individual loss as well as of a collective loss of humanity. Violence, she suggests, dehumanizes the perpetrator as well as the victim. First-hand accounts of women, not only rape survivors but those who took up arms as well as social workers and medical personnel, form the core of the book. These accounts, presented with a minimum of interpretive framing, form an archive in themselves, even as they fill gaps in official narratives of the war. Significantly, Saikia tries to link everyday forms of violence with the extraordinary violence of the war by presenting intergenerational narratives. She also breaks a longstanding nationalist silence by including the voices of so-called Bihari or Urdu-speaking women, who were targeted for violence because of the community's assumed collaboration with the Pakistani army. The absolute binary between victims and perpetrators, Bihari and Bengali, comes undone in the process.

At the same time, Saikia runs into a methodological difficulty familiar to feminist scholars. The stress on a common, deep structural vulnerability shared by women across ethnicity, class and religion runs the risk of reinscribing an absolute gender binary. Combined with the lack of contextual framing in the presentation of victim narratives, the analysis could be (mis)read as an unwillingness to confront the systematic, ideologically driven nature of mass rapes of Bengali women or an obliteration of the historical configurations of power that rendered Urdu speakers into a 'despised' other in the eyes of Bengali nationalists. *How do we unpack the binary of victim and perpetrator without erasing historically dominant relations of power?* For Saikia, Biharis appear to be the ultimate object of abjection and Bihari women the apotheosis of humanity. This valorization of Urdu speakers inadvertently refuses questions of scale and ideology, particularly the structural vulnerability of Hindu women.

Both D'Costa and Saikia include testimony from Firdousi Priyobhashini, a renowned sculptor and an extraordinarily courageous individual whose contribution to challenging dominant male narratives in Bangladesh cannot be underestimated. Priyobhashini's travails (the occasional charge of being a collaborator rather than a victim of sexual violence) point to the inability of (male) nationalist discourse to accommodate narratives that do not fit a straightforward script of passive female victimhood. Any acknowledgement of agency in negotiating the complex structure and practices of power risks disrupting the official narrative of male heroes and female victims.

I end this section with some speculative thoughts on the scandal over Sarmila Bose's 2011 volume, *Dead Reckoning: Memories of the 1971 War*. Numerous commentators have offered detailed critiques of this profoundly flawed and politically inflammatory book. There is no need to reproduce them here. I am interested in nationalist reactions to *Dead Reckoning* and other texts that, it seems to me, are symptomatic of a larger issue looming over debates on sexual violence, impunity and possible reparations for survivors.

Bose presents *Dead Reckoning* as the first available counter-nationalist—and so ostensibly neutral—narrative of the 1971 war. She attributes existing gaps in scholarship on 1971 or in the destruction of potential evidence of mass killing to Bengali laziness or self-interest (fears of undermining the claim of genocide prevents serious investigation on the topic, if we are to believe her). Bose claims her research did not unearth any evidence of the systematic use of rape as a weapon of war. Rather, that Bihari women were subject to sexual violence functions for her as a sign of the inevitability of sexual violence in wars and conflicts. In other words, heterosexual rape is a 'natural' male response in times of crisis. Bose blames an essentialized Bengali ethno-hatred for wartime violence against the Urdu-speaking population. She recycles colonial discourses of race and ethnicity to explain Bengali hostility to Urdu speakers and to justify the Pakistani state's unleashing of murderous violence. The discourse of equivalence to which she resorts relies on the erasure of power, politics and questions of scale. The logic Bose deploys erases the history of the Pakistani's state's use of Urdu speakers as a comprador class, and its strategy of playing populations against one another. Nayanika Mookherjee's excavation of colonial racial and gendered tropes as they were deployed in 1971 come to mind.

Dead Reckoning is easily dismissed as an instance of shoddy methodology and intellectually questionable epistemology in the garb of neutral scholarship. Yet, it may be worth interrogating the visceral register in which (some) reactions to Bose, but more significantly to the 2011 film *Meherjaan* (in which the Bengali heroine gives shelter to and falls in love with a deserter from the Pakistani army during the 1971 war), and Yasmin Saikia's 2011 book (which has not been published in Bangladesh) have been expressed. Such expressions, I suggest, signal something deeper than standard nationalist policing of political boundaries. For despite the wildly varying quality and goals of these three projects, by default, they unsettle the heroic narratives and tropes of victimhood central to Bengali ethno-nationalism.

It is worth recalling here that the writing of national history in Bangladesh is intimately entangled in statecraft and political legitimacy. History matters quite literally in everyday politics. The non-resolution of the 1971 question—no war trials for forty years, the presence of known collaborators in public political life and the ensuing contradictions over Bengali/Bangladeshi identity—makes it difficult ('dangerous' from some perspectives) to talk about the violence foundational to Bengali ethno-nationalism, especially given the tenuous hold of the 'hegemonic' narrative of the Bengali nation itself. The long-term manipulation and erasure of history set the stage for the production of often very partisan and selective histories. This context is critical in understanding the often hostile public reception to scholarship, journalism and cultural production that destabilizes or complicates heroic binary nationalist narratives. The fear of unsettling a hard-won and tenuous position may explain some of the calls for silence and censorship to the film *Meherjaan*, in which the female protagonist falls in love with a Balochi deserter from the Pakistani army, or to the journalist David Bergman's careful, detailed analysis on his blog of the numbers killed in 1971.[7] Violence against Bihari women is an especially incendiary issue in the circumstances.

AN OTHER GEOGRAPHY OF VIOLENCE

The exclusionary aspects of Bengali ethno-nationalism have been challenged most directly by various movements for indigenous rights centred on the CHT.[8] The region, granted 'protected' status under British colonialism, was incorporated into the territory of sovereign Bangladesh in 1971 by the contingencies of postcolonial politics. As with all such projects, the ethno-linguistic terms of Bengali nationalism were by definition exclusionary.[9] The state's political project hinged on the production of a culturally homogeneous population of ethnic Bengalis.[10]

The military dictatorship of Ziaur Rahman embarked on a counter-insurgency project in the CHT that involved the resettlement of poor landless Bengalis into an area with linguistically and ethnically distinct populations. The militarization of the CHT, which continued under Ershad, made the region a focus of the pro-democracy movement in the 1980s. Young Bengali activists in the post-Ershad period also turned their attention to the extensive human rights violations in the CHT. Texts such as *Between Ashes and Hope: Chittagong Hill Tracts in the Blind Spot of Bangladesh Nationalism* (Mohaiemen 2010) are keenly attentive to the sexualized nature of militarized violence in the area. The more recent ethnic privileging of Bengalis in the Constitution of Bangladesh has received relatively less attention.[11] Notably, indigenous men and women have been at the forefront of articulating resistance to Bengali cultural and military hegemony. Euro-American scholars working at the intersection of colonialism, ethnicity and identity have also produced a substantial body of literature on the CHT (see, especially, Van Schendel 2001).

Occupation rarely names itself as such (Visweswaran 2013: 3).

So it is the material violence and symbolic domination of everyday life in the CHT that are recast as matters of territorial and cultural integrity, economic development and national security. Narratives of militarism and counter-insurgency, interwoven with discourses of development and ecological sustainability, reproduce the CHT as a troubled space that must be tamed; they also serve to erase relations of power between Bengalis and others.

From the outset, Pahari/Jumma women featured centrally in 'counter-insurgency' measures, implicated in the everyday practices required to secure occupation and to reproduce the cultural/racial other of the Bengali nation.[12] Ironically, the emergence of a militant movement provoked increased use of sexual violence as a tool of repression (Naher and Tripura 2010).

Today, a complete imbalance in power enables Bengali settlers and others to appropriate indigenous land—through violent or non-violent means—with relative impunity. The marginality of indigenous groups within the nation-state is compounded by the culture of impunity that characterizes the sphere of justice in Bangladesh as a whole. To say that indigent Bengalis, or those with no patronage ties, have limited access to justice would be an understatement. Perpetrators with ties to powerful politicians or other wealthy patrons are rarely held accountable for crimes anywhere in Bangladesh. The perpetrators of illegal evictions, often carried out through (the threat of) abductions and sexual violence, and periodic massacres, act with the knowledge that Pahari grievances have little chance of redress under existing structures of power.[13]

Security personnel may account for the majority of rapes, but the conditions of occupation encourage and enable Bengali settlers to 'violently take over lands belonging to the Jummas, evicting hundreds from their homes, using sexual violence against indigenous women, and committing massacres' (Chakma and Hill 2013: 139).

Sexuality as a counter-insurgency measure may have a longer institutional history; reportedly, in 1983, army officers received a secret circular encouraging them to marry indigenous women. Nation building, in this imaginary, requires the literal occupation of indigenous women's bodies. Chakma and Hill (2013: 142) suggest that this memo functioned not only to encourage voluntary intermarriage, but resulted in a violent turn, with marriages between army officers and indigenous women taking place through intimidation and abductions. It is more than likely that the (talk of the) existence of the memo encouraged the dismissal or condoning of the coercive aspects of such marriages.

KALPANA CHAKMA AND HER SISTERS

Jumma women have consistently resisted such practices formally and informally, through poetry as well as politics. At one point in time, the Hill Women's Federation (HWF), of which Kalpana Chakma was the organizing secretary, epitomized such resistance in the political arena. The disappeared figure of Kalpana Chakma, 'lost but not forgotten', has come to be an important signifier in the struggle for indigenous rights in the CHT.[14] Kalpana's words of resistance continue to resonate powerfully in protests against Bengali domination of indigenous peoples. Her diaries have been serialized in vernacular newspapers. Meghna Guhathakurta (2001, 2004) has powerfully memorialized sections of Kalpana's diary to open up an analysis of structural violence, feminist movements and nationalism politics. The anniversary of Kalpana Chakma's abduction on 12 June 1996 is not simply a ritual marking the injustice done towards an individual woman, but has become an occasion to foreground continuing collective injustice in the CHT.

Kalpana Chakma's brief life and the afterlife of her disappearance are emblematic of the high cost of speaking out in the context of the power asymmetries and culture of impunity noted earlier. In an important analysis, Lamia Karim (1998) notes that at the time, it was easy for many middle-class Bangladeshis to dismiss the problem of a missing Chakma woman by appealing to a narrative of romance (rumours abounded that she had eloped with her supposed abductor) or a discourse of terrorist separatism (another rumour was that she had joined the insurgency and fled across the border). Karim argues that those whose identities were invested in/produced through the Bengali nation-state were deeply uncomfortable taking up the cause of someone whose political demands appeared to threaten territorial integrity. Activists fell back on a language of rights violation, without questioning the contours of Bengali nationalism. Karim observes that this line of argument assumes that all subjects enter the nation-state as full citizens and with the same rights. She writes, 'Although the body of the missing Chakma woman serves to bond the human rights activists and organizes them against the gendered violence of the state, it simultaneously immobilizes their action because the Chakma woman's stakes of self-determination, at least potentially, undermine the Bangladeshi nation-state' (ibid.: 314).

Karim wrote these words in 1998. The provenance of feminist and human rights activism in Bangladesh has expanded considerably since then. Today, 'the CHT problem' is firmly located within the orbit of the national question. It is instructive that the seventeenth anniversary of Kalpana Chakma's abduction was commemorated in 2013 at the auditorium of the Muktijuddho Jadughor (the Liberation War Museum), a bastion of secular Bengali nationalism.

Yet, inclusion is tenuous and conditional upon demonstrating loyalty to the Bengali nation. The anxiety this generates may explain the urgent quest on the part of some indigenous activists to locate Pahari freedom fighters in the 1971 war, for instance. Witness also the unfolding of the Shahbagh movement, in which indigenous activists tried to carve out a space for themselves but remained on the margins. Difference, 'sisterhood' and nationalism do not sit well together.

On the other side, the feminist activist Kabita Chakma cautions against the masculine militarist orientation of resistance that emerges from the twinning of the rape of the land and sexual violence against Pahari women (Chakma and Hill 2013: 156).

VEXING ABSENCES AND GAPS IN THE ACADEMIC RECORD

Two issues are conspicuous by their absence in the literature reviewed. First, strikingly little academic research has gone into exploring the violence entailed in mainstream development policies, especially in relation to the displacement and dispossession of ethnic minorities. It is only because of a handful of progressive NGOs and, increasingly, social movements that operate outside formal civil society structures (such as the National Committee to Protect Oil, Gas and Mineral Resources) that we know something of the coercion, sexual and otherwise, faced by communities living in localities where shrimp cultivation, eco-parks, open-pit coal mining and other multinational corporation-driven 'development' initiatives unfold. Meghna Guhathakurta's (2008) work on globalization and the shrimp industry in the south-east of Bangladesh remains a notable exception.

Until recently 'academic' and NGO research was driven by a donor agenda in which critiques of orthodox development policies had little space (see van Schendel and Westergaard 1997). Support of orthodox development models and support of the nation invariably folded into each other. The ground is beginning to shift, however. Independent academic research on issues such as struggles over open-pit coal mining, or the implications of microcredit, is beginning to emerge (Karim 2011; Siraj Annie 2010). Also missing is an analysis of contemporary forms of sexual violence in relation to the structural changes and inequities wrought by neo-liberal capitalism. Although there is a growing literature on sexual violence and harassment, the intersection of political economy and cultural formations in the making of male and female subjectivities in Bangladesh remains unexplored (see Siddiqi 2003a, 2003b, 2004 for efforts in this direction).

Second, the subject of sexual violence in sectarian conflicts involving minority religious communities (primarily Hindus) has barely been addressed in academic research. This is an astonishing and somewhat perplexing gap. NGOs as well as feminist human rights organizations and certain civil society institutions are at the forefront of documenting/making visible rights abuses against religious minorities, persistently challenging the silence or denial of official discourse. Yet, few academic books have been written on communalism in Bangladesh.[15] None that I know of address the question of sexual violence, with the exception of two essays written in the aftermath of retaliatory violence around the Parliamentary elections of 2001 (Guhathakurta 2002; Siddiqi 2007).

It may be that a *decontextualized* emphasis on violence enacted on the individual body obscures the structural factors and practices of violence. Individualizing violence also works to obfuscate the systemic violence against those perceived to belong to a particular collectivity (Paharis, Urdu speakers, etc.). Structural violence can then be relegated to the margins, if engaged at all, or even naturalized.

Custodial violence around which major feminist interventions coalesced (Sammilito Nari Samaj; Yasmin and Shima Choudhury murders) have not received much scholarly attention either.[16]

CONCLUDING THOUGHTS

It is no longer possible, if it ever was, to think of women in Bangladesh as a unitary category. As the analysis in this paper shows, the homogenizing effects of nationalist constructions of gender and violence have been consistently interrogated by a range of feminist scholars and activists. Nevertheless, the lines between what can be said and what 'must' remain unsaid call for further feminist engagement. In addition, considerations of class and inequality are rarely addressed in the existing literature. It is urgent to develop an intersectional critique that transcends a nationalist and developmentalist lens if feminists are to meaningfully challenge sexual violence and impunity, both in times of war and not-war.

NOTES

1. See, for instance, *Hidden Danger*, Roushan Jahan's important monograph on domestic violence, which came out in 1994.
2. These numbers are highly contested. I have quoted the available figures in their upper ranges to convey the extent of sexual violence at this time.
3. Islam applied critical discourse analysis to over fifty news reports and features published in one Bengali and one English language newspaper between December 1971 and 1972.
4. This account drew on my own experience of growing up in Bangladesh in the 1970s and 1980s, watching state-owned television, long before the days of privately owned satellite channels.
5. It is in these circumstances that new Bengali counter-histories began to be written, that the Liberation War Museum was set up in 1996, and that Tareque Masud began making his films on 1971.
6. In 2013, the volume was translated and published under the title *Rising From the Ashes: Women's Narratives of 1971*. One reason for the translation, as stated in the English language preface, is the evident importance of testimonies in the international sphere of wartime tribunals (Akhtar, Hossain and Kamal 2013: xvii). This documented research was formally handed over to Bangladesh's International War Crimes Tribunal by Sultana Kamal, the executive director of ASK, in 2013.
7. See his blog at http://bangladeshwarcrimes.blogspot.com (accessed 17 September 2015).
8. This section draws heavily on my forthcoming essay titled 'Against Forgetting: Gendered Justice in Postcolonial Bangladesh' .
9. See, especially, Mohsin (1997), one of the first texts to unpack the hegemonic tendencies of Bengali ethno-nationalism.
10. During his first visit to the CHT, Sheikh Mujib famously called on Paharis/Jummas to forgo their language and culture and *become* Bengalis and so, by implication, full citizens of the country. The 1972 Constitution did not recognize the existence of indigenous peoples inside Bangladesh; ethnicity and citizenship were folded into each other.

11. In 2011, Parliament passed the Constitution (Fifteenth Amendment) Bill, reinstating the principle of secularism. The amendment revised Article 6 of the Constitution, which proclaims: 'The People of Bangladesh shall be known as Bangalees as a nation and the citizens of Bangladesh shall be known as Bangladeshis.' By this definition, all non-Bengali speakers, including indigenous peoples, fall outside the horizon of the ethnic nation. National belonging and full citizenship rights hinge on cultural and linguistic assimilation to the dominant culture.
12. Naming or classification is a deeply fraught exercise in this and other contexts. Jumma, arising from *jhum* or swidden agriculture, is a relatively new political label embraced by many progressives. However, not all groups in the CHT were necessarily engaged in *jhum* cultivation and not everyone is comfortable with the term. In this essay, I use the terms Pahari (admittedly with negative connotations in Bengali circles) and Jumma interchangeably.
13. The CHT Peace Accord in December 1997, which ended two decades of armed struggle between the Shanti Bahini and security forces, did not change this fundamental asymmetry in power. The most important provisions of the accord—demilitarization, the settlement of land disputes, and the devolution of authority to indigenous institutions and representatives—remain partially implemented, if at all. The accord makes no provisions for survivors of sexual violence to seek redress or 'rehabilitation' (Mohsin 2003).
14. 'Lost but Not Forgotten' is the title of a blog post by Amnesty International blogger Lydia Parker on the subject (see Parker 2013).
15. Here I limit my observation to English language documents.
16. Elora Halim Chowdhury's *Transnationalism Reversed* (2011) is the first of hopefully many more considerations of the women's movement in a transnational frame.

REFERENCES

Ain o Salish Kendra (ASK). 2001 *Narir Ekattor: Juddhoporoborti Kothhokahini* (Women's '71: Post-War Voices/Stories). Dhaka: Ain o Salish Kendra.

Akhtar, Shaheen, Hameeda Hossain and Sultana Kamal (eds). 2013. *Rising from the Ashes: Women's Narratives of 1971* (translated by Niaz Zaman). Dhaka: University Press Limited.

Bacchetta, Paola. 2004. *Gender in the Hindu Nation: RSS Women as Ideologues*. New Delhi: Kali for Women.

Banerjee, Sukanya, Angana Chatterji, Lubna Nazir Choudhury, Manali Desai, Saadia Toor and Kamala Visweswaran (eds). 2004. 'Engendering Violence: Boundaries, Histories and the Everyday', *Cultural Dynamics*, 16(2–3): 125–39.

Bhasin, Kamla and Ritu Menon. 1998. *Borders and Boundaries: How Women Experienced the Partition of India*. New Delhi: Kali for Women.

Bose, Sarmila. 2011. *Dead Reckoning: Memories of the 1971 Bangladesh War*. London: Hurst.

Brownmiller, Susan. 1975. *Against Our Will: Men, Women, and Rape*. New York: Random House.

Butalia, Urvashi. 2000. *The Other Side of Silence: Voices from the Partition of India*. Durham: Duke University Press.

Chakma, Kabita and Glen Hill. 2013. 'Indigenous Women and Culture in the Colonized Chittagong Hill Tracts of Bangladesh', in Kamala Visweswaran (ed.), *Everyday Occupations: Experiencing Militarism in South Asia and the Middle East*, pp. 132–57. Philadelphia: University of Pennsylvania.

Chowdhury, Elora Halim. 2011. *Transnationalism Reversed: Women Organizing Against Gendered Violence in Bangladesh*. Albany: SUNY Press.

Copelon, Rhonda. 1994. 'Surfacing Gender: Reconceptualizing Crimes against Women in Time of War', in A. Stiglmayer (ed.), *Mass Rape: The War Against Women in Bosnia*, pp. 197–218. Lincoln: University of Nebraska Press.

D'Costa, Bina. 2004. 'Coming to Terms with the Past in Bangladesh: Naming Women's Truths', in Luciana Ricciutelli, Angela Miles and Margaret H. McFadden (eds), *Feminist Politics, Activism and Vision: Local and Global Challenges*, pp. 227–47. Toronto: Inanna Publications.

————. 2008. 'Victory's Silence', *Himal South Asian*, December. http://old.himalmag.com/component/content/article/3660-victorys-silence.html (accessed 8 June 2015).

———. 2011. *Nationbuilding, Gender and War Crimes in South Asia*. London: Routledge.

Das, Veena. 1995. 'National Honor and Practical Kinship: Unwanted Women and Children', in Faye D. Ginsburg and Rayna Rapp (eds), *Conceiving the New World Order: The Global Politics of Reproduction*, pp. 212–33. Berkeley: University of California Press.

Das, Veena, Arthur Kleinman, Margaret M. Lock, Mamphela Ramphele and Pamela Reynolds (eds). 2001. *Remaking a World: Violence, Social Suffering and Recovery*. Berkeley: University of California Press.

Guhathakurta, Meghna. 2001. 'Women's Narratives from the Chittagong Hill Tracts', in Rita Manchanda (ed.), *Women, War and Peace in South Asia: Beyond Victimhood to Agencies*. New Delhi: Sage.

———. 2002. 'Assault on Minorities: An Analysis', *Meghbarta* online journal. http://www.meghbarta.net/2002/january/minor.html#minor1 (accessed 5 September 2011).

———. 2004. 'Women Negotiating Change: The Structure and Transformation of Gendered Violence in Bangladesh', *Cultural Dynamics*, 6(2–3): 193–211.

———. 2008. 'Globalization, Class and Gender Relations: The Shrimp Industry in Southwestern Bangladesh', *Development*, 51(2): 212–19.

Ibrahim, Nilima. 1998. *Ami Birangona Bolchi* (I Am a War Heroine Speaking). Dhaka: Jagriti Prokashan.

Islam, Kajalie Shehreen. 2012. 'Breaking Down the Birangona: Examining the (Divided) Media Discourse on the War Heroines of Bangladesh's Independence Movement', *International Journal of Communication*, 6: 2131–48. http://ijoc.org/index.php/ijoc/article/viewFile/874/787 (accessed 8 June 2015).

Ivekovic, Rada and Julie Mostov. 2006. *From Gender to Nation*. New Delhi: Zubaan.

Jahan, Roushan. 1994. *Hidden Danger: Women and Family Violence in Bangladesh*. Dhaka: Women for Women.

Kabeer, Naila. 1988. 'Subordination and Struggle: Women in Bangladesh', *New Left Review*, 168 (March–April): 95–121.

Karim, Lamia. 1998. 'Pushed to the Margins: Adivasi Peoples in Bangladesh and the Case of Kalpana Chakma', *Contemporary South Asia*, 7(3): 301–16.

Karim, Lamia. 2011. *Microfinance and its Discontents: Women in Debt in Bangladesh.* Minneapolis: University of Minnesota Press.

Mani, Lata. 1987. 'Contentious Traditions: The Debate on Sati in Colonial India', *Cultural Critique*, 7: 119–56.

McClintock, Ann. 1995. *Imperial Leather: Race, Gender and Sexuality in the Colonial Contest.* London: Routledge.

Mohaiemen, Naeem. 2010. *Between Ashes and Hope: Chittagong Hill Tracts in the Blind Spot of Bangladesh Nationalism.* Dhaka: Drishtipat Writers' Collective.

Mohsin, Amena. 1997. *The Politics of Nationalism: The Case of Chittagong Hill Tracts, Bangladesh.* Dhaka: University Press Limited.

————. 2003. 'Women, Peace and Justice: A Chronology of Denial', *Journal of Social Studies*, 100: 58–71.

Mookherjee, Nayanika. 2004. '"My Man (Honour) Is Lost but I Still Have My Iman (Principle)": Sexual Violence and Articulations of Masculinity', in R. Chopra, C. Osella and F. Osella (eds), *South Asian Masculinities*, pp. 13–159. New Delhi: Kali for Women.

————. 2006. '"Remembering to Forget": Public Secrecy and Memory of Sexual Violence in the Bangladesh War of 1971', *Journal of the Royal Anthropological Institute*, 12(2): 433–50.

————. 2008. 'Friendships and Encounters on the Political Left in Bangladesh', in Heidi Armbruster and Anna Lærke (eds), *Taking Sides: Ethics, Politics, and Fieldwork in Anthropology*, pp. 65–87. New York: Berghahn Books.

————. 2011. 'The Absent Piece of Skin: Gendered, Racialized and Territorial Inscriptions of Sexual Violence During the Bangladesh War', *Modern Asian Studies*, 46(6): 1572–681.

Murthy, Laxmi. 2012. 'The Birangana and the Birth of Bangladesh', *Himal South Asian*, 20 March. http://himalmag.com/the-birangana-and-the-birth-of-bangladesh (accessed 7 June 2015).

Naher, Ainoon and Prashanta Tripura. 2010. 'Violence against Indigenous Women', in Naeem Mohaiemen (ed.), *Between Ashes and Hope: Chittagong Hill Tracts in the Blind Spot of Bangladesh Nationalism*, pp. 194–98. Dhaka: Drishtipat Writers' Collective.

Pandey, Gyan. 2001. *Remembering Partition.* New York: Cambridge University Press.

Parker, Lydia. 2013. 'Kalpana Chakma: Lost but Not Forgotten in

Bangladesh', Huffington Post Blog, 19 December (updated 18 February 2014). http://www.huffingtonpost.co.uk/lydia-parker/kalpana-chakma-bangladesh_b_4464852.html (accessed 8 June 2015).

Saha, Poulomi. 2012. 'Review of Yasmin Saikia *Women, War and the Making of Bangladesh: Remembering 1971*', *Interventions: International Journal of Postcolonial Studies*, 15(3): 450–51.

Saikia, Yasmin. 2011. *Women, War, and the Making of Bangladesh: Remembering 1971*. Durham: Duke University Press.

Siddiqi, Dina M. 1998. 'Taslima Nasreen and Others: The Contest over Gender in Bangladesh', in Herbert Bodman and Nayereh Tohidi (eds), *Women in Muslim Societies: Diversity within Unity*, pp. 205–28. Boulder: Lynne Rienner.

———. 2003a. 'New Trends in Violence: Sexual Harassment and Obstacles to Mobility in Bangladesh', in Salma Khan (ed.), *Role of NGO in Effective Implementation of PFA and CEDAW in Bangladesh*. Dhaka: NGO Coalition on CEDAW and Beijing Process (NCBP).

———. 2003b. 'Gender-Based Violence in Bangladesh: Political and Social Dimensions', in Salma Khan (ed.), *PFA and NFA Implementation in Bangladesh: Role of NGO*. Dhaka: NCBP. Page numbers not available.

———. 2004. *The Sexual Harassment of Industrial Workers: Strategies for Intervention in the Workplace and Beyond* (CPD-UNFPA Programme on Population and Sustainable Development, Occasional Paper 26). Dhaka: Centre for Policy Dialogue.

———. 2007. 'Communalizing the Criminal or Criminalizing the Communal? Locating Minority Politics in Bangladesh', in Amrita Basu and Srirupa Roy (eds), *Violence and Democracy in India*, pp. 223–49. New York: Seagull Press.

———. Forthcoming. 'Against Forgetting: Gendered Justice in Postcolonial Bangladesh', in Rita Manchanda (ed.), *Gender Justice in Post Conflict South Asia*. London: Sage.

Siraj Annie, Nasrin. 2010. '"What Else Do You Suggest Me to Do?" Local Perceptions of Human Security and Motivations to Join the Phulbari Social Movement, Bangladesh'. MA thesis, Department of Sociology and Cultural Anthropology, University of Amsterdam, Amsterdam, 2010.

Van Schendel, Willem. 2001. *The Chittagong Hill Tracts: Living in a Borderland*. Dhaka: University Press Limited.

Van Schendel, Willem and Kirsten Westergaard. 1997. *Bangladesh in the 1990s: Selected Studies*. Dhaka: University Press Limited.

Visweswaran, Kamala. 2013. 'Geographies of Everyday Occupations', in Kamala Visweswaran (ed.), *Everyday Occupations: Experiencing Militarism in South Asia and the Middle East*, pp. 1–28. Philadelphia: University of Pennsylvania.

2

The History of Sexual Violence, Impunity and Conflict

The Bangladesh Context

AMENA MOHSIN

> What difference does it make to the dead, the orphans and the homeless, whether the mad destruction is wrought under the name of totalitarianism or the holy name of liberty or democracy.
>
> (Mohandas K. Gandhi)

Gandhi perhaps could have added the term 'raped' to the list of war victims. But then, with all due respect to him, is not the omission quite typical and natural of this gendered society? The modern state is indeed a very gendered construction, and remains so in its notions of security, sacrifices and also suffering. In the process of 'nation' building, patriarchal values gain salience and are adopted as national values and ethos. A process, and at times a policy, of deliberate forgetting seems to be under way to erase or, if I may say so, undermine the contributions of women in the making of a state. One does not have to go too far to substantiate this. The case of Bangladesh is a testament to it.

While writing about the history of sexual violence, conflict and impunity in Bangladesh, one is overwhelmed not only with methodological issues and the location of the researcher vis-à-vis the researched, but also what is being researched. Ferdausi Priyobhashini stated it quite poignantly to me: rape is not sexual violence, it is violence of the most oppressive and exaggerated form; when one adds the epithet 'sexual', there is a human element to it, but rape has no human element, it is violence.[1] This sense of guilt and disempowerment is further complicated by the politics, institutions and processes surrounding the issue at hand, which in a way sanctions the 'violence' in a particular set of circumstances, but turns around and condemns the same when the perpetrator is the 'other'. In essence, surrounded by the history of politicization and power games, lies the her-story of this violence. Most disturbingly, the history of sexual violence in Bangladesh has been trapped within a nationalist paradigm, where the nation is privileged and the woman is valorized in the context of the nation, not in her own right as a woman and human being.

As a researcher and a woman, I also feel most incapacitated and disempowered by the enormity of the pain of the victims/survivors on the one hand, and the domain of power on the other. The power relations are woven into the social, psychological and political fabric of the system that we live in; it is systemic and thereby lived in. The impunity of the perpetrators is also to a large extent systemic. The state, under the rubrics of legalities, politics, religion and culture, provides this space to the perpetrators. The impunity, in other words, is not only political/legal but also social, starting at the level of the personal. While conflict is an act of politics between two nations, states or communities, sexual violence traverses the personal, societal and national.[2]

Mapping or defining what constitutes sexual violence is also problematic and is linked to the question of impunity. For most men and women in Bangladesh, prevailing attitudes play a dominant role when it comes to matters of impunity. With only sexual intercourse outside marriage under coercion being considered as rape, the discourse on sexuality and sexual violence is shrouded in in layers of legality and illegality, primarily religious rather than 'nationalist'.[3] Researchers have used different criteria to categorize violence. The predominant feature in all of this is the element of fear and the power of the perpetrator. This, as a social scientist, I would argue, is the criminalization of power and through it the criminalization of intent. Through the latter, a culture of silence surrounding sexual violence is created. The fear embedded in this violence is not limited to the body, but critically to the mind. In conventional societies, sex is regarded as not only intimate but also sacrosanct.[4] If a woman is violated, she is fearful of having lost her purity. I feel that this notion of purity and honour is fundamental, and is the key with which the system of power and violence can be unlocked. Fear displaces and dislocates a person; it permeates, as stated earlier, the layers of religion, culture, nation, state and the politics that keep on reproducing this systemic vice.

Violence has been categorized as: physical violence, for example slapping, hitting, kicking and beating; sexual violence, such as forced intercourse and other forms of coerced sex; and psychological violence, for instance, intimidation and humiliation (García-Moreno et al. 2005: 13). This categorization is indeed problematic, since the psychological aspect is integral to all forms of violence. A major element of the act of sexual violence is control, and the power inherent in patriarchy attempts to control the psychological and sociological makeup of women through these acts. In these, they are aided by cultural and religious norms and practices. A major consequence of this is the silencing of the victim and survivor. Notions of shame and honour are played and overplayed. The victims, their families and communities not only internalize these values, but often own and defend them. There is, thus, a silence that speaks out. It speaks of the constructed norms of patriarchy and masculinity; it also speaks of the hurt and the 'guilt' that the victim/survivor has internalized and continues to carry. The silence, perhaps, also provides a breathing space to society and the individual concerned during which narratives are created and deconstructed; more often than not, the humane element inherent in silence is politicized. The silence of the state is different from that of the victim/survivor, who might be trying to take control of her 'self'. The state, on its part, uses the silence as a tool of control and domination, which further recreates and perpetuates the culture of impunity.

This paper is an attempt to trace the her-stories of sexual violence in Bangladesh and the impunity surrounding it. Case studies from conflict periods, that is, the nine-month-long Liberation War of Bangladesh and the CHT, in Bangladesh, have been examined to trace both sexual violence and impunity. It is also important to note that Bihari women have also been violated during and in the immediate aftermath of the Liberation War, but the statist discourse and the mainstream women's movement have failed to integrate them in carving the history of Bangladesh and the mapping of sexual violence in 1971. Arguments have been made along the lines of state versus non-state, random versus targeted. It is contended here that these statist/nationalist and legalist binaries only help the culture of impunity through the acceptance of certain violence as 'normal'. The argument of 'us versus them' is a highly masculine and hegemonic discourse, which promotes a culture of hyper-masculinity and sexuality. Power and power relations cannot be fragmented. If we accept the principle of the universality of rights, along the same premise, I would locate sexual violence. This is a part of her-story that the state of Bangladesh needs to reckon with.

The paper is divided into three major sections. In the first, the question of impunity has been examined through a study of the 'secular' and 'religious' discourses that go into the makeup of statecrafting in Bangladesh. The second section delves into three case studies of *birangonas* or war heroines of 1971. The third section examines the violations committed in the CHT by Bengali military personnel and Bengali settlers.

IMPUNITY AND THE MODERN STATE

Impunity implies exemption from punishment or loss. In the international law of human rights, it refers to the failure to bring perpetrators of human rights violation to justice and, as such, itself constitutes a denial of victims' right to justice and redress. Impunity is especially common in countries that lack a tradition of rule of law; suffer from corruption or that have entrenched systems of patronage; or where the judiciary is weak or members of the security forces are protected by special jurisdiction or immunities.

It is argued that impunity of different kinds and degrees is embedded within the nation-state formation. This cuts across gender, class, religious and ethnic lines. Taking a critical look at the location of women within the nation-state construct, one observes a clear gender bias in its founding principles and institutions. The notions of nation-state and citizenship, major elements of the state, operate within a masculine paradigm that marginalizes women and puts them on the periphery. This gender bias itself is the dominant frame of impunity. The nation-state predicates itself upon the conception of a collective homogeneous identity that is the nation. This collective identity sets it apart from the other collectives. This supposedly homogeneous nation interacts with the external world through a political system called the state. This state is again sovereign, independent and autonomous—attributes associated with masculinity. The sovereign, however, legitimizes its power through the nation; hence, nation and state are often used interchangeably. This nation or collective in the discourse of nationalism has been likened to a clan or kinship. Authenticity of the clan members is, therefore, critical. In order to maintain the purity and authenticity of the nation, women are perceived as the biological and cultural bearers of this nation. They are also seen as the property and symbols of honour of the nation.

Women's freedoms are repeatedly curtailed in the guise of protecting the honour of the nation. As bearers of culture, they are burdened with upholding the image of being 'proper women', which itself is a social construct. This more often than not puts them in a marginalized position compared to men. Raping a woman's body is equated with dishonouring the 'other' or the enemy's property and honour. In order to defend that honour, the nation silences its 'own' women. This silencing provides impunity to the perpetrator, who is the 'other'. Meanwhile, the state that commits the crime protects its citizens who have committed these crimes, as during war/conflict periods, armed forces are given special powers and enjoy impunity under those powers. Thus, a culture of impunity is perpetrated through the very act of defending the idea of the nation-state, both by the violators and the violated.

These processes impinge on the notion of equality. A culture of normativity is created to regulate the behaviour of women, which, it is argued in the context of Bangladesh and in many other societies, has created a culture of shame and honour that violates women's rights as equal human beings. This is done through the control of women's bodies, their mobility and minds. An intertwining between the secular, that is, the ideology of nationalism, and institutionalized religion is observed here. One may liken nationalism to religion; to the nationalists, the control of women's bodies is critical since it is the emblem of the nation's honour and culture, and essential for the biological continuity of an authentic nation. This authenticity necessitates the control of women's bodies. There is a proverb in Bangla: '*lojja narir bhushon*' (shame/modesty is the apparel of a woman). Such proverbs are inculcated in women since their childhood. Their minds are disciplined to behave in certain appropriate ways defined by patriarchal norms. The boundaries and norms of religion too are defined through the same patriarchal lens, often taking the context out of the text.

The Constitution of Bangladesh gives equal status to women in public spheres. It does not allow discrimination against any citizen on the basis of religion, race, sex, caste or place of birth (Article 28 [1]); it guarantees women equal rights with men in all spheres of the state and public life (Article 28 [2]); it entitles all citizens to equal protection of the law (Article 27); and it endeavours to ensure participation of women in all spheres of national life (Article 10). It also mandates that nothing shall prevent the state from making special provisions in favour of women or for the advancement of any backward section of the population (Article 28 [4]).[5] The Constitution of 1972 had secularism as one of its state principles. The Proclamation of Order No. 1 replaced this in 1977 by the principles of absolute trust and faith in the Almighty Allah. Article 12, through which communal political parties were banned in Bangladesh, was also dropped. These changes were given effect through the Fifth Amendment to the Constitution in 1977. The changes took place in the wake of the military takeover of state administration in August 1975. The entry of the military into the political sphere itself is a highly masculine act that bolsters masculine notions of state and power. The induction of religion into politics and the revival of religious political parties further shrank spaces for women. The space given to religion-based political parties provided the space for a kind of politics that gave a distorted and patriarchal interpretation of religion. It resulted in a proliferation of fatwas against women by village religious and social leaders. Not only military regimes but subsequent civil regimes also depended on the patronage and support of these forces to create their support base at the local level. This in turn opened the gates for impunity. The Nurjahan case is a testimony to this (Guhathakurta 2003).

Despite the equality of women in public life on paper, the Constitution retained the provision of personal laws as codified by the British in 1937. Partha Chatterjee (1989) points out that the nationalists were too eager to retain the traditional and customary norms exalting them to the status of spiritual. Clear lines were drawn between the material and the spiritual, the nation being elevated to the level of the spiritual and women being the bearers of it. Men were the material part. During the Indian nationalist movement, women also wanted customary norms to be codified as laws. It was argued that the relegation of these as customs was derogatory and insulting for the communities concerned, and they were legislated by the British into laws in 1937. The insertion of this curtailed the rights of women on critical 'personal' matters. This discrimination on the basis of sex was in contravention of the terms set down in the Constitution of Bangladesh. The retention of personal laws has curtailed women's rights and claims to equality as is evident in marriage, divorce and child custody laws.

The provision of personal laws and guardianship for women creates a system of impunity as, according to the legal system, it is the woman's guardian—be it a father, brother, uncle or husband—and not the woman who has been subjected to sexual violence who decides if recourse to the justice system should be taken. Often, guardians have denied justice to a woman in the name of shame and honour, or out of fear.[6]

It is critical to note that religious texts are used to restrict the equality and freedom of women. This curtailment, it is argued here, is not in tune with the spirit of religion. Leila Ahmed (1992: 10) is quite pointed in her argument that there is an ethical vision of Islam as there is a pragmatic side, and as the religion spread, it absorbed local socio-cultural practices. The practices specifically pertaining to women came to be accepted as part of Islam. However, a dispassionate reading of the Quranic text and the Hadith based on the practices of the Prophet Mohammad reveals that women enjoyed much more freedom and rights during the days of the Prophet than later on. The Quran gives absolute equality of morality and spirituality to men and women:

> For men and women, —
> For believing men and women,
> For devout men and women,
> For true [truthful] men and women
> For men and women who are
> Patient and Constant, for Men

And women who humble themselves,
For men and women who give
In charity, for men and women
Who fast (and deny themselves),
For men and women who
Guard their chastity, and
For men and women, who
Engage much in God's praise, —
For them has God prepared
Forgiveness and a great reward.

(Sura 33: 35, cited in Ahmed 1992: 64–65)

The implications of the above, Ahmed (ibid.: 11) argues, are far-reaching. Both men and women, according to this, have identical virtues and qualities, and the concomitant rewards are the same. The equality of virtues implies the equality of men and women. In other words, the Quran makes no discrimination based on sex; it is the societal construction of gender through which discrimination creeps in between sexes. However, the tension between the spiritual/ethical and the pragmatic aspects of religion remains. If the pragmatic is based on the context, then to attain the true spirit of religion the ethical and spiritual ought to be emphasized where men and women are regarded as equal. The divide between the public and the private, and the construction of gender with prescribed spaces and roles have impacted women's lives and their rights most adversely. Human lives are regulated through everyday norms as well as personal ones, such as marriage, divorce, children, access to and control over property.

The free liberal economy in the age of globalization is also a major avenue of providing impunity. Though much is being said in the name of women's empowerment and women in development, in gender and development, and in gender mainstreaming, donors look for stability within a state, no matter how hegemonic and repressive the state is, for making investments in aid. This developmentalist model presumes women will be empowered once they are visible, but what is overlooked is the veiling of the mind. Autocratic regimes, be they civil or military, depend upon local forces, as suggested earlier, to strengthen or hold on to their power bases. These conservative forces only reproduce conservatism, which primarily affects women at the national level as well. The bolstering of non-democratic regimes, though elected, leads to further militarization and shrinks women's spaces. In the post-9/11 war on terror, donors have often supported forces that give vent to fundamentalism in the name of 'moderating' the forces.

Impunity, in other words, is an interlocking political, social and economic phenomenon. There is a political economy of it, which is personal, political and global.

Let us now turn to an examination of the her-story of sexual violence in Bangladesh in 1971.

BIRANGONAS AND THE BIRTH OF A NATION-STATE, 1971

Women's sacrifices, contributions, victimhood and agencies are central to an understanding of the roles and spaces they occupy in the edifice of nation formation. The state of Bangladesh, indeed, stands on the blood and ashes of one of the worst genocides committed in the history of humankind by the Pakistani military and its collaborators in 1971. I will not go into the debate on numbers, which I consider to be ethically and politically wrong since it boxes human beings and their pains into statistics that political states and researchers use as a tool for justifications.[7] I would argue that sexual violence committed in 1971 by Pakistani military personnel and its collaborators constituted an act of crime against humanity. In the International Crimes Tribunal for Rwanda (ICTR), the Appeals Chamber described rape as a 'form of aggression, the central elements of which cannot be captured in a mechanical description of objects and body parts' (Hoque and Fletcher 2012: 90). The Chamber compared rape to torture and argued that rape is committed to attain a prohibited purpose. Taking note of the cultural sensitivities involved in public disclosures of intimate matters, it further stated that:

> Sexual violence, including rape, is not limited to physical invasion of the human body and may include acts, which do not involve penetration or even physical contact. The Chamber notes in this context that coercive circumstances need not be evidenced by a show of physical force. Threats, intimidation, extortion and other forms of duress, which prey on fear or desperation, may constitute coercion. (ibid.: 91)

The Chamber argued that for an act to be charged as a crime against humanity, it must be committed as part of a widespread or systematic attack directed against a civilian population on discriminatory grounds (ibid.). There is no dearth of evidence that the sexual violence committed in Bangladesh in 1971 was discriminatory as the civil population was unarmed. Women were targeted as the 'other', which needed to be polluted and destroyed.

Sexual violence is also genocide, the ICTR stated: 'Rape and sexual violence … constitute genocide in the same way as any other act as long as they were committed with the specific intent to destroy in whole or in part, a particular group, targeted as such' (ibid.: 92). In 2008, the United Nations Security Council Resolution (UNSCR) 1820 noted that rape and other forms of sexual violence could constitute a war crime, crime against humanity or a constitutive act with respect to genocide.[8] In 2009, the UNSCR 1888 called for an end to impunity to such acts.[9]

Indeed, sexual violence and rapes were committed with a specific intent, which was to inflict severe bodily and psychological damage to the victims in order to destroy their personhood. As discussed earlier, women are considered to be the spiritual and cultural bearers of a nation, the honour of the community. By violating women of the 'other', the perpetrators were violating the honour, the authenticity of their culture, the very essence of nation. By impregnating the women, they were 'polluting' the nation. The sexual violence, including rape, was widespread and systematic. The studies of ASK, the War Tribunal Fact Finding Mission and others undertaken by individual authors and newspapers, as well as the testimonies in the Liberation War Museum attest to the heinousness and enormity of the crimes committed.

The narratives of the *birangona*s, how the state dealt with them and the war babies, not only iterate the limits of the nationalist paradigm, but also the legal and human rights paradigms, acts of crimes against humanity and acts of genocide. I will examine these by discussing three interviews: of a Tripura woman from the CHT, a tea worker from Sylhet and a Bengali woman from Borguna, in that order. The sequence of the case studies intends to deconstruct the dominant notion that the Bangladesh Liberation War was limited to ethnic Bengalis and also to demonstrate the widespread nature of the crimes committed. Then I will examine how the Bangladesh state has dealt with the *birangona*s.

CASE 1: Sanashri Tripura, Khagrapur, CHT

I interviewed Sanashri Tripura in 1997 as part of the 1971 women's narratives research undertaken by ASK. At that time, she was 55 to 60 years old. In 1971, she must have been 30 to 35. It was difficult to tell her age because poverty and the struggle for mere survival had taken its toll on her. She lived alone in a single-room mud house. A simple *chowki* (bed) was her only belonging. Her only son, Surendra Lal Tripura, and youngest daughter, Renuka, lived in the two mud houses adjacent to her's. She had three other daughters.

As argued earlier, a major contradiction of nation crafting is the glorification of the sacrifices of the women war victims at the level of political rhetoric, *maa boner ijjot* (honour of mothers and sisters), as a collective but on the other hand, the silencing of women as per societal norms at the individual level created a culture of silence. It, therefore, did not come as a surprise that though local people at the administrative level said that 400 to 500 women were violated in the CHT, I was able to locate and talk to only one woman, that too probably because she was poor and had no guardian as such. Though I had informed Shakti Prodo Tripura, the local union *parishad* (council) chairman of my work and had requested him to explain the purpose of my visit to Sanashri, when he was accompanying me to her house, he told me that he had been unable to do so since he had not known how to handle it. As we reached their yard, Shakti spoke to Sanashri's son in Tripuri, which I did not understand, and the son looked unhappy and kept on giving me suspicious looks. They went inside, while I was asked to wait. I was tense and disturbed, and had the feeling that it was their sheer poverty that had allowed me to intrude upon their personal lives, lives hitherto kept silent, though people were aware of their history. It was like a forbidden territory that I was invading and disturbing the apparent calm Sanashri had managed to establish over the years.

After a while, they came out and asked me to go inside. This time the son did not accompany us, which explained to me the burden that my presence had put on them. Sanashri looked visibly disturbed as I sat beside her on the floor, but soon she relaxed and started speaking to me. She spoke in Tripuri and Shakti Prodo Tripura translated for me. She looked very lost and as she spoke, it was like she was digging things that she had long buried.

In 1971, Sanashri lived with her son and four daughters. Her husband would be away often as he had business in Tripura, India. He never came back after 1971. She could not recall the exact month, but said that it had happened during the month of Ashar or Srabon, that is, the monsoon season. They came in the morning, two or three Pathans (the Hill people used this term to describe the Pakistani army). A few Mizos were also with them. They wanted to kill her son, but he ran away, as did her three older daughters. They also chased her niece, Chandra Lokkhi Tripura, who was staying with them. Sanashri was left alone in the house with her 1-year-old daughter in her lap. The Pathans entered the house while the Mizos stayed outside. The latter destroyed her banana and papaya trees. The Pathans did not hurt her child, but assaulted her. When I asked her about the nature of the assault, she looked very disturbed and simply said that they had hurt her. It was evident that she was reliving the pain and did not want to talk about it any more. They ate whatever food there was in the house and left. Since she did not have any material belongings, they could not take anything. They never came back.

She said that it changed her life completely. She remains traumatized and she faints whenever she thinks of it. She often has nightmares of the incident, but in the nightmares their faces become hazy, even though she remembers them distinctly. The haziness and remembrance of the faces is indicative of her continuing internal struggle. She said that she does not want to remember it so she keeps herself busy with her work and grandchildren. She never spoke of it or sought any consolation. She has carried on with her life, drawing her strength from her children. She felt that she needed to be there for them.

After the liberation, she never reported this incident. She was not aware of any rehabilitation centre or of any compensation. She did not hold anyone responsible for the incident; instead, she repeatedly pointed to her forehead, blaming her fate for what had befallen her. She was very bitter about it; ironically, she said that she had not been involved in the war and had not supported the Mukti Bahini (liberation forces). She posed a rather poignant question to me: 'How could I support the Mukti Bahini when I was struggling with poverty in my day-to-day life?' She pointed out that her neighbours had been very supportive and nobody ever asked her anything. In a resigned way she told me, 'Today I have twenty grandchildren. What is the point of talking about these things?' This was also indicative of an inner lament at the societal and political constructions that are forcing her to talk about the event at the fag end of her life, at a point when, despite having lost the most intimate part of herself, she had kept quiet for the sake of protecting herself and her children from humiliation and shame. The notions of shame and honour indeed need serious interrogation and dislocation.

I left Sanashri with a sense of loss and anger, thinking not only of her, her struggles and battles with life and living, but also questioning the very edifice of our statecraft and the manner in which histories are being written, glorifying leaders. Where does Sanashri locate herself in this vortex (Mohsin 2013)?

CASE 2: Poonohboti Khashi, Tea Worker, Sri Mongol, Moulvibazar, Sylhet

In narrating her experience of sexual assault in 1971, Poonohboti said that in 1971, she was 30 years old and worked in the tea gardens with her husband. They had one son and two daughters. One day, all of a sudden, the Pakistani army came and surrounded their tea garden. She could not recall the day or date. That morning, she had gone to the Rajghat tea garden to visit her parents. There was an army camp in Khejurchara. The same day, the military entered the Rajghat and Tiprachara tea gardens in different groups. Each group was composed of ten to twelve personnel.

> I was going from my parents' house to my husband's place. I could see the army all around. Suddenly, they confined me in front of the bungalow of the assistant manager of Khejurchara garden. They asked me in Urdu where I was going. I told them that I had gone to visit my parents, and then they asked me for my address. I told them that I work in the tea garden. Then they said to me that you are the leader of the garden, so I had to tell them who had blown off the Rajghat bridge. I answered that I was unaware of those things. Then they took me to their camp and locked me in a room. The incident took place at 10 AM. They

> left me there, saying that they would hold my trial in the evening around 5 PM.
>
> In the evening, the army subedar called me. Then he called the other army personnel as well. He said to me, 'Tell us. If your luck serves you, you will return alive from here, else you will not return.' I started praying and asking god what wrong I had done. Then the guard of the tea garden was called in to give evidence. His name was Bolram. He said that I was a tea garden worker and did not know anything. He further asked them to let me go. They got angry at the guard and shouted him out. Then they started questioning me about the bridge again. Despite my constant denials of any knowledge, they refused to accept my pleadings. [They kept saying] that since I was a leader of the garden, I must be knowing who had blown the bridge up. I was then a member of the central committee of the tea garden workers' union. Then they made me stand straight. One of the soldiers said that I should be allowed to go, as it wasn't my fault. Then the subedar thought for a long time and finally he asked me to leave. I walked back and around 8 PM reached home.

In her narrative, Poonohboti never mentioned that she was raped. When asked about it, she got perturbed and said, 'They did not spare me of anything, they locked me in around 10 AM. Around noon one army person came in and raped me. At that time I saw about ten or twelve army personnel standing outside.' When asked if they had tortured her physically apart from rape, she replied in the affirmative. She further stated they would beat her and then do whatever they wanted. They killed Lokkhi of Khejurchara before her after torturing her physically.

After returning from Khejurchara, Poonohboti could not go to work for a month. 'I was almost dead. The military had tortured me so much and inflicted so much fear in me, that I almost became numb, and had little awareness of whether I was alive or dead.' She did not recall how long she had been assaulted. She thought that the subedar was a good person, and because of him she managed to come back alive. With a sigh she stated that whenever she thinks of 'that Punjabi', the soldier who tortured her, she loses her self-control.

Since that incident, Poonohboti continued to be haunted by fear. She always felt that the military would come again. She would jump at every sound and freeze at the sight of the military. Her husband did not say anything to her after the incident. 'When he had heard that the army had taken me, he came to take me, but the army did not allow him to get in. The children were home and were all crying.' She added: 'Where should I seek justice? Who would give me justice?' But then, she followed it up saying that she would be prepared to go and give evidence. Though she had heard that many people had received help from the government, she had not. Her husband is now retired and both of them live on subsidy. (Hasan 2002: 194–96)

CASE 3: Jamila Khatun, Borguna

Jamila never came out when her mother was talking, though it was she who was to be interviewed. During the conversations with her mother, it was revealed that the Pakistani military personnel had also raped her mother. She constantly talked of Jamila's plight. Though very old, she seemed to have an inner strength while talking about her daughter. She finally called her daughter and asked her to narrate her own story.

Jamila had been a young girl of 11 to 12 when it happened. She had only had one menstrual cycle and she had not developed physically either. She was raped at a time when she was not even aware of the sexual act. She was taken away along with her mother who thought that perhaps the military would kill her mother and set her free, or they would set both of them free. Since she was unaware of the very notion of sexual acts and rape, she could not even imagine that something like that could happen. Then she saw other women and girls were being brought and raped. There was no end to it. The military personnel came in batches and the rapes continued day and night. They did not consider the women and girls to be human. Jamila was very young, yet she was repeatedly raped. She thought of death, but there was no way of escaping since there were always guards stationed there. She had lost all sense of time and could not remember how long they had been in confinement. All she remembered was fear—fear that those devils would come in any moment and jump on her. They used to bring in many girls, keep them for a few days and then they would kill them after raping them. They did whatever they wanted. There was no proper time for food or baths. The only thing that was done properly was their torture.

They did not do anything to Jamila the day she was taken, but her mother was tortured (raped). Both mother and daughter thought that perhaps Jamila would be spared because she was so young. Jamila narrated that the day the military approached her, no words can express the way her mother pleaded and cried to save her daughter's honour. Her mother was ready to give up everything, including her life, to save her daughter; yet, she could not save her daughter's honour. Jamila said that the pain and suffering that they experienced can never be put into words; death was better than that life. Due to continuous multiple rapes, she was almost half dead. It was her mother who took care of her over there. After they were allowed to leave the camp, they came to their *bari* (cluster of households). She was very sick; her father spent a lot of money to have her treated. The people of their *bari* were very rude and spoke ill of them. Nobody spoke to her; she was not allowed to enter the other households.

One of Jamila's uncles tried to settle the matter by talking to the elders in the village, but it didn't help. Then Jamila went with her mother to live in her maternal grandparents' place, where they were left in peace. In the meantime, the country became independent. During the war, their house had been looted and burnt down, but the people of her own village continued to speak badly of her, so she remained at her grandparents' and never went back to her own village. Her paternal grandfather came several times to take her back, but she refused to return. In the meantime, the family thought of marrying her off, but all the proposals broke down after the other side heard of her experience. Her maternal grandfather wanted to consider concealing Jamila's history, but her paternal grandfather did not agree. Finally, Jamila was married to someone who did not care about her history. The wedding took place at her maternal grandparents' place and she went with her husband to her father's house. Once again, the villagers tried to bring up her past to her husband, but he shut them up by saying that he knew about it.

'In my husband's place, except for my husband nobody knows about my past,' Jamila said. 'The children don't know anything.' She felt that there was no point in picking up these issues at this point in time because it would just disturb their lives again. She said, 'If you want to write history, write it, but please don't create any new problems. We have lost our honour, nothing can bring it back. Ask the government to bring them to trial. We only want justice' (Zahid 2012: 36–41).

There seems to be no end to the sorrows of victims of sexual violence. Jamila's plea for justice can only be a beginning for the healing of the sufferers; no legal justice can bring back what they lost. Not only the victims themselves, but their children too suffered the associated pains and stigmas. The new state of Bangladesh began its journey on a very strong nationalist ethos, but there was a process of silencing women, silencing the stories of how the Pakistani army and its collaborators had used rape as a war strategy to pollute and stigmatize the 'other'.

Islam (2012) points out that on 22 December 1971, immediately after the birth of the new nation, the government declared the women who had been raped during the war to be *birangonas* (war heroines). Through media content analysis of the immediate period following the war, she found terms like *lanchita* (shamed), *nirjatito* (oppressed/repressed), *biddhosto* (ruined) and *bibharanto* (confused) in Bangla dailies to describe the *birangonas*. English newspapers used the word 'oppressed'. There were repeated calls for paying respect to the *birangonas* and honouring them by marrying them. In other words, it became a marrying-off campaign. It was presumed that marriage was rehabilitation, and women would be fused, reintegrated and honoured through marriage. The patriarchal notions of statecrafting thus were very pronounced in the new state; the state lens was gendered and nationalistic. There was no element of liberalism or liberation for women as individuals.

Susan Brownmiller (1975), who came to Bangladesh after the war, has pointed out that Pakistani soldiers had raped about 200,000 Bengali women in 1971. Yet, the fourteen volumes of officially documented history of the war of independence carry only a few testimonies of rape. The government set up a rehabilitation centre in each district for the affected women. The centres, however, did not keep any records of the affected women. The idea at that time was to rehabilitate these women in society as quickly as possible. Therefore, at present no proper record of rape victims is available. They were never properly compensated either. According to Maleka Khan who was in charge of a rehabilitation centre in Dhaka, a doctor at the centre had told her that during the first three months of 1972, 170,000 rape victims underwent abortions and more than 30,000 war babies were born. This list, however, is not an exhaustive one and excludes the most marginalized women (Kabir 1998). Most of the war babies were given up for adoption despite protests and pleadings from their mothers. In this context, Neelima Ibrahim points out in her two volumes of *Ami Birangona Bolchi* (1998) that when she had called upon Sheikh Mujib, the first president of Bangladesh, to decide about the fate of these children, his response was: 'Send the children who have no identity of their father abroad. Let the children of human beings grow up like proper humans. Besides, I do not want to keep that polluted blood in this country.' This attitude of the Father of the Nation epitomized the gendered attitude of the state and society. It reified the privileged position of men in society and, more importantly, over women. Where was the voice of the women who had lost and suffered the most during those nine months? Who gave the state the right to snatch away their children? The state never made any attempt or created any space for these women to rehabilitate themselves psychologically. If prevalent social values meant that in order to grow up as proper human beings, one needed the identity of a father, why do we, then, glorify the mother figure in our nationalist construction? Are we talking of a mother sanctified and legitimized by a male? I leave it to readers to find answers to these questions.

Brownmiller (1975) has further pointed out that Bengali men were totally unprepared to accept these women; some women were rejected outright by families. The attempt to make them acceptable to society by giving them the title of *birangona* was resented by women's rights activists because it did not offer them anything; in other words, there was nothing beyond the title. Moreover, the expectation that the title would make them acceptable did not exactly work out. Instead, these women became marked.

Neelima Ibrahim (1998) has detailed the frustrations and agonies of *birangona*s with both state and society. In the seven cases narrated in her two volumes, the *birangona*s express their dismay at the state's role in silencing them. They point out that the sacrifices of the freedom fighters (mostly men) have been properly recognized and acknowledged by the state, roads have been named after them and memorials have been built. They are honoured in state functions and even their children continue to enjoy many state benefits. But the *birangona*s are nowhere. There are no memorials or roads to remind people of their sacrifices. They cannot even come out and state with pride that they are *birangona*s. A *birangona* has aptly summarized the contradictions and hypocrisy of our state and society by posing the following question: 'Why is it so? Is it only because we are women that we are unholy; whereas the Razakars and Al-Badars [Bengali collaborators of the Pakistani army], despite their sins have been accepted and today constitute the elites of the society?' (ibid.)

Hossain (2006) points out that support and hope was given to the rape victims and war widows by women's rights activists like Neelima Ibrahim, Bashonti Guhathakurta and Naushaba Sharafi who toured the countryside and met these survivors. Many informal groups gave welfare assistance, but in a war-torn country there was little scope for bringing about institutional or cultural changes. The demand for justice and trial for war criminals came around in the 1990s, with Jahanara Imam playing a leading role in it. By the mid-1990s, a space was also being created for the *birangonas* to have their voices heard. Researchers and scholars, both home and abroad, began asking questions. In this context, Mookherjee (2006) suggests that, apart from the domestic political context, which constituted of the protests against the political rehabilitation of the wartime collaborator Ghulam Azam, and the movement led by Jahanara Imam, the formation of the *gana adalat* (people's tribunal), also point to the international recognition of rape as a war crime in the 1990s. Within this national and international political context, it became imperative for women's and human rights activists to search for the stories of *birangonas*, to provide evidence for the institution of a war crimes trial. The print media played a critical role in women's activism, home and abroad, to bring these voices to the public domain and one must acknowledge that the taboo surrounding the *birangonas* is gradually giving way to acceptance and acknowledgement as *joyita*, the victorious.[10] It may be noted that the International Crimes Tribunal-2 (ICT-2, discussed later), on 23 December 2014, in its verdict on sentencing to death the former Jatiyo Party minister Syed Md Qaiser for his 1971 war crimes, described the victims of rape and the babies born out of these rapes as freedom fighters (Das 2014). It needs to be seen how this is translated into societal values, individual perceptions and state policies.

On 25 March 2010, the Awami League government announced

the formation of the ICT. It was composed of three judges, a seven-member investigation committee and a twelve-member prosecution team to hold the trials, according to the ICT Act of 1973, which provided for the detention, prosecution and punishment of persons for genocide, crimes against humanity, war crimes and other crimes under international law. Members of the Jamaat-e-Islami, and individuals who later joined the other mainstream parties like the BNP, Awami League and the Jatiyo Party, but were later identified as collaborators and perpetrators, are being tried under the tribunal.

It is argued that the conclusion of the trials, and the verdicts delivered and executed will determine where the state stands vis-à-vis its nation in terms of justice and impunity.

THE BANGLADESH STATE AND THE CHT

Marginalization and Conflict in the CHT

The CHT, situated in the south-east, occupies a physical area of 13,295 km^2, constituting 10 per cent of the total land area of Bangladesh. The region comprises three districts: Rangamati, Khagrachari and Banderban. It is surrounded by the Indian states of Tripura on the north and Mizoram on the east, Myanmar on the south and east, and Chittagong district on the west. Its population, according to the last census held in 1991, was approximately 974,000 (BBS, 1993). Out of this, Hill people constituted 500,000 and Bengalis 470,000. Eleven ethnic groups populate the CHT: Bawm, Chak, Chakma, Khami, Kheyang, Lushai, Marma, Mrung, Pankho, Tanchangya and Tripura. They closely resemble the people of North-East India, Myanmar and Thailand rather than the predominantly Bengali population of Bangladesh.

Women in the CHT, which witnessed more than two decades of armed violence as a consequence of insurgency and state military action, have also borne the brunt of this violence. But their sacrifices and sufferings have not been acknowledged. The peace accord signed between the Parbattya Chattagram Jonoshonghoti Samity (PCJSS), the political front that carried the movement on behalf of the Hill people, and the Government of Bangladesh (GOB) is extremely gendered, with no reference whatsoever to the woman question (Mohsin 2004).

The conflict had its roots in the adoption of Bengali nationalism as the basis of the new state. The entire population of the country irrespective of their ethnic backgrounds were to be known as Bengalis. The later identity might have a political connotation to it; but Bengali is also a cultural and linguistic identity having its roots in Bengali history and culture. Manobendra Narayan Larma, the lone representative of the Hill people in Parliament, refused to accept this constitution and formed the PCJSS in 1972, and later a military wing, the Shanti Bahini (SB), was added to it in 1973. The PCJSS, however, started its major activities after the assassination of Sheikh Mujib on 15 August 1975. Until then, Larma had hoped that he could carry on his bargaining at the political level with Mujib, but the military takeover on 15 August dashed those hopes.[11]

The CHT underwent full-scale militarization. The general officer commanding of Chittagong division was put in charge of its administration. The military controlled the political and economic lives of the Hill people. In the name of counter-insurgency and national security, massive violations of human rights took place, which had an adverse impact on the entire population, though women were the worst sufferers on sexual and ethnic grounds. The sexual politics during periods of conflict and war acquire very distinct targeted dimensions and women, thus, also suffered due to certain specific measures undertaken by the military in the name of counter-insurgency, such as clearing the jungles to search out members of the SB. Since CHT women collected many of their household essentials from the forests and also sold in the market, they were deprived of their traditional means of livelihood.

A peace accord signed between the GOB and the PCJSS on 2 December 1997 brought the armed hostilities to an end. But there is never an abrupt end to atrocities between the time of war/conflict and peace. Accords are no guarantee to sustainable peace unless they address the genuine and actual grievances of the aggrieved, which, this paper suggests, the CHT Peace Accord largely failed to do. It polarized the Hill community into pro-accord and anti-accord groups. This, along with the extremely slow pace of implementation, created a situation of uneasy peace in the region. Gunfire exchanges between the anti-accord United Peoples Democratic Front (UPDF) and the pro-accord PCJSS are still quite common.[12] Taking advantage of the ongoing conflict in the region, a group has emerged in the Hills in whose economic interest it is to keep the conflict going. There is, thus, a political economy of conflict, which further marginalizes the chances of peace and, as argued earlier, perpetuates, widens and deepens a culture of impunity.

Sexual Violence in the CHT

> I hated my mother. She used to force me to talk to the military officials who visited our house frequently. I was very young and quite beautiful. The military personnel loved to talk to me [and] my mother knew what their intentions were. Yet, she would force me to go and talk with them. The military had taken away my father; my mother hoped that if I befriended the military, they would release my father.[13]

This is how Kabita Chakma, former president of the HWF, narrated to me her childhood experience. She does not blame her mother any more. Having grown up and experienced a political movement, she blames the state for her mother's attitude. She believes that at that point in their home, her mother was helpless and the survival of the entire family, including her father who was in army captivity, was her only priority. In moments like these, notions of privacy break down. This brings in question the notion of the state as a guarantor of citizens' rights and also the issue of citizenship. How equal are we as citizens? Conflict, insurgencies and violence, as stated earlier, are the creations of state policies. The attempt to change people's lives through state power in the name of law and national interest takes away their lives from them. The resistances take varied forms. In this example, Kabita's mother, a homemaker, tried to salvage the family by appeasing the military. In other words, the military derived its impunity socially by creating fear within the family.

Violence against indigenous women is considered one of the major concerns in the CHT today. The perpetrators also enjoy impunity due to lack of access to justice. Military personnel are given impunity as they are tried in military court. Kalpana Chakma's case, discussed later, is a glaring example of this. The numbers attest to the continued and widespread nature of the violence. Though I do not agree with the politics of numbers in instances of violence, but here numbers have been used purposely to demonstrate that despite the accord violence continues. Between January 2007 and October 2012, there were 160 reported incidents of violence against indigenous women all over Bangladesh of which at least 96 per cent were cases of sexual violence (Kapaeeng Foundation 2013). It is widely believed that Bengali and security personnel in the CHT have used violence against women, particularly in the form of rape, as a weapon against Hill women. According to a report of the CHT Commission, over 94 per cent of cases of rape of Hill women between 1991 and 1993 were by security personnel. Over 40 per cent of these women were under 18 years of age (CHT Commission 1997: 9). In May 2011, Sujata Chakma was brutally killed, allegedly after rape by Ibrahim, a settler at Ultachhari village of Rangamati district. In 2012, a total of seventy-five indigenous women and children across the country were violated, out of which fifty-five were from the CHT and twenty from the plains.

Despite the CHT Peace Accord, the Hill women continue to be sexually harassed and assaulted by Bengali security personnel and Bengali settlers. During the conflict period, many Hill women were also abducted. The HWF has worked to take up cases of rape by security personnel and bring them to public forums. Kalpana Chakma, in fact, is a symbol of the Hill people's struggles and sacrifices within the state of Bangladesh. According to them, one hears of incidents of sexual harassment and rapes almost every week. Age is no longer a factor, young girls aged 10 and 12 to women in their 50s are being raped. The opening of the hills for tourism has added to the crimes. Violence against women takes varied forms—sexual assault, rape, murder after rape, suicide following rape, kidnapping, stalking and more. Some of the Hill people have indicated that there have been incidents of intra-community violence as well. Modernity, technology and development, along with lack of good governance and a reliable justice system, are contributing to the increase in violence against women.[14]

Case Studies of Violence against Women

In May 2011, Sujata Chakma was brutally killed, allegedly after rape, by Ibrahim, a settler at Ultachhari village of Rangamati district. A major impediment to women getting justice and fair treatment is lack of legal assistance. On 26 August 2003, the Bengali settlers burnt down fourteen Adivasi villages. Complaints came of the rape of ten women during that attack. A representative team of the Permanent Committee for the Ministry of CHT Affairs along with many human rights organizations investigated the incident, but they maintained a silence about the incidents of rape. On 28 April 2012, a group of Bengali settlers assaulted and robbed an indigenous woman, Alpana Chakma, in Rangamati district. The victim was seriously wounded and later a case was filed against seven unidentified Bengali settlers at the Longadu police station. Two of them were arrested. However, the perpetrators threatened the indigenous people, asking them to withdraw the case. Again, on 30 May 2012, a Bengali settler, Md Amir Hossein (45), and his two sons, Md Jasim (21) and Md Ibrahim (18), of Amtala in Rangamati district beat up three indigenous villagers, including a woman. The victims belonged to one family and the intention of the perpetrators was to forcibly grab their land.[15]

The Abduction of Kalpana Chakma

Kalpana Chakma, an indigenous and women's rights activist, and organizing secretary of the HWF, was kidnapped on 12 June 1996 from her village home at New Lallyaghona, Baghaichari, Rangamati, CHT. She was 23. There is still no word of her whereabouts, nor is there any indication of whether she is alive.[16]

Her abduction came at a time when she was active in highlighting the plight of indigenous women who were routinely being tortured, abducted, raped, discriminated against and often murdered. She had been threatened with rape and assassination earlier, and though apprehensive, she had refused to back down. On that night, several hours before the seventh national elections, Kalpana had returned home from campaigning for the independent candidate, Bijay Ketan Chakma, a senior presidium member of Pahari Gana Parishad, supported by the indigenous people. Her brothers were eyewitnesses to the crime, and named Lieutenant Ferdous of the Bangladeshi army, Nurul Haque, a commander of Village Defence Party (VDP), and Saleh Ahmed, a member of the same organization, as the main culprits.

The day after Kalpana was taken, her brothers went to the army camp to search for her, but were forced to leave. Over the years, three separate investigations have been undertaken, but these have failed to even consider eyewitness evidence of the family members. Her family was later pressured by the military to leave the village. The army is also believed to be responsible for spreading rumours that Kalpana had 'eloped' with her captor. Gunshots were fired at a crowd that had gathered to protest her abduction two weeks after the incident.

Kalpana Chakma's diaries were published five years after her abduction. In them, she talks of persecution and threats of rape of Hill women. Subsequent administrations have at best neglected the case and at worst sheltered the guilty army personnel from prosecution. The executive director of the Bangladesh Human Rights Commission (BHRC) falsely claimed that Kalpana Chakma was safe in Tripura and that the accused armed forces members were just used as cover-ups by her family to hide the fact that she had eloped. Lieutenant Ferdous has been promoted and still serves in the military in the same area. The case demonstrates the extent of violence, the arrogance of power and the impunity enjoyed by the military personnel.

As a result of this case, Kalpana Chakma became a symbol and an inspiration for the Hill women's cause. Her abduction became a national issue and the HWF networked with the mainstream women's organizations and the left movements to bring it to the fore. It needs to be emphasized here that the fate of many Bengali women is no different; however, I am fully conscious of the difference between rapes committed in peacetime and rapes committed during war/conflict. In the latter case, one is not only targeting a woman but also an enemy woman; the means to seek justice (if at all there can be any) are also limited or non-existent. More importantly, the dynamics of nationalism are at play. Talking to the rape survivors was very difficult for me while carrying out research in the CHT as they refused to talk or even be identified. However, I did manage to talk to two of them.

Shushoma, Khagrachari, May 2007

Shushoma, now 45, came forward voluntarily. She told me categorically that she had nothing more to lose. She did not want any more wars, referring to the continuous fights between the PCJSS and the UPDF, which was why, for the sake of her people, she was opening up after twenty years of silence. She did not want any other woman to suffer like her. Shushoma was a family planning worker. Her husband was a government servant. In 1984, there were often raids in their village. The military would come and beat up the men, take away the food and accuse the villagers of helping the SB. The men would mostly spend the nights outside, either in relatively safe localities or hide in the jungles. Shushoma used to be alone in the house with her 2-year-old daughter. One night when the military entered the village, everybody ran for their lives. But Shushoma could not as her daughter had high fever. The Bengali settlers were with the military. They entered her house, damaged everything and then shouted at her, accusing her of supporting the SB secretly. They enquired about her husband as well. By that time, she was almost senseless out of sheer fear and she thought that she would die. She could not say a single word and her daughter was crying. Next she remembers two Bengali settlers on top of her. She regained her senses the next morning. Her daughter was lying near her, fast asleep. The house was in a mess and the village was almost deserted. Her neighbours consoled her and took care of her. She realized that people knew about what had happened, but nobody said anything. Her husband returned after many days, but he refused to even look at her. That hurt her the most. The village elders talked to him and made him understand, but Shushoma could never go back to him. With tears in her eyes, she told me that she lived on only for her daughter's sake. She blamed her husband for not being there on that fateful night; yet treating her like a piece of dirt after his return. She never talked about it, but within her she had changed. She does not trust any man any more or even the institution of marriage. She believes that we are all lonely in this world and one needs to accept that. After all, she has lived a life of loneliness and trauma herself. Her daughter is a schoolteacher at present. She wants her to be independent and take her own decisions in life. Before winding up with me, she told me, 'Look, I am an independent woman today, but at what cost? I don't want any other woman to buy her independence at this cost.'

Shushoma's dreams of a peaceful non-violent CHT are, however, far from being realized. Even today, in post-accord CHT, women continue to be raped.

Kalashona, Khagrachari, July 2004

Kalashona, aged 45, hails from Mohalchari, where, following a dispute between a Bengali settler and the Hill people, the settlers killed a man, wounded twenty-five others, raped nine women and torched about four hundred houses in twelve villages on 26 August 2003. About 2,000 Hill people were rendered homeless as a consequence.[17] Kalashona was one of the rape victims.

When we met, she broke down and, seizing my hands, she kept repeating that she could not stay in her house as the military was looking for her, that she had sneaked out to see me. Sobbing, she told me that on that fateful day, she had been working in the field when she saw fire in the neighbouring villages. At first she thought that the Bengali settlers would not come to their village, but they did. People began to run for their lives, some even on boats. She too accompanied them. Her 20-year-old daughter and 9-month-old granddaughter were also with her. The settlers and the army got hold of the boats and took them to the cremation place in the mountains. There they beat up people mercilessly. The settlers had got hold of her daughter, who was shouting for help. Kalashona snatched the baby from her daughter and asked her to run. Then eight of the army people attacked her and two of them raped her. They strangled the baby to death. There were many witnesses to this incident. They brought the body of the baby back and buried her. Many other young girls were raped, but they didn't speak about it since they were young and had their future before them. Kalashona, however, despite all the risks, wanted the world to know.

The military is looking for her, presumably to keep her from talking. Her husband is angry with her, yet, as a woman, she feels that she has this obligation to other women. Her daughter is almost insane with grief over the loss of her daughter and the fate of her mother, but Kalashona continues to hold on. She does not want any compensation: 'You cannot compensate for certain things in life, but you can fight it, and opening up is my mode of fighting back.'

I could not but be impressed by her agency and will to resist and fight back.

As suggested earlier, creating fear and controlling women and, therefore, society through it is a major objective of sexual violence, of rape more specifically. Samari Chakma wrote on 12 June 2014, the eighteenth anniversary of Kalpana Chakma's abduction:

> I grew up in the Hills during the military rule. In those days, one of the strategies of Bengali rule was the threat of raping Pahari [Hill] women.... Our lives were highly controlled.... It was more the fear of being raped, rather than its actual occurrence, which gnawed at our insides.

She goes on to discuss how societal values and responses have changed in the post-accord situation. During the conflict period, there was no means of knowing if a Hill woman had been raped, but if the HWF came to know about it, its members would go, investigate and write reports about it. But there was no reporting of it in the newspapers. If the HWF had news that army personnel in a particular area had made lists of young Hill women, they would then go and discuss with the residents how to resist sexual harassment. But this is no longer so in the post-accord scenario. An attitudinal change has come about in Hill society towards women and rape, which marks a major shift and threat for women. The word *dhorshon* (rape) was non-existent in the Chakma language, but now Hill men are also raping Hill women. In the 1980s, if a Chakma woman was raped, *lajja* (shame) or the loss of chastity was not an individual or family affair; it was considered to be a community/village affair. The villagers, including the *karbari* (village head), would sit together and decide upon how to resist the assaults. In the post-accord setting, Bengali values have entered into the Hills. While rape is continuing unabated, it is now seen as the raped woman's loss of chastity and honour, not a community affair. This, indeed, is a major threat for women.

In the CHT, the military enjoys impunity through the Special Powers Act of 1947, given to it during the insurgency. Since the accord remains only marginally implemented, the military continues to enjoy these special powers and uses the Act extensively, particularly in conflict-prone areas, whether it is in the plains or hills, as a weapon of oppression. The Act established preventive detention and since 1974, successive governments in Bangladesh have made use of it to detain individuals who might commit 'prejudicial acts' against the state. Under Section 2(f) of the Act, these include undermining the sovereignty or security of Bangladesh, creating or exciting feelings of enmity and hatred between different communities, and interfering with the maintenance of law and order. The Act provides no guidance on the burden of proof necessary for the government to conclude that an individual is likely to commit such an act. As a result, detentions under the Special Powers Act generally rely on allegations, with very little evidence. There are few, if any, institutional checks against its abuse by government officials. Detention under the Act is generally performed at the behest of the district magistrate or additional district magistrate in the area. In most districts, the district magistrate is also the district administrator, as Article 115 of the Constitution of Bangladesh provides that subordinate courts are to be under the control of the executive. In the absence of true separation of powers, detentions are often politically motivated within the districts. The Ministry of Home Affairs is supposed to provide a report within thirty days stating the grounds for detention of an individual. The Act allows for initial detention of a period of one month; after this time an advisory board can indefinitely extend the detention for a period of six months at a time. Additionally, detainees are denied the right to legal representation before the advisory board.

Impunity is also enjoyed through the ethnic divide. Sectarian violence is a major cause of sexual violence against women in the Hills. The burden of evidence also is a part of impunity. Samari Chakma (2014) writes that as a practising lawyer in Khagrachari, she had the opportunity of closely observing legal cases concerning rape in 2014. She was disturbed to find that none of the medical reports attest to the woman or girl being raped. On closer examination, she found that doctors were being pressured by both the military and the civil administration not to attest or confirm reports of rape. The ethnic divide is very clear here: government doctors are instructed that if Bengali settlers have raped Hill women or girls and it is found to be true, 'communal harmony' in the CHT would be disturbed. Thus, once again, women are being sacrificed at the altar of 'national security'.

CONCLUDING REMARKS

Impunity is a major challenge in women's battles against sexual violence. This is not an easy fight. The patriarchal norms regulating our lives accept impunity as a given in many instances. This analysis has traversed the paths of the personal, social, political, national and global. The dominant paradigms of the secular and religious come together on the societal construction of gender. The power of this construction itself is a major obstacle in the deconstruction of impunity. While legal measures are a necessary step, it is only the beginning. What is required is the unveiling of the minds of both men and women, and the establishment of a knowledge system to bring a paradigm shift in the dominant discourses. When Gayatri Spivak (1994) posed the question on whether the subaltern can speak, its value addition to the body of knowledge and lived lives opened new windows of thoughts. Interventions are required from the personal to the global levels to scope out the voices of both women and men to deconstruct the hegemony of masculinity, power and control violence based on sex. The culture of impunity needs to be broken by breaking the culture of silence and changing the established notions of shame and honour. Samari Chakma's (2014) writing is not only a piece on the CHT, but maps the limits of modernity, the importance of attitude. It is the mind where war begins and it is the mind where, through activism at various levels, the violence of impunity will be fought. The task is difficult, but the voices speaking out are also loud and clear.

NOTES

1. Interview with Ferdausi Priyobhashini, 29 May 2014.
2. Interview with Dr Meghna Guhathakurta, executive director, Research Initiatives, Bangladesh, 12 June 2014.
3. Interview with Dr Firdous Azim, head, Department of English and Humanities, Brac University, 28 May 2014.
4. Interview with Dr Hameeda Hossain, human and women's rights activist, 18 May 2014.
5. Constitution of the People's Republic of Bangladesh, as modified up to 31 May 2000.
6. Interview with Dr Meghna Guhathakurta, 12 June 2014.
7. I take strong issue with Sarmila Bose's 2011 work, *Dead Reckoning: Memories of the 1971 Bangladesh War*, on methodological grounds.
8. See the full text at http://www.un.org/en/ga/search/view_doc.asp?symbol=S/RES/1820%282008%29 (accessed 3 June 2015).
9. See http://www.un.org/en/ga/search/view_doc.asp?symbol=S/RES/1888%282009%29 (accessed 3 June 2015).
10. The daily *Prothom Alo* used this terminology on the occasion of International Women's Day in March 2014.
11. For details, see Mohsin (1997).
12. For details of the post-accord situation, see Mohsin (2003).
13. Personal interview with Kabita Chakma, Dhaka, 18 February 2010.
14. Findings from the author's field visits to the CHT in 2013 and 2014.
15. Based on different reports and the author's field visits.
16. Based on field visits and reports in the *Dhaka Tribune* (http://www.dhakatribune.com/juris/2014/feb/14/searching-17-years#sthash.6RqfqfPz.dpuf [accessed 6 June 2015]).
17. As reported in the *Daily Star*, Dhaka, 19 March 2004.

REFERENCES

Ahmed, Leila. 1992. *Women and Gender in Islam: Historical Roots of a Modern Debate*. New Haven: Yale University.

Bose, Sarmila. 2011. *Dead Reckoning: Memories of the 1971 Bangladesh War*. Columbia University Press.

Bangladesh Bureau of Statistics. 1993. Statistical Pocketbook of Bangladesh. Government of the People's Statistical Division, Republic of Bangladesh, Ministry of Planning. Dhaka.

Brownmiller, Susan. 1975. *Against Our Will: Men, Women and Rape*. Harmondsworth: Penguin Books Ltd., p. 79.

Chakma, Samari. 2014. 'Are We All Equal in the Eyes of Law?' (translated by Rahnuma Ahmed), *New Age*, 12 April. Dhaka.

Chatterjee, Partha. 1989. 'The Nationalist Resolution of the Women's Question', in Kumkum Sangari and Sudesh Vaid (eds), *Recasting Women: Essays in Indian Colonial History*, pp. 233–53. New Delhi: Kali for Women.

CHT Commission. 1997. *Life is Not Ours: Land and Human Rightsin the Chittagong Hill Tracts, Bangladesh*, International Work Group for Indigenous Affairs, Copenhagen.

CHT Commission. 2000. *Life is Not Ours: Land and Human Rights in the Chittagong Hill Tracts, Bangladesh*, International Work Group for Indigenous Affairs, Copenhagen.

Das, Tapos Kanti. 2014. 'Qaisar Sentenced to Death for War Crimes', *New Age*, 24 December.

García-Moreno, C., H.A.F.M. Jansen, M. Ellsberg, L. Heise and C. Watts. 2005. 'WHO Multi-Country Study on Women's Health and Domestic Violence against Women'. Geneva: World Health Organization. http://www.who.int/gender/violence/who_multicountry_study/Introduction-Chapter1-Chapter2.pdf (accessed 2 June 2015).

Guhathakurta, Meghna. 2003. 'Religion, Politics and Women: The Bangladesh Scenario'. http://www.academia.edu/6303274/Religion_Politics_and_Women_the_Bangladesh_Scenario (accessed 2 June 2015).

Hasan, M.A. 2002. 'War and Women'. War Crimes Fact Finding Committee (Trust) and Genocide Archive & Human Studies Centre, Dhaka.

Hoque, Mofidul and Laurel E. Fletcher (eds). 2012. 'Colloquium on Accountability of Sexual Violence Crimes and Experiences of the International Tribunals'. Liberation War Museum, Dhaka.

Hossain, Hameeda. 2006. 'Women's Movement in Bangladesh: The Struggle Within', *Daily Star*, 5 February.

Ibrahim, Neelima. 1998. *Ami Birangona Bolchi* (I am a War Heroine Speaking). Dhaka: Jagriti Prokashoni.

Islam, Kajalie Shehreen. 2012. 'Breaking down the Birangona: Examining the (Divided) Media Discourse on the War Heroines of Bangladesh's Independence Movement', *International Journal of Communication*, 6: 2131–48.

Kabir, Shahriar. 1998. *Ekatture Birangona: Bhindeshi Nayanikar Obhiggota* (Heroines of '71: The Experience of Foreigner Nayanika). Dhaka: Janokontho.

Kapaeeng Foundation. 2013. *Human Rights Report 2012 on Indigenous Peoples in Bangladesh*. Dhaka: Kapaeeng Foundation.

Mohsin, Amena. 1997. *The Politics of Nationalism: The CHT, Bangladesh*. Dhaka: University Press Limited.

————. 2003. *The CHT, Bangladesh: On the Difficult Road to Peace* (International Peace Academy Occasional Paper Series). Boulder: Lynne Rienner.

————. 2004. 'Gendered Nation, Gendered Peace', *International Journal of Gender Studies*, 11(1): 43–64.

————. 2013. 'Experiences of Two Indigenous Women, CHT', in Shaheen Akhtar, Hameeda Hossain and Sultana Kamal (eds), *Rising From the Ashes: Women's Narratives of 1971* (translated by Niaz Zaman), pp. 85–89. Dhaka: University Press Limited.

Mookherjee, Nayanika. 2006. '"Remembering to Forget": Public Secrecy and Memory of Sexual Violence in Bangladesh War of 1971', *Journal of the Royal Anthropological Institute* (New Series), 12(2): 433–50,

Spivak, Gayatri Chakravorty. 1994. 'Can the Subaltern Speak?', in Patrick Williams and Laura Chrisman (eds), *Colonial Discourse and Postcolonial Theory: A Reader*, pp. 66–111. London: Harvester Wheatsheaf.

Zahid, Surma. 2012. *Ekatture Nirjatito Narider Itihash* (The History of the Tortured Women [of 1971]). Dhaka: Onnesha Prokashon.

3

Birangona

Bearing Witness in War and 'Peace'*

BINA D'COSTA

On a mild September morning in 2011, three members from the ICT investigation team came to my house. The traffic in Dhaka city was horrendous. The investigators decided to make use of precious time by interviewing me on our way to the ICT. They were interested to hear about my work with the women who, by bearing witness to sexual and gender-based violence in the 1971 war, became its icons—*birangona*s—and those children who were born through violence, bearing witness to reproductive crimes—the war babies. While I have much respect for everything that they were doing to include the experiences of *birangona*s and war babies in their investigations into the violence during the war, I was quite taken aback by the abruptness of their questions. 'How many did you find? Where? Give us their contact details please...'

---

*This is an updated and revised version of an essay published in 2005, titled, 'Coming to Terms with the Past'. My thanks to Hameeda Hossain, Amena Mohsin and Justine Chambers for their comments on the drafts.

My insistence that not many would be keen to share their stories publicly, especially with police investigators, was not so seriously considered; yet I did not give in so easily. Women's testimonies self-consciously serve within a liberation lineage where the most oppressed and 'invisible' subject is the powerful speaking woman, in this case the *birangona*. The narrating of history by *birangona*s and by other witnesses of sexual and reproductive crimes before the ICT importantly gives voice to the sexual and psychological torture used as a strategy by the Pakistani war machine during the war in 1971.

Waiting to testify for long periods before providing evidence and then having to face the accused and the defence team are not easy tasks. Yet *birangonas* testified in front of the ICT in an attempt to share their experiences in a public tribunal in 1992. They also testified in other women-friendly platforms, such as the Liberation War Museum in Bangladesh, at the Extraordinary Chambers in the Courts of Cambodia (ECCC) in 2012 and at the Comfort Women's Public Tribunal in 2000, also known as the Tokyo Tribunal.

Uncovering the truth from a shroud of erroneous national consciousness is a prerequisite for a nation's reconciliation with its own past. When the wall of silence that surrounds abuses of women's human rights breaks down with testimonies and evidence, how do we then translate emotions and passions into practical actions? This chapter addresses this query by focusing on the vulnerability of women survivors of the 1971 war whose needs both the state and the civil society have failed to address in a meaningful and responsive way.

The chapter begins by examining women's experiences of sexual violence and torture in the *muktijudhyo* (the Liberation War of 1971). It then goes on to provide a brief account of the war and the responses to *birangona*s in the immediate aftermath of the war. Through a brief analysis of the Peoples' Tribunal of 1992, this chapter then argues for a gender-sensitive and safe space for women to share their memories of sexual and gender-based violence during this time. The final part of the chapter discusses the broader contexts of women's advocacy in the region and elsewhere in redressing rape and sexual violence.

THE CONTEXT: RECOVERING THE PAST

The Cambodian Defenders Project in partnership with the Victim Support Section of the ECCC convened the Asia-Pacific Regional Women's Hearing on Gender-based Violence in 2012. Testimonies were presented by survivors and witnesses of sexual violence perpetrated during the conflicts in the region—Cambodia (1975–79), Bangladesh (1971), Nepal (1996–2006) and Timor-Leste (1974–99) (Cambodian Defenders Project 2012). Saleha Begum, 55 at the time of the hearing, was 14 years old in 1971. She recounted how the Pakistani army and their local collaborators, the Razakars, abducted her, her sister and one of her neighbours. 'The soldiers committed all kinds of sexual orgy on us,' she recalled, which included sodomy (ibid.: 17). Begum was also a witness to the torture, rape and murder of many girls during the conflict. She was raped repeatedly and brutally for two months in front of her sisters and other girls, which caused severe vaginal bleeding and permanent scars. Then she was transferred to the Golmari Camp in Khulna where she remained for another two months. Begum, her sister, and six other girls and women who became pregnant were taken to a nearby bridge to be killed. Although she was shot in the leg, she survived, but her sister and the other rape victims died that day. Begum gave birth four months after liberation, resulting in abandonment by her family and the community.[1]

Begum started working as a domestic help and got married following Bangladesh's independence. She told her husband about her ordeals in 1971 and he first wanted to divorce her but was deterred by the fact that she was pregnant again at that time. She gave birth to a daughter. Begum's in-laws abandoned her and rejected the daughter, who was unable to meet her paternal grandparents until she was 14 years old. Begum's daughter is very proud of her mother for speaking out (ibid.: 17–18, 39).

Mosamma Rajia Khatun Kamla, 55, in her testimony at the same hearing, said she was only 13 years old when she suffered rape, sexual slavery, unlawful confinement and torture (ibid.: 38). She was married off by her parents to protect her from the Pakistani soldiers and was sent to stay with her in-laws. When the Pakistani army attacked the village, she escaped to the forest along with her mother-in-law. She learnt the next day that her father had been killed, along with many other relatives. She was separated from her mother-in-law, and a Razakar tricked her into going to a military camp. There, she was stripped naked and tied to a pillar. She was raped by six soldiers one after another and was left tied to the pole for the entire night. Her vagina had been permanently damaged due to the brutal sexual violence. She was detained in the camp for fifteen days and repeatedly raped during that time. When her rapists were no longer able to perform vaginal sex because she was very swollen, they performed anal and oral sex, spreading the semen over her face. She witnessed many rapes, torture and executions at the military camp. After a fortnight, she was ordered to work as a cleaner in the camp and given the task of washing the Pakistani army uniforms although she could barely walk because of the injuries to her anus and vagina. She managed to escape by hiding in a pond. When the soldiers could not find her, they randomly shot into the pond.

Naked, she made her way to the other side of the pond with a bamboo stick. There, she found the house of an old woman, and the two hid together. The old woman gave her some bananas and clothes, and advised her to go to India as a refugee. On the road with others to India, she witnessed many atrocities, including rape and murder perpetrated by the Pakistani military and their Bangladeshi collaborators. Eventually she met *muktijodhya*s (freedom fighters) on the road who took her to a safe haven and provided her with medical care. When one of the *muktijodhya*s took her to his own house, the woman there refused to allow her in. With no food, she slept in a cow shed and survived as she could in hiding by begging (ibid.: 17–18). She recalled, 'After liberation, I could not find work because people could see from my scars that I was a rape victim, and no one gave me food or shelter.'

The report further documents how Rajia Khatun was deceived by a man into working in a brothel. He assured her that it was a place for rape victims to get help. The report notes that at first the brothel owner, Shushuma, was much kinder than many others she had asked for help, giving her food and shelter, and allowing her to bathe. She was provided medical treatment for her vaginal injuries. She stated, 'Then I realized she was treating me so that she could use me as a prostitute' (ibid.: 18). When she refused to have sex with her first customer, she was beaten brutally. She was trapped and forced to stay for three years, where she eventually met her husband as a customer. After buying her from the brothel owner, he brought her to his house, where she discovered he already had one wife and three children. She was rejected by his family. Still, she remained and gave birth to two sons. When her sons were still young, one an infant and the other 5 years old, her husband died. She and her children were thrown out by her in-laws. With nowhere else to turn and two sons to support, she returned to prostitution. She said: 'I still remember those days, though forty years have passed, and still I have not received justice.' Her sons, now grown, have faced stigma throughout their lives because their mother was raped during the Liberation War. She concludes, 'I came here to share my story, but it is not about me only, but about the millions, all those who were killed, tortured and raped in 1971' (ibid.: 18–19).

These two testimonies vividly articulate the strategic use of rape as a genocide tactic in the *muktijudhyo* (D'Costa 2011, 2014). Although no accurate statistics are available, in Bangladesh it is generally accepted that in 1971 an estimated 200,000 Bengali girls and women were raped by soldiers. This figure has also been cited by feminist scholars elsewhere (Copelon 1995: 197; Manchanda 2001:

30). Scholars also cite that some 25,000 were forcibly impregnated (Brownmiller 1975: 84; Copelon 1995). Based on my own research, especially interviews with medical practitioners, social workers and government officials who worked at that time in Bangladesh, I believe that a very large number of women and girls, both Bengali and of other ethnic groups, such as the Biharis, were targeted during 1971 (see Siddiqi 2013). Yet, women's narratives that directly speak to the war crimes of 1971 have been excluded from the official construction of history making. Feminist authors, filmmakers and cultural activists from Bangladesh, on the other hand, meticulously recorded women's stories in their representations (Akhtar 1999, 2006; ASK 2001; Bobby 2015; Gazi and Lutfa 2014). In this context, certain narratives were privileged and valorized, while other narratives were silenced in order to create an 'acceptable' national story (Chowdhury 2015; Hossain 2010; Matsui 1998; Puja 1998, 2001).

National interpretations of rape and forced impregnation of women saw these experiences as being less about women themselves than about the challenge to Bengali nationalist and masculine identity (D'Costa 2014). While the war ended Pakistani rule in Bangladesh, existing power relations, political hierarchies, and limited political and cultural ties with Pakistan persisted. The inevitable struggle for power in the years following the war, divisions between liberation leaders and the heavy dependence of the governments on political and economic alliances, in particular with the Middle East, allowed conservative groups who sided/collaborated with Pakistan during 1971 war to re-establish a power base and a limited legitimacy. It was in this context that the culture of impunity in Bangladesh developed. After the war ended on 16 December 1971 with Indian army intervention, the three states involved in the war, India, Bangladesh and Pakistan, began prolonged negotiations over the release of approximately 93,000 Pakistani prisoners of war (POWs), including 15,000 civilian men, women and children captured in Bangladesh/East Pakistan (Burke 1973: 1037) but detained under Indian authority. The matter was complicated by the Bangladeshi prime minister Sheikh Mujibur Rahman's insistence on trying 1500 Pakistani POWs for war crimes and the Pakistani president Zulfikar Ali Bhutto's reluctance to agree to it (ibid.: 1037–38). On 28 August 1973, India and Pakistan signed a treaty with Bangladesh's support, which provided repatriation of all POWs except 195 prisoners who Bangladesh insisted on prosecuting for genocide (for various statistics, see LaPorte 1972; Ministry of External Affairs 2000) and other war crimes (*Statesman Weekly*, 1 September 1973). Post-war tripartite diplomacy between India, Pakistan and Bangladesh, such as the 1973 India–Pakistan agreement and the Bangladesh–India repatriation proposals, stipulated that Pakistan would investigate and have the obligation to try those Pakistanis who were found guilty of war crimes. Pakistan also made similar promises in its submissions to the International Court of Justice on 11 May 1973. Unfortunately, these undertakings were not fulfilled afterwards.

Bangladesh's unwillingness and inability after 1975, when Sheikh Mujibur Rahman was brutally killed, to hold the perpetrators responsible for war crimes led to a brittle peace in the post-war state. There was growing frustration and resentment among its citizens about the fabrication of history through textbooks and government-sponsored media to serve the need of authoritarian regimes in the post-1975 period until Ershad's resignation in 1990. Also, there were various kinds of international, regional and domestic pressures, including by families of persons stranded in Pakistan.[2]

Bangladesh's history has been written and revised during each change of political regime, a process further complicated by the influence of military and religious elites. Eventually, the reinstatement of some of the infamous pro-Pakistani political leaders who were directly responsible for the genocide committed in 1971 led to the construction of separate and parallel histories: one that exists in the official discourse and others that exist in micro-narratives, in memory and in lived experience. While the gender aspects of this deliberate suppression of women's experiences of sexual violence during conflicts have been investigated at length by feminist researchers (ASK 2001; Butalia 1995a, 1995b, 1998; Das 1994, 1995; Hossain 2010; Ibrahim 1998; Menon and Bhasin 1996, 1998; Menon 1998 in South Asia, for example), what remains is the question of how to bargain with a patriarchal state without compromising the agenda for justice should suppressed stories come out. Local initiatives by Bangladeshi feminist or civil society organizations made several attempts to organize platforms for silenced voices to be heard, but they remain marginalized and unstable. The Peoples' Tribunal proceedings in 1992 (discussed later in the chapter) and the oral history publication by the ASK that came out in 2001 are two examples where pro-liberation civil society and feminist human rights organizations made efforts to bring women's voices to the foreground.[3] Before discussing these initiatives, it is important to first elaborate on the historical events of the 1971 war and the initial responses to *birangonas*.

MUKTIJUDHYO: 1971

Anti-colonial nationalism reached its peak in South Asia after World War II. Finally, on 3 June 1947, the British government announced the Mountbatten Plan, a policy statement that recognized the inevitability of the partition of India. The plan was implemented with the birth of Pakistan on 14 August 1947 under the provisions of the British Indian Independence Act 1947. Pakistan was composed of five provinces in two regions: Punjab, Sindh, the North-West Frontier Province (NWFP) and Baluchistan in West Pakistan, and East Pakistan that became Bangladesh later on.

During their years of union, the two regions of Pakistan enjoyed an uneasy partnership marked by intermittent regional, economic, political and cultural conflicts. Tension reached its peak after a national election in 1970 escalated into an armed conflict in March 1971. For over nine months, the Pakistani army tried to subdue the rebellious civilian Bengali population. A guerrilla insurgency began in March and with Indian armed assistance, Bangladesh finally attained its independence in December 1971. Much has been written on this war, and in recent times various accounts have also documented women's diverse experiences of it.[4]

The Liberation War of Bangladesh was very much a story of women. Although the exact number is unknown, many women participated as active combatants in the war. They also assisted freedom fighters in a range of ways, for example, by hiding them in their houses in times of crisis, and providing them with food and medicine. When men in local communities fled in fear of army persecution or to fight in the guerrilla war, women took care of families.[5] After the war, many widows were responsible for the children and elders. Finally, women were targeted for rape and forced impregnation by the Pakistani military.

The 22 December 1971 proclamation of the People's Republic of Bangladesh declared the wartime victims as *birangona* (Gayen 2015).[6] Soon after his return to Bangladesh in 1972, the first prime minister of Bangladesh, Sheikh Mujibur Rahman, popularly known as Bangabandhu, acknowledged that women made grave sacrifices for the 'freedom of the country' and emphasized that rape victims should be treated with honour and respect. In his speeches and in private conversations, Mujib reiterated his promise to rehabilitate women and used the word *birangona*. The literal translation of the word is 'war heroine'. Originally, however, it was intended to honour all women—political activists, freedom fighters, rape survivors and so on—who participated in the national struggle (Kamal 2001). The term was also intended to give rape survivors an honorary status and to provide them with equal access to privileges in the public sector, such as the education and employment rights granted to male freedom fighters (Pereira 2002).

The term *birangona*, however, became a distinct marker or a boundary that identified these women as victims of rape and often subjected them to humiliation and abuse. As Faustina Pereira (ibid.) points out, by its very nature, the term was a restrictive privilege. So strong was the stigma of rape in Bangladesh that most women did not take advantage of the title, 'because to do so would be tantamount to focusing on the scar of rape on the victim, thus forcing her to risk a social death' (ibid.: 62). However, it was not only the naming that added to the stigma but Bangladeshi society's rejection of the women and girls who were subjected to sexual torture in 1971. The presence of the *birangona* is a stinging reminder to the state of how the norm of purdah, or female seclusion, collapsed during the war when men were unable to defend their women. Not only were women left unprotected and exposed to sexual violence, many were abandoned by their families after the war. Rahnuma Ahmed (2015) notes that through the discursive production and reproduction of ultranationalist forces, *birangonas* become socially vulnerable, ideologically marginal and eventually silenced.

As a response to this complex situation, concerned Bengalis, especially the cultural elite of the country, recently coined a new term: *nari jodhya* or women combatants. Men who fought in the Liberation War were referred to as *muktijodhya*, *mukti* meaning freedom and *jodhya* combatant. The most common translation of this is 'freedom fighters'. In October 2014, the Jatiya Muktijodhya Council (JMC, National Freedom Fighters' Council) formally recognized *birangonas* as freedom fighters.[7] Parliament, on 29 January 2015, passed a bill to recognize *birangonas* as freedom fighters by preparing a list of their names. Monirul Islam the lawmaker from Jessore-2 constituency placed the proposal before the national parliament. Liberation War Affairs Minister A.K.M. Mozammel Huq said, 'The Ministry of Education has been requested to include *birangonas* in the textbooks. Moreover, it has been discussed in making their allowance Tk 10,000' (*Daily Star*, 30 January 2015). While this bill was passed unanimously, the house rejected another lawmaker's proposal to rename *birangona* to *bir konya* (brave girl/woman). The minister commented, 'It will not be wise to rename Birangona as it was named by Bangabandhu Sheikh Mujibur Rahman.'

The Ministry of Liberation War Affairs published a gazette notification on 12 October 2015 formally recognizing forty-one women as freedom fighters. Figure 3.1 is a snapshot of a table published in the *Dhaka Tribune* on 13 October 2015, providing a crucial acknowledgement for the brave women of 1971 by naming them. This is significant for various reasons. It brings with it some forms of economic justice that the *birangona*s have demanded for decades. Those awarded the status will now receive an honorarium, rations and medical services.[8] It is also interesting that while *birangona*s and women's rights activists in their advocacy emphasized that Bangladeshi society must break the taboo and silence related to sexual violence, the government followed the usual line that women usually do not want to come forward. The minister explained: 'We are in a discomfort as many of them do not want to publish their names due to social reasons.... However, the list will be updated regularly and their names will be published 30 years later so that they do not have to deal with social taboo' (*Dhaka Tribune*, 13 October 2015).

Figure 3.1: List of War Heroines Published in a National Daily

LIST OF WAR HEROINES RECOGNISED AS FREEDOM FIGHTERS					
MYMENSINGH		THAKURGAON		27	Rahela Begum
1	Moymuna Khatun	12	Sumi Bashugi	28	Lili Begum
2	Halima Khatun	13	Maleka	SIRAJGANJ	
3	Zahera Khatun	14	Moni Kisku	29	Aymona
4	Fatema Khatun	15	Niharani Das	30	Asiya Begum
HOBIGANJ		16	Nurjahan Begum	31	Surjo Begum
5	Majed Begum (alias Majeda Khatun)	17	Hafeza Begum	32	Komola Bewa
SYLHET		CHAPAINAWABGANJ		33	Joygon
6	Eshnu Begum	18	Rabiya Begum	34	Suraiya Khatun
	Kushtia	19	Maleka Begum	35	Mahela Begum
7	Elejan Nesa	20	Hasina Begum	36	Hamida Bewa
8	Momena Khatun	21	Jolo Begum	37	Hasna Begum
9	Doljan Nesa	22	Sofeda Begum	38	Srimoti Rajubala Dey
10	Mojiron Nesa	23	Ayesha Begum	39	Rohima Bewa
RANGPUR		24	Renu Begum	40	Chamena Khatun
11	Monsura Begum	25	Hajera Begum	41	Shamsunnahar Bewa
		26	Arbi Begum		

Without an informed plan of action to change patriarchal traditions and societal norms from which the stigma emanates, the introduction of new or innovative terms such as *nari jodhya* or these new measures might not prove enough to positively address justice for the *birangonas*. Although *jodhya* (a fighter) in its conventional interpretation implies an active combat role, the current regime has recognized various actors in the war as freedom fighters (see Note 7). Those *birangonas* who want to be recognized must be gazetted. At the time of writing, there were a total of 124 applications that the JMC had received, among which 80 were approved, verified and then recommended to the ministry for recognition. Even though both the JMC and the ministry included female officials in the process, the verification process involves several complex bureaucratic steps.

In addition, the conventional interpretation does not take into account the experiences of many women whose lives were changed dramatically by war outside this paradigm. Indeed, their sacrifice has virtually gone undocumented (not unseen). Despite some attempts to respond to their economic and security needs, the state has so far been unable to counter the social rejection of the *birangona*. On the other hand, the minister's reiteration of social taboo and stigma implicitly reinforces the belief that being raped in the war (even if it is for the nation) is something to be ashamed of, while fighting in the war is heroic. Shame and honour thus essentially shape *birangona*/*nari jodhya* construction by the Bangladeshi state.

LOOKING BACK AT VICTORY'S SILENCE

On 4 April 1971, the Bangladesh Armed Forces was formed with Bengali-manned battalions of the East Bengal Regiment (EBR) under the command of Colonel M.A.G. Osmani, a retired officer of the Pakistani army. During the first Bangladesh Sector Commanders Conference in July 1971, the battle zones throughout Bangladesh/East Pakistan were divided into eleven sectors for better management and coordination. Each sector had Bengali commanders in charge of the military operations; all of them had defected from the Pakistani armed forces. Tajuddin Ahmed, the prime minister of Bangladesh's government-in-exile, on 11 April 1971 in a speech on Free Bangla Radio stated, 'Today, a mighty army is being formed around the nucleus of professional soldiers from the Bengal Regiment and EPR [East Pakistan Rifles] who have rallied to the cause of the liberation struggle' (Ministry of External Affairs 2000: 282–86). The Mukti Bahini (Liberation Army) faced no personnel problem as Bengalis volunteered by the thousands—estimated at 175,000—to join them. This also included a large number of deserters from the EPR, EBR and the Bengali police force (Rizvi 1987).

Internally, the overwhelming support for the Mukti Bahini created a sense of insecurity among the Awami League leadership, resulting in the setting up of yet another exclusive guerrilla force, the Mujib Bahini (named after Sheikh Mujibur Rahman), which comprised diehard supporters of both the Awami League (AL) and Mujib (*Far Eastern Economic Review*, 4 September 1971; *The Times*, 20 May 1971, 15 June 1971). As Bangladeshi society transitioned from violence towards a more democratic or liberal political system, various forms of masculinities continued to influence post-war society, forming yet another patriarchal social order. Countless *muktijodhyas*, those who surrendered arms and returned to their civilian lives, lived in dire poverty. There were also those who continued to carry weapons and either became involved in criminal activities or were slowly absorbed by political parties. In addition, in the first five years of Bangladesh's sovereign life, the parallel politics between the Mujib Bahini and the Mukti Bahini created factionalism in its politics, which influenced the consciousness of Bangladesh's armed forces.

While both women and men participated in the struggle for independence as *muktijodhyas*, women were generally excluded from most honorific titles and awards, and the highest bravery decorations of the Bangladeshi state were reserved for those who served in the armed forces. Acknowledging the courage and sacrifice of male *muktijodhya*s, the government also awarded them with public service quotas to enter into various government departments. Bangladeshis commemorated them through patriotic songs, poems and literature. On the other hand, women were not beneficiaries of the actual or symbolic rewards. While there were no awards, even for women who were commended for their roles as active combatants, the government introduced a scheme for monthly pensions/grants and job quotas. Although neither men nor women participated in the Liberation War with benefits in mind, the government's ill-planned and biased policies created frustration within the community.

Immediately after independence, some *birangona*s were treated with respect. *Muktijodhya*s in formal and informal conversations with me indicated that they helped the women rescued from the rape camps in any way they could, such as offering them food, water and medicine, and taking them to health care units or back to their families.[9] Between 2001 and 2010, I have conducted a number of interviews with *birangona*s, war babies, *muktijodhya*s and the families of the victims. One of the freedom fighters I spoke with clearly stated, 'We always treated the women with respect and we were genuinely concerned about their suffering'.[10]

In contrast, the initial responses of the women's families were not positive. In middle-class families, the issue of rape was treated with secrecy and many families never revealed their daughters were 'taken' by the Pakistani army. A shroud of silence covered their stories. Some families took pregnant women to clinics for abortions. When asked, Respondent B said:

> It still remains as a scar in my heart. The government allowed abortion on a mass scale. They did not want any Pakistani child. Either they were to be aborted or to get out of the country as soon as possible. We had incubators and we were prepared to take the premature babies.[11]

Those families that could afford to exile their daughters to neighbouring India or one of the Western countries preferred abortions in order to quietly get rid of their family 'shame'. If the women were in an advanced stage of pregnancy, they were left in rehabilitation centres or clinics to give birth, after which the babies were given up for adoption.[12] When I asked Geoffrey Davis, who worked as a physician in Bangladesh immediately after the war, if there were some women who were reluctant to have abortions or give up their babies for adoption, he said, 'Well… a few of them did…'[13] When asked if he knew what happened to them, he answered:

> I have no idea. [The] ISS [International Social Service] was there to get as many babies as they could. Because there were less and less babies available for adoption in America and Western Europe and they wanted to get as many babies as they could get.

As I stated earlier, 25,000 cases of pregnancy were reported after the war. However, no official or unofficial statistics exist to my knowledge indicating the number of women who had abortions or the number of babies sent to other countries.

Several political developments could be identified that have contributed to the silence surrounding rape in Bangladesh. While the reintegration and rehabilitation of women into society was given the highest priority, rape as a sexual and reproductive crime received no significant attention from the government and the political elite despite its inclusion as a crime in the International Crimes Tribunal Act 1973. Bangladesh signed the Rome Statute on the Establishment of an International Criminal Court (ICC) on 17 July 1998 and now formally recognizes that rape, sexual aggression and gender-specific violence constitute war crimes and crimes against humanity. Bangladesh became the first South Asian state that ratified the Statute on 23 March 2010. Also, as mentioned earlier, post-war diplomacy between India, Pakistan and Bangladesh compromised the trial of war criminals and their collaborators, which had serious consequences for seeking justice. Pakistan never kept its promise to carry out the trials against those who were charged. In addition, the gradual rehabilitation of Bengali collaborators of the Pakistani army into the Bangladesh political scenario at both local and state government levels silenced the micro-narratives through direct or indirect coercion. In particular, with the lifting of the ban on religious political parties (Jahan 1995: 97), the *birangona* issue was buried further.

In spite of the Mahila Parishad's and other senior women's strong support for rehabilitation, there was little space for protest and advocacy for women's justice during the fifteen years of military dictatorship. Instead of the advocacy for gender justice, senior women policymakers and practitioners were more focused on getting the *birangona*s reintegrated in the wider Bangladeshi society. The demand for justice for sexual and reproductive crimes of 1971 was occurring in the larger context for demanding justice for all Bengali victims of war crimes, but not in the context of gender justice. Consequently, there was no coordinated and sustained feminist movement/consciousness to make available a 'pro-gender justice' political language at this time.

While in the Pakistani context 'purity' meant creating a 'proper' Muslim identity that would fit the Muslim Pakistani imagination, in the context of Bangladesh, it meant 'purging' the state of Pakistani blood. Children were vivid reminders of the attack on a 'pure' Bengali identity. Therefore, the Bangladeshi state responded to the issue of wartime pregnancy in a way it perceived as legitimate: it exercised its authority over women's bodies and their maternal role through abortion and forced adoption programmes. The needs of the women were insignificant in this nationalist construction of identity. Clinics, international adoption agencies and religious organizations facilitated these programmes, acting as surface mechanisms for arms of the state, often against the wishes of some of the women, thereby victimizing them for a second time. As far as Bangladesh was concerned, the task of flushing out 'impure' Pakistani blood was necessary for the honour of the new nation. The abstract notions of purity and honour are dangerous rationales for which women often pay heavily. The appropriation of birth, denying it and, when possible, stopping it through state abortions demonstrates the power of the state over women's bodies when they have little or no control (Das 1995: 55–83).

During this time women were symbolically distanced from birth by the nation-state's narrative. The abortion and adoption programmes carried out by the Bangladeshi government following the war indicate the forcible appropriation of women's bodies for the interest of the nation. In the context of the mass suicide of women during the partition of 1947, Urvashi Butalia (1998) argued that these actions were approved because women were protecting the purity of the community whose borders they constituted.[14] Similarly, in 1971, the issue of 'choice' became even more problematic in terms of the complex intersections of gender, religion and national interests in which women were trapped. Social workers, government officials and medical staff working in the rehabilitation centres and clinics were, like the *muktijodhyas*, genuinely compassionate towards the survivors. Geoffrey Davis recalled many women's stories:

> Some of the stories they told us were appalling. Being raped again and again and again by large Pathan soldiers. You couldn't believe that anybody would do that! All the rich and pretty ones were kept for the officers and all the other ones were distributed among the other ranks. And the women had it really rough. They did not get enough to eat. When they got sick, they got no treatment. A lot of them died in those camps. There was an air of disbelief about the whole thing… but the evidence clearly showed that it did happen.[15]

In my interviews, I was particularly interested in knowing if the *birangona* women had a choice in the matter of pregnancy and the high rates of terminations that took place. When I asked Davis if the social workers and the medical personnel involved respected women's choices to have an abortion or not, he replied:

> Nobody wanted to talk about it. You could not ask questions and get an answer. Quite often it would be that they couldn't remember. And the men didn't want to talk about it at all! Because according to them the women had been *defiled* [emphasis mine]. And women's status in Bangladesh was pretty low anyway. If they had been defiled, they had no status at all. They might as well be dead.[16]

Given the nature of social relations and family attitudes towards women, both Nilima Ibrahim and Maleka Khan, prominent social workers heavily involved in the rehabilitation programme of *birangonas*, in their interviews with the ASK oral history team, noted that women effectively had no choice.

The attitudes of and decisions taken by the social workers and medical staff in the rehabilitation centres similarly reflected patriarchal, traditional values about family, community norms and state policies, and they thus endorsed decisions to reintegrate women into society as soon as possible by keeping their trauma and ordeal a secret, contributing to the silencing in official documents and personal narratives. Respondent B, who worked in the rehabilitation projects and was particularly involved in the adoption programmes, commented: 'There was a wound. We tried to rehabilitate them, tried to accept the situation they were in. And we would never write names, neither addresses. Stigma would remain if people knew.'[17]

In the aftermath of the war in Bangladesh, Badrunnesa Ahmad, Bangladesh's first minister of education (1973–75), and Nurjehan Murshid, state minister for health and social welfare (1972–73) and minister of social affairs and planning (1973–75), in Parliament demanded justice on behalf of the *birangonas*. Yet there also existed a vast power discrepancy between the *birangonas* and the social workers, government officials or others who were involved in the rehabilitation programmes undertaken by the government. The shame and stigma attached to sexual violence were not challenged. Instead, there was an implicit charity-focused approach that denied women the opportunity to voice their protests if they were unwilling to go ahead with the state's prescribed policies. Women were cast as victims and only as victims did they deserve the state's assistance. In these contexts, it was almost impossible for them to speak out as strong and outspoken survivors.

On 7 January 1972, in response to the development of women's movements, the government set up the Central Organization for Women's Rehabilitation to institutionalize women's rehabilitation programmes and place them under the management of the national central women's rehabilitation board, which coordinated the government's post-war policies with regard to women. Sufia Kamal was the chairperson, who, along with Taslima Abed, Shahera Ahmed, Hajera Khatun and others, started the rehabilitation programmes in two houses in Eskaton, Dhaka (Scholte 2014). In 1974, the name of the board was changed by legislation to the Bangladesh Women's Rehabilitation and Welfare Foundation. Eventually, the government changed the profile of the foundation and merged it under the Women's Division of the Women and Children Affairs Ministry. Schemes such as those 'to free women from the *unchosen* [emphasis mine] curse of motherhood' (Gafur 1979: 555) and to encourage men to marry *birangonas* (ibid.: 429) reveal that patriarchal and traditional beliefs played out in decisions made in relation to these rehabilitation programmes.[18] The state-sponsored abortion and adoption programmes clearly aspired to prioritize the national identity of Bengalis, identifying the children carrying Pakistani blood as liabilities to the purity of the nation-state. In an atmosphere filled with nationalistic passion and hatred towards Pakistanis, *birangonas*, who were already vulnerable and relied on the state's prescribed policies, were unable to articulate resistance if they had any.[19] Since the pregnant body was a vivid reminder of the Pakistani father, *birangonas*' reproductive rights belonged to the nation.

As such, the primary goal of the state's rehabilitation programmes in relation to *birangonas* was not emancipative, but to reintegrate the women into the traditional gender roles they had previously performed as housewives, mothers or daughters, effectively silencing their experiences during the conflict. Women's own silence on the other hand guaranteed that the state's rehabilitation programmes remained unchallenged. This silence also ensured that the elite narrative construction of the past gained official acknowledgement.[20] However, there were significant efforts made by notable individuals to reclaim the voices of women in the attempted prosecution of war criminals in the early 1990s. After the fall of Hussain Muhammad Ershad, women's groups and a range of civil society actors were much more explicit in their demand for gender-sensitive justice for crimes committed in 1971 and for crimes against minority women, such as in the CHT.

QUESTIONING THE CULTURE OF IMPUNITY

The 1971 war in Bangladesh led to a complete breakdown of state and community. The question of justice assumed great urgency, but there was no common understanding of how to achieve it. In the absence of legal norms or any nationally organized political forces, there were several individual and local efforts to respond to the demands for justice. The most successful of all these efforts were led by a single woman, Jahanara Imam. Rumi, her son, participated in the war as a *muktijodhya* and was brutally tortured and killed by the Pakistani army in 1971. Her book *Ekatturer Dinguli* (Those Days of '71) is an autobiographical record of the violence and was published in 1986.[21]

Popularly known as *shahid jononi* (martyr mother), Jahanara Imam began a crusade in January 1992 directed against Golam Azam and other collaborators who had supported Pakistan during the 1971 war, and engaged in atrocities and sexual violence against Bangladeshi civilians (Ghosh 1993: 703–4).[22] On 29 December 1991, Golam Azam was appointed the *aameer* (chairperson) of the Jamaat-e-Islami (hereinafter Jamaat), an Islamic nationalist party of Bangladesh (Kabir 1993: 11) that did not support the liberation movement of Bangladesh, which had its roots in secularism and Bengali national identity.[23] The Jamaat members actively collaborated with the Pakistani army during the war (Jahan 1980: 58) and, as a consequence, along with some other religious parties, the party was banned after 1971 (ibid. 1995: 94). Following significant political changes in Bangladesh, in particular with the amendment in the Constitution in 1977 and the pro-Islamic tilt in the Zia and Ershad regimes, the Jamaat got involved in Bangladeshi politics once again (for details, see Shehabuddin 2008).[24]

Under her leadership, the pro-liberation movement was coordinated and people from various corners, such as the intellectuals, students, freedom fighters (both men and women) of the 1971 war, war widows and families, especially children whose parents had been killed organized under Projonmyo Ekattur (Generation '71), supported a massive movement to hold a symbolic people's tribunal to bring Golam Azam and other war criminals to trial. Imam was elected chairperson of the Ghatok Dalal Nirmul Committee (Committee for the Elimination of Killers and Collaborators) created on 19 January 1992 (Kabir 1993) to demand trials of war criminals. Under her, the National Coordinating Committee for Realization of Bangladesh Liberation War Ideals and Trial of Bangladesh War Criminals of 1971 was formed in February 1992, integrating the political parties in opposition and the cultural elite of Bangladesh to hold the people's tribunal. In Jahanara Imam's words: 'prompted by our commitment to the values of the Liberation War and love for our country and aggrieved by the failure of the government to try the war criminals', the committee decided to unearth 'evidence of complicity of all collaborators of war crimes, crimes against humanity, killings and other activities' (cited in Ziauddin 1999).

After three months of intensive organizing and activism, the people's tribunal was held in Dhaka on 26 March 1992 and nearly 200,000 people from all over the country participated as witnesses (*Dhaka Courier* 1992). This massive popular movement demonstrated that Bangladeshis were indeed interested in seeking justice for 1971. Unfortunately, however, the quality of the commission's reports was very poor, the language emotive rather than reasoned, and it lacked details that would lead to any possible criminal prosecutions (Ziauddin 1999). After Imam's death in 1994, political differences significantly weakened the movement.

Despite the intervening years, the silence surrounding the rape of women in 1971 was still prevalent and sexual violence remained a well-guarded secret within the affected families. Some viewed the 'digging into the past' as an unnecessary exercise that would cause them more pain and misery, especially because no organized effort to seek redress had been made in the country. Moreover, various interest groups ignored the sensitive nature of the women's stories and the fact that disclosing their identities might contribute to the stigma they were forced to bear by their communities. For example, at the Dhaka People's Tribunal in 1992, the court was not able to hold the hearings of the testimonies of victims and survivors of the 1971 war due to a government-sponsored assault by the police on the organizers (Kabir 2000: 29).[25] The government also filed cases of treason against the organizers (ibid. 1999: 20) that stagnated the movements afterwards.

The three rape survivors who were brought in from the rural areas of Kushtia, a southern region in Bangladesh, to provide testimonies were also unable to narrate their experiences. None of them had clear ideas about the tribunal proceedings, what their testimonies actually signified and what implications these public testimonies might have in their present lives (Begum 2001: 82, 86). The local activists who brought them to Dhaka did not ask them if they wanted to testify either (ibid.: 102) and they were left in the dark. Yet their photos and stories appeared in national newspapers the next day (Begum 2001; *Dhaka Courier* 1992). As a consequence, because of strong ideas around purity and honour, these women were subsequently persecuted and excluded from participating in the life of their communities.[26]

Their ordeals were featured in the print media in 1996 (*Daily Shongbad*, 11 November 1996) and fresh interest in their stories brought them into the public arena again. This experience had a significant impact on the women's increasing reluctance to speak with 'outsiders'. In addition, women's organizations became very sceptical about bringing *birangona* women to speak openly and testify about their experiences at public platforms. Most women still do not feel comfortable talking about the pain and trauma of 1971. Their discomfort is a combination of traumatic memories, traditional parameters of shame and purity, the stigma attached to the rape experience, the need to reintegrate into their society, and to address basic requirements for survival. In combination, all these have led the women to create their own negotiated survival techniques 'just to get on with their lives'.[27]

In 1994, Nilima Ibrahim published a two-volume book, *Ami Birangona Bolchi* [This is the *Birangona* Speaking], the only available collection of testimonies of women survivors in print until 2001 when ASK published its oral history volume. In the preface of the 1998 edition, Ibrahim writes:

> I promised my readers to publish the third volume of *Ami Birangona Bolchi*. However, I no longer want to do so, for two reasons. First, my physical condition: Writing about the Birangona affected me both physically and emotionally. Second, the present society's conservative mentality. They [society] do not hesitate to call the Birangona sinners. Therefore, I don't want to insult those women all over again who were not allowed to live an easy and normal life even 25 years ago.... In addition, many compassionate people requested me for their [*birangonas*'] contacts. I believe, it wouldn't be right to rub salt on the wounds of those who we coldly banished from our community one day.

In December 1996, the Shommilito Nari Shomaj (a broad network of feminist activists in Bangladesh, hereinafter SNS) organized four women's testimonies from Ibrahim's book to be read on Bangladesh Television (BTV). After the telecast, a few *birangona*s contacted Nilima Ibrahim and the SNS to share their stories.[28] There was a newspaper report on this, revealing that the SNS was approached by one of the women who bluntly said, 'I was raped by Pakistani army in 1971' (Khan 1997). When the SNS activists asked the women why they were coming forward after twenty-six years of silence, one of them replied, 'Because now I am getting the courage to do so' (ibid.). Several others gave similar explanations. One rape survivor stated, 'I was raped and I would like to tell my son about it but do not know how to do so' (ibid.). These women wanted the Pakistani government and its collaborators to be brought to trial internationally. It was the crucial factor in their decision to communicate with Ibrahim and other social workers, whom they trusted. Despite the reactions of *birangona*s as a result of the TV show, with the memory of the previous trial in 1992 still fresh, women's groups remained sensitive in bringing the women to face the public.

Until her death in June 2002, Ibrahim refused to reveal any personal information about the women. In her conversation with me in 2000, she mentioned that she was very concerned about the renewed interest in publicizing the stories of *birangona*s. I realized that she wanted to protect the women's privacy and did not want to cause any further harm to them.[29] This reaction was not surprising, considering the way in which women's stories have been exploited or used without any legal, financial or moral support being offered in return.

Nonetheless, their testimonies are crucial for war crime trials to demonstrate the gendered nature of the 1971 war and the state policies afterwards. It is my contention that a gender-sensitive space can be provided for the *birangona*s to speak about their experiences in a way that keeps them and their stories safe from further persecution and violence. As I specify later in the chapter, informed strategies, in particular learning from women's groups and movements elsewhere in South Asia, can assist Bangladeshi women's groups to pursue this sensitively, with the *birangonas*' interest foremost in mind.

A small but significantly important number of *birangona*s have been prepared to come forward and document their narratives. Although women's groups did not pursue the issue, *birangona*s have also still maintained their demands for justice. Ferdousi Priyobhashini, another courageous *birangona* woman who came forward with her story wrote: 'I am one of the 250,000 raped women of '71. I am telling you these stories because those who killed 3 million Bengalis in '71 and raped 250,000 women still have not been brought to justice' (1999: 67).

When I visited Bangladesh in 2002 and spoke with Halima Parveen, she reiterated the demands of other women.[30] Halima *apa* (sister) fought in the war and was raped in captivity. She indicated that she would testify and encourage other women to do so and stated, 'I will fight with even the last bit of strength I have in my body to demand justice from Bangladesh government and from Pakistan.'[31] It is evident that despite the hardship and possible consequences of disclosure, if an appropriate forum is provided, women will come forward to speak. Their desire to tell their stories is evidence that if an action-oriented network is organized to seek justice for crimes committed during the 1971 war, some *birangona*s would be interested in participating. Sharing their war memories in a woman-friendly environment, sensitive to their traditional and cultural restrictions, can help facilitate the participation of many *birangona*s in this kind of network.

The Muktijuddho Jadughor (Liberation War Museum, LWM) in Bangladesh has undertaken the initiative to record the experiences of *birangona*s. In documenting women's experiences of the war, LWM researchers have used gender-sensitive approaches such as maintaining confidentiality and conducting closed-door interviews. In several conferences and public events, LWM speakers such as

Mofidul Hoque have raised the importance of ensuring justice for *birangonas*.

Although making women visible is necessary, by itself it is not enough to enable feminists to provide a full analysis of women's exploitation within the nation-state system (Rai 2002; Waylen 1996). While it is possible to arrive at a macro-level understanding of nationalism's gender-blind approach, without looking at micro-level and regional politics, a feminist scholarship of post-conflict situations will be unable to address the 'woman question' in diverse locations. Similar to other regions in South Asia, cultural and regional experiences of women vary immensely and women respond quite differently—and sometimes from contradictory positions—according to their backgrounds, education and politics. *Birangonas*, especially those who live in rural areas, might lack the means to reflect upon and to articulate their own experiences except through the socially accepted norms with which they are already familiar. Focusing on the lived reality of women and offering them choices so that they can decide for themselves whether or not they have been silenced in the national history making of the state may be more important. This might create the social awareness necessary to serve as the driving force behind a common platform of action.

FRAMING WOMEN'S ISSUES IN BANGLADESH

Despite holding diverse views, Bangladeshi women's organizations have successfully raised numerous feminist issues. The space of social activism is occupied by activists well versed in the social and political movements of South Asia. As political activists, Bengali women contributed to the anti-colonial nationalist struggle for the independence of the Indian subcontinent. During both the anti-colonial movement against the British and the Bangladeshi national liberation movement, Muslim Bengali women appeared in public and participated in protests, demonstrations and other forms of political campaigns for the freedom of their land. Their visibility became an important symbol in the Bengali national movement.

During the national movement of independence for Bangladesh, women organized and participated in protests against the repressive measures taken by the military regime of Pakistan. The military regime detained numerous political activists and leaders without trial during 1966–70. A group of young women activists, most of whom were associated with leftist organizations, approached the AL, the strongest political party in East Pakistan, and with the help of political leaders, formed a joint women's action committee to organize protests by the wives and mothers of political prisoners for their release (Jahan 1995: 93). The Bangladesh Mahila Parishad (Women's Caucus, BMP) in 1972, which is the oldest and largest women's organization in Bangladesh, also started as an offshoot of the Communist Party of Bangladesh.

Movements for national liberation are rarely extended to the autonomy and liberation of women (Moghadam 1994: 2). Both during the liberation struggle in 1971 and in the aftermath of the creation of Bangladesh, women activists enthusiastically expressed their solidarity in the construction of the new nation-state. However, as Rounaq Jahan (1995) observes, despite their significant role in the war, the new government soon marginalized women. The policies for the rehabilitation programmes in Bangladesh after 1971 were introduced irrespective of women's wishes and consent. While these were often justified as pragmatic alternatives in order to counter stigma and social rejection experienced and feared by rape victims, these practices are evidence of the ways women's rights are subsumed and subordinated under national 'rights'. Generally, women's liberation has been regarded as being unfavourable to the identity and existence of the nation (Kumar 1993; Menon-Sen 2002; Sobhan 2003). During the 1971 nationalist struggle, Muslim Bengali women went out on to the streets in active resistance. This liberating gesture served several purposes: it demonstrated to the Pakistani rulers that Bengali culture was different from West Pakistani traditions, that Bengalis shared similar cultural values irrespective of whether they were Hindu or Muslim, and that Bengali women were more liberated than West Pakistani women. Many Muslim Bengali women participated as activists in their country's national movement. Their unique cultural identity became their symbol and the use of the phrase 'Muslim Bengali woman' had a political rather than a religious connotation.

Although their political activism played a crucial role in achieving independence, after their country was born, these women were encouraged to go back to their traditional roles as wives, mothers and daughters, and as protected and vulnerable beings. Moreover, the national movement was not concerned with women's 'actual' emancipation. As a result of their exclusion, the Liberation War failed to achieve freedom for all of its citizens. Nationalist rhetoric had served to consolidate emotion in order to create an active struggle against the Pakistani army using the situation of women, but in reality, women were still seen to belong in the private sphere, situated in a complex construction of traditional, religious and cultural values.

Traditionally, the honour of the family is linked to the virtue of its women and men are responsible for protecting this honour (Kabeer 1998: 100). The image of Bengali women as cherished and protected mothers, wives and daughters was, over the years, challenged by an awareness that women are subordinated in the hierarchical gender relations in Bangladesh, which denies them both social power and autonomy over their own lives. The experience of 1971 helped women raise their concerns about their subordination. The norm of female seclusion and the so-called 'safety' of the private sphere was shattered in 1971 when women could not be protected by their men against aggression and were then abandoned, through no fault of their own (Jahan 1995: 102).

Since the Liberation War, a Bengali ruling class comprising an unstable class alliance of an underdeveloped bourgeoisie, the military and the bureaucracy has been in power (Kabeer 1998: 99).

Though regimes have changed, increasing impoverishment and social differentiation, and a steady rise in aid dependency have persisted. At the same time, increased violence against women in both the public and private spheres has helped develop a greater awareness of the position of women in Bangladesh. This awareness has also been informed by developing communication with other states and increased participation in transnational feminist programmes, including attendance at international conferences, workshops and dialogues, and a significant interest worldwide in addressing gender inequality.

Interestingly, the nascent women's movement did not work actively to mobilize support for rape victims. In reflecting on the reasons for this, women leaders offer a variety of perspectives. Many groups and individuals were hesitant to challenge the society's strong patriarchal traditions and feared that doing so would invite a backlash that could hurt the victims more. There were very few groups, with limited scope and membership, and as such still quite vulnerable. Even some organizations, such as the BMP, which later vocally and successfully challenged the government's stand on gender violence, did not articulate a position on rape at this time.[32] Some organizations and individuals also wished to remain 'apolitical', implying that even after more than three decades of independence, the stories of women can make some powerful groups 'uncomfortable' and 'angry'. Cautioned by the drastic curtailment of women's rights in Iran and Pakistan that accompanied the rise of political power of Islamists (Jahan 1995: 98), the Bangladeshi women's movement sought to build public opinion in support of secular politics. During the United Nations Decade for Women (1976–85), Bangladesh's governments invited women's groups to advise in preparing official reports for intergovernmental discussions and agreements that provided the opportunity to women's groups to articulate their positions in the government agenda (ibid.). With gender equity and poverty alleviation programmes at the forefront of development planning,

Bangladeshi women researchers and NGO employees were invited to voice their opinions in international conferences and workshops. This opened up the possibilities of cross-border dialogues. To serve the interests of their development policies, governments encouraged dialogue and the sharing of views and information with women's groups in other countries. Despite the changing political situation in Bangladesh, this facilitated dialogues among women inside Bangladesh and enabled them to create partnerships with women's organizations overseas in order to address specific issues, especially development and women's empowerment.

While an increase in women's status is essential for gender equity, the issue of violence against women has also been addressed strategically by women's organizations. For example, ASK, the Bangladesh Legal Aid and Services Trust (BLAST), Shaishob, Shakti and Naripokkho publicized cases of dowry-related family violence and murder, acid throwing and rape (including rape in police custody and rape of adolescents), creating a public outcry. Their history, activism and the contemporary politics of Bangladeshi nationhood within which a vibrant feminist movement thrived, saw these organizations adopt agendas that addressed violence against women, patriarchal dominance, common class problems, labour exploitation and unequal economic arrangements within specific national contexts. The activism of non-state actors organized into local networks has had a positive impact in agenda setting, framing and spreading norms, and changing state practices.

The similarities of women's movements in the Indian subcontinent derives from the fact that India, Pakistan and Bangladesh have a shared colonial national past that utilized the situation of women for the existence of the nation-state. Furthermore, regional workshops, conferences and academic exchanges between activists and scholars regarding women's rights have contributed to the growth of a shared and coherent women's networking and intellectual activism in South Asia. Based on common cultural and traditional backgrounds, and on the shared history of nation building in different states, these networks have exchanged ideas, formulated strategies and developed new ways of addressing the historical abuse of women and seeking restitution in the present (Bunch and Reilly 1994; D'Costa 2011; Keck and Sikkink 1998; Puja 2001; Thompson 2002).

Feminist analyses have contributed to our understanding of sexual violence in armed conflicts, women's roles in peace building, masculinities and violence, gender and national identity politics, and testimonies and memory (Askin 1997; Chinkin 2006; Seifert 1993). However, an assessment of jurisdiction, law and evidence validate that these remain a challenge in prosecuting sexual and gender-based violence as an international crime. In a conference marking the tenth anniversary of the ICTR judgement on the Akayesu case, Navanethem Pillay, the UN High Commissioner for Human Rights, who also served as a member of the Trial Chamber, explained:

> Rape and sexual violence are sustained by the patterns of gender inequality which cut across geo-political, economical and social boundaries. Justice is needed on the individual and national level to redress rape and other expressions of sex inequality that women experience as a part of their everyday lives, as well as on the international level for sexual violence and other crimes perpetrated in times of conflict and war that are not effectively addressed at the national level. (2010: xiv)

This case significantly expanded the international community's ability to prosecute gender-based war crimes; and the jurisprudence provided by this has been taken as a starting point to review rape laws elsewhere (ibid.: xv). A collection of essays that came out from the ICTR tenth anniversary conference provides critical appraisal of recent developments in rape laws, across a range of diverse jurisdictions. Various national jurisprudence considered in this collection reveal that wide-ranging efforts have been made, allowing a diversity of approaches and traditions.[33] The authors contributing to this volume explain national and international rape law concerns and developments. A particular insight offered by a number of authors and relevant to this discussion is that constant pressures from feminists have led to rape law reforms. For example, in post-conflict Croatia, voices of feminism and women's activism have been crucial in placing concerns of sexual violence in the political agenda (McGlynn and Munro 2010: 168–82; Radacic and Turkovic 2010), and in both Australia and the US, sustained feminist activism achieved changes in the formal laws and policies on rape (McGlynn and Munro 2010: 10–11). It is also noted that England and Wales have one of the lowest rape conviction rates in Europe, and despite feminist pressures and reforms and convictions, the sentencing of individuals has been inadequate. Some of the prejudices of national law, such as the divide between private and public spheres, that usually left family relations and abuse in the domestic sphere and outside the protection of national law, is also present in foundational international law, which considers the treatment of citizens as a private matter for each state (Cole 2006; McGlynn and Munro 2010: 45–50).

It took decades for the international community to seriously consider and investigate sexual crimes. Four international criminal justice institutions, namely, the ICTR, the ICT for the Former Yugoslavia (ICTY), the Special Court for Sierra Leone (SCSL) and the ICC played a key role in acknowledging that rape, forced marriage, sexual slavery and forced prostitution are war crimes, crimes against humanity and in some instances acts of genocide.[34] The ground-breaking Akayesu case before the ICTR was the first time when an international court recognized that rape constituted an act of genocide.[35] The text of the Akayesu judgement made a discursive shift by naming both women and girls as victims of violence. The Tadic case before the ICTY was the first where a defendant was specifically charged with rape and sexual violence as crimes against humanity and war crimes.[36] Also, the Kunarac (Foca) case before the ICTY resulted in the first international conviction for rape, torture and enslavement of women and girls as crimes against humanity.[37] However, legal precedents are not enough to oppose sexual and gender-based violence. The capacity of women to be involved in designing their own empowering activities is crucial in any effective justice approach.

CONCLUDING REMARKS: INTERNATIONAL CRIMES TRIBUNAL AND *BIRANGONA* TESTIMONIES

Birangona experiences have been used in Bangladesh by the ICT in various cases. A prosecution witness in the trial of A.T.M Azharul Islam, assistant secretary general of the Jamaat-e-Islami party and the commander of the Rangpur district unit of Al-Badr in 1971, testified that he, along with three Pakistani army personnel, tortured and raped a pregnant woman for about nineteen days at Rangpur Town Hall in 1971.[38] As a result, she lost her six-month-old foetus in womb. Mujibor Rahman Master, the eighth witness of this case to the ICT-1, mentioned in his testimony that he had heard about this incident from the victim. Azharul Islam was found guilty on five counts of mass murder and rape, and was sentenced to death.

On 8 May 2014, Abu Asad, third prosecution witness in the case against the Jamaat leader Abdus Subhan, told the ICT how he was forced to work with Subhan who carried out atrocities in Pabna during the war. Asad, a member of Mujaheed Bahini, a collaborating paramilitia unit stated, 'I also witnessed how the Pakistani army had raped wives and daughters before their husbands and fathers and shot the raped women.' At this point, he broke down and verified, 'Subhan Saheb was present with the army at that time.' Subhan has also been sentenced to death for his involvement in targeting Hindus during 1971.

Another witness, Momena Begum, gave her testimony in an in-camera trial that eventually led to the sentencing of Kader Mollah, another Jamaat leader. Mollah was executed in 2014. Momena Begum, like the women whose narratives are introduced earlier in the chapter, was only a young girl (12 years old) during the war. Similar to other minors, she was a witness to the war. Her name was not disclosed when the original verdict of life sentence was announced. However, her testimony was publicized and her name disclosed when the Appellate Division converted his life sentence to a death sentence. Her testimony came under direct attack from critics of the tribunal who asked whether a young girl of that time could identify Mollah so easily. A senior justice campaigner in Bangladesh told me, 'We have talked to many victims. Unfortunately, the ICT accidentally disclosed her name. This was quite traumatic for Momena in particular.' As the chapter argues, women who were victims in 1971 and agreed to provide their testimonies must be protected first to ensure justice.

Even as the increased recognition of rape and other forms of sexual violence as international crimes is lauded as furthering the commitment to address gender-based violence in Bangladesh, it also sparks concerns. Some of the prosecutions provided even less hospitable experience for victims of sexual violence as there was no trauma counselling available. Momena's case described earlier also demonstrates a lack of gender sensitivity and maintaining the confidentiality of victims. While *birangona* experiences were included in trials, they had very limited agency in the inherently masculine court environment, which used its jurisdiction for international crimes of sexual violence to promote its own justice agenda. Hirsch and Sarkis (2015: 518) argue that 'if a nation uses sexual violence prosecutions to advance its own policies, agendas, and ambitions, women's experiences of violence will be discounted as will the overall struggle against sexual violence'. There is a need to recognize and change traditions that violate women's human rights in both public and private spheres. It is also critical to ensure that after the ICT proceedings conclude, *birangona*s are not forgotten, as was the case after the 1992 Peoples' Tribunal. They need protection from the state. Economic resources are finally trickling down to some of them following the recognition of their freedom fighter status. Their equal participation in matters important to them, such as economic justice, livelihood, health, and education and employment access for their children, must be ensured. Lessons learned from their experiences in the aftermath of the war are invaluable in improving reporting and investigation; to enable future prosecution in domestic criminal courts as well. As such, *birangonas*, as victims, survivors and witnesses of 1971, could truly be the icons for prevention of any kinds of violence against women in Bangladesh.

NOTES

1. At this point, Begum became emotionally overwhelmed and ended her testimony. She left the hearing accompanied by a psychosocial support person.
2. For details, see D'Costa (2011).
3. The ASK initiated the Oral History Project. Some of the important interviews were published in *Narir Ekattor* in 2001. In Bangladesh, the term 'pro-liberation' (*shadhinotar pokhye*) and 'anti-liberation forces' (*shadhinotar bipokhyo shokti*) have been invoked by the media, activists and academics to differentiate between interest groups such as civil society actors, political leaders and others who supported the justice campaigns and who advocated against revisiting the atrocities of 1971. Many in the pro-liberation lobby either participated in the war or are sympathetic to it. Individuals in the anti-liberation lobby have often been accused of collaborating with the Pakistani army or showing some bias towards the religious right. After the ICT proceedings began, these terms have acquired new meanings in the war of rhetoric and propaganda campaigns.
4. On women's experiences, see ASK (2001); D'Costa (2005, 2011); Mookherjee (2008, 2015); Saikia (2011).
5. This is particularly evident from Respondent A's (who wishes to remain anonymous) interview. I spoke with her in Kolkata, India, in January 2000. She played a major role in the rehabilitation of the women. She mentioned that they focused on female-headed households after the war as their numbers had increased. She said:

> We also did some rehabilitation work for women on the other side of the Buriganga [a river next to Dhaka]. All were Hindu women. No men, no grown-up boys. The army killed all the men. They dug up a big hole where they buried all the men. And also the grown-up boys. Women were left alone. We started a programme for helping the women. I gave each woman [money] to do some small business. They made a little extra. Afterwards, they continued to work with that small savings. Then we gave them geese, ducklings, chicks and goats. For the next three years we helped them to stand on their [own] feet. That is how Jagoroni [a handicrafts shop in Dhaka city run by Catholic nuns] came into being. It was the Widows' Programme.

6. Nayanika Mookherjee (2015: 129) also notes that Minister Kamruzaman used this nomenclature in December soon after his arrival in Dhaka.
7. It is estimated that over 100,000 people took part in the war against Pakistan. In a recent interview, the Liberation War Affairs Minister A.K.M Mozammel Haque provided a list of freedom fighters, which included in the Laal Muktbarta, India's list of Bangladeshi fighters; freedom fighters certified by Prime Minister Sheikh Hasina; those who crossed over into India and registered for training; servicemen who worked to create public opinion for the Liberation War; the Mujibnagar government employees; members of the armed forces, police, then East Pakistan Rifles, Ansars who fought in the war; MLAs and MPs of the wartime government. In addition, artists and performers of Swadhin Bangla Betar; journalists who played leading roles after the liberation; Swadhin Bangla football team members; and doctors, nurses and their assistants who treated the wounded freedom fighters and officials at offices under the Mujibnagar government too will be eligible for the status. The minister also mentioned that those who were at least 15 years old on 26 March 1971 could apply for the status.
8. The monthly allowance for a freedom fighter aged over 65 is USD 129 (BDT 10,000). The war-wounded gazetted freedom fighters also get tax exemption for an annual income of up to USD 5,490 (BDT 425,000). In addition, children and grandchildren of freedom fighters

will be entitled to receive reserved quotas in public recruitment and enrolment in educational institutions.

9. Interviews with social workers, medical practitioners and *birangonas*, 1999, 2000.
10. Interview, 2000.
11. Interview with Respondent B, social worker, 7 February 2000, Kolkata, India.
12. Ibid.
13. Interview with Geoffrey Davis, 1 June 2002, Sydney, Australia. Davis worked with International Planned Parenthood in Bangladesh in 1971–72. I gratefully acknowledge Roger Kilham's assistance in tracking down Geoffrey Davis.
14. The partition of India in 1947 sparked violent communal riots between Hindus, Muslims and Sikhs. In March 1947, four months before the actual partition, some Sikh villages in the Rawalpindi area of Punjab had been attacked in retaliation of Hindu attacks on Muslims in Bihar. The story of ninety women who drowned themselves by jumping into a well at Thoa Khalsa, a small village in Rawalpindi, when their men were no longer able to defend their honour is still discussed today in tones of admiration and respect. For details, see Butalia (1998: 146–84).
15. Interview with Davis, 2002.
16. Ibid.
17. Interview with Respondent B, 2000.
18. For details on sexual and reproductive programmes, see Hossain, Ahmed and Khan (1973). I thank Rahnuma Ahmed for alerting me to this important publication.
19. It is not my contention that many *birangonas* did not want to go through abortions or the adoption programmes. However, without recovering the voices of the women themselves, we would not be able to decipher the meaning of choice that could be either voluntary or coercive, especially when motherhood that belonged previously in the private domain was now controlled by the state.
20. The Bangladesh government gradually eradicated the programmes principally designed for *birangonas* and is said to have allegedly destroyed their records.

21. The book was translated into English in 1991 with the title *Of Blood and Fire: The Untold Story of Bangladesh's War of Independence.*
22. Golam Azam fled East Pakistan just before it became Bangladesh. In 1978, he returned to Bangladesh and has lived there since as a Pakistani national. The ICT found him guilty of five charges and sentenced him to ninety years in prison. He died in late 2014. On 21 March 1981, there was a demand from freedom fighters under the banner of Bangladesh Muktijodhya Shongshod (Freedom Fighters' Association) to try Golam Azam and other collaborators for war crimes in a people's tribunal (Kabir 1993: 15–19). This movement faltered due to government intervention.
23. It was founded on 26 August 1941 by Syed Ab'ul Ala Maududi as a movement to promote social and political Islam. After independence, it began to operate in Bangladesh as Bangladesh Jamaat-e-Islami. On 1 August 2013, the Bangladesh Supreme Court declared the registration of the Jamaat illegal, ruling the party unfit to contest in elections.
24. In May 1977, Article 38 of the Constitution banning the use of religion for political purposes was revoked, clearing the way for religion-based parties to get back into Bangladeshi politics (Anisuzzaman 2000: 59).
25. The Bangladesh Nationalist Party-led government was against this symbolic tribunal. The BNP won the election on 27 February 1990 with 140 seats and formed the government with the support of the Jamaat.
26. The three women come from rural and traditional areas where purdah and *izzat* (honour) have very strong social meanings. The tribunal organizers were not sensitive to this.
27. Interview with *birangona*, 1999.
28. Field notes from interview with Nilima Ibrahim, social worker, 14 January 2000.
29. Ibid.
30. My sincere thanks to Shaheen Akhter for introducing me to Halima Parveen.
31. Interview with Halima Parveen, *muktijodya* (woman combatant), 25 December, 2002.

32. Maleka Begum differs on this and noted that both herself and Begum Sufia Kamal were advocating for women's justice since Bangladesh became a state.
33. See, generally, McGlynn and Munro (2010: 137–251).
34. For details, see Walsh (2013: 62–65). For an overview of the jurisprudence addressing sexual violence in international courts and hybrid tribunals, see D'Costa and Hossain (2010).
35. *Prosecutor v. Jean-Paul Akayesu*, ICTR, case no. ICTR-96-4-T, 2 September 1998.
36. *Prosecutor v. Tadić*, ICTY, case no. IT-94-1-A, 15 July 1999.
37. Dragoljub Kunarac was one of the eight individuals named in the first indictment, issued in June 1996, dealing with sexual offences. This significant indictment covers the brutal regime of gang-rape, torture and enslavement, which Muslim women and girls of Foca and elsewhere were subjected to between April 1992 and February 1993 by Bosnian Serb soldiers, policemen and members of paramilitary groups, including some coming from Serbia and Montenegro. *Prosecutor v. Kunarac* (Trial Judgement), ICTY, case nos IT-96-23-T and IT-96-23/1-T, 22 February 2001.
38. Islam was 61 years old at the time of writing, which makes him 17 during the war.

REFERENCES

Ahmed, R. 2015. 'History as Ethical Remembrance: Dhaka University, Shaheed Minar, and CP Gang's "Bessha" Banner, Part IV', *New Age*, 14 November. http://newagebd.net/175123/history-as-ethical-remembrance-dhaka-university-shaheed-minar-and-cp-gangs-bessha-banner-iv/ (accessed 20 November 2015).

Akhtar, S. (dir.) 1999. *Itihash Konya* (Daughter of History) (film).

————. 2006. *Taalash* (the Search). Dhaka: Mowla Brothers.

Anisuzzaman, M. 2000. 'The Identity Question and Politics', in R. Jahan (ed.), *Bangladesh: Promise and Performance*, pp. 45–63. Dhaka: University Press Limited.

Ain o Salish Kendra (ASK). 2001. *Narir Ekattor: Juddhoporoborti Kothhokahini* (Women's '71: Post-War Voices/Stories). Dhaka: Ain o Salish Kendra.

Askin, Kelly. 1997. *War Crimes Against Women: Prosecution in International War Crimes Tribunals*. The Hague: Kluwer Law International.

Boby, F. (dir.). 2015. *Bish Kantha* (The Poison Thorn) (documentary).

Begum, S. 2001. 'Masuda, Elijan, Duljan, Momena: Kushtiar Charjon Grihobodhu' (The Four Housewives of Kushtia), in Ain o Salish Kendra (ASK), *Narir Ekattor: Juddhoporoborti Kothhokahini*, pp. 80–107. Dhaka: ASK.

Brownmiller, S. 1975. *Against Our Will: Men, Women and Rape*. New York: Bantam Books.

Bunch, C. and N. Reilly. 1994. *Demanding Accountability: The Global Campaign and Vienna Tribunal for Women's Human Rights*. New York: Centre for Women's Global Leadership and UNIFEM.

Burke, S.M. 1973. 'The Postwar Diplomacy of the Indo-Pakistani War of 1971', *Asian Survey*, 13(11): 1036–49.

Butalia, U. 1995a. 'Muslims and Hindus, Men and Women: Communal Stereotypes and the Partition of India', in T. Sarkar and U. Butalia (eds), *Women and Right-Wing Movements: Indian Experiences*, pp. 58–81. London: Zed Books.

————. 1995b. 'A Question of Silence: Partition, Women and the State', in R. Lentin (ed.), *Gender and Catastrophe*, pp. 92–109. London: Zed Books.

————. 1998. *The Other Side of Silence: Voices from the Partition of India*. New Delhi: Penguin Books.

Cambodian Defenders Project. 2012. 'Asia-Pacific Regional Women's Hearing on Gender-Based Violence in Conflict: Report on the Proceedings'. http://gbvkr.org/wp-content/uploads/2013/01/Asia-Pacific-Regional-Womens-Hearing-on-GBV-in-Conflict-2012-Report.pdf (accessed 7 October 2015).

Chinkin, C. and H. Charlesworth. 2006. 'Building Women into Peace: The International Legal Framework', *Third World Quarterly*, 27(5): 937–57.

Chowdhury, E.H. 2015. 'When Love and Violence Meet: Women's Agency and Transformative Politics in Rubaiyat Hossain's Meherjaan', *Hypatia*, 30(4): 760–77.

Copelon, R. 1995. 'Gendered War Crimes: Reconceptualizing Rape in Time of War', in J. Peters and A. Wolper (eds), *Women's Rights*

Human Rights: International Feminist Perspectives, pp. 197–214. New York: Routledge.

Cole, A. 2006, 'International Criminal Law and Sexual Violence: An Overview', in C. McGlynn and V.E. Munro (eds), *Rethinking Rape Law: International and Comparative Perspectives*, pp. 47–60. New York: Routledge.

Das, Veena. 1994. 'Moral Orientations to Suffering: Legitimation, Power, and Healing', in L.C. Chen, A. Kleinman and N.C. Ware (eds), *Health and Social Change in International Perspective*, pp. 139–70. Boston: Harvard School of Public Health.

Das, V. 1995. *Critical Events: An Anthropological Perspective on Contemporary India*. Oxford: Oxford University Press.

D'Costa, Bina. 2005. 'Coming to Terms with the Past in Bangladesh: Naming Women's Truths', in Luciana Ricciutelli et al. (eds), *Feminist Politics, Activism and Vision: Local and Global Challenges*, pp. 227–47. London: Zed Books.

———. 2011. *Nationbuilding, Gender and War Crimes in South Asia*. London: Routledge (second edition, 2013).

———. 2014. 'Once Were Warriors: The Militarized State in Narrating the Past', *South Asian History and Culture*, 5(4): 457–74.

D'Costa, B. and S. Hossain. 2010. 'Redress for Sexual Violence before the International Crimes Tribunal in Bangladesh: Lessons from History and Hopes for the Future', *Criminal Law Forum*, 21(2): 331–59.

Gayen, K. 2015. 'Women, War and Cinema: Construction of Women in the Liberation War Films of Bangladesh', *French Journal for Media Research*, 3: 1–25.

Gafur, M.A. 1979. *Shomaj Kolyan Porikroma* (Critical Survey of Social Welfare). Dhaka: Pubali Prokashoni.

Gazi, L and S. Lutfa. 2014. *Birangona: Women of War* (play), directed by F. Ozcan.

Ghosh, P.S. 1993. 'Bangladesh at the Crossroads: Religion and Politics', *Asian Survey*, 33(7): 697–710.

Hirsh, S. and C. Sarkis. 2015. 'Establishing Rape as a Crime against Humanity: Innovations and Reactions from African Nations', in M.M. Kurtz and L.R. Kurtz (eds), *Women, War and Violence: Topography, Resistance and Hope*. Denver: Praeger Press.

Hossain, H. 2010. 'Overcoming the Trauma of War, Contesting

Controls, the Struggle Beyond 1971', in *Freedom from Fear, Freedom from Want? Rethinking Security in Bangladesh*, pp. 12–38. New Delhi: Rupa.

Hossain, T., J.U. Ahmed and N.I. Khan (eds). 1973. *Proceedings of the Seminar on Family Planning, November 21–25, 1972*. Dhaka: Bangladesh, Ministry of Health and Family Planning.

Ibrahim, N. 1998. *Ami Birangona Bolchi* (This is the *Birangona* Speaking). Dhaka: Jagriti Prokashoni (first published in 1994).

Imam, J. 1986. *Ekatturer Dinguli*. Dhaka: Sandhani Publications. (Translated as *Of Blood and Fire: The Untold Story of Bangladesh's War of Independence*, Dhaka: Academic Publishers, 1991.)

Jahan, R. 1980. *Bangladeshi Politics: Problems and Issues*, Dhaka: University Press Limited.

————. 1995. *The Elusive Agenda: Mainstreaming Women in Development*. London: Zed Books.

Kabir, S. 1993. *Gonoadaloter Potobhumi* (Background of the Peoples' Tribunal). Dhaka: Dibyo Prokash.

————. 1999. 'Introduction', in S. Kabir (ed.), *Ekatturer Dushoho Smriti* (Those Terrible Memories of '71), pp. 7–30. Dhaka: Ekatturer Ghatok Dalal Nirmul Committee.

————. 2000. *Ekatturer Gonohotya: Nirjaton ebong Judhyaporadhider Bichar* (Genocide of '71: Trials of the War Criminals for the Suffering). Dhaka: Shomoy.

Kabeer, N. 1988. 'Subordination and Struggle: Women in Bangladesh', *New Left Review*, 168 (March/April): 95–121.

Kamal, Sultana. 2001. 'Potobhumi', in S. Akhter, S. Begum, H. Hossain, S. Kamal and M. Guhathakurta (eds), *Narir Ekattur o Judhyo Porobortee Kothyokahini*, pp. 14–20. Dhaka: Ain o Salish Kendra.

Keck, Margaret E. and Kathryn Sikkink. 1998. *Activists beyond Borders: Advocacy Networks in International Politics*. Ithaca: Cornell University Press.

Khan, N. 1997. 'War Crimes against Bengali Women by Pakistani Army and Their Collaborators in 1971: The Rape of a Nation', *Daily Star*, 12 December.

Kumar, Radha. 1993. *The History of Doing: An Illustrated Account of Movements for Women's Rights and Feminism in India, 1800–1990*. London: Verso.

LaPorte, R. 1972. 'Pakistan in 1971: The Disintegration of a Nation', *Asian Survey*, 12(2): 97–108.

Manchanda, R. 2001. 'Where Are the Women in South Asian Conflicts?', in R. Manchanda (ed.), *Women, War and Peace in South Asia: Beyond Victimhood to Agency*, pp. 9–41. New Delhi: Sage.

Matsui, Y. 1998. 'History Cannot Be Erased, Women Can No Longer Be Silenced', in I.L. Sajor (ed.), *Common Grounds: Violence against Women in War and Armed Conflict Situations*, pp. 26–32. Philippines: Asian Center for Women's Human Rights (ASCENT).

McGlynn, C. and V.E. Munro (eds). 2010. *Rethinking Rape Law: International and Comparative Perspectives*. New York: Routledge.

Menon, R. 1998. 'Reproducing the Legitimate Community: Secularity, Sexuality, and the State in Post-Partition India', in P. Jeffrey and A. Basu (eds), *Appropriating Gender: Women's Activism and Politicized Religion in South Asia*, pp. 15–32. New York: Routledge,.

Menon, R. and K. Bhasin. 1996. 'Abducted Women, the State and Questions of Honour: Three Perspectives in the Recovery Operation in Post-Partition India', in Jayawardena Kumari and M. De Alwis (eds), *Embodied Violence: Communalizing Women's Sexuality in South Asia*, pp. 1–31. London: Zed Books.

————. 1998. *Borders and Boundaries: Women in India's Partition*. New Delhi: Kali for Women.

Menon-Sen, K. 2002. 'Bridges over Troubled Waters: South Asian Women's Movements Confronting Globalization', *Society for International Development*, 45(1): 132–36.

Ministry of External Affairs. 2000. *Bangladesh Documents*. Madras: B.N.K. Press Private.

Moghadam, V. 1994. 'Introduction: Women and Identity Politics in Theoretical and Comparative Perspective', in V. Moghadam (ed.), *Identity Politics and Women: Cultural Reassertions and Feminisms in International Perspective*, pp. 3–26. Boulder: Westview Press.

Mookherjee, N. 2008. 'Gendered Embodiments: Mapping the Body-Politic of the Raped Woman and the Nation in Bangladesh', *Feminist Review: Special Issue on War*, 88(1): 36–53.

————. 2015. 'The Spectral Wound. Sexual Violence, Public Memories and the Bangladesh War of 1971'. Durham: Duke University Press.

Pereira, F. 2002. *The Fractured Scales: The Search for a Uniform Personal Code*. Calcutta: Stree.

Pillay, N. 2010. 'Foreword', in Clare McGlynn and Vanessa Munro (eds), *Rethinking Rape Law: International and Comparative Perspectives*, pp. xiv–xv. New York: Routledge.

Priyobhashini, F. 1999. 'Onek Mrityo Dekhechi, Nari Nirjatoner Kotha Shunechi Kintoo Kokhonou Bhabini Ami Tar Shikar Hobo' (Have Seen Many Deaths, Heard about Violence against Women but Never Thought I Would Be a Victim of Such Violence), in S. Kabir (ed.), *Ekatturer Dushoho Smriti*, pp. 67–86. Dhaka: Ekatturer Ghatok Dalal Nirmul Committee.

Puja, K. 1998. 'Backlash against the Comfort Women Issue: Moves against History Textbook References', in I.L. Sajor (ed.), *Common Grounds: Violence against Women in War and Armed Conflict Situations*, pp. 198–204. Philippines: Asian Center for Women's Human Rights (ASCENT).

Puja, K. 2001. 'Global Civil Society Remakes History: "The Women's International War Crimes Tribunal 2000"', *Positions: East Asia Cultures Critique*, 9(3): 611–20.

Radacic, Ivana and Ksenija Turkovic. 2010. 'Rethinking Croatian Rape Laws: Force, Consent and the Contribution of the Victim', in Clare McGlynn and Vanessa Munro (eds), *Rethinking Rape Law: International and Comparative Perspectives*, pp. 168–82. New York: Routledge.

Rai, S.M. 2002. *Gender and the Political Economy of Development: From Nationalism to Globalization*. Cambridge: Polity Press.

Rizvi, H.A. 1987. *The Military and Politics in Pakistan*. Lahore: Progressive Publishers.

Saikia, Y. 2011. *Women, War, and the Making of Bangladesh: Remembering 1971*. Durham: Duke University Press.

Scholte, M. 2014. 'Liberating the Women of 1971', *Daily Star*, 8 December. http://www.thedailystar.net/liberating-the-women-of-1971-54154 (accessed 8 October 2015).

Seifert, R. 1993. *War Rape: Analytical Approaches*. Geneva: Women's International League for Peace and Freedom.

Shehabuddin, E. 2008. *Reshaping the Holy: Democracy, Development and Muslim Women in Bangladesh*. New York: Columbia University Press.

Siddiqi, D. 2013. 'Left behind by the Nation: "Stranded Pakistanis" in Bangladesh', *Sites*, 10(1): 1–33.

Sobhan, S. 2003. 'The Women's Movement of Southern Asia', *Canadian Dimension*, 37(1): 26.

Thompson, K.B. 2002. 'Women's Rights Are Human Rights', in S. Khagram, J.V. Riker and K. Sikkink (eds), *Restructuring World Politics: Transnational Social Movements, Networks and Norms*, pp. 96–122. Minneapolis: University of Minnesota Press.

Walsh, Annelotte. 2013, 'International Criminal Justice and the Girl Child', in Lisa Yarwood (ed.), *Women and Transitional Justice: The Experience of Women as Participants*, pp. 54–74. London: Routledge.

Waylen, G. 1996. 'Analysing Women in the Politics of the Third World', in H. Afshar (ed.), *Women and Politics in the Third World*, pp. 7–24. London: Routledge.

Women's International War Crimes Tribunal on Japan's Military Sexual Slavery. 2000. Tokyo. http://www1.jca.apc.prg/vaww-net-japan/e_new/judgement.html (accessed 20 November 2015).

Ziauddin, A. 1999. 'What Is to Be Done about the Pakistani War Criminals and Collaborators?', *Daily Star*, 3 December. http://www.bangladeshmariners.com/HmdrRprt/what.html (accessed 24 May 2004).

Newspapers cited:

Daily Shongbad, 11 November 1996.

Daily Star, 30 January 2015.

Dhaka Courier, No. 3-16 April 1992.

Far Eastern Economic Review, 4 September 1971.

Statesman Weekly, 1 September 1973.

The Times, 15 June 1971.

The Times, 20 May 1971.

4

The Unbearable Tedium of Rightslessness

FAUSTINA PEREIRA*

BACKGROUND

This essay tackles a paradox of our times. We live in an age which sees the highest ever application of rights language and moral grammar both in private and public discourse. At the same time, we observe the widest spectrum of rights violations, leaving open spaces where a condition of rightslessness manifests itself upon persons, processes and structures. It could be argued that the worth of the human person now is more starkly measured through an

---

* I would like to thank the ASK for organizing two focused group discussions for me with women's and human rights activists of various age groups in Bangladesh whereby I was able to gain much insight into the evolution of the movement over four decades, and to test my own assumptions of some of the challenges and lapses. In particular, I would like to thank Dr Hameeda Hossain for taking the time to answer some critical questions and comment on my paper, and Dr Amena Mohsin and Dr Dina M. Siddiqi for kindly reviewing this paper and providing critical feedback.

unapologetic capitalist and hetero-patriarchal lens, especially when seen in the backdrop of apparent rights consciousness worldwide. We live in a generation that has seen the largest wealth creation in human history, yet four billion of the planet's seven billion people live outside the protection of the law, not having even the basic recognition of existence—a legal identity through which claims to rights and its attendant benefits can be made.

By looking at specific cases of absence or abuse of rights drawn from the work of various rights-based organizations, either collectively or individually, I wish, first, to look at the elements that produce the condition of rightslessness. Having quickly uncovered the structures, processes and breach of state obligations that create, uphold and normalize rightslessness, I shall move on to an area that is much less discussed.

I would like to take a self-critical look at 'rights upholders'—institutions and mechanisms, individuals or legal aid, and justice service delivery groups—to see whether we, despite the best of intentions, may also be contributing to the sense of routine in the manner in which we deal with rights abuse. I would like to hold a mirror to ourselves to see whether this results, at the very least, by not challenging the mundanity of rightslessness and reinforcement of impunity. How often do we look at the problems of justice merely symptomatically and not question its deeply embedded tensions? What, if any, are the day-to-day challenges that get in our way of doing so?

If one were to trace the origins of justice services in Bangladesh since its independence in 1971, we would find that due to various contours in financial aid architecture and other socio-political waves, not least the impact of neo-liberal assertions, the whole 'rights culture' has been co-opted by a very narrow lens of 'service delivery'. This lens is often detached from the larger canvas of human development. I would further enquire whether NGO-ization or project-ization of grassroots movements and aid politics in Bangladesh has not played a role in justice delivery groups and organizations sometimes lapsing into intellectual and moral laziness, which in turn has allowed a larger systemic problem of impunity by state institutions to go unchallenged. I answer these self-imposed questions by trying to understand how the rights-based movement in general and the women's rights movement in particular has evolved through major political and socio-economic shifts and continues to be the fulcrum upon which citizens negotiate their rights with the state.

UNCOVERING THE FACE OF IMPUNITY AND SEXUAL VIOLENCE IN BANGLADESH

The Stories

Of a Warrior: Ravaged Over and Over, She Fights on for Justice

> They raped her daughter, ruined her husband's business and ravaged her face with acid but they couldn't silence her. In the face of overwhelming odds, Nasima Akhtar has steadfastly demanded one thing: justice. Armed with nothing but an iron will, Nasima has been waging a lonely war against influential opponents and an apathetic system, refusing to be silenced by the traditional taboos that say rape is too shameful for a woman to speak of. 'Jiddi', her husband calls her—'stubborn'.
>
> Nasima vividly remembers the night her daughter was attacked. It was barely a year after she and her husband Yousuf, a marine spare parts dealer, had moved to Cox's Bazar in search of a better future. That evening, Nasima had taken her five-year-old daughter Tumpa to the doctor, leaving 11-year-old mentally challenged Jhumur alone at home. With her husband away on business, Nasima had no alternative.
>
> The round trip to the doctor's surgery took almost two hours. When Nasima returned, she saw a knot of people outside her door. 'Fear gripped my heart,' recalls Nasima. 'My first thought was, "Something has happened to my daughter!"'

Jhumur lay in a foetal position on the bed, crying her eyes out. The neighbours gathered round the bed and told Nasima what had happened. The electricity had gone out around 7.30 PM when they heard a single scream from Jhumur.

'We tried to open the door but it was bolted from inside,' said Nasima's neighbour Mariam, in a statement to police. 'We called Jhumur but heard nothing. About half an hour later, the door opened and out walked Yousuf's business partner, Aziz. He walked away quickly, pressing the keypad on his mobile phone. We rushed inside and found Jhumur bleeding and barely conscious, her clothes in disarray.'

The rape occurred on August 4, 2006. The next day Nasima lodged a case with Cox's Bazar Model Police Station. After investigating, the police filed a charge sheet implicating Aziz. The case went to trial a couple of months later.

But for Nasima and her family, the ordeal had just begun. Inexplicably, the alleged child molester Aziz was never arrested. 'They are locals—wealthy and influential,' said Nasima. 'We were from another district and were poor. We were no match for them.'

Nasima was about to discover how prejudice, government inactivity and deficiencies in the criminal justice system throw up formidable obstacles for women who try to obtain justice following sexual offences. From the very beginning, Aziz's family pressured Nasima to withdraw the allegations. But when faced by a stream of threats, Nasima remained determined. 'I want justice for my daughter,' she said repeatedly. She was to pay a high price for her defiance.

September 1, 2008 is a date that will live with Nasima forever—it is burnt into her memory and her face. She had gone to court with her sister and brother-in-law to testify in the case. Before she did so, the defendant's brother, Hakim, approached her with a settlement offer. He insisted that she talk to him privately, so Nasima accompanied him to a secluded corner of the court premises. Hakim gave Nasima a stark choice. Take some cash and drop the case—or face vengeance.

'He had a wad of cash in his right hand,' says Nasima. 'When I refused, he took a bottle out of his left pocket and poured its contents over my body. I felt like I was on fire. I saw flesh melting before my eyes. I fell to the ground and screamed and screamed...'

Hakim was nabbed on the spot and turned over to the police. But astonishingly, he was soon back on the streets. The police found no case against him. In his final report, Inspector Mohiuddin, Officer-in-Charge of Cox's Bazar police station wrote, 'It appears the plaintiff poured acid on herself in an attempt to frame the defendant, against whom she had a prior grievance...'

For Nasima, incarcerated in the burns unit of Dhaka Medical College Hospital, it was an insult heaped on injury. The acid had burnt the left side of her face, neck and breasts. She had difficulty eating and was in constant pain. 'I was burnt for demanding justice,' she mumbled through her tears.

Three long months and two operations later, Nasima was discharged from hospital. Her family had long ago fled Cox's Bazar and returned to their hometown in Khulna.

'The acid destroyed the skin on my neck,' laments Nasima. 'I have trouble swallowing or talking. My breasts have almost melted away. I avoid looking in the mirror these days.'

The story of Nasima's plight and her unrelenting courage in the face of adversity has drawn the attention of human rights campaigners. BRAC has come to her aid. Through the NGOs' human rights and legal aid services programme, BRAC lawyers have given the family legal assistance—help that the financially crippled Nasima desperately needs. The Acid Survivors Foundation (ASF), another NGO that campaigns against acid violence, helped pay for Nasima's surgery. BRAC and ASF both contributed to the cost of buying a dairy cow for the family.

Aside from the disfigurement, the psychological damage is enormous. It has taken months for Nasima to work up the courage to go outside. She keeps all the doors and windows locked, is terrified by unexpected callers and is frightened to make hot drinks because of the memories it revives. For months she couldn't bear to have a shower because the feeling of liquid moving across her body revolted her.

But she is determined not to give up. 'I want others to learn from this and to refrain from committing these crimes. I believe that rape is a crime against the whole society, not just a crime against my mentally challenged daughter.'

'My wife is strong-willed,' says Yousuf. 'There were times when I weakened and wanted to settle, but she wouldn't allow it. "We want justice, not handouts," she kept saying.'

Nasima's courage may be extraordinary, but the facts of the case—the rape, the vengeful defendants, the cup of industrial-strength sulphuric acid—are all too familiar in a country that sees upward of 150 acid attacks and 400 rapes every year.

Nasima wants to encourage other women to fight for justice. But she acknowledges that her own battle has been harder than she ever imagined.

'We are cowering in fear. My husband has lost his business and I have lost everything. Meanwhile the culprits are still going about their daily lives.'

The details of how she lost her dreams, her identity and almost her life will stay with Nasima forever. While her attackers walk free, Nasima has nothing but her scars.[1] (al-Mahmood 2010)

'Religion' Saved, with it Rapists

Gang-rape victim Serafina Mardi (age 11) gave up her life in protest at the settlement by the community leaders and Surshunipara Catholic Church in Godagari that forced her family to stay away from legal proceedings.

Police, family members of the indigenous victim and the community leaders said the settlement was done at a time when

Serafina's rape case was under trial and for the sake of protecting the religion.

In the settlement, it was fixed that the rapists would give an amount of Tk 1.4 lakh to the family as compensation while Serafina [was] to wed Nirmol Murmu, one of the rapists.

Reverend Bernard Tudu, a priest of the church, said the families of the nine rapists attempted to leave the Amtulipara village following the filing of the rape case. The local community leaders initiated the settlement in a bid to protect the village where 36 indigenous Christian families have been living since 2005.

He denied the involvement of the church while talking to *The Daily Star* at Rajshahi Caritas office.

Revd Tudu said the settlement took place on the church premises weeks after the rape incident on April 24 last year. He only kept the fine money to hand it over to the victim's family on February 11.

S.M. Rokon Uddin, Superintendent of Police (SP) in Rajshahi, said the church authorities called all the rapists to the church and performed their confessions.

The SP said police had pressed charges against all the nine accused on August 11 last year but the rapists were acquitted as no prosecution witness appeared before the court.

Police is yet to take actions against the people involved in the out-of-court settlement although the rapists are allegedly threatening the victim's family not to file any more cases.

'We have recorded an unnatural death case following Serafina's suicide,' said the SP.

The rapists are still at large, said the villagers.

M. Noor Khan, one of the directors of Ain O Salish Kendra, said there is no scope for out-of-court settlement during the legal proceeding of rape incidents and the involvement of the leaders of any religion in the settlement is a punishable offence.

'The entire process of the settlement was illegal as it was done to avoid court trial. All those who are involved in it must be punished,' observed Khan.

Visiting Serafina's house at Amtulipara yesterday *The Daily Star* experienced a feeling of deep shock and silence among the family members. The family buried Serafina overnight.

'If the priest asks me to accept the settlement, what else can I do? I have to live here with three other daughters having the rapists as neighbours,' said victim's father Cornelius Mardi, a farm labourer.

Revd Tudu, however, denied that he ever met Serafina's father.

Cornelius alleged that Moheswar Soren, Lobin Hembrom, Jotin, Monir Murmu, Amin, Bhawani, Fabian Murmu, Moti Mardi were among the village leaders who forced him to accept the judgement of the settlement.

Serafina's mother Susana Soren alleged that instead of taking actions against the rapists, the community leaders on the next day of the rape incident fined her husband with Tk 1,200 for publicly yelling at the rapists.[2] (Priyo News 2011)

When a Girl Is Executed... for Being Raped

A 14-year-old Bangladeshi girl, Hena, allegedly was ambushed when she went to an outdoor toilet, gagged, beaten and raped by an older man in her village (who was actually her cousin). They were caught by [the] wife of the alleged rapist, and the wife then beat Hena up. An imam at a local mosque issued a fatwa saying that Hena was guilty of adultery and must be punished, and a village makeshift court sentenced Hena to 100 lashes in a public whipping.

Her last words were protestations of innocence.... [I]n interviews with family members, parents [said that they] 'had no choice but to mind the imam's order. They watched as the whip broke the skin of their youngest child and she fell unconscious to the ground.'

> Hena collapsed after 70 lashes and was taken to the hospital. She died a week later, by some accounts because of internal bleeding and a general loss of blood. The doctors recorded her death as a suicide. (Women and girls who are raped are typically expected to commit suicide, to spare everyone the embarrassment of an honor crime.)...
>
> A court ordered the body exhumed after word leaked out, and an examination revealed severe injuries. Lawsuits are now underway against the doctors who had called her death a suicide, and several people have been rounded up—including the alleged rapist... But Hena's family is under police protection because of concern that other villagers will take revenge at them for getting the imam and others in trouble. (Kristof 2011)

These cases, just a sample representation of many 'sensational' ones that make the headlines, are in a sense 'easier' to unpack if one is to trace system failures, organizational lapses and the cycle of forgetfulness at the state and non-state level. And yet, there are many that fall under the daily, routine, mundane cluster—the everyday cases of rape, incest and brutality within the home, silent or silenced cases that either do not attract the attention of an outside intervener or keep percolating through the system of criminal or social justice in near perpetuity. It is not necessarily the horrific ones outlined here, but the day-to-day nitty-gritty issues that snowball into what can almost be termed as a 'white noise' of the justice system—the din of voices seeking redress, culminating in a muffled, camouflaged chatter that creates the backdrop for daily existence, casting a sense of normality on a redress-less existence.

This culture of the absence of redress is hardly trapped at the household or immediate community level. With larger issues of political economy and compulsions of the market, more women than ever before are actively present in the public sphere. Silences that fuel impunity have been pushed beyond the household or the personal and on to the public sphere. Sexual harassment and violence faced by women in the garments industry in Bangladesh is a case in point (Fair Wear Foundation 2013). According to the Dhaka Metropolitan Police reports, whereas female garments workers account for only 2 to 3 per cent of the total population of women in the metropolitan area of Dhaka, they make up 11 per cent of rape cases. These workers, usually very young, unmarried and trapped in low-skill and low-income jobs, are prey to sexual violence within and outside their factories. Such has been the rise of sexual violence against women in the workforce, particularly of female garments workers, that the High Court Division of the Supreme Court of Bangladesh recently asked the government to explain why it should not be directed to 'frame rules and use of technological devices to arrest the criminals and prevent rape, stalking and eve-teasing of garment workers' ('Mirpur DC, OC Summoned over Rape' 2014; 'Too Many Incidents of Rape' 2014). This was in response to a writ petition filed by a rights-based organization praying for the court to pass necessary orders upon the government to protect garments workers who are targets of sexual violence. The petition made specific reference to an incident in July 2014 where a 19-year-old female garments worker was gang-raped in a microbus in Mirpur on her way home from the factory. She was forcibly picked up in the vehicle in the city's Darus Salam area by three people, including her neighbour Farid, 35, who used to stalk her.

Understanding the Scale and Cost of Sexual Violence and Impunity

The passage of the Domestic Violence (Prevention and Protection) Act in 2010 was an important turning point in clarifying once obfuscated notions of what behaviours could and should be recognized as domestic violence. The categories of violence set out in the Act, namely, violence in the form of physical, sexual, psychological or economic abuse, helped set the scene to more methodically understand, sometimes through survey experiments, the attitudinal dimensions surrounding violence, the parameters of violence, and the services and response mechanisms available. It also paved the way to better determine risk factors such as age, location and literacy in shaping the understanding of the nature of violence and the landscape of impunity surrounding sexual violence faced by women, children and sometimes men in Bangladeshi society.

This Act is an important piece of legislation to have in place in the face of rather dismal success with the previous law (which still exists) addressing criminal (or cognizable) offences against women, girls and children, namely, the Nari o Shishu Nirjatan Daman Ain (Suppression of Violence against Women and Children). However, the path to effective implementation of this 'enlightened' Act is not devoid of obstructions. Most notable is a perception failure as to the object of the law. It will be a mistake to delink the historical problems of effective implementation of the Nari o Shishu Nirjatan Daman Ain from the lack of implementation of the Domestic Violence Act. Quite apart from procedural weaknesses, both suffer from a fundamental perception failure—one that perceives the operations of laws more to 'break the family' and 'disrupt social order' than one of justice, reparation and redress. Much more systematic advocacy efforts are necessary to build a critical mass of awareness, together with practical and accessible services and tools for redressal. This will require a parallel investment in capacitating duty bearers and service providers.

The mindset that rape, though a 'social crime', is 'sometimes right and sometimes wrong', is not too far from the outlook that justifies violence of women at the hands of men, particularly of wives by husbands in the domestic sphere.[3] Let us take a moment to look at some numbers to remind ourselves of the pervasive and normalization of violence against women in Bangladesh, particularly sexual violence.

In an attempt to estimate the economic costs to the nation arising from direct costs associated with spousal violence in the form of health care, displacement, social service, legal service and criminal justice, the Centre for Policy Dialogue (CPD) arrived at a total of BDT 3,783,312 and a cost per victim of BDT 18,917 for the year 2009 (CPD 2009). The study says that the costs could be even higher if intangible expenses like pain, suffering and morbidity were taken into consideration. It also points out that there is a larger impact of this economic cost because had there been no spousal violence, the victims could have used the money for other productive purposes.

In-house reports for BRAC in 2013 of complaints reported to the Community Empowerment Programme (CEP), which is just one unit of BRAC's several rights-based programmes, depict sobering trends. Of the total 3221 incidents that year, the most frequently reported forms of violence were (highest to lowest): murder, rape, suicide, physical torture and attempted rape (BRAC 2013). Some significant findings of this report are as follows:

- Of the reported cases, 73.5 per cent of the incidents involved women or girls as victims/survivors, which means almost three out of every four victims/survivors are women or girls.
- An overwhelming majority (86 per cent) of the victims/survivors are children (0–17 years) and youth (18–35 years).
- Almost half of the victims are youths.
- Nearly half of the reported victims/survivors were poor and one-third were middle class; meanwhile, the ultra-poor were subjected to rape more than any other forms of violence.[4]
- Seven out of every ten perpetrators were men.
- More than half of the perpetrators (56 per cent) belonged to the middle class, while almost half of them had been fugitives when the case was reported.
- Thirty-five per cent of the perpetrators were family members of the victims/survivors, while 31 per cent were their neighbours.

An authoritative study (Siddique 2011) on the cost and consequences of violence at the household level finds that the cost of domestic violence represents about 12.5 per cent of Bangladesh's national annual expenditure or about 2.1 per cent of gross domestic product.

If we stop for a moment to take a look at the number of people seeking redress against sexual and other violence (such as physical assault and burning), an alarming picture emerges, as presented in Table 4.1. These numbers are from the data maintained by the Multisectoral Programme on Violence against Women of the Ministry of Women and Children Affairs for the One Stop Crisis Centres (OCCs) in eight medical college hospitals (MCHs) across the country as of August 2014. According to these government-maintained statistics, only one in about five incidents is filed as a case in the formal legal system, of which judgement has been pronounced in roughly one-seventh of the cases, of which penalty has been imposed in just ninety-six out of seven hundred and eight cases.

By far the most alarming statistic of all points to the reality that the scope, scale and depth of impunity around sexual and other violence is faced by women in this country in their very own homes. A nationwide survey titled 'Violence against Women Survey 2011' conducted by the Bangladesh Bureau of Statistics in collaboration with the United Nations Population Fund found that 87 per cent married women suffer domestic violence; 77 per cent of those tortured faced violence in the past twelve months, meaning that they were regularly beaten; 50 per cent of the victims needed medical help; while one-third of the women were raped by their husbands (Islam 2014).

Do all of these numbers and the tales of claims not redressed add up to a culture of impunity? If so, who is to be held accountable and to what degree? Of course, the state must be held up as the primary and ultimate duty bearer. What role, if any, do non-state actors such as rights-based (human rights, feminist, development, environmental, civil society) organizations play in redressing these wrongs? How far, if at all, can non-state organizations be held responsible?

Table 3.1: OCC Clients up to August 2014

Category	*OCC, DMCH*	*OCC, RMCH*	*OCC, CMCH*	*OCC, SMCH*	*OCC, KMCH*	*OCC, BMCH*	*OCC, FMCH*	*OCC, RpMCH*	*Total*
Physical assault	2,983	4,430	1,917	2,045	2,172	1,069	187	201	15,004
Sexual assault	1,728	539	721	1,284	337	353	70	37	5,069
Burns	218	45	14	19	54	20	4	5	379
Total	**4,929**	**5,014**	**2,652**	**3,348**	**2,563**	**1,442**	**261**	**243**	**20,452**
No. of filed cases	1,856	514	622	669	364	445	68	70	4,608
No. of judgements announced	276	172	59	85	32	79	3	2	708
Cases where penalty imposed	43	31	13	02	03	04	0	0	96

Source: http://www.mspvaw.org.bd/index.php?option=com_content&view

According to experts in international human rights law, given the sheer number of cases waiting for remedies, it does indeed amount to a systematic failure of the state to redress sexual violence and, therefore, to impunity. The UN Commission on Human Rights (UNCHR) (2005) defines impunity as:

> The impossibility, de jure or de facto, of bringing the perpetrators of violations to account—whether in criminal, civil, administrative or disciplinary proceedings—since they are not subject to any inquiry that might lead to their being accused, arrested, tried and, if found guilty, sentenced to appropriate penalties, and to making reparations to their victims.

The UNCHR further goes to state that impunity, therefore, implies a political and social context in which laws against human rights violations are either ignored or perpetrators inadequately punished by the state. The duty to combat impunity rests firmly with the state.

It is said that a person stands a better chance of being tried and judged for killing one human being than for killing 100,000 (Opotow 2001). Similarly, we seem to swirl within a well of moral exclusion, letting the state off the hook for its routine failure to protect citizens in their daily lives. We overlook or do not effectively hold accountable the state for its neglect, incapacity, incompetence and amnesia, which allows the daily accretion of failures and lapses, rendering a dehumanized and normalized state of daily existence of violence, injustice and absence of redress.

But it would be a mistake to examine impunity around sexual violence in Bangladesh as detached from a widespread culture of pervasive impunity as a whole. Insidious financial corruption, political collusion, lack of freedom of speech, organized crime in electoral politics, amassing of wealth through political positions, abuse of power by law enforcement agencies, abductions, mass killings, illegal detentions, extrajudicial killings, non-accountability of institutions, in particular criminal justice institutions, religious persecution, redressing historical wrongs, such as on issues of war crimes, and violations of every spectrum of the rule of law is the backdrop against which we assess the state's unwillingness, inability or negligence towards sexual violence suffered by its citizens.

Even when the Bangladeshi state does formally engage on the issue of impunity around sexual violence, it does so in a most selective and detached manner. It does not fully take into account or acknowledge the day-to-day violations and the accumulation of countless cases of non-redressal as impunity. For example, the government has taken a strong position on 'breaking the cycle of impunity on sexual violence' in the context of the Global Summit to End Sexual Violence in Conflict held in London in June 2014.[5] The government pledged to 'lead by example in breaking the global culture of impunity by bringing to justice the perpetrators of sexual violence and crimes against humanity during Bangladesh's 1971 War of Liberation'. During this summit, the foreign minister of Bangladesh said in his statement:

> 43 years after 200,000 Bengali women were subjected to crimes against humanity of horrendous proportions, including systematic and widespread rape, sexual torture, enslavement and forced pregnancy by occupying military forces and their auxiliary forces in 1971, Bangladesh has taken the bold step to break the cycle of impunity and bring the offenders to justice in a domestic war crimes trials.

While it is necessary to condemn impunity for sexual violence in times of conflict and extraordinary historical moments, it does not justify silence during 'peace' for the very same crimes that are perpetrated not by enemies of the state, but its citizens and institutions, including law enforcement authorities.

We see this unease around addressing violence of a sexual nature in other arenas of state response as well. For example, Bangladesh appears to be more comfortable to talk about recognition and protection of the rights of the transgender community than those of the gay, lesbian and bisexual one; and would much rather openly speak about the rights of sex workers to protection with regard to housing, livelihood and voter's rights, than the rights of women to be protected in their homes from marital rape or children from incest. This asymmetrical approach towards sex, sexual violence and sexuality is not partial to the government. While the rights-based discourse and service delivery mechanism in Bangladesh has progressed widely, it has mainly addressed sexual violence as violence and engaged with it within a criminal justice or a health and reproductive rights framework. The rights-based movement in Bangladesh has a long way to go in adapting its perspectives and activities in recognizing sexuality as a vital aspect of development, and also acknowledging the centrality of sexual rights to well-being (Gosine 2005).

LIVING WITH IMPUNITY: INSIGHTS INTO A CULTURE OF BARGAINING WITH PATRIARCHY

It has been argued that the perceived benefits of abiding by the rules of classic patriarchy may motivate women to internalize its norms (Kabeer 1988; Kandiyoti 1988). Some of the statistics seem to point towards the interpretation that the pressures and benefits of classic patriarchy induce compliance (Kabeer 1988), even to the extent that a wife's transgressions be seen as disobedience and a husband's violence as justifiable punishment (Yount and Li 2009; see also Browne-Miller 2012). It should, therefore, not be surprising that more than 80 per cent of married women in some Bangladeshi villages have reported that wife beating is right or acceptable (Schuler and Islam 2008).

Women's high and variable rates of justifying intimate partner violence (IPV) have been explained largely on substantive grounds (Yount et al. 2013). Scholars have argued that women may internalize certain norms of patriarchy even if they ostensibly contradict their interests (ibid.; Kabeer 1988). This internalization, in theory, is more likely under family systems that: (*a*) ascribe women to be financially dependent and obedient; (*b*) ascribe men to be providers and enforcers of obedience; and (*c*) promise benefits to compliant women (Kandiyoti 1988; Yount et al. 2013).

A combined reading of the findings of four empirical documents —the Demographic and Health Survey (DHS) for Bangladesh as of 2011 (NIPORT, Mitra and Associates, and ICF International 2013), the 2014 survey by the Bangladesh Bureau of Statistics on domestic violence (Islam 2014), the national survey on Cost of Domestic Violence (Siddique 2011) and the 2014 study on estimating women's contribution to the economy ('Women's Unaccounted Labour Significant' 2014) help us track not just who the actors across the spectrum are in Bangladesh, but at which stage these actors 'give in' to systemic or new pressures, thus allowing duty bearers (whether individuals, institutions or the state) to get away with their rent-seeking or criminally negligent behaviour. These findings help us link the personal experiences of women to a political analysis of their subordination. One issue that comes through persistently in these findings, and indeed the women's rights movement of Bangladesh, is that women's bodies and spatial existence continue to be sites of oppression and vested negotiation.

It could be argued, therefore, that an important contributing factor to impunity, consistent with Deniz Kandiyoti's (1988) theory of bargaining with patriarchy, is that the women whose reported attitudes most reflected classic patriarchal norms were the ones who had fewer opportunities and exposures than women whose reported attitudes most contradicted these norms. Qualitatively, the former group was older on average, were less likely to have had any schooling, had fewer mean grades (1.5 versus 3.8), had worked outside the household less often, had less exposure to the media, were less likely to have belonged to a community organization, had husbands with fewer mean grades, and were less likely to make decisions alone about daily purchases (Yount et al. 2013).

Do these women make active and strategic survival decisions; and do these 'decisions' transform their status from victims to survivors? If it is really a daily mindful choice between omissions or commissions that either avert or trigger victimization, then are these women acting upon their inherent agency? We shall look more closely at these questions later in this paper. For now, we can leave this point by recalling what Nancy Fraser (1998) calls, in her Integrated Theory of Justice, 'bivalent categories' whereby problems of recognition (culture, sex, ethnicity, class) or rejection become entwined with deprivation of various forms, including resource, mobility and voice, to produce particularly intractable forms of loss, exclusion, injustice, impunity or poverty.

Globally, the field of feminist politics is rich and developed on the subject of language and the interlinkages between the politics of redress and the positionality of the individual or site of injustice. Bangladeshi feminism too has developed its own understandings of victimhood, survivorship and victimization. For a large part, it understands victimhood as a state of being and recognizes it as distinct from victimization, which is a process of being victimized. Therefore, it has developed its own language (*protikar*, *protirodh*, *uttokto*, *khomotayon*) and actions accordingly, recognizing women as functioning as unequal citizens, where their bodies continue to be sites of struggle and are subverted by larger politics (Huq 2003).

We are, therefore, cautious not to draw a simplistic correlation between culturally evolved or socialized impunity where victims operate within an accepted silence with situations where victims are actively silenced. In other words, we must strive to analytically distinguish day-to-day silences that feed into a norm of rightslessness from the kind of impunity where a person who has been raped or criminally violated and actually wants to access justice cannot do so. We need to see these two forms of impunity as operating at two very different levels. One is more a cultural issue where women are socialized into thinking that it is okay to be hit by their husbands or punished for transgressing social norms. The other is the structural impunity and political patronage buttressed by the state's active or neglectful absences that operate against victims who actively seek redress and look for a way out of a rights vacuum. Each form of impunity, operating at the varied levels, poses different analytical problems or a different project of feminism and the rights-based movement.

Ayesha Jalal, in her essay 'The Convenience of Subservience' (1991), provides an exceptionally insightful treatment of the issue of women who navigate through the channels of impunity, whether at home or in the government. Jalal and others caution against making a linear assumption that a woman who lives in the midst of violence or rightslessness is unaware of impunity or her role in it. We are told that if she is living within a structure of violence, she is making a choice. We cannot deny her her agency where, if she finds an opportunity or legitimation to challenge impunity, then she will do so. At the same time, we cannot elide the cultural contexts and moral economies in which she functions necessarily with her silence as acceptance of impunity.

One might question the notion that women living within a daily cycle of impunity inevitably have 'choices' or options available to them in the first place. What we consider choices may in fact have much more ambiguous consequences—and they may be more Hobson's choices rather than Faustian bargains (Hickey and du Toit 2007).

I see an interesting parallel between the feminist analysis of silences in impunity with contemporary readings in poverty studies, particularly those that examine the processes of adverse incorporation and social exclusion that trap people in poverty. The concept of adverse incorporation, it is argued, captures the ways in which localized livelihood strategies are enabled and constrained by economic, social and political relations over both time and space, in that they operate over lengthy periods and within cycles, and at multiple spatial levels, from local to global. These relations are driven by inequalities of power (ibid.).

Without labouring this parallel too far, it could be concluded that a key contribution of this analogy is that the concepts and praxis of impunity, injustice and poverty are multidimensional. They are, in the language of Axel Honneth, 'thick, multilayered and historically developed' (Lovell 2007), and refer to particular forms of interaction involving the individual, state, market, community and household. They all draw explicit attention to the terms of inclusion in individual as well as institutional forms, and thus to the relations that keep people poor, excluded, neglected and in abeyance within a state of rightslessness over time.

THE STRUGGLE WITHIN: UNDERSTANDING THE ORGANIC AND STRUCTURAL LIMITATIONS OF RIGHTS-BASED ACTORS TO ADDRESSING SEXUAL VIOLENCE AND IMPUNITY

Like most rights-based movements throughout the world, the Bangladeshi women's and human rights movements too have been far from monochromatic, in either their formation or modes of resistance to patriarchal internalization and statist compulsions. Yes, we speak of *a* human rights movement or *the* women's rights movement in Bangladesh. The formation of various rights-based movements has grown organically and fluidly, and is multifaceted. Yet, they all feel sufficiently linked to basic goals to feel ownership towards *a* larger movement.

An analysis of our rights movement(s), from 1947 or earlier onwards to today's globalized reality, brings up a complex and multilayered journey of struggle against equally complex processes and structures responsible for the accretion of failures in the making of a widespread culture of impunity. Of course, the processes and structures that have failed and continue to fail have not always been statist. They are the combined result of a cyclical failure of a myriad forces, societal mindsets, economic swings and geopolitical shifts.

If we take a closer look at the women's movement as a case in point, we see the combined effects of the inner tensions within a larger canvas of shifts and interests. These tensions help account for how not just the women's rights movement but the wider human rights movements approached issues of state failure to address violence, injustice and lack of choice. In describing the modes of resistance in Bangladeshi women's struggle for freedom and justice, Hameeda Hossain (2006) sums it up best:

> Women's struggles cannot be compressed into a monolithic, homogenous movement, because our lives are caught within a complex mosaic of religious, ethnic, caste hierarchies and class interests. While our first experience of subordination is in the family, gender relations of power are mirrored in communities, labour markets, political and legal systems. As in the rest of South Asia, women in Bangladesh have engaged with populist movements for independence and democracy with some expectation that the promise of freedom and equality would extend to gender relations. But the reformist agenda of the newly independent state, despite its commitment to constitutional rights, failed to challenge entrenched relations of power within the family and the community.

From the time of Bangladesh's emergence as an independent nation in 1971 to the present day, an abiding theme of the women's movement has been to negotiate within the democratic space to bring to the forefront the historically sidelined 'woman question'. Much has changed in four decades since independence to raise the social and economic status of all citizens, most visibly women, through progressive economic steps. Women are considered significant drivers of the three thrust sectors (agriculture, readymade garments and migrant labour) of Bangladesh's enigmatic progress from a 'bottomless basket' to a near-middle-income country, having hit almost every millennium development goals (MDG) target.[6] And yet, we are still battling that very basic premise of women's freedom, where women and girls are free from social and state-perpetuated gender hierarchies that rob them of the opportunity to live full and meaningful lives.

A decade-by-decade analysis of the struggles and gains of the women's movement in Bangladesh brings to light a fascinating portrayal of shifts and trends in the changing nature of claimants and the very state itself. In the first and second decades (1970s and 1980s) since independence, we see women's concerns framed through the demands of the time—angst over sectarian and communal divides, economic exploitation, political disenfranchisement, nation-building efforts to rise from the ashes of a war-torn economy, rampant poverty, hunger, disease, and near non-existent infrastructure and political instability. Almost true to a Maslowian model of progression, by the early 1990s we observe a shift in women's demands from basic needs to something more. These demands focused on women's mobility in the public sphere, freedom from physical and economic violence, and clearer rights within the family and community.

An important bridge between the 1980s and 1990s was the toppling of an authoritarian military regime through mass uprisings. Women's groups actively joined university students and other organized bodies in the mass movements, which culminated in the overthrow of General H.M. Ershad and ushered in the first ever democratic elections in 1991. Perhaps the promise of participating in a democratic framework provided women's groups the impetus to craft their demands from a rights-based, legislature-driven angle. We see, therefore, the rise throughout the 1990s of the demands for legislation on a uniform family code, and the criminalization of dowry, polygamy and acid violence, among other issues. This was also the time that saw the emergence of unique socio-political configurations. For example, not only was there almost instinctive mobilization by women's rights groups on a wide array of issues, but also the emergence of service delivery-driven civil society group formations, such as legal aid organizations, convergence of women's and environmental issues in national development discourse, and rise of print media groups.[7] These groups systematically and effectively challenged the series of structural failures by different institutions of the state, whether it was the home ministry, police, court, jail administration, hospital authorities or local government representatives. We see this in such cases as the fatwa incident against Nurjahan of Chatakchara in Sylhet on grounds of alleged sexual transgression, or the case of teenager Shima Choudhury of Chittagong, who was raped by police and died in 'safe custody' (Amnesty International 1997).

As we move on to the fourth decade of women's mobilization in Bangladesh, from early 2000 onwards we notice that our response has become more disparate; rapid mobilization of activism has become more difficult. We notice the encroachment of extraneous push-and-pull factors, such as projectization of activist agendas and competition for funding and media attention, which have blunted the visibly strong and unified urges of activism for justice. Whereas even until the late 1990s, rights-based response was more cohesive, it has become more splintered, a contiguous mass giving way to an 'island cluster' formation. Organizational identity has become more prominent, some groups drifting further away from the centre than others. Indeed, what constitutes the centre is not so clear any more. By the end of the fourth decade, most 'activism' seems to have become more about service delivery and not so much about changing structure.

What has brought about this fundamental shift? Having spoken to women's rights activists across three generations, some answers come to light. One consistent theme emerging from a broad analysis is the impact of neo-liberalism on gender politics. A sub-theme of this finding is that the persistent and overarching failures that form the very basis of engagement with or dissent from the state have also shifted. These shifts have been along the lines of market-driven development, increasing encroachment of radical Islamization in social and institutional settings, and the visible costs and opportunities of living with globalization.

The one characteristic that has not changed for the women's rights movement has been its frenetic pace—irrespective of the decade and form in which the activism takes place, women's and rights-based activists continue to perform in a firefighting mode, with little time or space to conduct rigorous analysis or academic examination of the gains and losses and trajectories of the movement. Having said this, feminists on the ground are quick to point out that while inward-looking scrutiny is certainly important and necessary, we must be cautious to not become so self-flagellating as to exonerate the state from its indispensable obligations to its citizens. Of course, neither the nature of rights-based movements nor the very state from which it derives its claims have been static. Given domestic and geopolitical shifts, and the push-and-pull factors of market and social variables, it is all the more necessary to analyse shifts and trends against the backdrop of the changing nature of claimants and duty bearers, whether they are the state, national institutions or corporations, or influential individuals.

CONCLUSION

We live in a very particular moment of rights. The dichotomy between rights bearers and rights holders, like the nature of the state in which they function, is ever evolving. Never before has the dramatic rise in rights consciousness and the disillusionment with the rights discourse collided so resoundingly.

Justice actors too, like many others that interact in the domains of rights, the human body as a site of oppression and resistance, governance and the state, formal law and cultural norms are revisiting and reimagining notions of justice. In Bangladesh, feminist and development movements are constantly finding ways to challenge the culture of impunity. Or rather, they address the many cultures of impunity—whether sexual, political, financial or institutional. With regard to addressing sexual violence and challenging impunity in Bangladesh, we certainly must continue our existing modes of resistance through a 'more of the same' approach. In addition, I would like to offer three specific and self-prescribed 'corrective' measures as we go forward.

Correct the Erroneous Conflation of Legal Aid with Access to Justice

Many of us in the 'legal aid movement' in Bangladesh tend to make a correlation between access to legal aid as access to justice. This assumption is faulty insofar as it fails to take into account the full remit of justice. By addressing only one of the many steps that lead to justice, we leave the victims of sexual violence wide open to further victimization by systemic failures on every other front. This conflation stems from a lack of a holistic understanding of victims' multidimensional paradigms of exclusions and disadvantages. We as service providers are either not aware or do not sufficiently acknowledge the 'webs of influence' and entrenched political clientelism within which victims of sexual or other violence come to us or are served by us. Nor is there a full understanding, despite functioning in a society where not just financial but varied dimensions of corruption forms the principal language of negotiation, of how victims and their immediate communities suffer as they do not have the basic cultural capital required to negotiate and advance their claims (Gupta 1995).

Meld the 'Rights'-Based and 'Needs'-Based Approaches to Development and Justice Services

This unique phenomenon in Bangladesh of a clear dichotomy between 'activist' and 'development' camps in terms of operations (not so much in ideology) emerged from the early to mid-1970s, since the formation of various non-government, civil society and issue-based associations. There are only a handful of organizations that adopt and apply both approaches in their interventions. And that too, almost every case has come about through the dynamism and charisma of the founding heads of the organizations, rather than any conscious melding of the two paradigms. In some cases, the two streams have looked at and continue to look at the other with disdain or distrust, or both. 'Development' organizations have been mainly operating on a 'needs'- or 'welfare'-based model of service delivery, not necessarily taking into account the entitlement, agency or centrality of the person whose needs they serve. On the other hand, rights-based groups have, with almost evangelical zeal, focused primarily on the 'demand' or 'rights' perspective of the issue, without taking into account the day-to-day lived reality and 'needs' of the person whose cause they serve. Being caught in a classic divide between being either the 'objects' of development goals or 'subjects' of justice services, the 'victim' hardly makes the journey to 'survivorship', and in many cases is left exposed to the forces of rent seeking, unaccountability and routine neglect, which become part of their daily existence.

Yes, we function in a reality where different societal and political interests can manipulate our operations and the operations of the state. But in our mode of service delivery—whether needs or rights based, we go about our functions as if we live in a Weberian ideal of the state—a goal-oriented, unitary institution discrete from society, with an undisputed sovereignty in its spheres of jurisdiction and with a clear separation of powers between a judiciary, a legislative and an executive branch of government (Berenschot 2010).

The Need for Re-engaging

Women's rights, human rights, development and environmental movements, together with the media, make up the bulk of civil society voices in Bangladesh. Beyond the individual claimants of justice, civil society actors also exert influence and contest the market and the state as a means to challenge impunity and injustice. But those of us who function within these spheres of contestation would do well to remember that even for civil society, there is a front door and even a back door and revolving door of operation. It is certainly a wonderful idea for seeking redress from a liberal state, but we constantly have to engage amongst ourselves to examine whether the state as we know it is going to be useful for us. Yes, it is true that within women's rights and human rights activism, structural issues often get sidelined because of immediate ones that need to be addressed. As activists in these spheres, we find ourselves having to deal with one case and move to the next. Nevertheless, I would urge that we find ways to devote dedicated time and energy to undertake an ecosystemic and self-reflective study of our work, and look more critically at our engagements with the structures, processes and shifts that we function within.

For feminist circles in particular, I believe that it is important to take another look at the nature of feminist engagement with the ecosystem in which it functions. Those of us who address sexual and systemic violence need to look at how the nature of the quest for justice continues, morphs and changes over the years.

A justice-centric battle against impunity, whether carried out by individuals, groups or wider movements, brings best results when efforts remain undisturbed by internal schisms. Overcoming the ailment of sexual violence and the impunity around it is an old, worldwide goal. Not all have succeeded at overcoming this obstacle, and certainly not at the same rate. In Bangladesh, we undoubtedly have not got there yet. But it is important more than ever before to acknowledge and build upon the small but significant progress so far that has come through the collaborative efforts of many actors, both at the grassroots and at the centre, including some segments of the government.

This quest for justice is more than simply addressing the violence at the moment it happens and then moving on. This is an important moment in Bangladesh when we are questioning our histories, our own interventions and our own actions in dismantling impunity. We need to seize this historical moment the best we can.

NOTES

1. Some names have been changed to protect the privacy of victims.
2. Also see Ali (2011).
3. The controversial remark about rape being 'sometimes right, sometimes wrong' was made by the Indian minister Babulal Gaur in response to criticism for failing to visit the scene and for accusing the media of hyping a story where two young girls, cousins aged 12 and 14, were gang-raped and hanged in Uttar Pradesh (Molloy 2014).
4. BRAC's understanding of the 'ultra-poor' are those people who are caught in a below-subsistence trap from which it is difficult to break free using available resources and mechanisms. More often than not, ultra-poverty tends to be chronic and intergenerational. The ultra-poor spend most of their income on food, yet fail to afford their basic calorific need. Ultra-poverty, especially in South Asia, has a distinctly gendered face; many of the ultra-poor households tend to be headed by women, having been widowed or abandoned. See, for example, Matin, Sulaiman and Rabbani (2008). For a fuller understanding of BRAC's approach to addressing this target group, see the Challenging the Frontiers of Poverty Reduction/Targeting the Ultra Poor (CFPR-TUP) programme at http://tup.brac.net/ (accessed 20 June 2015).
5. See http://www.banglanews24.com/en/fullnews/bn/93300.html (accessed 13 June 2014).
6. 'Bottomless basket' was a dismissive term used by Henry Kissinger, former US foreign secretary, in 1974, referring to the newly independent nation. See, however, 'Bangladesh: Out of the Basket' (2012).
7. For example, the *Daily Star*, *Prothom Alo*, *Janakantha*, *Financial Express*, *Bhorer Kagoj* and *Manabzamin*.

REFERENCES

'Bangladesh: Out of the Basket'. 2012. *The Economist*, 2 November. http://www.economist.com/blogs/feastandfamine/2012/11/Bangladesh (accessed 21 June 2015).

'Mirpur DC, OC Summoned over Rape of Garment Worker'. 2014. *Daily*

Star, 9 July. http://www.thedailystar.net/mirpur-dc-oc-summoned-over-rape-of-garment-worker-32575 (accessed 18 June 2015).

'Too Many Incidents of Rape'. 2014. *New Nation*, 30 July 2014. http://thedailynewnation.com/news/16459/too-many-incidents-of-rape.html (accessed 18 June 2015).

'Women's Unaccounted Labour Significant, Needs Recognition: Study'. 2014. Centre for Policy Dialogue. http://cpd.org.bd/index.php/women-unaccounted-contribution-to-economy-significant-needs-recognition-study (accessed 21 June 2015).

al-Mahmood, Syed Zain. 2010. 'Of a Warrior: Ravaged Over and Over, She Fights on for Justice', *Daily Star*, 8 March. http://archive.thedailystar.net/newDesign/news-details.php?nid=129180 (accessed 20 June 2015).

Ali, Anwar. 2011. 'Out of Court Settlement of Rape: Priest, 9 Others Arrested', *Daily Star*, 24 February. http://archive.thedailystar.net/newDesign/news-details.php?nid=175298 (accessed 20 June 2015).

Amnesty International. 1997. 'Bangladesh: Failure by State Protects Alleged Rapists', ASA 13/05/97. https://www.amnesty.org/download/Documents/160000/asa130051997en.pdf (accessed 8 October 2015).

Berenschot, Ward. 2010. 'Everyday Mediation: The Politics of Public Service Delivery in Gujarat, India', *Development and Change*, 41(5): 883–905. http://www.academia.edu/822937/Everyday_Mediation_The_Politics_of_Public_Service_Delivery_in_Gujarat_India (accessed 21 June 2015).

BRAC. 2013. 'Brief Report on Rights Violations 2013'. A Brief Analysis of the Human Rights Violation Incidents Identified and Reported by CEP during 2013, Stop Violence Initiative (SVI) Community Empowerment Programme, BRAC.

Browne-Miller, Angela (ed.). 2012. *Violence and Abuse in Society: A Global Crisis*. Praeger.

Centre for Policy Dialogue (CPD). 2009. 'Domestic Violence in Bangladesh—Cost Estimates and Measures to Address Attendant Problems'. Report No. 97. http://www.cpd.org.bd/pub_attach/DR97.pdf (accessed 21 June 2015).

Fair Wear Foundation. 2013. 'Standing Firm against Factory Floor Harassment, Government of the Netherlands and UN Women'. http://www.fairwear.org/ul/cms/fck-uploaded/documents/fwfpublications_reports/StandingFirmReportFWF2013.pdf (accessed 8 October 2015).

Fraser, Nancy. 1998. 'From Redistribution to Recognition? Dilemmas of Justice in a "Post-Socialist" Age', in Cynthia Willett (ed.), *Theorizing Multiculturalism: A Guide to the Current Debate*, pp. 19–49. Malden: John Wiley & Sons.

Gosine, Andil. 2005. 'Sex for Pleasure, Rights to Participation, and Alternatives to AIDS: Placing Sexual Minorities and/or Dissidents in Development'. IDS Working Paper 228. http://www.ids.ac.uk/ids/bookshop/wp/wp228.pdf (accessed 22 June 2015).

Hickey, Sam and Andries du Toit. 2007. 'Adverse Incorporation, Social Exclusion and Chronic Poverty'. Working Paper 81, Chronic Poverty Research Centre. http://www.chronicpoverty.org/uploads/publication_files/WP81_Hickey_duToit.pdf (accessed 21 June 2015).

Hossain, Hameeda. 2006. 'Women's Movements in Bangladesh: The Struggle Within', *Daily Star*, 5 February. https://www.mail-archive.com/sacw@insaf.net/msg00441.html (accessed 21 June 2015).

Huq, S.P. 2003. 'Bodies as Sites of Struggle: Naripokkho and the Movement for Women's Rights in Bangladesh', *Bangladesh Development Studies*, 29(3/4, special issue on Citizenship and Rights in Bangladesh): 47–65. http://www.bids.org.bd/bds/XXIX%203&4.pdf (accessed 21 June 2015).

Islam, Zyma. 2014. 'Most Abused at Homes', *Daily Star*, 26 January. http://www.thedailystar.net/most-abused-at-homes-8422 (accessed 20 June 2015).

Jalal, Ayesha. 1991. 'The Convenience of Subservience: Women and the State of Pakistan', in Deniz Kandiyoti (ed.), *Women, Islam and the State*, pp. 77–114. Philadelphia: Temple University Press.

Kabeer, Naila. 1988. 'Subordination and Struggle: Women in Bangladesh', *New Left Review*, 1(168). http://newleftreview.org/I/168/naila-kabeer-subordination-and-struggle-women-in-bangladesh (accessed 8 October 2015).

Kandiyoti, Deniz. 1988. 'Bargaining with Patriarchy', *Gender & Society*, 2(3): 274–90.

Kristof, Nicholas. 2011. 'When a Girl is Executed… for Being Raped', *New York Times* Blog, 30 March. http://kristof.blogs.nytimes.com/2011/03/30/when-a-girl-is-executed-for-being-raped (accessed 20 June 2015).

Lovell, T. 2007. 'Nancy Fraser's Integrated Theory of Justice: A

"Sociologically Rich" Model for a Global Capitalist Era?', *Law, Social Justice & Global Development Journal*, 1. http://www.go.warwick.ac.uk/elj/lgd/2007_1/lovell (accessed 21 June 2015).

Matin, Imran, Munshi Sulaiman and Mehnaz Rabbani. 2008. 'Crafting a Graduation Pathway for the Ultra Poor: Lessons and Evidence from a BRAC Programme', Working Paper No. 109, March, Chronic Poverty Research Centre.

Molloy, Antonia. 2014. 'Indian Politician Says of Rape, "Sometimes it's Right, Sometimes it's Wrong"', *Independent*, 5 June. http://www.independent.co.uk/news/world/asia/indian-politician-says-of-rape-sometimes-its-right-sometimes-its-wrong-9494981.html (accessed 21 June 2015).

National Institute of Population Research and Training (NIPORT), Mitra and Associates, and ICF International. 2013. *Bangladesh Demographic and Health Survey 2011*. Dhaka and Calverton, MD: NIPORT, Mitra and Associates, and ICF International. dhsprogram.com/pubs/pdf/FR265/FR265.pdf (accessed 16 September 2015).

Opotow, Susan. 2001. 'Reconciliation in Times of Impunity: Challenges for Social Justice', *University of Massachusetts Boston Social Justice Research*, 14(2): 149–70.

Priyo News. 2011. '"Religion" Saved, with it Rapists'. news.priyo.com/law-and-order/2011/02/23/religion-saved-it-rapists-20509.html (accessed 20 June 2015).

Schuler, Sidney Ruth and F. Islam. 2008. 'Women's Acceptance of Intimate Partner Violence within Marriage in Rural Bangladesh', *Studies in Family Planning*, 39(1): 49–58. http://www.ncbi.nlm.nih.gov/pubmed/18540523 (accessed 21 June 2015).

Siddique, Kaniz. 2011. 'Domestic Violence against Women: Cost to the Nation', CARE Bangladesh. http://www.carebangladesh.org/publication/Publication_9287219.pdf (accessed 20 June 2015).

United Nations Commission on Human Rights. 2005. 'Set of Principles for the Protection and Promotion of Human Rights through Action to Combat Impunity', 8 February. http://www.derechos.org/nizkor/impu/principles.html (accessed 20 June 2015).

Yount, Kathryn M. and L. Li. 2009. 'Women's "Justification" of Domestic Violence in Egypt', *Journal of Marriage and Family*, 71(5): 1125–40.

Yount, Kathryn M., Nafisa Halim, Sidney Ruth Schuler and Sara Head. 2013. 'A Survey Experiment of Women's Attitudes about Intimate Partner Violence against Women in Rural Bangladesh', *Demography*, 50(1): 333–57. http://www.ncbi.nlm.nih.gov/pmc/articles/PMC3716289 (accessed 21 June 2015).

5

Medico-Legal Evidence in Rape Prosecutions in Bangladesh

Legal and Policy Reform to End Impunity

ISHITA DUTTA

INTRODUCTION

Despite stringent laws penalizing rape, the right of rape survivors in Bangladesh to access justice is routinely denied. Social stigma also prevents many from disclosing violations and seeking redress. Where they do seek redress, protracted and adversarial court proceedings and insufficient institutional support often combine to deny justice. Inadequacies in the laws and policies surrounding medico-legal evidence collection that inhibit prosecution are a key barrier. This paper provides an account of the present state of medico-legal evidence based on investigations on the ground, and discussions with medical and legal practitioners, and with feminist activists who have been involved in supporting survivors and campaigning for change in these laws and policies. Following this, it highlights concerns regarding the existing laws and policies on medico-legal evidence collection, with special emphasis on the continuing use of the physically invasive and legally unsound two-finger test. It concludes with a stocktaking of the movement for law and policy reform currently under way in Bangladesh that seeks to create uniform, gender-sensitive and victim-centric policies, practices and protocols for medico-legal evidence collection in rape prosecutions.

This paper emanates from the research and advocacy experience of BLAST on medical evidence laws and practices, and its ongoing intervention under the Growing Up Safe & Healthy (SAFE) project focused on reform of laws, policies and procedures to create a more rights-sensitive and victim-friendly process for collection of medico-legal evidence in cases of rape. In developing this paper, research was conducted in the form of interviews with women's rights activists who have been involved in the campaign for the reform of medico-legal evidence-collection procedures in Bangladesh, judges, lawyers and medical practitioners. Further, a literature survey was conducted to set forth the context, and legal research was conducted to analyse the trends in the use of medico-legal evidence in reported judgements. Last, existing research, reports and background papers developed under the SAFE project were utilized to provide anecdotal information on the use of medico-legal evidence in criminal prosecutions.

BACKGROUND AND CONTEXT

According to police reports, an average of 3,300 people are raped every year in Bangladesh (Ahmed 2011). In another study, about 24 per cent of urban women and 30 per cent of rural women reported that their first sexual experience was forced (Fulu et al. 2013). While physical violence is well documented, very few studies have investigated sexual violence. Especially with respect to the issue of access to justice for women survivors of rape, studies have repeatedly highlighted the social ramifications—such as rejection by society and family, and feelings of shame that survivors experience—as major factors contributing to underreporting of the crime (Naripokkho and Bangladesh Mahila Parishad 2005). However, very little has been written about the 'medico-legal gauntlet' that a survivor inevitably has to face in order to access justice (Ahmed 2011).

Some information is available on the procedural barriers that a survivor faces in securing a successful rape prosecution, primarily from findings of studies carried out by local NGOs dealing with the issue of VAW. One thing that has been discussed is delays in trial proceedings, often due to difficulties in collecting statements by individuals such as the investigating officer. This delay impacts the efficacy of the prosecution's case by providing time for the defendant's lawyer or family members to intimidate witnesses (Naomi 2009). From 1998 to 2000, the Naripokkho 'Pilot Study on Violence against Women' (Azim 2000) addressed these delays by collecting reports of rape from national dailies and then following up with twenty-two policy stations and two hospitals in Dhaka to ensure that cases were dealt with efficiently (UNFPA 2013).

In a separate study, Naripokkho, a women's activist group working with violence survivors since the 1980s, found that the gender- and victim-insensitive behaviour of medical officers, as well as the lack of counselling and trained staff to work with survivors, prevents many women from seeking medico-legal support. The inability to make individuals feel comfortable results in even fewer rape cases being brought to trial (Bairagi et al. 2006).

Medico-Legal Evidence as a Barrier

Few papers discussing the procedural barriers to prosecution expressly reference the limitations of medico-legal evidence. Where such limitations are discussed, they refer either to procedural critiques such as the late medical examination of survivors, or critiques of the way medico-legal evidence is deployed in court, such as how lack of evidence of physical resistance is used as an indication that rape has not occurred.

Delay in medically examining the survivor after the assault to obtain evidence was the main procedural issue discussed in the literature (Islam and Islam 2003; Naomi 2009). A study on the examination of the socio-demographic characteristics of 230 sexual assault victims in Dhaka stated that the majority of survivors (61.3 per cent) were not examined on the day of the assault (Islam and Islam 2003). In a rural setting, an even lower proportion of the survivors surveyed, only 3.41 per cent, were examined on the day of the assault (Barek 2010). Individuals who are examined days after the assault have bathed, often washing away evidence, which is not helpful in building a legal case against the assailant.

Another problem discussed is that doctors who have examined a survivor may get transferred to different areas of the country, which results in them not receiving court summons. For this reason, on average, it takes seven or eight months to get the evidence from the doctor to the court (Naomi 2009). Further, the requirement for a physical medical examination often exposes women to shame and social disgrace, and may discourage them from going forward with the process (Zaman 1999).

Studies have also talked about the relevance of evidence of physical resistance in determining whether rape took place. One problematic study written by a physician at Dhaka Medical College surveyed 176 cases of reported rape at the Sher-e-Bangla Medical College, Barisal, and used medico-legal evidence in combination with character evidence to give an opinion on which cases were rape and which cases were not.

The study concluded that 73.8 per cent of the sample was considered not rape based on '*the victim's history of love affairs, leaving home secretly with their fiancés, living with them for many days, absence of physical signs of resistance prior to coitus*, sometimes their direct admission that they had sexual intercourse with consent and will and without any duress' (Barek 2010, emphasis added). This study provides an insight into the harmful institutional understanding of rape offences held by the medical community.

In particular, this conclusion perpetuates the idea that a victim's character and past sexual history should determine the validity of their complaint.

Referring to the difficulties in obtaining medico-legal reports and the preference that judges have for seeing marks of physical assault to decide in favour of a rape victim, reports have also critiqued the practice of Bangladeshi courts of using the lack of evidence of physical resistance to indicate whether rape had occurred (Naomi 2009).

Interventions have also attempted to address some of the problems with obtaining medico-legal evidence for rape victims. One example is UNICEF's Woman Friendly Hospital Initiative, developed in 2002, which addresses the treatment of women in hospital settings, including how they are treated during collection of evidence in the hospital (Du Mont and White 2007, citing Afsana, Rashid and Thurston 2006; Haque 2001; Haque and Clarke 2002). The main intervention included training hospital staff to offer respectful care to victims with the intention of increasing women's usage of services, allowing evidence to be documented correctly (ibid.).

LEGAL FRAMEWORK

The colonial-era Penal Code 1860 defines and penalizes the offence of rape in Bangladesh. The definition and penalty under it were further supplemented by the enactment of the Suppression of Violence against Women Act 2000 (hereinafter the SVAW Act) (as amended in 2003). The Criminal Procedure Code 1898 and the Evidence Act 1872 govern procedural and evidentiary issues relating to the prosecution of rape. In addition, the SVWA 2000 contains provisions specific to medico-legal evidence collection in cases of VAW.

Definition of Rape

Section 9(1) of the SVAW Act read together with Section 375 of the Bangladesh Penal Code 1860 define the offence of rape.[1] According to this definition, if a male, not being married to a woman above 16 years of age, has sexual intercourse against her will or without her consent or with consent obtained by putting her in fear or by deceitful means, or with a woman below 16 years with or without her consent, shall be presumed to have raped such a woman. Under the existing laws of Bangladesh, the offence of rape can only be established where there is 'forced penetration of the male sexual organ in the female vagina' (Naripokkho and Bangladesh Mahila Parishad 2005).

Globally and even regionally, definitions of rape have evolved from requiring proof of force or violence to requiring proof of consent (UN Division on the Advancement of Women 2010). Unfortunately, these trends do not appear to be reflected in the current law or its interpretation in Bangladesh.

Collection of Medico-Legal Evidence

The collection of medical evidence in rape cases is governed by provisions of the Evidence Act 1872 and the SVAW Act 2000 (as amended in 2003). Section 45 of the Evidence Act is the umbrella provision that provides for 'opinions of experts' to be sought in relevant cases. This includes medical experts. Also of relevance in the context of rape prosecutions and medico-legal evidence is Section 155(4) of the Evidence Act. It forms part of a section titled 'Impeaching the credit of the witness' and states that in prosecutions of rape, the victim's testimony may be discredited by showing that she was of 'generally immoral character'. This section is considered to provide the legal basis for introducing evidence about a rape survivor's sexual history in a trial. Another vestige of the colonial regime, this legal provision is based on the presumption that the victim has engaged in consensual sex unless there is enough evidence to corroborate her claim that the sexual intercourse was non-consensual and she had been raped. This presumption of consent/non-consent based on sexual history has a direct bearing on the administration and findings of the 'two-finger test' conducted as part of medico-legal examinations of rape survivors. This is discussed in greater detail later.

The first express provision with respect to medico-legal evidence collection in cases of VAW was articulated in Section 32 of the SVAW Act. Notably, the provision does not apply to cases of rape only, but to all offences under the Act. The section stipulates that medical examinations shall be conducted in a government hospital or private hospital recognized by the government for the purpose. The medical officer at any such hospital, if approached by a survivor of violence, shall quickly conduct a medical examination and furnish a certificate to the concerned person and inform the local police station about the commission of the offence (SVAW Act, Section 32[2]). Where such medical examination is not conducted within a reasonable time period, it shall be deemed to amount to misconduct and such a person shall be subject to penalties in accordance with organizational service rules and policies (Section 32[3]).

POLICY FRAMEWORK

Two years after the enactment of the SVAW Act and consequent to persistent advocacy by Naripokkho, the Ministry of Health and Family Welfare, Government of Bangladesh, issued a circular dated 16 September 2002 setting out 'the Guidelines' for medical examinations of women and child survivors of violence pursuant to Section 32 of the SVAW Act (Basu 2013).

The 'Preamble to the Guidelines' states that they have been enacted pursuant to the state's obligation to prevent incidents of VAW and provide remedies where such incidents do occur. It further states that the guidelines are being enacted for the implementation in practice of provisions relating to the *medical treatment and medical examination* of survivors of violence, contained in Section 32 of the SVAW Act, Section 43(2) of the Acid Control Act 2002 and Section 29 of the Acid Crimes Prevention Act 2002.[2] The police headquarters reportedly finally received these guidelines in September 2008.[3]

These guidelines contain the following provisions with respect to medical examinations:

1. According to Clause (a) of the guidelines, a woman or a child victim of rape or any other form of violence who approaches, even without any police reference, a physician on duty at a government medical hospital/establishment, or at a government-recognized health centre run by any voluntary organization, has to be examined by such physician. At the minimum, such an examiner should be a medical officer.
2. The medical examiner shall conduct the examination in accordance with the rules made in this respect and forward the medical certificate to the relevant district magistrate and local police station. A copy of the certificate should also be provided to the person being examined.

The significance of the guidelines is threefold. First, they clarify that all government or non-governmental hospitals authorized in this respect may conduct medical examinations. Second, they explicitly do away with the requirement of filing a criminal complaint with the police prior to the medical examination. This is a marked improvement, as previously it was mandatory to obtain court orders in order to have a medical examination conducted. This was subsequently changed to allow the examination upon the filing of a police complaint (Bairagi et al. 2006). Third, the guidelines recognize the importance of health care for a survivor of violence. It states that all necessary services should be provided by a physician and his/her assistant to a woman or child survivor of violence.

MEDICO-LEGAL EVIDENCE RECORD FORMAT

A standard general format for the collection of medico-legal evidence, developed in accordance with the guidelines issued by the

Ministry of Health and Family Welfare in 2002, was released five years later in February 2007. Reportedly, the medico-legal record (MLR) form was circulated to the various government hospitals at the district and *upazila* levels in July 2007 (Naomi 2009).

The MLR form makes provision for recording several details concerning a survivor of violence. Significantly, it includes a provision for 'description of genital organs, including hymen and vaginal canal'. The findings of the 'two-finger test' used by medical examiners to make observations regarding the hymen and vaginal canal are recorded here.

CHALLENGES IN CURRENT POLICY AND PROFORMA

The most significant concern with respect to the current legal regime on medico-legal evidence collection is undoubtedly the requirement of conducting the highly invasive and insensitive 'two-finger test'. The use of this test to examine the vaginal canal is highly problematic not only due to inherent inaccuracies associated with it but also with the manner in which such findings are used to discredit women's testimonies. Apart from being physically invasive, it is legally unsound. Criminal law experts, lawyers, police and forensic scientists all over the world have concluded that this kind of test has no evidentiary value, no scientific merit, breaches national and international human rights standards, compounds the victim's trauma and, paradoxically, amounts to a further sexual assault (HRW 2010: 18).

While the form does require that the woman's consent be taken before any examination is performed, the relevant entry is drafted in cursory terms and does not expressly state that such consent has to be 'informed' and 'free'. Specifically, it seeks the victim's consent in accepting that the results of the examination may go for or against her. This results in further ambiguity regarding the medical officer's obligation to accurately inform the survivor of the invasive nature of the tests and reasons thereof prior to conducting them.

Finally, the form is drafted in such a manner that medical evidence may be collected only from women and girl survivors of sexual violence. Thus, it cannot be used for other groups of persons vulnerable to sexual violence, such as male children or transgendered persons.

The 'Two-Finger' Test

The 'two-finger' test is a medical examination 'in which the examining doctor notes the presence or absence of the hymen and the size and so-called laxity of the vagina of the rape survivor and comments about whether she is "habituated" to sexual intercourse' (ibid.).

The earlier discussion regarding the MLR form suggests that the 'two-finger test' is still prescribed by the government and applied in the investigation of rape cases. It also remains on the syllabus of medical schools and is taught in the major obstetrics and gynaecology departments in medical colleges in Bangladesh. An exploratory study conducted in 2011 found that the test was being carried out as a matter of routine practice at the One Stop Crisis Centre at the Dhaka Medical College Hospital, the country's foremost government medical institute, and by the same measure a relatively gender-sensitive and victim-friendly institute (Ahmed 2011; also see Rougerie 2013).

A research study carried out in 2011–12 by BLAST confirmed the widespread prevalence and routine use of the test in other parts of Bangladesh. This study analysed case records in sixty-one instances of rape from fifteen districts and found that the test was conducted in all but nine cases, including on a victim found to be twenty-six to twenty-seven weeks' pregnant. Additionally, in twelve cases, the test was conducted on minor/child victims. The study also found that in three of the nine cases in which it was not conducted, the examining officer found signs of forceful sexual intercourse as well as signs of physical injuries, indicating that although routinely conducted, such tests are not necessarily required to arrive at a conclusion of forced sexual intercourse (Bairagi et al. 2006).

As discussed earlier, there appears to be a prevailing attitude both among the medical and legal communities that women have the upper hand in rape cases, that they have the power to make false accusations. This leads to a perception that institutional mechanisms should be wary of women's accounts of rape. The test is, therefore, justified partly on the basis that it is the price that has to be paid for making an allegation of rape and partly on the basis, as stated earlier, that it acts as a deterrent to false allegations. This is problematic for a number of reasons, not the least of which is that it further serves to fuel the patriarchal hegemony in the treatment of rape survivors in Bangladesh, which advocates suspicion of women's motives over sensitive and rehabilitative treatment. Worryingly, anecdotal experience suggests that the test dissuades women and their families from seeking medical or legal services in the first place, or from continuing with the medical examination once they are told of the nature of the test (Islam 2013; Moni 2010, cited in Basu 2013).

No Dignity for the Rape Survivor

The most jarring aspect of the medico-legal examination of rape survivors is that from the start these examinations are not viewed as routine medical procedures. Understandably, for the survivor, the experience is fraught with difficulties. What is less apparent is the near-prurient interest with which not only medical officers but also the police and lawyers view medical examinations. I use the term 'near-prurient' as there may not be a sense of enjoyment in the doctor carrying out the test, but there is the absence of a clinical approach that such an examination merits. This interest is what leads to a medical officer probing a rape survivor aged 12 years, who was taken away from a bus station by a driver and helper, and raped in a moving vehicle, to find out whether the reported incident was her 'first exposure'.[4] This near-prurient interest is what makes a doctor 'want' to conduct medical examinations even where there are junior medical officers available to do so.[5] Such an attitude, prevalent in a society that attaches the highest value to covering the female body in order to keep its honour intact, is ironic at best and perverse at worst. It is also a reflection of the unpleasant curiosity that surrounds the female body in our society.

The Good Girl–Bad Girl Dichotomy

> You don't understand. All types of cases come: genuine cases where a *bhalo meye* [good girl] suffers as well as false cases which involve a *kharap meye* [bad girl] who is used to [it]. (Medical officer, Dhaka Medical College Hospital)

A very high value is placed on the chastity of women. Girls are conditioned to be ashamed of their bodies. Thus, good girls hide their bodies and bad girls show their bodies. This notion of *bhalo meye, kharap meye* permeates our combined social psyche to the deepest extent possible. So much so that when a woman who worked as a sex worker for the better part of her life and later became an NGO worker was reduced to tears of shame and embarrassment when she had to undergo a routine gynaecological examination conducted by a male doctor. Her only poignant words of explanation were, '*Amar khub lojja laglo*' (I was deeply ashamed).[6] This value placed on social perceptions of good and bad character gives rise to this extreme dissonance, by which a sex worker is a *kharap meye* and should have no qualms about showing her body, but causes extreme shame in an NGO worker who is a *bhalo meye*.

These perceptions are also the reason why conversations with most judges, lawyers and medical practitioners dealing with rape cases invariably turn to the perceived character of the woman making the accusation of rape. This turns judges and lawyers into bastions of truth, whose focus shifts from ascertaining the guilt of the accused to deliberating on whether the survivor was chaste enough to have made a true accusation. In the case of medical practitioners, it forces them away from making a medical catalogue of injuries to a legal inference of rape. The only means remaining then to test the merit of the survivor's allegation is a medico-legal examination and this is taken to be the primary determiner of whether rape occurred, irrespective of all the gaps.

Institutional Gaps

The guidelines and medical evidence form issued by the Ministry of Health and Family Welfare, despite their apparent deficiencies, represent an important step towards standardizing policies and procedures. However, the ground reality is that in practice even these basic minimum standards are not being uniformly implemented. The primary reason for this is the lack of awareness and dissemination of the guidelines and the form among both medical organizations and law enforcement agencies.

More troubling are situations where doctors in urban medical centres are unable to conduct examinations in line with the ministry's guidelines and form due to a lack of personnel and resources. For instance, a newspaper article published in a leading national daily in April 2013 and a suo moto rule issued by the High Court Division, Supreme Court of Bangladesh, consequent to the article highlighted the fact that all medical examinations at the Dhaka Medical College Hospital were being conducted by male doctors with the assistance of male medical support staff in clear contravention of the guidelines ('HC Summons DMCH Director, Forensic Head' 2013). It was later reported that this is true of other national leading medical institutions as well ('Comprehensive Strategy Needed' 24 April 2013). If this is indeed true of the major establishments located in the capital of the nation, the situation in other relatively remote and backward regions of the county can well be imagined.

For women survivors of sexual violence outside district towns, access to even basic medico-legal services is negligible. Despite government efforts to scale up service delivery, such medical examinations are still only conducted at the district level, which are often at extensive distances from where the incident occurs or where survivors reside. This is partially due to a lack of adequate resources or facilities or a lack of awareness at the local level about the guidelines requiring all government medical colleges, district hospitals as well as police station-based health complexes to carry out the tests. Further, tests are conducted during office hours. There is no possibility of being able to seek and receive medico-legal services past 5 PM (Bairagi et al. 2006; also see BLAST 2013b).

The role of medical officers does not end with completing the examination of a rape survivor. They are subsequently required to appear in courts to present expert testimony on whether forcible sexual intercourse took place. Often, medical officers report not having received any court summons. They are in general reluctant to conduct tests as they do not want to get involved in protracted court proceedings (Bairagi et al. 2006; also see Naomi 2009). Even in cases where women are able to access medico-legal services and get medically examined, it is not necessary that the report issued will be authentic. For example, a case study (Hossain 2012) by the BMP, the largest national women's human rights organization in Bangladesh, demonstrating the effect of a medical re-examination on a rape prosecution revealed that a medical officer had falsified the findings due to pressure from the accused. Such instances occurring in other cases, especially where the accused has social or political clout, are certainly not inconceivable.

Problems are compounded due to a lack of knowledge and awareness among women and girls with respect to the procedure to follow in case an incident of rape occurs. Survivors contaminate or wash away the evidence by bathing or urinating, or due to long delays in being able to approach the police or doctors for assistance. Further delays in medical examination often occur due to attempts at settlement of rape cases through mediation within the community or due to the fact that medical facilities are at extensive distances (ibid.)

MEDICO-LEGAL EVIDENCE AND WOMEN'S ACCESS TO JUSTICE

Globally, definitions of rape have evolved from requiring proof of force or violence to requiring proof of consent. Unfortunately, these trends do not appear to be reflected in the current law or its interpretation in Bangladesh. To illustrate, in *Shahjahan v. State* the Hon'ble High Court described 'rape' as follows: 'The word "rape" literally means *forcible seizure* and *that element is [a] characteristic feature of the offence*.'[7]

Medico-legal evidence-collection practices and procedures in rape cases in Bangladesh are plagued with inefficiencies, both procedural and institutional. This asks the question why the criminal justice system puts such overwhelming emphasis on medico-legal evidence in rape cases at all. Discussions with judges, lawyers and women's rights activists reveal that the criminal justice system views this as the only 'scientific evidence' of rape. It is believed to unequivocally speak to the veracity of the accusation. Thus, it is not viewed as evidence that is corroborative to the testimony of the victim; rather, it is a verification of her accusation.

Starting from this standpoint, it does not come as a surprise that the High Court Division, Supreme Court of Bangladesh, quoted with approval a seventeenth-century English case stating, 'Rape is an accusation easily to be made and hard to be proved and harder to be defended by the party concerned.'[8] It then went on to acquit the appellant, noting that the alleged victim delayed in filing a First Information Report (FIR), was not medically examined and did not have her clothes chemically analysed. There were also no bruises or marks of violence on her body. Ruling that in the absence of enmity between the parties, the court must insist upon proof of the charge, the appellant was acquitted.[9]

This is symptomatic of the deeply entrenched patriarchal attitudes and rape myths that prevail in Bangladeshi society and that have seeped into institutional understandings of the offence of rape. It is critical to highlight that such barriers in medico-legal evidence collection emanate from these social and legal constructions of the definition of rape.

An analysis of the decisions of the higher judiciary in Bangladesh on the relevance of medical evidence in rape prosecutions is illustrative of the traditional understanding of the offence, whereby signs of force and injury are deemed necessary to the occurrence of rape. Also pervasive in the judgements are the entrenched notions of shame, morality and honour. These play out in obvious ways such as testimonies of 'older, divorced women' requiring corroboration by medico-legal evidence and testimonies of 'helpless women' being beyond reproach.

In *Biplob v. State*, the conviction of the accused, Biplob, was overturned in appeal.[10] The victim had been married and divorced prior to the incident. The court held that an accused may be convicted on the basis of uncorroborated testimony only when it finds that that the testimony is unimpeachable and inspires confidence. Where the alleged victim is a grown-up or married woman, it is safe to insist on corroboration. The delay in filing the FIR as well as no signs of rape being found upon medical examination cast doubt on the victim's testimony.

Conversely, in *Monirul Islam (Md) v. State*, the court held that the medical examination, which was made several days after the incident, was of no value since an adult married woman is unlikely to bear any trace of rape after such a long period.[11] The high court nonetheless affirmed the conviction on the grounds that the court can base a conviction for rape on the testimony of a sole witness, given that the witness is credible. In this case, the victim, who was a helpless village woman, did not have any reason to make false allegations and suffer the ignominy of rape. The victim also knew the accused and used to call him '*kaka*'. This gave further credibility to her testimony.

Equally insidious and common in some decisions are insinuations about a woman's age, class and character. These factors determine the worth of a victim's accusation and whether it needs corroboration with medico-legal evidence. Even though it is clear from a cursory reading of the judgements that the findings of a medico-legal examination are critical to the finding of rape, it is also apparent that the interpretation of such evidence is based on seemingly extraneous factors such as the victim's family background and the victim's reputation. Accordingly, in one case, the court took note of the fact that an alleged victim had intercourse with the appellant some fifteen or sixteen times, and did not disclose this to her parents until she was three months' pregnant. It quashed the conviction of the appellant as the victim was not 'virtuous', and concluded based on the circumstances that both parties had consented to intercourse.[12]

In *Misti v. State*, the appellants, prior to kidnapping and raping the accused, had called for a *shalish* (local mediation) meeting to deal with the victim's 'unsocial' behaviour.[13] The high court found the accused guilty and noted that an offence can be proved by the evidence of a solitary testimony with no corroborating evidence if that testimony is beyond reproach. In cases where the victim is from the lower strata of society or of ill repute, the testimony will not inspire confidence as the family's honour is not at stake. The courts must seek corroborating evidence in such cases. In this particular case, as the victim's family came from a respectable educated family, corroborating evidence was unnecessary.

However, in *Hossain Shially (Fakir) v. State*, the high court held that corroboration of evidence of the prosecutrix is necessary in cases where the victim has attained majority.[14] The sole testimony of a prosecutrix who has attained majority was not considered sufficient evidence to base a conviction for rape. In addition, the medical examination was conducted more than thirty days after the alleged incident and the medical officer did not notice any marks that suggested rape on the victim's body. Thus, the high court quashed the conviction. The court in this case also made reference to the fact that the FIR was filed more than twenty-five days after the alleged incident as there had been an attempt to settle the matter by *shalish*. However, it overlooked the fact that this is a legitimate cause for delay in the context of Bangladesh where rape cases continue to be 'settled' within the community despite clear legal strictures prohibiting this practice. Further, as noted earlier, a necessary consequence of these cases in which a *shalish* is held is that there is loss of medico-legal evidence due to the delay. This leads to an inference of 'no rape' by courts.

Additionally, there is significant variance in the stance of the higher judiciary vis-à-vis the corroborative value of medico-legal evidence. On the one hand, the High Court Division has quashed the conviction of an accused where there was no sign of rape and the victim was habituated to sex as per the medical certificate. These facts were deemed to raise doubts as to the victim's testimony.[15]

On the other hand, the finding of rape in a medico-legal examination has also been held to require corroboration. In *Safazuddin v. State*, the high court set aside the conviction of the appellants Safazuddin and Mohsin for rape and abetting the commission of rape respectively.[16] The ruling was based on the facts that the FIR was filed eleven days after the alleged incident. Moreover, the MLR report was filed thirty-four days after the examination and noted that the victim had been subjected to forceful sexual intercourse. However, *the delay in filing the report places doubt on the veracity of its findings.*

The court has also noted that the absence of injury on the private parts of the victim cannot lead to the conclusion that rape was not committed.[17] This does not, however, appear to be the prevailing viewpoint. Concerns remain even among lawyers working in criminal law that the 'two-finger test' can lead to doctors' reports being conflicting, which, because they automatically go in favour of the accused, further jeopardize the chances of conviction. In fact, there has been at least one instance where a lawyer expressly advised Naripokkho that when some time has elapsed since the alleged offence of rape, a case of 'outraging modesty' may be filed in order to 'successfully achieve justice'. Thus, in terms of outcomes in rape cases, there is no 'justice' without medico-legal evidence.

This is also in conformity with the opinion of other lawyers who have stated that in many cases a 'doctor's evidence is decisive', and that 'if a doctor opines that a victim is sexually habituated [*sic*], then there is automatic acquittal'.[18]

WINDS OF CHANGE: CAMPAIGN FOR LAW AND POLICY REFORM

For over a decade now, women's rights organizations in Bangladesh have been advocating for law and policy reform to make medico-legal evidence-collection practices and policies victim and gender sensitive. What essentially began as an advocacy exercise for the adoption of a minimum set of standards for medico-legal evidence collection has now snowballed into a full-fledged campaign for law and policy reform involving several civil society organizations.

Naripokkho first approached the issue as part of a bigger initiative of facilitating access to justice for women survivors of violence in the late 1990s. In monitoring individual cases of violence against women, it was realized that medico-legal evidence plays a crucial role in the criminal justice system. Accordingly, Naripokkho approached the issue from the supply side, undertaking activities to capacitate medical professional and law enforcement agencies to provide support to women survivors of violence in a gender-, rights- and victim-sensitive manner. As the next step to this capacity building, Naripokkho started an institution-building campaign, demanding that the state formulate uniform guidelines laying out the medico-legal evidence-collection procedure. As a result, the Ministry of Health and Family Welfare formulated such guidelines for the first time in 2002. Naripokkho continued its work with government institutions, targeting the dissemination of these guidelines to all government hospitals and police stations. This was finally achieved in 2008.

In 2010, a consortium of six organizations, comprising BLAST, the International Centre for Diarrhoeal Disease Research, Bangladesh, Marie Stopes Bangladesh, Nari Maitree, Population Council and We Can Alliance began implementation of the SAFE project.[19] A key feature of the project is its effort to address barriers to women's access to justice, including but not limited to cases of violence against women. As part of this project, BLAST undertook to look at the issue of medico-legal evidence collection from the survivors' perspective, choosing mainly to highlight the negative impact that malpractices in medico-legal evidence collection, such as the 'two finger test', have on women's access to justice.

A national conference on 'Medical Evidence in Rape: Policies, Practices and Procedures' was organized in Dhaka in February 2013 by BLAST and the SAFE project. The conference resulted in the adoption of a statement demanding comprehensive reforms to the law, policies and institutions governing the collection of medico-legal evidence in Bangladesh. Undoubtedly, the highlight of the conference and the consequent statement is that it brought together over a 100 experts from various fields, including forensic science, medicine, law, law enforcement, health and human rights, who unequivocally demanded the abolition of the 'two-finger test'.[20] This statement was sent to the Bangladesh National Human Rights Commission in the form of a memorandum on behalf of eight human rights and women's rights organizations in March 2013.

Thereafter, a memorandum was sent to the secretary, Ministry of Health and Family Welfare, the government agency with direct jurisdiction over the subject of medico-legal evidence collection. This, in turn, outlined the laws and procedures relating to medical evidence collection in rape cases, and set out some urgent concerns in this regard, concerning:

1. limited compliance with the Ministry of Health's 2002 circular, which provided that women and girl complainants in rape cases, among others, are entitled to immediate physical examination, and to receiving copies of any medico-legal examination;
2. provisions in the MLR report, which call for unnecessary and immaterial information to be recorded; and
3. the so-called 'two finger test', which results in complainants facing cruel and degrading treatment.

After these advocacy measures failed to produce the desired changes from policymakers, the judiciary was approached. On 8 October 2013, a writ petition was filed in the public interest by six human rights and women's rights organizations, namely, BLAST, ASK, BMP, BRAC, Manusher Jonno Foundation and Naripokkho, and two individuals, Dr Ruchira Tabassum Naved and Dr Mobarak Hossain, before the High Court Division, Supreme Court of Bangladesh. The petitioners prayed that the so-called 'two-finger test' should be declared to be without lawful authority and of no legal effect, and that a failure to prohibit the test was resulting in discriminatory and arbitrary treatment against women and girls, and that it should be declared to be a violation of fundamental rights as guaranteed by Articles 27, 28, 31 32 and 35(5) of the Constitution.

After moving the petition, on 10 October 2013, a division bench of the High Court Division, Supreme Court of Bangladesh, comprising Justice Mirza Hussain Haider and Justice Khurshid Alam Sarkar, issued a Rule Nisi upon the respondents, namely, secretary, Ministry of Health and Family Welfare; secretary, Ministry of Home Affairs; director general, Directorate of Health Services; and the inspector general of police, returnable within four weeks. The court further directed the secretary of the Ministry of Health and Family Welfare

> to set up a Committee including experts on forensics, criminal justice, public health and experience in providing support to women and girls survivors of violence, to develop a comprehensive guideline for police, physicians and judges or the Nari o Shishu Nirjaton Domon Tribunals on examination and treatment of women and girls subjected to rape and sexual violence, and to submit a detailed report thereof to this court *within three months from the date of receipt of this order*, for dealing with same in accordance with the law.[21] (emphasis added)

The Ministry of Health and Family Welfare finally constituted a committee under the chairmanship of the additional secretary, public health, Ministry of Health and Family Welfare, on 1 January 2014. The committee held its first meeting on 12 January 2014 and later constituted a subcommittee that is drafting the guidelines (Uzzal 2014).

CONCLUSION

Institutional responses to rape, including with respect to medico-legal evidence collection, mirror the prevalent notions in society about the causes and consequences of rape, including a 'general suspicion of women's claims of rape and an inclination to down play the perpetrators' responsibility and criminality while shifting blame towards the victim based on her behaviour and personal characteristics' (Du Mont and White 2007). Widespread gender discrimination and biases within the law and institutions liable to enforce the law in Bangladesh mean that the right of access to justice for rape survivors remains unrealized. Policies and institutions that require corroboration of a survivor's testimony by less-than-credible medical evidence and view practices such as the 'two-finger test' as necessary tribulations towards seeking a conviction in effect reinforce a climate of impunity and perpetuate gender discrimination.

In order to make access to justice a reality for women in Bangladesh, it is essential to keep up the demand for law and policy reform towards according a rape survivor's testimony the weight it deserves in a court of law. However, given the current importance attached to medical evidence in rape prosecutions and the dilatory pace of law reform, it is of utmost urgency that initiatives be undertaken to ensure that medical evidence is recorded in a way that is accurate, efficient, gender sensitive, victim friendly and respectful of human rights.

NOTES

1. Nari o Shishu Nirjatan Domon Ain 2000 (as amended in 2003), Section 9(1) states: 'If a male person without marital relationship has sexual intercourse with a woman above sixteen years of age *without her consent or with consent obtained* by putting her *in fear* or *deceitful means or with a woman of age below sixteen years with or without her consent* he shall be presumed to have raped such woman.'

   The Bangladesh Penal Code, Section 375, Rape: 'A man is said to commit "rape" who except in the case hereinafter excepted, has sexual intercourse with a woman under circumstances falling under any of the five following descriptions:

   'Firstly, Against her will.

   'Secondly, Without her consent.

   'Thirdly, With her consent, when her consent has been obtained by putting her in fear of death, or of hurt.

   'Fourthly, With her consent, when the man knows that he is not her husband, and that her consent is given because she believes that he is another man to whom she is or believes herself to be lawfully married.

   'Fifthly, With or without her consent, when she is under fourteen years of age.

   'Explanation: Penetration is sufficient to constitute the sexual intercourse necessary to the offence of rape.

   'Exception: Sexual intercourse by a man with his own wife, the wife not being under thirteen years of age, is not rape.'

2. Unofficial English translation of the guidelines is available at http://www.blast.org.bd/content/report/moh-circular2002-translation-3-2-13.pdf (accessed 22 June 2015).
3. Information received from Naripokkho.
4. BLAST interview with Dr Sharmili Paul, lecturer, Dhaka Medical College Hospital, 7 July 2014.
5. BLAST interview with Kamrun Nahar, member, Naripokkho, 21 July 2014.
6. BLAST interview with Adv. Habibunessa, member, Naripokkho, 12 July 2014.
7. *Shahjahan v. State*, 10 BLC (2005) 195.
8. *Sobuj v. State*, 11 MLR (HC) 2006 (284).
9. Ibid.
10. *Biplob v. State*, BLC (2001) 632.
11. *Monirul Islam (Md) v. State*, 8 MLR (HC) 2003 (27).
12. *Sohel Rana (Md) v. State*, 57 DLR (2005) 591.
13. *Misti v. State*, 6 MLR (HC) 2001.
14. *Hossain Shially (Fakir) v. State*, 8 MLR (HC) 2003 (355).
15. *Firoz Chokder v. State*, 11 MLR (HC) 2006.
16. *Safazuddin v. State*, 27 BLD (HCD) 2007 (321).
17. *Al Amin & Ors v. State*, 51 DLR (1999) 154.
18. BLAST interview with Md Khurshid Alam Khan, Dhaka, 4 July 2012.
19. The SAFE project is testing an intervention for promoting sexual and reproductive health and rights (SRHR), and reducing violence against women and girls in the Dhaka slums. It seeks in particular to foreground women's and girls' rights to choice and consent with regard to marriage, sex and childbearing. Details available at http://www.safeprojectbd.org/what-we-do/advocacy/ (accessed 23 June 2015).
20. Refer to the webpage 'News on Medical Evidence Laws and Justice for Rape Victims', http://www.blast.org.bd/news/news-reports/472-blastnews (accessed 23 June 2015). Also see BLAST (2013a).
21. See the webpage 'Two Finger Test on Rape Survivors Challenged', http://www.blast.org.bd/component/content/article/28-nr/484-news (accessed 23 June 2015).

REFERENCES

'Comprehensive Strategy Needed'. 2013. *New Age*, 24 April, Dhaka. http://newagebd.com/detail.php?date=2013-04-24&nid=47025 (accessed 19 December 2014)..

'HC Summons DMCH Director, Forensic Head'. 2013. *Daily Star*, 17 April, Dhaka. http://archive.thedailystar.net/beta2/news/hc-summons-dmch-director-forensic-head (accessed 19 December 2014).

Afsana, K., S.F. Rashid and W. Thurston. 2006. 'Challenges and Gaps in Addressing Domestic Violence in Health Policy of Bangladesh'. Paper presented at the World Conference on Prevention of Family Violence, 23–26 October, Banff, Canada.

Ahmed, Maimuna. 2011. 'The Two-Finger Test: About Character or Consent?', *Forum Magazine*, 5(11). http://archive.thedailystar.net/forum/2011/November/finger.htm (accessed 18 December 2014).

Azim, S. 2000, 'Pilot Survey on Violence against Women in Bangladesh'. Unpublished report, Naripokkho, Dhaka.

Bairagi, G., B.K. Chanda, N. Naher, D.N. Talukdar, K.M. Salim and S.K. Ghosh. 2006. 'One Stop Crisis Centre: A Model of Hospital-Based Service for Domestic Violence, Burn & Sexual Assault Survivors in Bangladesh', *ORION Medical Journal*, 25 (September): 407–10.

Bangladesh Legal Aid and Services Trust. 2013a. '100 Experts Demand Change in Medical Evidence Laws and Justice for Rape Victims', press release, 2 February 2013. http://www.blast.org.bd/content/pressrelease/press-release-nc-2-2-2013.pdf (accessed 18 December 2014).

———. 2013b. 'Conference Report: National Conference on Collection of Medical Evidence in Rape Cases: Practices, Procedures and Policies'. 2 February 2013, Dhaka.

Barek, Abdul. 2010. 'A Study on Pattern of Alleged Rape Cases at SBMC, Barisal', *Anwer Khan Modern Medical College Journal*, 1(1): 15–18.

Basu, Asmita (ed.). 2013. *Medical Evidence in Rape Cases: Law and Practice in Bangladesh*. Dhaka: Bangladesh Legal Aid and Services Trust.

Du Mont, Janice and Deborah White. 2007. *The Uses and Impacts of Medico-Legal Evidence in Sexual Assault Cases: A Global Review.*

Geneva: World Health Organization. http://www.svri.org/medico.pdf (accessed 19 December 2014).

Haque, Y.A. 2001. 'The Woman Friendly Hospital Initiative in Bangladesh: A Strategy for Addressing Violence against Women', *Development*, 44(3): 79–81.

Haque, Y.A. and J.M. Clarke. 2002. 'The Woman Friendly Hospital Initiative in Bangladesh: Setting Standards for the Care of Women Subject to Violence', *International Journal of Gynecology & Obstetrics*, 78 (Supplement 1): S45–49.

Hossain, Sara. 2012. *CEDAW Bench Book Bangladesh*, December. Dhaka: Ministry of Law, Justice and Parliamentary Affairs.

Human Rights Watch (HRW). 2010. 'Dignity on Trial: India's Need for Sound Standards for Conducting and Interpreting Forensic Examinations of Rape Survivors'. http://www.hrw.org/sites/default/files/reports/india0910webwcover.pdf (accessed 19 December 2014).

Islam, M.N. and M.N. Islam. 2003. 'Retrospective Study of Alleged Rape Victims Attended at Forensic Medicine Department of Dhaka Medical College, Bangladesh', *Legal Medicine*, 5 (Supplement 1): S351–53.

Islam, Udisa. 2013. '"Two-Finger Test" Deters Rape Victims from Seeking Justice', *Dhaka Tribune*, 1 September. http://www.dhakatribune.com/law-amp-rights/2013/sep/01/%E2%80%98two-finger-test%E2%80%99-deters-rape-victims-seeking-justice (accessed 19 December 2014).

Moni, Jharna. 2010. 'Bangladesh: Why Dhaka's Rape Survivors Give Up on Justice', Women's Feature Service, 8 February. http://periodicals.faqs.org/201002/2035982201.html (accessed 19 December 2014).

Naomi, Sharin Shajahan. 2009. 'The Legal Challenges on the Way to Judicial Remedy in Rape Cases: The Role of Human Rights and Legal Services Programme of BRAC', BRAC Research Report, April. http://research.brac.net/reports/the%20legal%20challenges_new.pdf (accessed 19 December 2014).

Naripokkho and Bangladesh Mahila Parishad. 2005. 'Baseline Report Violence Against Women. International Women's Rights Action Watch Asia Pacific Research Report'. http://www.iwraw-ap.org/aboutus/pdf/FPvaw.pdf (accessed 19 December 2014).

Rougerie, S.M. 2013. 'BLAST Exploratory Study', in Asmita Basu (ed.), *Medical Evidence in Rape Cases: Law and Practice in Bangladesh*. Dhaka: BLAST.

UN Division on the Advancement of Women. 2010. *Handbook for Legislation on Violence against Women*, July. http://www.un.org/womenwatch/daw/vaw/handbook/Handbook%20for%20legislation%20on%20violence%20against%20women.pdf (accessed 19 December 2014).

Fulu, Emma, Xian Warner, Stephanie Miedema, Rachel Jewkes, Tim Roselli and James Lang. 2013. *Why Do Some Men Use Violence against Women and How Can We Prevent it? Quantitative Findings from the UN Multi-country Study on Men and Violence in Asia and the Pacific*, 10 September, UNDP, UNFPA, UN Women and UNV. http://unwomen-asiapacific.org/docs/WhyDoSomeMenUseViolenceAgainstWomen_P4P_Report.pdf (accessed 19 December 2014).

Uzzal, Moniruzzaman. 2014. 'Deadline Over for Readying Guideline on Treating Rape Victims', *Tribune*, 14 February, Dhaka. http://www.dhakatribune.com/law-amp-rights/2014/feb/14/deadline-over-readying-guideline-treating-rape-victims#sthash.Tgrcn2oT.dpuf (accessed 19 December 2014).

6

Bringing Women's Lives to Order

Challenging Impunity in the Community

HAMEEDA HOSSAIN*

> If women's rights are a problem for some modern Muslim men, it is neither because of the Koran nor the Prophet [Muhammad], nor the Islamic tradition, but simply because those rights conflict with the interests of a male elite.
>
> (Mernissi 1991)

INTRODUCTION

Political changes do not spark social transformation. It takes a concerted struggle to challenge customary social norms and dismantle traditional hierarchies. Following the war of independence, Bangladesh adopted a liberal constitution in 1972 that set goals of a secular and democratic state. But the claims for equality and justice have remained subordinate to the interests of class, kinship and gender, and the struggle to achieve these goals has been ongoing.

In rural areas in particular, religious leaders and community elders have continued to set markers to regulate social relations and

* With acknowledgement to Kazi Tamanna Ferdush for field research.

control sexual behaviour, particularly of subaltern groups. Isolated by class and gender, poor women who deviate from community norms have been forced to submit to brutal physical penalties or to social ostracism imposed by fatwas or by *shalish* decisions.[1] In some cases of a couple revoking a divorce and wanting to remarry, sexual violence was inflicted on the woman by forcing her into conjugal relations with another man (see discussion on *hilla* later in this paper). Such acts of sexual violence were justified by reference to religious traditions.

Although fatwas are not legal in Bangladesh, they are observed in rural society as guides to religious rituals. Professor A.M. Serajuddin defines a fatwa as:

> Specialist opinions of competent jurisconsults on any legal or religious matter where the rules of law are not clear, or because the issue or situation is novel, the existing rules do not provide an answer. The person who gives a *fatwa* is a *Mufti* who must be of an unimpeachable character, have deep insight into Islamic theology, be well versed in the original sources of law, have mastery over the languages of the original works and competence to form an informed independent judgment. (2011: 210)

This chapter is about women's resistance to the violence that was sought to be sanctified by fatwas and *shalish* decisions to regulate and constrain their autonomy, sexuality and choice in accordance with regressive interpretations of Sharia tenets or customary practices. It examines how the social and legal impunity of village patriarchs (religious clerics, community elders or *shalishkar*s) owe to their religious or political status in the village, their class and kinship networks within the community. After providing an overview of the prevalence of fatwas, I will illustrate through case studies the paths of women's resistance.

When women activists stepped in to protect individual victims from fatwa-instigated violence, they sought intervention from the courts on grounds of its criminality as well as a violation of their constitutional and human rights. From a reading of media reports on the incidence of fatwas, case studies and investigative reports by several legal aid organizations and knowledge gained from my participation in women's movements, I will discuss how the strategies adopted by women activists and human rights defenders sought to protect the survivors, criminalize perpetrators, counter religious dogma and contest the impunity of village patriarchs. Women's resistance against fatwa edicts thus evolved into a collective struggle against patriarchal impunity. Even before independence, women had pursued legal reform and sought judicial interventions to contain gender-based violence. In the 1980s, collective campaigns against violence on women at local and national levels by the BMP and seventeen other women's organizations came together under the banner of Oikkyo Boddho Nari Samaj (United Women's Society) and led to the enactment of deterrent and punitive legislation by the state. The Dowry Prohibition Act 1980 and the Nari O Shishu Nirjaton Daman (Suppression of Violence against Women and Children) Act 2000 became their tools of resistance. On international platforms, women's advocacy led to the adoption by Bangladesh of General Recommendation 19 of the UN Convention on the Elimination of All Forms of Discrimination against Women (CEDAW), the Declaration to Eliminate Violence against Women at Vienna (1993) and the Beijing Platform for Action (1995).[2]

Reports of brutal and humiliating penalties on women imposed by fatwas in the 1990s alerted women activists to a socially and politically complex terrain of gendered controls. The challenges that these moral strictures presented to the women's struggle for equality and justice were made more complex by the rural observance of rituals, a traditional subordination of women, and the passivity of the state in intervening in community disputes or enforcing the law.

SOURCES OF IMPUNITY

Women's lives in Bangladesh are subject to multiple legal frameworks, which have not been liberating, notwithstanding the promise of reforms. Article 27 of the Constitution declared equality for all citizens under the law, but equality for women was limited by Article 28 to matters of the state and the public sphere only, while inequality in personal rights was derived from provisions in religious precepts.

The principle of secularism could not be translated into state policies because of social conservatism, and no legal reforms were introduced for gender equality in the first few years. On the other hand, after 1975, the state moved further away from its founding principles. Thus, in 1977, the Constitution was amended, under military rule, by replacing secularism with 'faith in Allah'.[3] In 1987, the next military ruler, General Muhammad Ershad, went even further to introduce 'Islam as a state religion' under the Eighth Amendment. Later, in 2010, an elected government introduced an ambiguity in the Fifteenth Amendment by restoring secularism in the Preamble but retaining Islam as a state religion in Article 2A. This has been used by religious groups/leaders to claim a right to freedom of religion and expression.

The silence of the state in mediating relations of power has allowed traditional practices and structures to persist. Several studies have reported that local government bodies, or informal traditional mediations, have been a more accessible option for village women than the formal courts because the negotiations are held promptly, in nearby locations, and do not call for lawyers' assistance. But in the absence of a structural transformation, the traditional justice system has remained gender discriminatory. Official *shalish* or mediation committees constituted by the union *parishad* chairman and members have often transgressed the laws when settling land and family disputes and even used coercion or imposed excessive fines.[4] Informal mediation committees constituted by influential village elders or professional *shalishkar*s remain patriarchal in bearing and ideology, and have been reported to adopt unjust customary practices in arbitrating women's options, contrary to the law.

Women's campaign for enactment of uniform family laws or reform of personal laws has found little support from political leaders or Members of Parliament, thus allowing the opinions of leaders of different religious communities to prevail. Article 41 of the Constitution, which protected freedom of religion and religious institutions, has allowed religious leaders to dominate their communities and impose religious laws in matters of marriage, divorce, inheritance and guardianship.

The Muslim Family Laws Ordinance (MFLO) 1961 had introduced a few changes in personal laws for Muslims to make polygamy conditional on a wife's consent and to facilitate a divorce by a woman.[5] This provided for a clause to be inserted in the *nikahnama* (marriage contract) whereby a Muslim woman could be delegated the right of divorce by her husband. Aside from these changes, Muslim women's rights in marriage, divorce, inheritance or guardianship have remained inferior to those of men. Hindu law is even more discriminatory, as women have no right to divorce or inheritance, and most male leaders have resisted reforms. Christian women may be only slightly better off under the laws prescribed by the Church (Huda 2011; Pereira 2011; Tamanna, Hossain and Haq 2011).

Rural communities have remained in a time warp of feudal and patriarchal values that allowed religious clerics or village leaders to regulate the lives of villagers.[6] Even though fatwas were not, and are not, legally enforceable in Bangladesh, there was, and continues to be, a common practice amongst Muslim villagers to seek guidance from clerics on religious rituals and customs, or to abide by decisions of village mediators. *Shalish* committees constituted by members elected to the union *parishad*, or unofficially by *shalishkar*s, tended to impose decisions on poor women and their families rather than to mediate disputes. The community's compliance came at a cost to women—of physical oppression and social stigma or exclusion. Thus, poor women and their families did not, or were unable, to defy controls imposed by powerful male village leaders.

In appointing themselves as moral guardians of the community, religious clerics and village leaders drew upon scriptures or traditional practices to justify their control over women's lives, sexual choice and livelihoods. That these edicts were not isolated acts became evident with the frequency of fatwas reported in the media after 1995 (Table 6.1). The fatwas coincided with more aggressive attacks by the religious right on institutions that promoted women's economic and social activities in defiance of state policies. The clergy in some districts incited local mobs to attack NGO-run educational or health institutions, obstruct women's participation in income generation schemes, or stop them from voting (Falguni 2001).[7] At the national level, fundamentalist political parties and organizers publicly accused some well-known writers of apostasy. They also demanded the enactment of a blasphemy law to replace existing colonial-era criminal laws on grounds of 'hurting religious sentiment' and the introduction of Sharia laws.[8]

TABLE 6.1: Incidents of Fatwa-/*Shalish*-Instigated Violence on Women (1995–2014)

	1995–2000	*2001–5*	*2006–10*	*2011–14*
No. of fatwas and *shalish* decisions	158	193	151	160
Cases filed	47	38	35	51
Hilla	24	37	34	25
Lashes/caning	81	53	49	13
Social boycott/ ostracization	28	59	46	42
Physical/mental torture	16	42	22	74
Suicide	11	9	4	27
Death	5	–	3	2

Not only were women's livelihoods at risk, but the threat of far-reaching structural regression in the state and society prompted collective resistance by women's rights and human rights defenders. There may have been little protest by victims and survivors in the community, but women activists, supported by NGOs and some voluntary community groups, adopted a multilayered strategy: to protect victims by stalling implementation of fatwas and questioning their legality; to raise citizens' awareness through public campaigns against gender injustice; and to hold local government bodies responsible for violations.

In negotiating between these multiple systems unjust to women, progressive women and human rights defenders have taken up a social challenge to democratize the *shalish.* At the same time, they have pursued law and policy reform through the formal justice system.

They sought enforcement of constitutional guarantees of equality and non-discrimination (Articles 27 and 28), their rights to freedom of life, livelihood and choice (Articles 31, 32 and 35).[9] They expected protection under existing personal laws (MFLO 1961) and the BPC 1860. They also demanded that state institutions uphold international guarantees of the right to life and liberty, and freedom from torture (International Covenant of Civil and Political Rights and Convention on Torture, ratified by Bangladesh).

Their struggles led in 2011 to the Appellate Division of the Supreme Court declaring illegal penalties pronounced by fatwas or *shalish.*[10] The Supreme Court also gave directions that fatwas or religious edicts could only be pronounced by 'persons properly educated in religious matters', and could not violate the rights, reputation or dignity of any person protected under the law. This landmark decision offered a legal and constitutional framework that has detracted from the social impunity of religious clerics and community elders to impose their notions of Sharia law.[11]

As media alerts spread across the country and beyond, powerless women persecuted in the villages found some protection from intervention by activists. When these incidents became public knowledge, the women's struggles were supported not only by national organizations and the media, but also by regional and international networks as a measure of their resistance to violence against women. Women Living under Muslim Law, a network of women's organizations in Europe and Asia, was particularly supportive in disseminating information and raising alerts from Bangladesh.

This did not imply, as has been assumed by some scholars (Riaz 2005), that the resistance in Bangladesh was an extension of a global 'clash of civilizations' or a strike for modernity. Perhaps similar incidents elsewhere may have raised parallel but separate responses. As Siddiqi argues, 'Global readings tend to frame local conflicts as though this were about Islam versus modernity. The local, national and international are complexly intertwined.'[12]

In Bangladesh women's support for fatwa victims was first directed to protect individuals from violence; their legal action was a response to the violation of their rights. Beyond this, the women's resistance challenged the political agenda propagated by religious parties for Sharia law and an Islamic state because they saw it as undermining citizens' rights and changing the structure of the state. They had contested the use (or distorted use) of religion even earlier, before independence, when their campaigns for legal reform led to the MFLO in 1961, or when they challenged the provision of polyandry and resisted an attempt by the Jamaat-e-Islami to reject a woman's candidacy for presidential elections in 1965. In their engagement with the national movements for independence or against military rule, progressive women's movements had pressed for secular state laws. In 1987, Naripokkho, a feminist group, filed a petition in the high court to challenge the validity of the Eighth Amendment to the Constitution that declared Islam as the state religion. While there was no controversy in accepting the right of an individual to her personal beliefs, the progressive women's movements had campaigned for a uniform set of laws that would provide an alternative platform for equal rights for women in all communities.[13]

THE NARRATIVE BEGINS WITH NURJEHAN

The narrative of women's resistance to fatwas began in 1993, when a young woman, Nurjehan, was reported to have committed suicide in Chattokchora, a remote village in Moulvi Bazar, in the north-east of Bangladesh, after Maulana Mannan, a local cleric, supported by nine men, pronounced a fatwa indicting her for marrying for the second time without a 'proper' divorce. Nurjehan and her husband were made to stand waist deep in a pit, and pelted 101 times with small stones. Her parents were also punished for abetting in the marriage. The humiliation drove Nurjehan to suicide. Punishment was meted out even though no laws were transgressed and the arbiters had no judicial authority. The state played no role in registering her marriage or divorce.

The news caught the attention of the national press and through it of women's organizations in different parts of the country. A local member of the BMP, the oldest and largest women's organization in Bangladesh, assisted Nurjehan's father to file a case in the local court.[14] Several women's groups monitored the court proceedings to ensure that reports by police and other agencies were filed in record time and held rallies to gain public support. The accused were arrested in April and criminal charges filed. It took three years of court hearings before Maulana Mannan and his nine accomplices were sentenced on charges of abetment of suicide (under Sections 114/306 and 504 of the BPC) to seven years of rigorous imprisonment and another year's imprisonment in lieu of payment of a fine of BDT 2,000.[15]

The judgement did not recognize the legitimacy of 'traditional jurisdiction' or religious prescription; it enforced criminal liabilities under state laws. In the three years that it took to sentence Maulana Mannan, a rash of fatwa episodes revealed how women were penalized by imams, madrasa superintendents, or locally elected or influential persons.

JURY OR PERPETRATORS: CRIMES OF 'TRADITIONAL JUSTICE'

Within a few months of Nurjehan's death, in May 1993, male members of two families held a *shalish* in the village of Madhukhali in Faridpur district, which accused a woman of *zina* (Arabic for adultery). The next morning, she was reported to have been burnt at the stake. The case was dismissed by the Madhukhali District Court, but upon an appeal by the BMP, the high court ordered a fresh investigation. In another incident in Shatkhira, a 16-year-old Muslim woman, a shrimp worker, committed suicide after she was condemned by a local *shalish,* constituted by the superintendent of a madrasa, the chairman and member of the union *parishad,* for her relationship with a Hindu man. The prosecution was not able to bring the perpetrators to justice and the illegitimate exercise of their power remained uncontested in the community (see Figure 6.1).

From the first few cases, it was assumed that these sporadic incidents occurred in remote villages, away from administrative controls. That these were not isolated incidents particular to any one community became evident from the geographical spread of decrees penalizing women for extramarital or premarital relations, refusal of offer of marriage/love by a woman, filing a case against a rapist, family disputes, attending literacy classes, talking with a stranger, inter-communal marriage, choosing a marital partner, oral divorce followed by remarriage and so on (Begum 1997; Helie-Lucas and Kapoor 1996).[16] In each case, the woman was charged with a sexual transgression according to the cleric's interpretation of religious norms/rules. In defiance of Article 7 of the MFLO 1961, the clerics insisted on the practice of an intervening marriage (*hilla* in Arabic) in order to revoke a divorce.

FIGURE 6.1: A Poster Produced by Probortna to Publicize the Punishment of Feroza in Shatkhira in 1996

FATWAS AND THEIR CONSEQUENCE

In a country where violence is widespread, comparative figures for marital violence, rape and even acid burns are, understandably, far higher than violence perpetrated by fatwa edicts.[17] Nevertheless, the latter created alarm as penalties were carried out in public (however small the audience), apparently with the community's acquiescence. The fatwa givers or *shalishkar*s faced little protest from the family or dissent from bystanders. Thus, a poor village woman was shamed into submitting to punishments either out of fear of the village patriarchs, in deference to religious prescriptions or due to her isolation; she found few defenders in her own community (Shehabuddin 2008).

The sentencing of Maulana Mannan by the high court did not put a stop to fatwas, nor did community elders cease censuring women. Over a period of nineteen years from 1995 to 2014 (see Table 6.1), 662 incidents of penalties prescribed by fatwa or by a *shalish* were reported in the national media. During this period, fifty-one of the women against whom fatwas had been issued were reported to have committed suicide and ten had died as a consequence of the violence. These figures may reflect an increase in reportage rather than in the number of actual incidents, but they indicated that village norms and practices were subject to the impunity of the informal system of retribution and that the formal justice system had less impact.

Figures 6.2 and 6.3 give us a comparative picture of the districts in which penalties were inflicted by fatwa on women in 2002 and ten years later in 2012. The same districts were prone to such incidence over a period of ten years.[18] Four districts in the north and east (Nilphamari, Rangpur, Bogra and Brahmanbaria) appeared to be more prone to fatwas, which could be due to the presence of a powerful religious leader, political strength of religious parties or proliferation of madrasas.

Figure 6.2: Map of Bangladesh Showing Districts where Fatwa- and *Shalish*-Related Violence Occurred (2002)

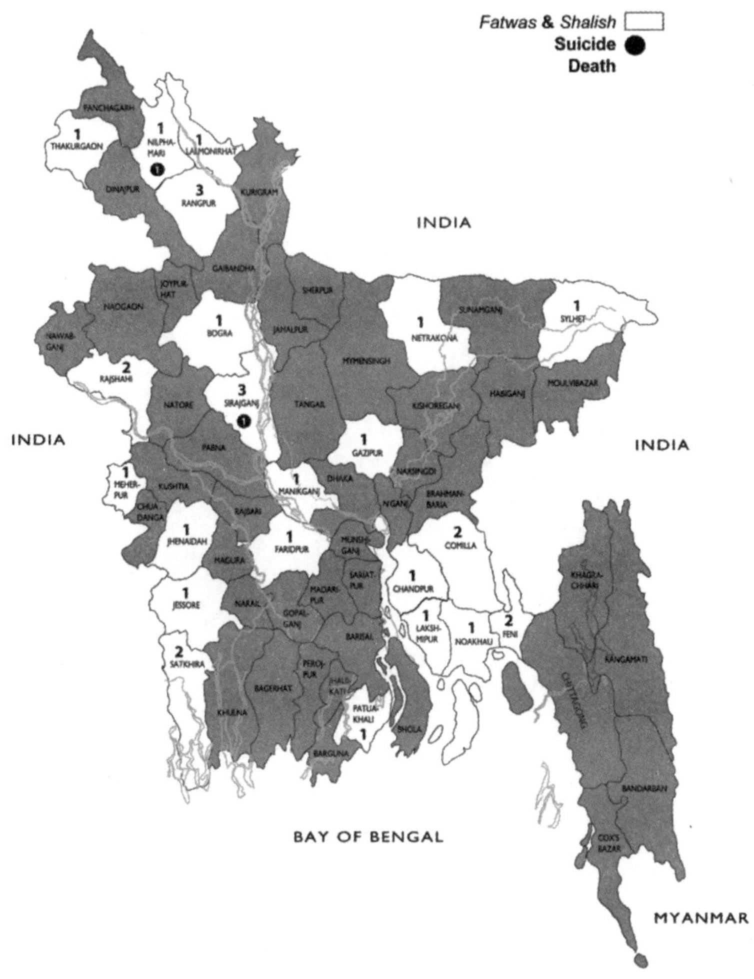

FIGURE 6.3: Map of Bangladesh Showing Districts where Fatwa- and *Shalish*-Related Violence Occurred (2012)

THE WOMEN'S RESPONSE

Women's activism thus faced multiple challenges: to hold the state responsible to establish criminal liability for extrajudicial penalties, to maintain rule of law so that customary practices did not violate the rights and dignity of women, and to meet Bangladesh's constitutional and international commitments; to make the community respect the Constitution, comply with national laws and prevent arbitrary or extrajudicial penalties.

Women activists and human rights organizations strategized through public campaigns, institutional interventions at the grassroots level and legal petitions in formal courts. Although there was no significant decline in fatwas between 1995–2000 and 2011–14, an increase in the number of legal cases (thirty-five in 2005–10 to fifty-one in 2011–14) suggests that women were beginning to seek legal retribution and challenge the authority of the village decision makers. Media reports also showed that physical penalties were less common, being replaced by less severe penalties of social boycott of women victims or their families.

TRANSFORMING THE *SHALISH*

Since the 1980s, several organizations had tried to reform and adapt the traditional *shalish* by making it more gender sensitive. Their strategies were directed to include women representatives in mediation committees and to invoke legal rights as a basis for mediation. The Madaripur Legal Aid Association (MLAA) had pioneered the training of several NGOs and women's organizations in mediation techniques and informed them about their rights under the law as opposed to customary practice.[19] Mediations by the MLAA and Nagorik Uddyog offered space to both sides to settle disputes within the law; they maintained written records of the settlement, which provided an alternative standard to the arbitrary processes of the traditional *shalish*. These procedures became precedents for the UNDP/World Bank reform of alternative dispute resolution strategies (Golub 1997, 2003, 2013), precisely because local institutions were seen as being far more accessible to rural disputants.

National organizations such as the ASK, BLAST, BRAC and Nagorik Uddyog were followed by women's organizations in the districts such as Banchte Shekha (Jessore) or Association for

Community Development (Rajshahi) to disseminate knowledge on legal rights and to advocate for the use of existing laws rather than the Sharia in settling disputes. Women disputants found these committees more responsive. Records of the Nagorik Uddyog's *shalish* proceedings explain how settlements were encouraged on the basis of legal rights rather than by an involuntary submission to arbitrary decisions.[20] Mediations conducted by panel lawyers and district coordinators of national organizations such as BLAST and BRAC were able to promote a fairer settlement for women.

Another approach used by the ASK was to activate local volunteer groups by creating awareness of legal rights so that they could monitor complaints of gender and social injustice and assist in dispute resolution. A panel of local lawyers was also motivated to provide free legal aid in local courts.[21] A publication by two volunteer monitoring groups (Manabadhikar Shangrakhan Parishad and Manabadhikar Nari Samaj 2011: 12) relates the experiences of members in pursuing complaints in police thanas, local *shalish* committees and in lower courts. Case studies maintained by local volunteers illustrate how dialogues and discussions with local elected representatives, administrative agencies and other influential persons on legal rights or legal consequences of their violations helped deter arbitrary and illegal acts. The emphasis on citizens' voluntary actions challenged arbitrary and illegal impositions, and created a space for peaceful settlement of disputes.

In order to persuade village leaders and local officials to observe the laws, legal aid organizations and human rights defenders organized dialogues and discussions to explain the laws governing divorce so that village leaders and local officials could not plead ignorance. The volunteers monitored human rights violations in their localities and were helped by lawyers to file cases. While many religious leaders remained adamant about observing Sharia precepts, others were persuaded to retract their decisions and respect the legal regime.

Dialogues and discussions proved to be useful reformative

tools. In one case, members of the Manabadhikar Shangrakhan Parishad in Gaibandha (a northern district) intervened to prevent the implementation of a decree of *hilla* marriage pronounced by the secretary of the Jamia Masjid (ASK 2014). They contested his insistence on an intervening marriage with threats of legal action in case he issued directions that violated given laws. This was followed by dialogues between lawyers from Dhaka and influential members of the local community. In another village in Mymensingh in 2006, both the MSP and MNP organized discussions between ASK lawyers and local imams and madrasa superintendents and were able to convince the community members that *hilla* marriages had been invalidated by the MFLO 1961, and that there was no reason why the couple could not stay together (ASK 2007).

The convergence of local women's activism with legal aid and human rights organizations strengthened structural support to victims. There were, however, social constraints. BRAC's Shebika (literally, a carer) programme was started with the expectation that knowledge of legal rights would motivate village paralegals to: (*a*) take action when their rights were infringed, and (*b*) set up local forums, especially women's forums, to provide space for poor people to claim their rights and entitlements. However, a study by Alim and Rafi (2011) reported that the paralegals were afraid to speak out as they found themselves an unequal match to challenge the power of the village patriarchs. The study's survey of Shebikas showed that many were inhibited from countering the power of class and kinship without support from a national organization or solidarity of women's groups. It underlined the importance of a wider national movement to challenge the politics of the religious right.

CLAIMS FOR GENDER JUSTICE

The resistance to fatwas inflicted on village women from a largely urban base has been critiqued by some feminist scholars on the grounds that defiance alienated the survivor from her community and isolated her. It had also been suggested that the alternative of observing the prescribed penance (*tawbakora*) would allow the woman to be reintegrated into the community.

The argument against external intervention is that a compromise with community norms would facilitate a survivor's reintegration into her society since she had no viable or sustainable choice outside her own community.[22] The example was given of a young woman who was rescued by a women's legal aid organization prior to execution of a fatwa and had to be kept in safe custody, first in jail and then in a women's shelter, to evade punishment in the village. Her stay in the shelter was indeed confining and isolating, with no prospect of economic or social engagement, which made her opt to accept the penalty so that she could rejoin her family and return to her village. She told her hosts that she would seek pardon (*tawba*) by submitting to the penalty and by subordinating herself to the community's terms. It did not serve to challenge the arbitrary imposition of moral strictures without support in the community.

Such an option, however, strips a woman of dignity and there is no guarantee that life in the village would not be without further risk of violence and social humiliation. An external intervention in such decision-making processes became necessary to overcome the vulnerability of village women.

The following two cases illustrate the outcome of intervention both in the traditional jurisdiction and in a formal court. In a case that occurred in 1994 in a Noakhali village, a local *shalish* committee ordered a woman who had conceived following a consensual sexual relationship with a married man to be flogged and that she marry the man in order to legitimize the child. The man was not penalized. An imam was invited to approve this decision. Following a media report on an impending implementation of this decision, a team of lawyers from ASK persuaded the police to stop the enforcement of the penalty. They then met with the parties concerned (the woman and man, local mediators, elected representatives and administration) and negotiated a settlement whereby the man was asked to transfer some land to the woman by way of compensation instead of marriage. Because the publicity from the *shalish* had made her a target of humiliation, she was moved to a shelter in a neighbouring village, where she was also given an opportunity for self-employment. It is possible that given time she could exercise her right to return to her own village.

This settlement has been critiqued on grounds that the woman was alienated from her own community. Siddiqi (2011b) quotes a criticism of the lawyers' intervention because it alienated the woman but did little to change the internal power dynamics in the village. While this may be true, since a single action cannot transform age-old social customs, the view that 'punishments' (whether they were legitimated through fatwas or not) served the basic function of restoring 'social harmony' does not take into account that such social harmony comes as a result of coercion and subordination of the woman to the power of the village patriarchs, and may in fact reinforce their authority and that of family patriarchs. In this case, marriage with a married man was preferred as a path to respectability, with no consideration of its consequences either for the victim or for the first wife. In cases of premarital pregnancy or rape, marriage is arranged not as an abiding relationship but solely with the purpose of legitimizing the child. The formality over, the woman is often abandoned, with little concern shown for the first wife.

Women activists have challenged the notion of an enforced 'social harmony' because it undermines a woman's integrity and dignity. They have intervened to redress individual wrongs so as to enable a survivor to resist oppression. Obviously, a single such act may not set a standard, but it offers a precedent towards a process of social transformation. Their collective actions in support of the survivor become an important part of their resistance against social domination.

The second case concerns a 12-year-old girl in Brahmanbaria raped by the son of a locally influential person. When her pregnancy became known, the man's family called a *shalish*, at which a maulana from a local madrasa issued a fatwa accusing her of *zina* (adultery or fornication) while ignoring the man's role. The BMP took the young girl into their shelter in Dhaka. The father filed a case against the rapist but no case was filed against the fatwa giver. The court, however, dismissed the rape charge for insufficient evidence. The young girl may not have got justice from the court, but in the meantime, she stayed in a Mahila Parishad home where she was educated by the organization. Later, she married and was able to support her daughter to study music.

THE LEGAL CHALLENGE

The legal challenge has been taken up at different tiers of the judicial system by legal aid and human rights organizations in support of women's campaigns. Challenging these incidents in formal courts has not been easy for survivors because of social inhibitions, inaccessibility of judicial institutions and prosecution lapses. Newspaper reports indicate that not many cases are filed in lower courts. The maximum number of cases filed were twenty out of fifty-nine reported incidents in 2011 (Table 6.1). Since the brief news reports on these cases were not followed up with more details, it is difficult to assess if the process was taken to its conclusion with police investigations or the filing of charges. Nor do the reports tell us of further court decisions.

Claiming Citizens' Rights

Legal complaints did, however, challenge traditional authority by bringing fatwas to the notice of the formal justice system, even in claims of citizenship rights. Between 1994 and 1996, women sought the court's intervention to exercise their constitutional right to vote. The Constitution had provided for women to be elected to reserved seats in Parliament and they had voted along with the men in national elections. Yet, in 1994–96, women in

Mahamaya union (of Chagalnaiya thana, Feni district), in Chandra Dighalaya (Gopalganj district), and in Jhaodi and Kalikapur unions (Madaripur district) were disallowed from voting due to revival of an age-old fatwa. Even though they had exercised their right to vote under a colonial regime since 1925 (Falguni 1996), leaflets were distributed instructing that it was un-Islamic for women to appear in public or to vote in elections. Local women voters protested this discriminatory practice, which was imposed in the name of traditional fatwas. With legal support from a women lawyers' group and as a result of their own initiatives, they were able to overcome the fatwa and vote in local and national polls.

In 1994, in Chagalnayia district, women were able to vote in local polls only after twenty-nine women voters complained in writing to the officers presiding over the election and to the candidates competing for the post of union *parishad* chairperson. The Bangladesh National Women Lawyers' Association (BNWLA) filed a petition in the high court on behalf of one of the women voters. In some unions in Madaripur and Gopalganj, women voters had not been registered to vote for over thirty years. Between 1994 and 1996, local women, supported by feminist and legal aid organizations, became active in filing complaints with the Election Commission and reclaimed their constitutional rights to vote in such cases.

Challenging the Tyranny of *Hilla*

Muslim clerics and orthodox leaders have generally rejected initiatives for reform. Earlier under Pakistani rule, the MFLO 1961, promulgated by General Ayub Khan, had led to massive street protests by religious parties in Pakistan. Women had welcomed the reforms even though the ordinance did not go all the way in granting equal rights in marriage and divorce or inheritance. Article 7 of this law (Serajuddin 2011: 207–12) introduced procedural steps to regulate divorce. The husband was required to notify the union *parishad* chairperson to allow for a reconciliation within a three-month waiting period. This was to deter arbitrary and impulsive decisions by husbands. This reform did away with an archaic Sharia ruling for a woman to undergo an intervening marriage and its consummation (*hilla* marriage), in case the oral divorce was revoked and they wanted to remarry.

Notwithstanding this reform, some Muslim clerics in villages, long after the independence of Bangladesh and till today, continue to ignore the law. Their edicts were not only demeaning to women but disrupted family relations. In the majority of cases when oral divorces were brought to the notice of the fatwa givers, women were made to undergo *hilla* marriage. Disobedience led to social boycott and ostracism.

Following the publication of a news item in the *Daily Jugantar* on 30 July 2007 about three incidents of *hilla* in a single village in Narail district within a period of three months, ASK conducted an investigation in Chachori village in Narial district. ASK's reports describe how local imams exploited popular belief in religious tradition to force couples to undergo intervening marriages.[23] It was only after media publicity that the local administration stepped in and the union *parishad* chairperson was approached to resolve the matter. Investigations into the Narail incidents revealed that the influence of religious leaders in a conservative society was a major reason for the community's compliance with fatwa directions. A woman member of the local union *parishad*, Salma (a pseudonym), as well as some educated youth explained to ASK's investigators that restrictions imposed on cultural and educational activities had created a confining environment.[24] To quote Salma, 'The influence of the *huzur*s [a mark of respect for a religious leader] and their disciples in the locality prevented me from interceding.' A local schoolteacher said, 'The *huzur*s and imams are not learned in the Quran, but take advantage of popular faith to propagate their edicts as representing the message of the Prophet. This is neither Islamic nor legal in Bangladesh.' A police officer interviewed by the ASK's investigator attributed the lack of administrative action to a delay in receiving news and the status of fatwa givers in the community.

Women's public campaigns had served to draw the attention of both the media and the judiciary (see Figure 6.4 for a clip from the documentary *Grahankal*). A report in the *Bangla Bazar Patrika,* a national newspaper, on 2 December 2000, detailing an incident of a *hilla* marriage in Naogaon, led the high court bench to issue a suo motu show cause notice in January 2001 to the district commissioner of Naogaon, the magistrate and the police to explain why they had failed to act in a case where one Haji Azizul Haq had ordered a divorced woman to undergo a *hilla* marriage in violation of Section 7 of the MFLO.[25] All three persons were summoned to appear before the court. The BMP (the largest women's organization) and ASK, acting as intervener, submitted

Figure 6.4: A Clip from the Documentary *Grahankal* (Eclipse) of a Protest Rally in Dhaka

detailed documentation to show that the prevalence of fatwas against women was in violation of law, and undermined women's dignity and security.

The high court's judgement declaring that all fatwas were illegal and unconstitutional, and directing that only courts could interpret laws was met with both a street and legal resistance from the religious right. A strike (*hartal*) on 3 July 2001, engineered by two fundamentalist political parties (Jatiyo Islamic Jote and Ulemai Mushaika), led to violent street demos in Dhaka resulting in some deaths, including that of a policeman (Hossain 2014). Their slogans, 'Fatwas will stay' and 'No room for apostates', were held out as a threat to the judges as well.

The legal response was made by two *mufti*s claiming to be learned in Sharia, who filed a third-party petition for leave to appeal before the Appellate Division of the Supreme Court (Hossain 2014) on grounds that the high court verdict violated their freedom of expression and freedom of religion.[26] The judgement was stayed pending hearing by the Appellate Division. In the meantime, the religious right propagated their message that the court's verdict was un-Islamic through *wazmahfil*s (sermons), at public gatherings and in mosques in different parts of the country. Since it was, and is, a common practice for villagers to seek explanation by way of fatwas on simple religious rituals, a total ban as indicated by the court directly challenged their day-to-day and well-embedded practices. The appellants also argued that the judgement violated their freedom of expression and freedom of religion. It became a challenge for the state to establish the primacy of the Constitution and legal institutions in view of the lived reality.

Legal aid and human rights organizations continued to press for application of constitutional guarantees for freedom of life, liberty and movement. Five organizations filed three writ petitions in 2009 and 2010 with detailed documentary evidence of the incidences of extrajudicial punishments inflicted upon women by fatwa declarations, arguing that they breached constitutional guarantees.[27]

The petition drew upon a brief by the International Commission of Jurists based on international human rights law.[28] The petition was also strengthened with submissions by international religious scholars, who pointed to the diversity of practice in Muslim countries where Sharia law prevailed and others where it was not applicable.

The High Court Division of the Supreme Court held hearings on these petitions for three days in June 2010 and in a judgement on 8 July 2010 declared illegal fatwas that inflicted penalties. It issued directions to the effect that law enforcement agencies, union *parishads* and *pouroshabhas* were responsible for preventing such actions as well as for prosecuting in the event of such an act.[29] It directed the local government ministry to disseminate the judgement to all administrative units and for the education ministry to include educational materials on the Constitution and national laws in schools, colleges, universities and madrasas.

Leading jurists appeared for each side and the Supreme Court heard the opinions of nine amicus curiae who spoke in favour of the primacy of constitutional and international rights over religious law or precepts, and on the criminality of imposing penalties.[30] On the other hand:

> Five *Olayma Kerams* were invited through the Director General of Islamic Foundation for their views on: (i) what is *fatwa*? (ii) status of *fatwa*, (iii) the application of *fatwa* in Bangladesh and its legality and (iv) the position of *fatwa* vis-a-vis our law and accordingly, they appeared and made their submissions.[31]

The latter argued for legitimization of fatwa under the Sharia and invoked Article 2A of the Constitution in claiming their right to exercise freedom of religion and freedom of expression.

The Appellate Division, after hearing the appeal of 2001 over eight days in March, April and May 2010, issued a short order in June 2011 to the effect that:

1. '*Fatwas* on religious matters only may be given by the properly educated persons which may be accepted only voluntarily but any coercion or undue influence in any form is forbidden.'
2. 'But no person can pronounce *fatwa* which violated or affected the rights or reputation or dignity of any person which is covered by the law of the land.'
3. 'No punishment including physical violence and /or mental torture in any form can be imposed or inflicted on anybody in pursuance of *fatwa*.'
4. 'The declaration of the High Court Division that the impugned *fatwa* is void and unauthorized is maintained.'

The full judgement of the Appellate Division was finally issued in December 2014. The four-year delay had been a matter of concern, since it could have been used to justify administrative ambiguity in implementation or to encourage a counter-mobilization by the religious right. The effect of this judgement has been evident in a decline in reported incidents. In 2014, there were thirty-two incidents of fatwa- or *shalish*-instigated violence, but no case of *hilla* was reported. In 2015, only five incidents were reported, which included a fatwa prescribing *hilla*. These few incidents could be attributed to the social impunity of the village leaders or to the distance of the formal regime of rights from the lives of ordinary citizens who remain ignorant of legal developments. The inefficiency of state agencies in implementing court judgements may have been an important factor.

The judgement has been used with some effectiveness by the five petitioners along with other organizations to circulate a leaflet to police stations and local administration categorizing specific penalties for violation of particular sections of the BPC and the liability of those who issue fatwas in breach of this order. They have also pressed for implementation of the court order by state agencies.

The final judgement by the Appellate Division did not ban the practice of fatwas outright but limited them to 'opinions' that were not enforceable. It upheld women's rights under the law of the land by declaring that:

> The issuance of *Fatwa* involving a finding of an 'offence against *shari'at*' and resulting in imposition and execution of extra-judicial penalties by persons is not in accordance with law. The kind of offences for which women have been subjected to lashing and beating or 'talking to a man', 'pre-marital relations', 'having a child outside the wedlock'. None of these is an offence under the prevailing Bangladesh laws. The trial of any offence and the imposition of penalties may only be given by established courts and tribunal. To the extent that traditional dispute resolution or alternative dispute resolution takes place, it is required to be carried out in accordance with law, and thus cannot involve the imposition of penalties that are not recognized by Bangladesh laws.

The judicial outcome owes largely to the women's struggle, which was sparked by an incident in a village and that became a cause for justice across the nation. In response, the formal justice system laid the legal framework for protection of women's rights within the Constitution (Articles 31, 33 and 35). It has also interpreted the state's responsibility in meeting commitments to international guarantees for dignity and security of citizens. Even though there is no explicit rejection of religious rituals and practices, the court's decision denies legal impunity to fatwa givers who transgress the laws of the land by issuing arbitrary, cruel and inhuman punishments.

This decision of the apex court has become a significant tool for women's groups to challenge arbitrary moral strictures controlling their social and sexual choices. It may not have put a complete stop to the social impunity of religious or other community leaders; nevertheless, grassroots women's organizations are now able to seek administrative action to enforce judicial decisions.

Women's activism on the ground has spurred judicial intervention, to facilitate the transformation of the traditional justice system and ensure that the law prevails over customary practices or norms that do not respect individual integrity. This alone may not put an end to the social and political impunity of the village patriarchs, but it has created a space for women to challenge such decrees that limit their autonomy and censure their sexual choice. With solidarity and support from human rights defenders, women have taken a strategic path towards freedom, dignity and justice.

APPENDIX A: DIFFERENT FORMS OF VIOLENCE ON WOMEN, 1995–2014

Year	*Rape/ attempted rape*	*Dowry violence*	*Acid burns*	*Fatwa or* shalish	*Domestic violence*	*Total*	*Fatwas as per cent total reported incidents of violence*
1995–99	3,571	302	511	127	1,095	5,606	2.27
2000–2005	5,420	650	1,211	224	1,933	9,438	2.37
2006–10	2,426	785	473	151	1,574	5,409	2.79
2011–14	2,821	552	223	160	1,354	5,110	3.12

APPENDIX B: BANGLADESH LAWS VIOLATED BY PENALTIES IMPOSED BY FATWA

Penalty imposed by fatwa	*Breach of law*
Lashing or stoning	Sections 323–26, BPC
Hilla	Section 508, BPC
Ostracism/restriction on movement	Sections 341–42 , BPC
Shaving of hair, putting shoe garland around neck	Section 354, BPC

Penalty imposed by fatwa	***Breach of law***
Social ostracism or being forced to seek forgiveness (*tawbakora*)	Section 508, BPC
Oral divorce	Section 7(2), MFLO 1961

NOTES

1. *Shalish* is the traditional system of mediation in villages to resolve marital or land disputes.
2. General Recommendation 19 of CEDAW affirmed that, 'Gender-based violence is a form of discrimination that seriously inhibits women's ability to enjoy rights and freedoms on a basis of equality with men.' The Declaration on the Elimination of Violence against Women, adopted by the UN General Assembly in its Resolution 48/104 of 20 December 1993, recognized an 'urgent need for the universal application to women of the rights and principles with regard to equality, security, liberty, integrity and dignity of all human beings'. A twelve-point Platform for Action was adopted by states at the Beijing UN Conference for Women in 1995. These international treaties, which created state obligations, were cited in the petitions filed in the Supreme Court.
3. General Ziaur Rahman, having taken over power in 1975, amended the Constitution in 1977 by inserting 'Bismillahi Rahman o Rahim' and replacing secularism with 'faith in Allah'. Socialism, another founding principle in the Constitution, was replaced with social justice.
4. The union *parishad* is the lowest tier of local governance comprising locally elected representatives and officials.
5. Earlier, the Shariat Application Act 1937 had been codified under colonial rule.
6. Several legal aid and women's rights organizations have tried to change this unfair system by setting up informal structures of dispute resolution.
7. In Bogra and Brahmanbaria in particular. See Helie-Lucas and Kapoor (1996: 40–47) for a chronological breakdown of incidents.
8. A draft to amend Section 295A (the blasphemy law) of the BPC

introduced by Matiur Rahman Nizami, secretary of the Jamaat-e-Islami, was patterned on the law in Pakistan.

9. Articles 27 and 28 of the Constitution of the People's Republic of Bangladesh guarantees equality in matters of the state and public life, while Articles 31, 32 and 35 provide guarantees for protection under the law, of the right to life and liberty.
10. In Civil Appeal Nos 593–94 of 2001.
11. The short order issued by the Supreme Court is discussed later in this chapter. The full judgement was given in 2014.
12. Personal communication with D. Siddiqi. See also Siddiqi (2011a, 2011b).
13. The demand for secular uniform laws governing women's personal lives was included in the manifesto of the Oikkyo Boddho Nari Samaj and in subsequent drafts prepared by feminist groups as part of their election campaigns.
14. Without her assistance the father may not have filed the case.
15. For abetment to suicide, for the abettors' presence at incident and for intentional insult with intent to provoke breach of peace.
16. Penalties included physical punishments (101 lashes or pelting with 101 stones), public shaming (shaving the victims' heads, parading them around the village) and social ostracism, all to humiliate women, supposedly as an example to others.
17. See Appendix A.
18. See Appendix B.
19. These organizations included ASK, BLAST, BRAC, BNWLA, Nagorik Uddyog, Banchte Shekha, Association for Community Development and several others.
20. By 2013 Nagorik Uddyog had formed 837 *shalish* committees in ninety-three unions.
21. Youth volunteers known as the Manabadhikar Shangrakhan Parishad (Association for the Protection of Human Rights) and women's volunteers known as the Nari Manabadhikar Parishad (Women's Rights Defenders) monitor human rights or *shalish* proceedings in forty unions after they are oriented to legal rights. Members of the Ainjibi Manabadhikar Parishad (Lawyers' Human Rights Association) offer free legal aid.

22. See Siddiqi (2011b) for an interpretation of an intervention by women lawyers to reverse *shalish* decisions consequent to a premarital pregnancy in Noakhali.
23. ASK's investigators did a fact finding into these incidents at Chachuri village of Narail district on 1 and 2 August 2007. Their findings were included in writ petition No. 5863/2009 filed by BLAST, ASK and other petitioners.
24. The youth mentioned in particular that they were not allowed to read Nazrul Islam's poems or philosophical texts by Aristotle or Plato.
25. *Editor,* Bangladesh Patrika *v. District Magistrate and Deputy Commissioner Naogaon.* On the basis of a news report that an imam in Naogaon had issued a fatwa instructing a woman to undergo *hilla* marriage, and no action had been taken by the magistrate and police.
26. See Hossain (2014) for information on Mufti Mohd Tayeb appellant in Civil Appeal No. 593/01 and Mufti Abul Kalam Azad appellant in Civil Appeal No. 594/01.
27. The five organizations were BLAST, Bangladesh Mahila Parishad, ASK, BRAC and Nijera Kori in WP 5863 of 2009, 754 of 2010 and 4275 of 2010 (reported at 63 DLR 1).
28. These included the state's duty to prevent, prohibit and punish cruel, inhuman and degrading treatment or punishment, and to enforce the universal prohibition against torture.
29. The *pouroshabha* is a tier of local governance.
30. The judgement cited Article 7 of the International Covenant on Civil and Political Rights, Articles 2 and 16 of the Commission against Torture and General Comment No. 7 of the Human Rights Committee, as well as UN CEDAW's concluding observations to Bangladesh's Sixth and Seventh Report (UNCEDAW C/BGD/CO) 2011, paras C (1 & 20) that violence against women impairs or nullifies the enjoyment by women of human rights and fundamental freedoms under general international law (para 37). The court noted that it could refer to these as an aid to interpretation to determine rights implied in the right to life and liberty but not enumerated in the Constitution, and also cited Article 25 of the Constitution (para 38).
31. See Supreme Court of Bangladesh CA Nos 593–94 of 2014, pp. 42–43.

SELECT BIBLIOGRAPHY

Ahmad, N.R. 2002. 'Women, Popular Culture and Islam in Bangladesh'. University of Texas, mimeo.

Alim, M.A. and M. Rafi. 2011.'An Assessment of NRLE Shebika with a Focus on Their Effectiveness', Research Monograph Series No 47, July, BRAC.

Ain o Salish Kendra (ASK). 2007. 'Salma Case Study 3'. Report by the Gender Gender and Justice Unit, internal memo.

————. 2014. *ASK Bulletin*, December.

Begum, M. 1997. *Fatwa 1991–1995*. Dhaka: Shikha o Sanskriti Charcha Kendra.

Falguni, A. 1996. 'Narir Bhot Odhikar Longhon' (Women's Voting Rights Violated), *ASK Bulletin*, February.

————. 2001. 'Fatwa', *ASK Bulletin*, March.

Golub, S. 1997. 'A Measure of Choice: Strategic Review for MLAA, Impact and Future Direction'. Report Prepared for the Ford Foundation, the MLAA, the Norwegian Agency for Development Cooperation and the Asia Foundation.

————. 2003. 'Non-State Justice Systems in Bangladesh and the Philippines'. Paper prepared for the United Kingdom Department for International Development, January.

————. 2013. 'The Political Economy of Improving Traditional Justice System: A Case Study of NGO Engagement with Shalish in Bangladesh', in H. Cisse, S. Muller, C. Thomas and W. Chenguang (eds), *The World Bank Legal Review: Legal Innovation and Empowerment for Development*, pp. 67–68. Washington, DC: World Bank.

Helie-Lucas, M.A. and H. Kapoor (eds). 1996. *Fatwas against Women in Bangladesh*. Grabels: Women Living under Muslim Law.

Hossain, H. 2001. 'Ei Shobghotna Shangbidhanke Botei Deshe Prochilito Anonya Ainke Langhan Kore Cholche', interview, *ASK Bulletin*, March.

Hossain, S. 2014. 'From Fatwas to Freedom from Violence: Experiences of Domestic Litigation in the Bangladesh Courts'. Mimeo, School of Oriental and African Studies, May.

Huda, S. 2011. *Combating Gender Injustice: Hindu Law in Bangladesh*. Dhaka: South Asian Institute of Advanced Legal and Human Rights Studies.

Karim, F. 2011. 'Bangladeshi Family Tells of Grief over Girl Whipped to Death', *Guardian*, 4 February.

Khanam, A. et al. 1997. *Fatwa Boli Chattokcharar Nurjehan*. Dhaka: Mahila Parishad.

Manabadhikar Shangrakhan Parishad and Manabadhikar Nari Samaj. 2011. *Kaaj Amar Kotha Amar* (My Work My Words). Manabadhikar Shangrakhan Parishad and Manabadhikar Nari Samaj.

Mernissi, Fatima. 1991. *The Veil & the Male Elite: A Feminist Interpretation of Women's Rights in Islam* (translated by Mary Jo Lakeland). New York: Perseus Books.

Khan, A.H. 2012. 'Putting an End to Fatwa Violence', *Forum*, 6 (March).

Pereira, F. 2011. *Civil Laws Governing Christians in Bangladesh*. Dhaka: The South Asian Institute of Advanced Legal and Human Rights Studies.

Riaz, A. 2005. 'Traditional Institutions as Tools of Political Islam in Bangladesh', *Journal of Asian and African Studies*, 40(3): 171–96.

Rahman, U. 2001. *Fatwa*, ASK *Bulletin*, March 2001.

Serajuddin, A. M. 2010. 'Judicial Activism and Family Law in Bangladesh', *Journal of the Asiatic Society of Bangladesh*, 55.

———. 2011. *Muslim Family Law, Secular Courts and Muslim Women of South Asia*. Karachi: Oxford University Press.

Shehabuddin, E. 2008. *Reshaping the Holy*. New York: Columbia University Press.

Siddiqi, D.M. No date. *Paving the Way to Justice: The Experience of Nagorik Uddyog*. London: One World Action.

———. 2003. 'Quest for Gender Justice'. ASK, mimeo.

———. 2011a. 'Islam, Gender and the Nation', in D. Heath and C. Mathur (eds), *Communalism and Globalisation and Its Diaspora*, pp. 181–203. London: Routledge.

———. 2011b.'Transnational Feminism and "Local" Realities: The Imperiled Muslim Woman and the Production of (In)Justice', *Journal of Women of the Middle East and the Islamic World*, 9: 84–88.

Tamanna, N., S. Hossain and M.A. Haq. 2011. *Muslim Women's Rights under Bangladesh Law: Provisions, Policies and Practices Related to Custody and Guardianship*. Dhaka: South Asian Institute of Advanced Legal and Human Rights Studies.

7

Eighteen

The silent witnesses of Kalpana Chakma's abduction speak, eighteen years after her disappearance

'I think it is natural to expect the caged bird to be angry at those who imprisoned her. But if she understands that she has been imprisoned and that the cage is not her rightful place, then she has every right to claim the freedom of the skies!'

Newspaper collage of Kalpana's portrait and a page from her diary. Bhorer Kagoj

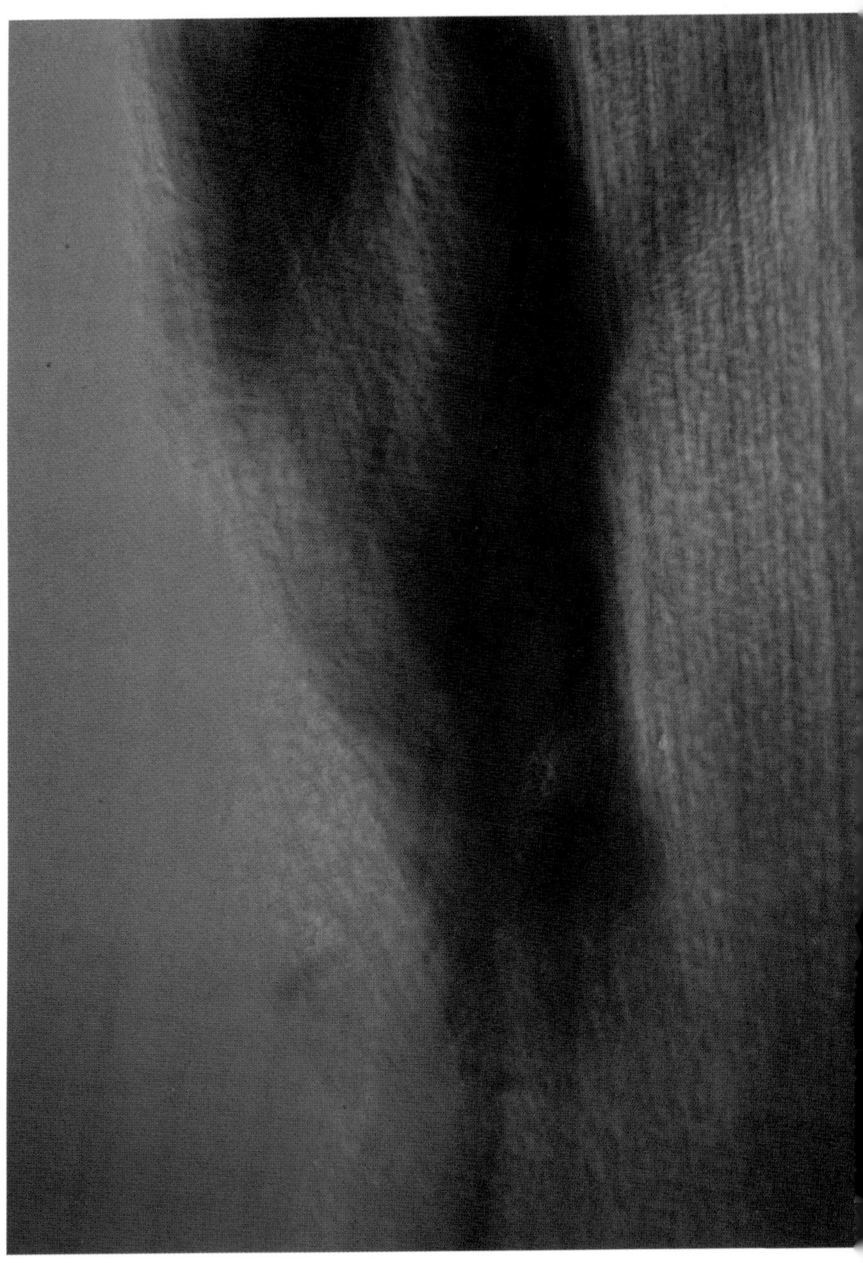

Kalpana's dress

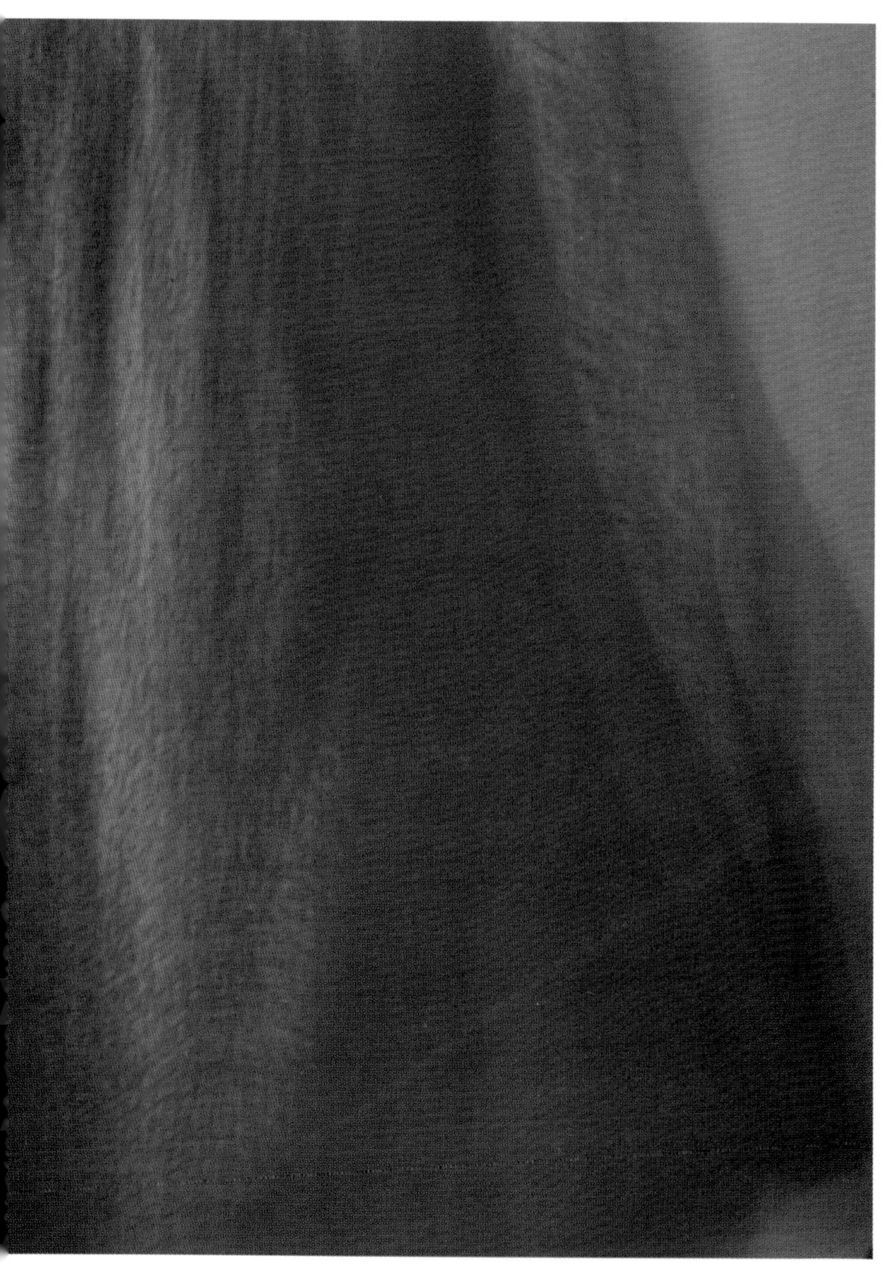

Kalpana Chakma was a fiery, courageous young indigenous woman of the Chittagong Hill Tracts in Bangladesh. Twenty years ago, she dared to demand her rights. She had the audacity to speak out against military occupation and harassment by her own country's army. She had the temerity to insist that, as a citizen of a free nation, she too needed to be treated as an equal.

Then in the early hours of 12 June 1996, she was abducted at gunpoint by the Bangladesh military. She never returned. The principal accused, Lieutenant Ferdous, has never been questioned by the police. He too has 'disappeared'.

Almost two decades later the photographer and activist Shahidul Alam, through found objects, her personal belongings and in-depth interviews, pieces together an unseen document, a forbidden history.

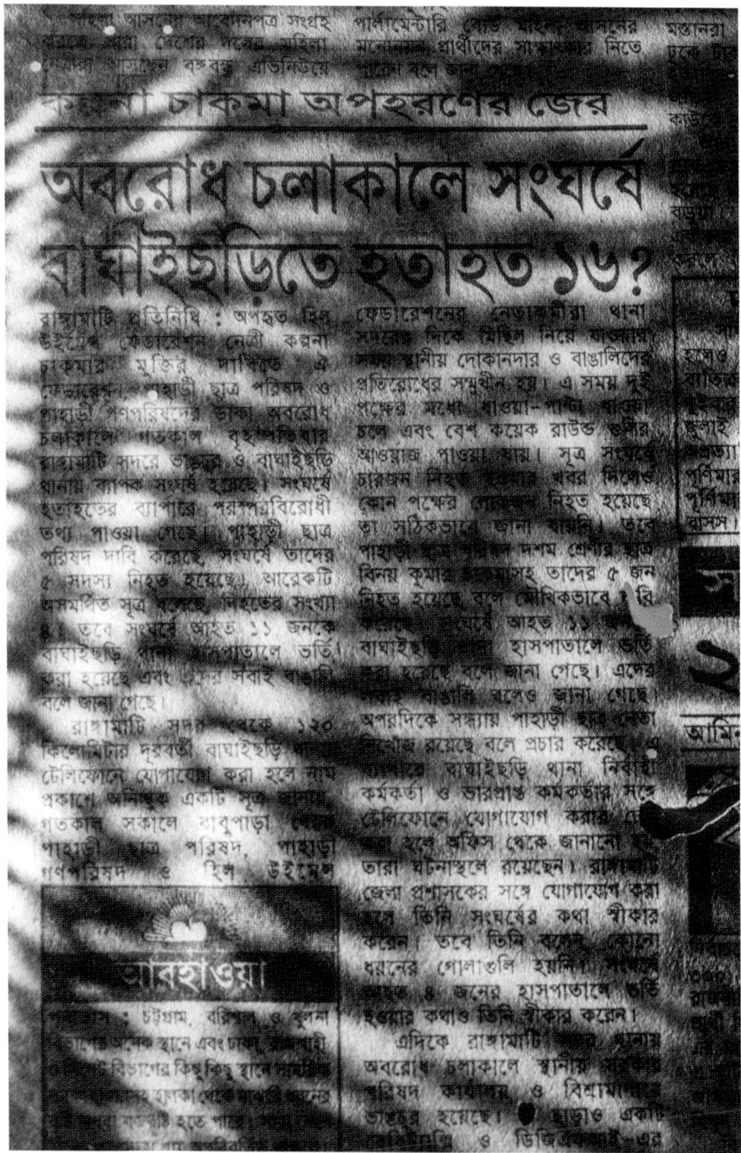

কল্পনা চাকমা অপহরণের জের

অবরোধ চলাকালে সংঘর্ষে বাঘাইছড়িতে হতাহত ১৬?

আবহাওয়া

Newspaper report on clashes after Kalpana's disappearance where 16 people are said to have died.

Cover of book on Lenin, part of Kalpana's personal collection

Back cover of book on Lenin, lists Marx, Engels and Lenin

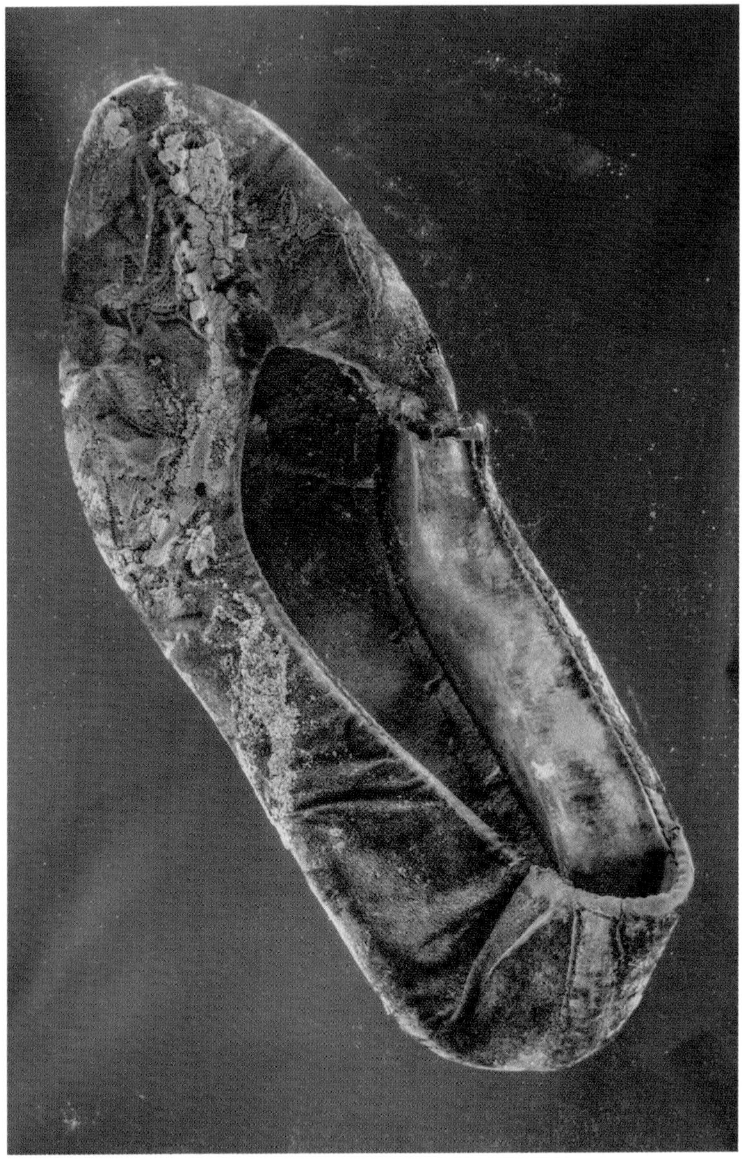

Kalpana's shoes

I will resist, I shall defy
Will you do as you please?
You turned my home into sand
It was a forest where I stand
You made daylight go dark
Left it barren never a spark

I will resist. I shall defy
You strip me of my land
On my women, your hand
No longer shall I see
No longer will I be

Abandon, neglect, rage
A throbbing womb, my stage
I curl, I tear asunder
Awake, I search, I wander

I am who I am
And I will resist
I shall defy

Poem by Kabita Chakma
Translation by Shahidul Alam

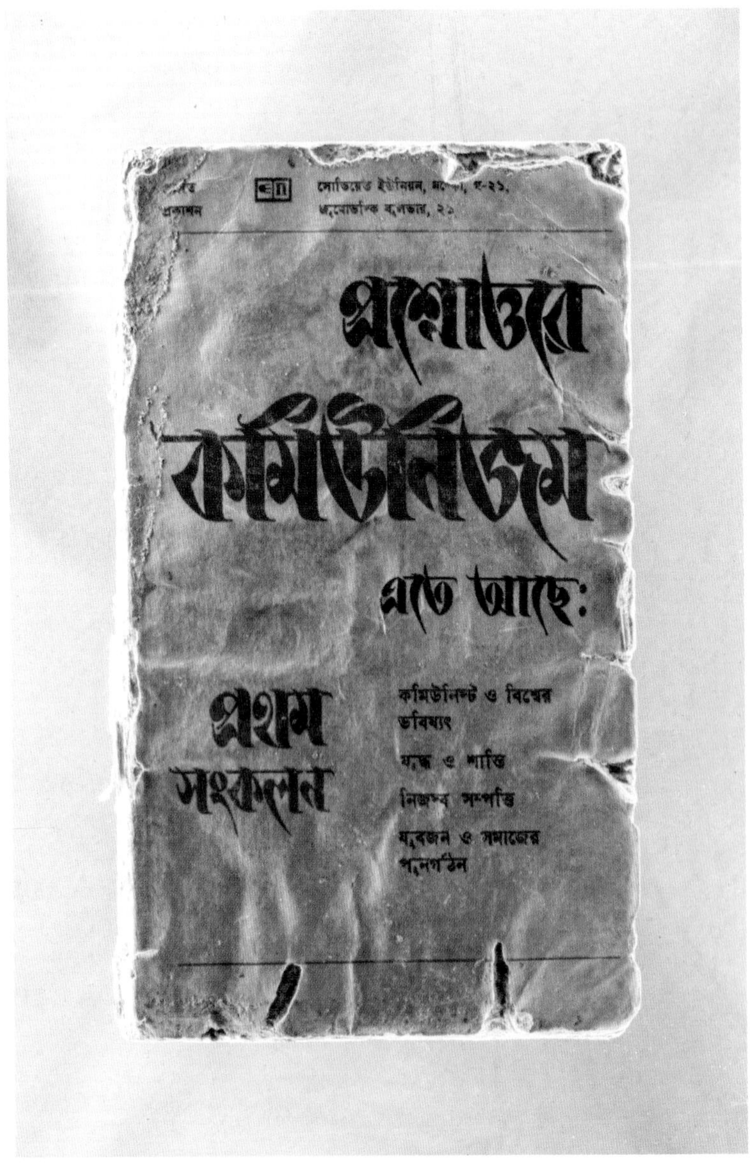

Questions and answers on communism. Part of Kalpana's personal collection

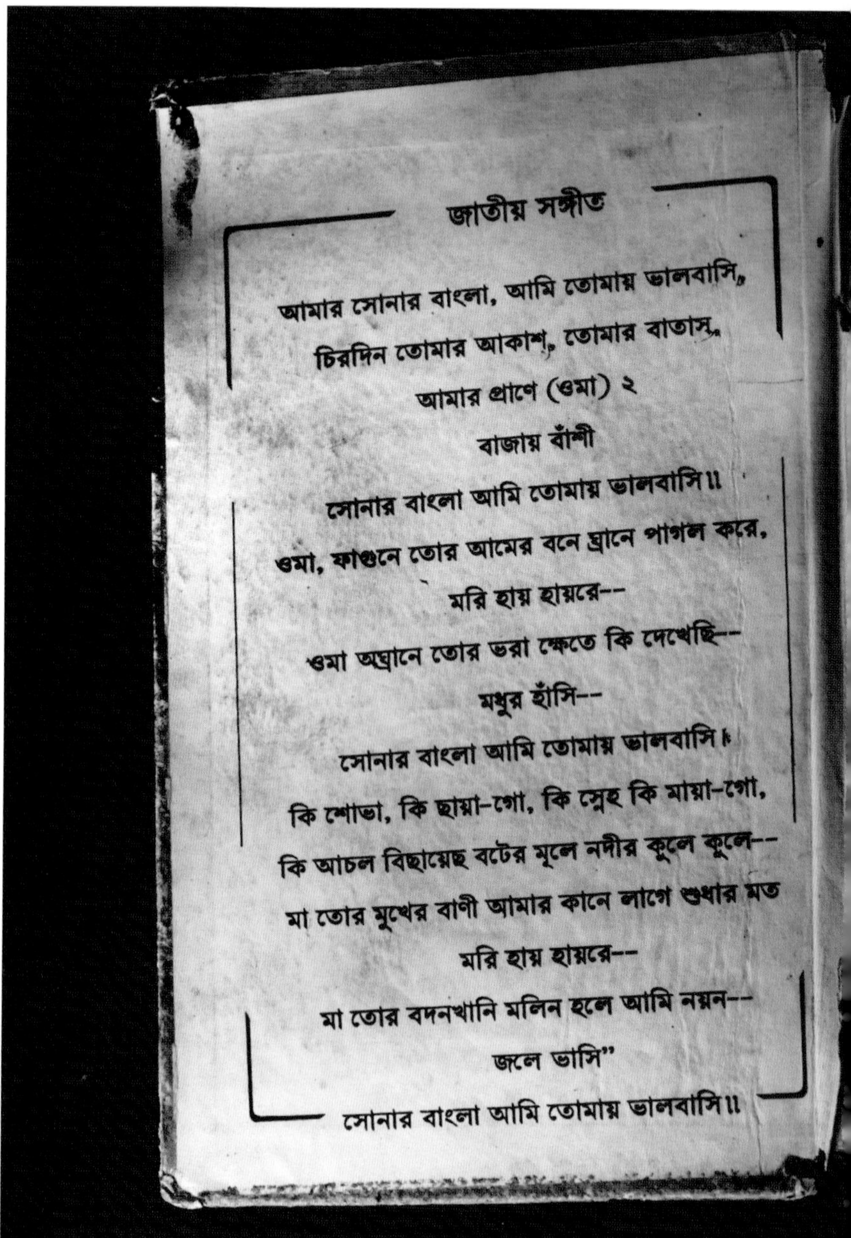

জাতীয় সঙ্গীত

আমার সোনার বাংলা, আমি তোমায় ভালবাসি,
চিরদিন তোমার আকাশ, তোমার বাতাস,
আমার প্রাণে (ওমা) ২
বাজায় বাঁশী
সোনার বাংলা আমি তোমায় ভালবাসি॥
ওমা, ফাগুনে তোর আমের বনে ঘ্রানে পাগল করে,
মরি হায় হায়রে--
ওমা অঘ্রানে তোর ভরা ক্ষেতে কি দেখেছি--
মধুর হাঁসি--
সোনার বাংলা আমি তোমায় ভালবাসি।
কি শোভা, কি ছায়া-গো, কি স্নেহ কি মায়া-গো,
কি আচল বিছায়েছ বটের মূলে নদীর কূলে কূলে--
মা তোর মুখের বাণী আমার কানে লাগে শুধার মত
মরি হায় হায়রে--
মা তোর বদনখানি মলিন হলে আমি নয়ন--
জলে ভাসি"
সোনার বাংলা আমি তোমায় ভালবাসি॥

Kalpana's diary

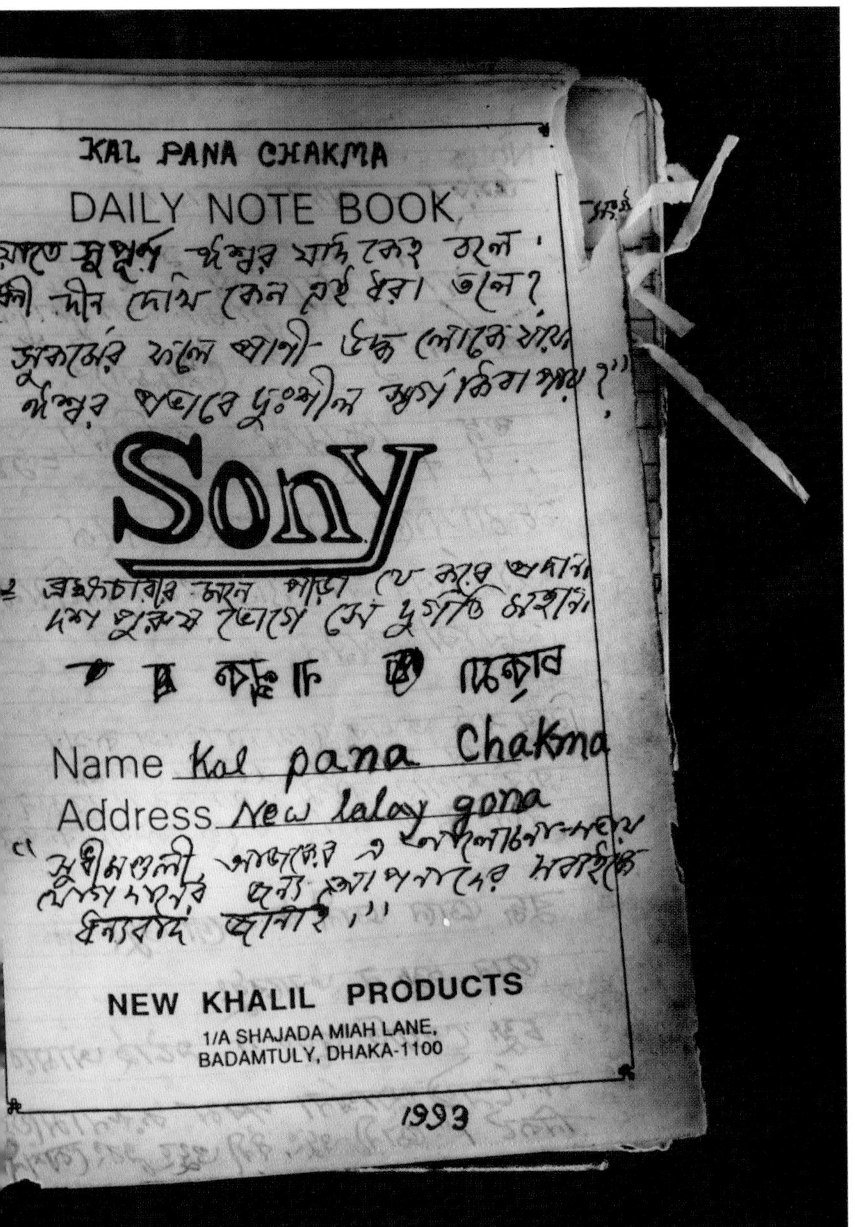
KAL PANA CHAKMA
DAILY NOTE BOOK
Sony
Name Kal pana Chakma
Address New lalay gona
NEW KHALIL PRODUCTS
1/A SHAJADA MIAH LANE,
BADAMTULY, DHAKA-1100
1993

Eighteen. The legal age to vote. The age of sexual consent. The threshold of adulthood when one ceases to be a child. Eighteen. The sections of the Mahabharata. Eighteen armies fighting over eighteen days. Eighteen, the number of years we have waited for justice. Eighteen years that you have been gone, Kalpana, my sister.

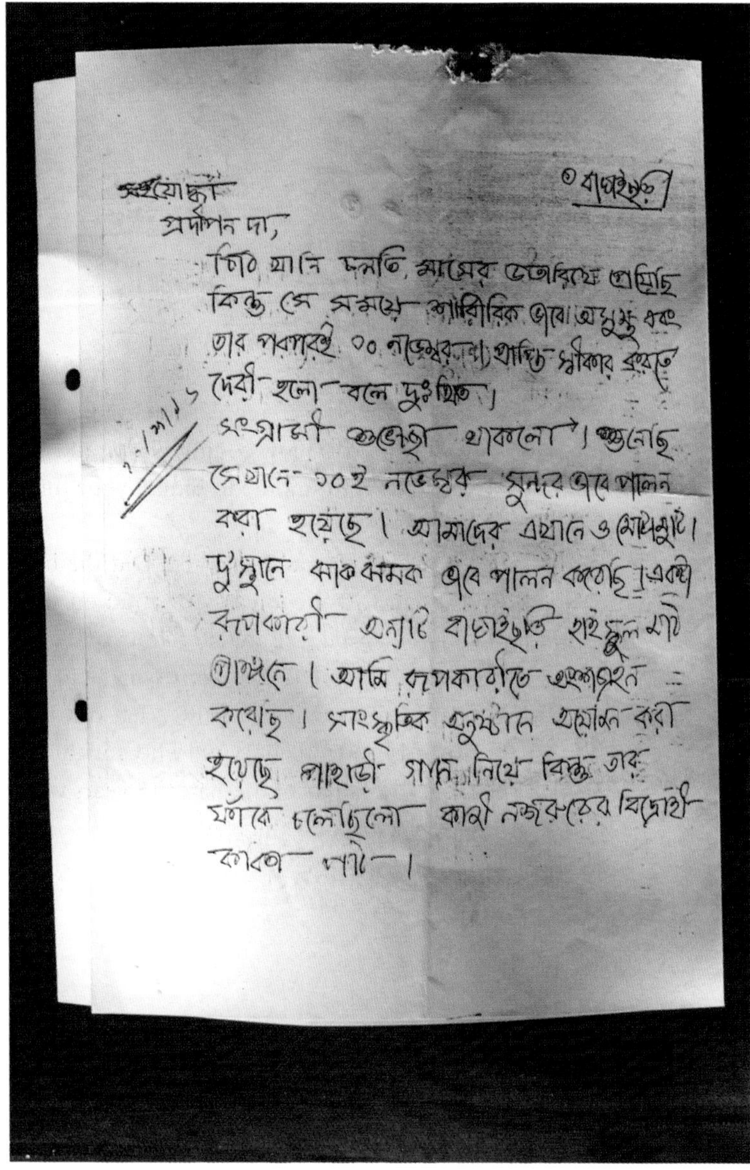

সহযোদ্ধা ৩ বাঘাইছড়ি

প্রদীপন দা,

চিঠি খানি চলতি মাসের ৩ তারিখে পেয়েছি কিন্তু সে সময়ে শারীরিক ভাবে অসুস্থ এবং তার পরপরই ১০ নভেম্বর নিয়ে থাকাতে স্বীকার করতে দেরী হলো বলে দুঃখিত।

সংগ্রামী শুভেচ্ছা থাকলো। শুনেছি সেখানে ১০ই নভেম্বর সুন্দর ভাবে পালন করা হয়েছে। আমাদের এখানেও মোটামুটি। দু'স্থানে জাকজমক ভাবে পালন করেছি। একটা রূপকারী অন্যটি বাঘাইছড়ি হাইস্কুল মাঠ প্রাঙ্গনে। আমি রূপকারীতে অংশগ্রহন করেছি। সাংস্কৃতিক অনুষ্ঠান আয়োজন করা হয়েছে পাহাড়ী গান নিয়ে কিন্তু তার মাঝে চলেছিলো কাজী নজরুলের বিদ্রোহী কবিতা পাঠ।

Kalpana's letter to a colleague and friend

I wonder what you'd look like today? Would you have mellowed with age, become wiser, more astute. Would you have spoken out with the same raw courage, or would you now have waited for the right moment, biding your time?

What did you see on that fateful last walk? Did the bark you leaned on respond to your touch? The mud on your shoes, the hole on your *orna*, the folds of your petticoat, what secrets do they bear? Did the words echo in the woods as you cried out to your brother? What did they do to you, my sister? What made you, who fought for justice and freedom, the enemy of the state? 18 years we've waited, Kalpana. For justice, for the truth.

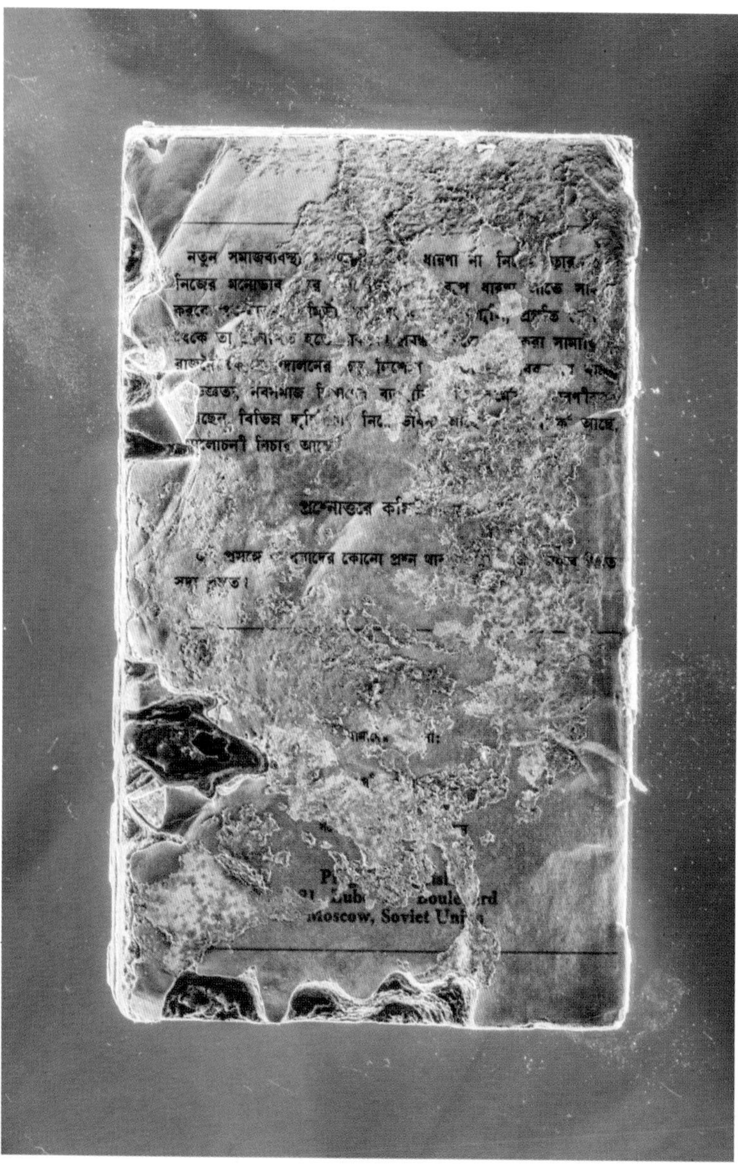

Back cover of booklet on communism

Hole in Kalpana's orna *(also called dupatta in other parts of the Indian subcontinent, commonly used with shalwar kameez and the kurta, used to cover a woman's breasts)*

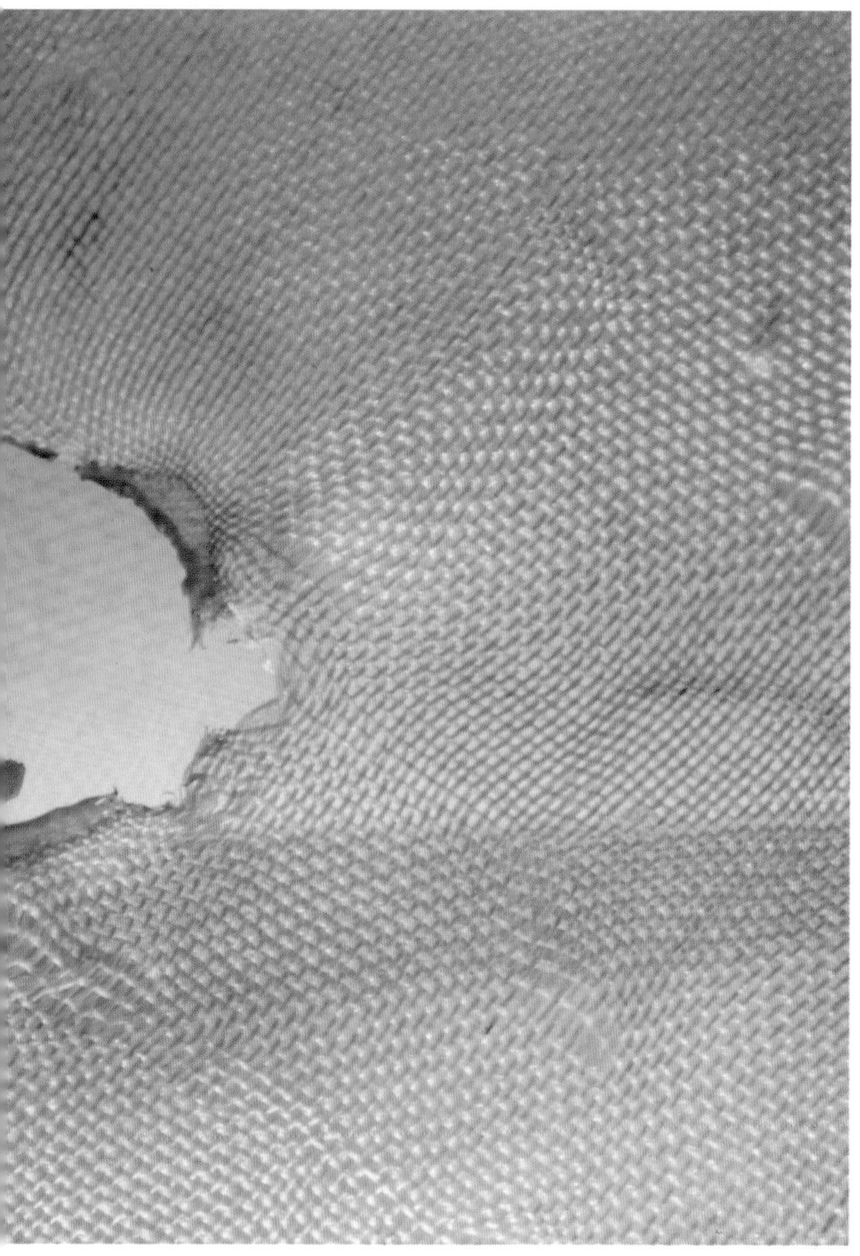

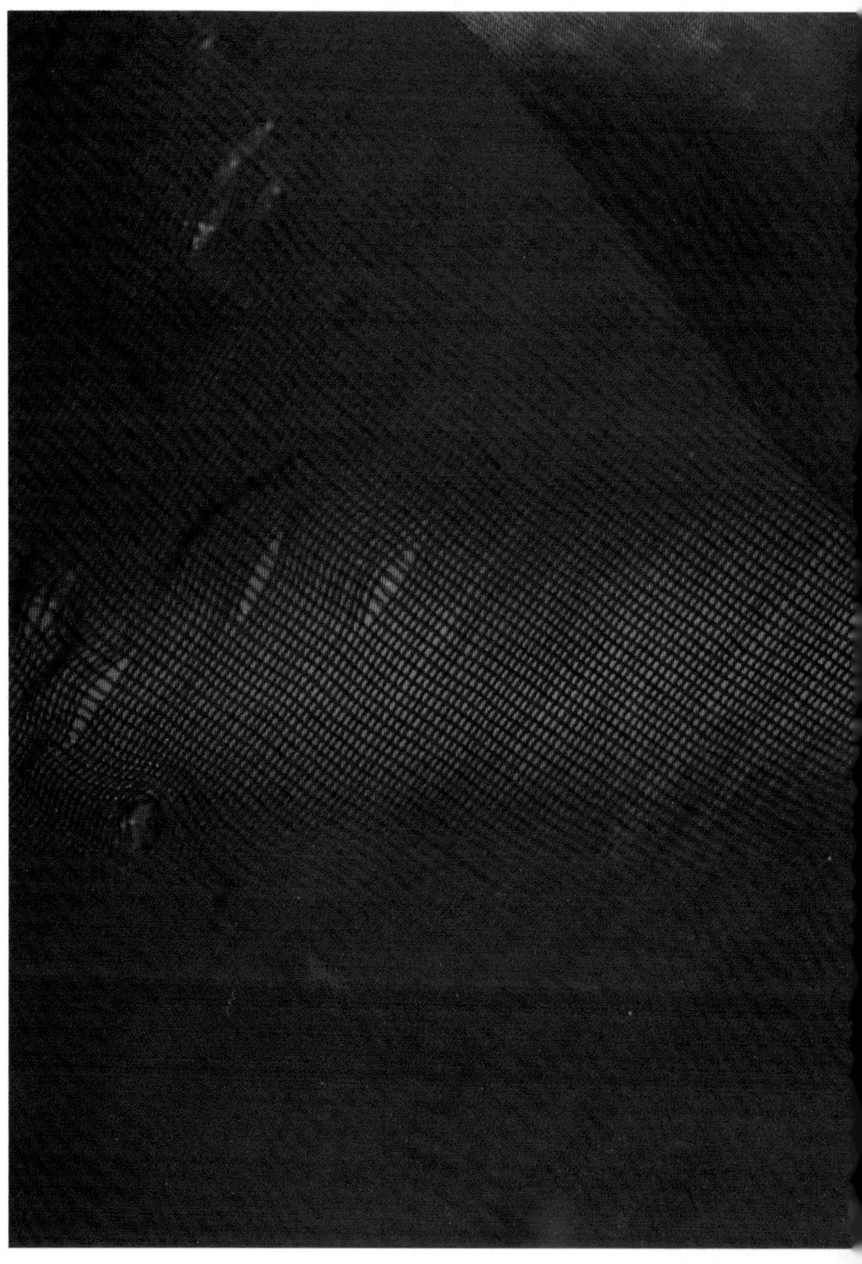

Kalpana's shawl

Objects collected from the path that Kalpana's abductors took her along, the last day she was ever seen.

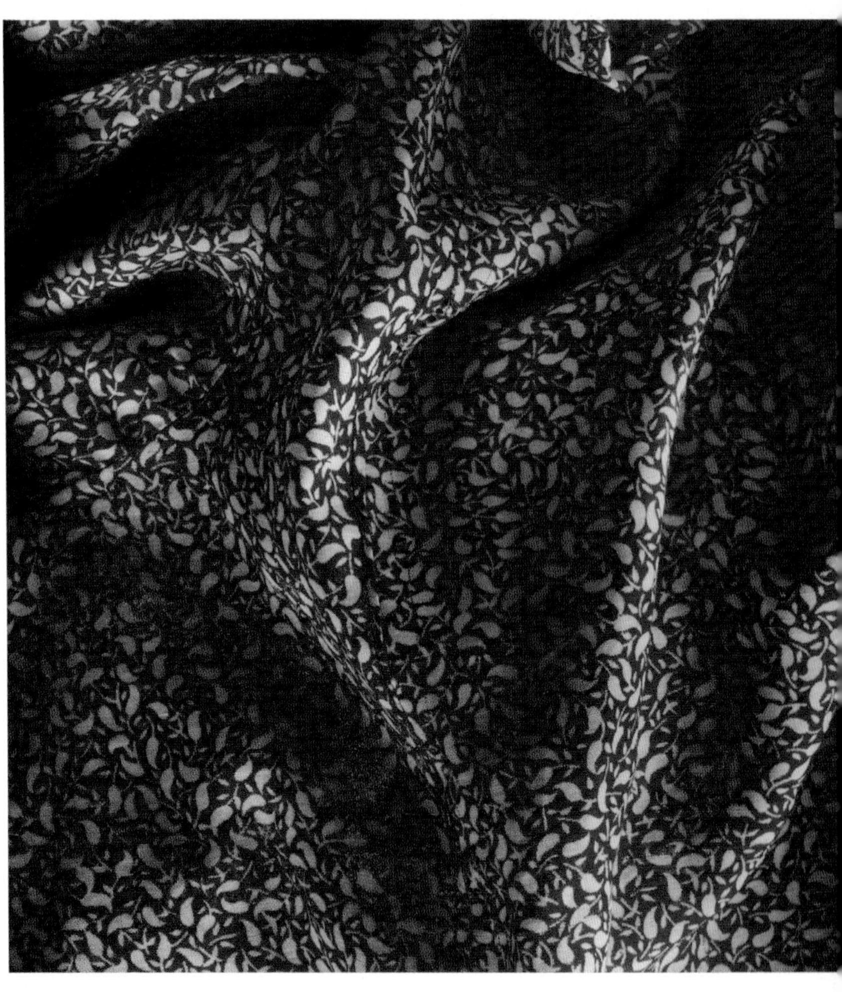

Kalpana's dress

There is no grave in Lallyaghona. No monument for its most famous daughter. But your voice still reverberates in the hills. They call out to rise. To resist.

As the streams glisten in the moonlight, they hear your call:

No more settlers
No more soldiers
No more murders
No more cowering in fear as muddy boots tread over freshly caked mud floors.
No more constitutions that deny equal rights.
No more waiting for justice. No more disappearances.

They await your return

8

Journeys through Shadows

Gender Justice in the Chittagong Hill Tracts*

BINA D'COSTA

INTRODUCTION

Feminist scholars working in areas that have traditionally been overlooked in international politics, especially peace and conflict research, such as gender, race and class, have examined the discipline's inadequacy to address these through a gender-sensitive framework. Feminist analyses have explored in detail sexual violence experienced by women; children and war; masculinities and violence; gender and national identity politics; and testimonies and memory (Butalia 1998; Menon and Bhasin 1998; Charlesworth and Chinkin 2000; Moghadam 1994, 2005; Kandiyoti 1991, 2005; Manchanda 2001). Employing a feminist perspective, this chapter articulates deeply embedded tensions within existing justice frameworks and indigenous rights. Also, by analysing the role of civil society networks in gender justice strategies in the CHT in

---

My sincere thanks to Prashanta Tripura for his feedback on the

Bangladesh, this chapter recommends a different and possibly more productive way of thinking about gendered experiences of justice in South Asia.

I use feminist methodology to analyse the nature of sexual and gender-based violence (SGBV) and gender justice in the CHT (D'Costa 2006). For this purpose, first, by placing the survivors of SGBV during and after conflicts at the core of research, this chapter suggests that centring the marginalized yields otherwise inaccessible theoretical insights to the question of justice, and ask ethical and substantive questions that impact not only the research design, but more fundamentally, the research question itself.

Insights from interviews conducted over the last six years in the CHT with survivors of gender-based violence, families of victims and survivors, indigenous leaders including circle chiefs, advocates and activists, indigenous political leaders, religious leaders, *karbari*s (village heads), Bengali settlers, members of the security forces such as the police and the military, and party officials have been included here. I have also carried out interviews in Chittagong and Dhaka with various stakeholders in gender justice processes for indigenous women and girls. For confidentiality and ethical reasons, none of the respondents have been named.

Second, this chapter discusses the role of civil society in responding to gender-sensitive needs of indigenous women and girls. Though they are not necessarily united in the questions of truth and justice, the roles and responsibilities of civil society in Bangladesh need to be discussed in the context of effective gender justice measures. Networks, NGOs, scholars, activists, religious leaders and other civil society groups often represent the way justice is perceived by communities. These groups also serve as the bridge of communication between people who are at the periphery of power and the elite, who are at the centre.[1] Civil society's role in gender justice and peace building, especially after a peace accord has been signed, is crucial, and that flexibility and ability to address trauma and suffering without political constraints are its major strengths.

However, Bangladeshi civil society groups involved in peace politics are often restricted in the political choices available to them.[2] In the CHT, women activists reflect how the broader women's movement in Bangladesh has failed to respond to the causes of indigenous women during the armed conflict.[3] Either in collaborative or adversarial relation to national governments, civil society groups play a vital role in diffusing universally applicable norms relevant to gender justice. Consequently, in the concluding section of this chapter, I provide a framework for effective civil society collaboration in promoting gender-sensitive justice measures in the CHT. The chapter is both theoretically and methodologically informed by recent developments in women's human rights, and peace and conflict scholarship.

Women's Human Rights Discourse

Feminist scholars focusing on human rights have often used gender justice interchangeably with notions of 'gender equality', 'gender equity', 'women's empowerment' and 'women's rights'. Those who have worked on the intersection of rights and development have also often conceptualized gender justice as a process that requires that women are able to ensure that power holders—whether in the household, community, market or state—can be held to account for actions that limit, on the grounds of gender, women's access to resources or capacity to make choices (Goetz 2007: 30–31). Contemporary concepts of gender justice in women's human rights discourse encompass human agency, rights and capabilities in political philosophy (Ackerly and Okin 1999; Nussbaum 2000; Okin 2004); debates within politics, anthropology, sociology and law about democratization, citizenship, constitutionalism, 'women's rights as human rights' and cosmopolitanism (Charlesworth and Chinkin 2000; D'Costa and Lee Koo 2013; Reilly 2009); and in the field of law, judicial reform and practical matters of access to justice (Sieder and McNeish 2013). Women's human rights discourse enables a focus around a common issue (with recognized variation) and has been aided with the use of the political tools of lobbying, caucusing and networking (Ackerly and D'Costa 2008; Keck and Sikkink 1998). While there have been attempts to create solidarity in feminist spaces, there are debates within feminist circles about these attempts as elitist, imperialist or merely disconnected from the lives of most of the world's women (Ali 2002; D'Costa 2006; Flax 1995; Mohanty 1991, 2003; Okin 1994; Spivak 1988).

Although there is much scholarship on women's activism, there has been little or no effort to include indigenous women's issues in mainstream feminist research. Most of the discussion involving indigenous women's rights and gender justice takes place within the broader indigenous rights discourse. Also, women's human rights experts are involved in designing and implementing projects that are meant to empower vulnerable populations and yet indigenous women and girls are often treated as victims with little say in these project designs and processes. While this scholarship has deepened the understanding of women's empowering gender justice, it has also left questions unanswered. How are indigenous women's activists and advocates on the ground framing their concerns in the global language of human rights? How best can international and national mechanisms and organizations meet their needs? When nation-states and custodians of cultural norms have resources to circumvent the power of human rights activism, undermining its local legitimacy, how do indigenous women strategically employ human rights approaches to address injustices? I examine how, in the context of these internal politics, experiences and challenges, activists and women's groups attempt to negotiate local complexities and those made central by the gender justice and protection mandate of the international community.

Peace and Conflict Discourse

In his analysis of militarization of Latin America, David Mares suggests that violent peace is

> the use of officially sanctioned military violence across national boundaries when war is not the intended result. War might occur, but as a result of escalation dynamics unknowable, unforeseen, or miscalculated by those who made the initial decision to use military force ... the decision to use military force should be thought of as a bargaining tactic rather than a decision to settle an interstate dispute through war. (2001: 7)

Political transition, healing and reconciliation and economic recovery are all closely interlinked with other security dynamics such as defusing spoilers of the peace process, integrating various factions, demobilizing former combatants appropriately and resettling displaced people.[4] Protracted militarization processes, the perpetual fear and insecurity of people, illegal transmigration programmes of the Bengalis in the CHT, and displacement of the indigenous populations make the region one of violent peace. This chapter argues that militarization has seriously affected the culture of impunity in the CHT, thereby deepening and reinforcing a violent peace in the post-accord CHT.

For Catherine Lutz, militarization includes

> a range of discursive and material processes through which societies prepare for war, and has become pervasive in the lives of contemporary national security states, spinning out through multiple related institutional domains—political, economic, juridical and familial—thereby intersecting with the existing social inequalities and cultural tensions and impacting combatants as well as non-combatants who are not otherwise caught up in military endeavours and preparedness routines. (2002: 723)

The enduring reproductions of militarization are predicated on, and justified through, a range of ideological logics of order and chaos, revolts and counter-insurgency measures that advance and legitimate military action. A variety of repressive strategies of militarization have been employed by the Bangladeshi state in the CHT, affecting the indigenous peoples, in particular women and girls. First, through a huge military presence in the region and the deployment of other security forces such as the police, including: the Rapid Action Battalion (RAB), an elite anti-crime and anti-terrorism unit of the Bangladesh police; the Border Guard Bangladesh (BGB), a paramilitary force; the Village Defence Party (VDP), a voluntary paramilitary force recruited largely from Bengali settlers and trained by the police; and the intelligence agencies, in disproportionate numbers.[5] Second, policies were put in place deliberately aimed at changing the demography of the indigenous areas through different government-sponsored transmigration programmes of Bengali settlers from the plains to the CHT region. The Bengali settlements enjoy the protection of the security sector and have frequently been involved in crimes in the CHT. During my interviews, survivors of SGBV noted that the Bengali settlers also have the protection of the police forces and the health officials.[6] And, finally, discriminatory practices, such as restricted access to educational, social and health care services for Adivasis, especially the smaller ethnic groups, living in remote and rural areas of the hills, as well as rigid funding regulations for international organizations, NGOs and community groups.

Militarization has also had an impact on impunity in the CHT (D'Costa 2010a; Roy 2004; IWGIA 2012). Relationships with law enforcement agencies are vitally important in resolving the culture of impunity. Local authorities and police stations in the hills are often subject to more political influence due to corruption, money politics, illegal timber trade and other cross-border activities, and have fewer resources than authorities and police stations in the plains. All of these factors are obstacles in addressing SGBV. Victims face many hurdles in seeking accountability. Intimidation and repressive actions by the police, the army and/or both Bengali settler and Pahari gangs involved in criminal activities, in many cases protecting the interests of the business sector, also contribute to the culture of impunity.

Land grabs contribute to an increase in the rate of gender-based violence as dispossession of land from women leaves them dependent on male relatives and more vulnerable to violence and sexual abuse.[7] Acres of indigenous land grabbed by the business sector, especially tobacco companies, the tourism industry and the security sector, under the pretext of providing better services and improving the livelihood of communities have also contributed to women's increased marginalization and vulnerability. SGBV has often been used to intimidate indigenous people to sell their land at bargain prices.[8] In some cases, the land is resold to military personnel and their families who have accumulated vast wealth in the CHT and invested in the tourism industry, contributing to the cycle of militarization in the region. These land grabs also affect women disproportionately as they are deprived of the livelihood they earn through small-scale agriculture.

South Asian feminists have explored various aspects of the 'woman question' in conflicts, such as how much attention do women's interests receive after conflicts have ended (Butalia 1998; Menon and Bhasin 1998; De Mel 2001; Manchanda 2001; Guhathakurta 2001, 2004; Khattak 2004; Hossain and D'Costa 2010; Chakma 2011).[9] Women who have taken part in nationalist movements and in the construction of their communities' identities in post-conflict periods have often done so in accordance with parameters or through an agenda largely framed by the elite, which largely comprises men. The position of women has, therefore, always revolved around performing supportive tasks in their communities. In South Asian conflict zones, state-initiated rehabilitation programmes aimed at enabling women to generate income have all been heavily built on the sexual division of labour, with women performing traditional feminine roles within their communities, such as sowing, cooking, paddy husking or even secretarial jobs.[10]

New feminist research also questions women's role in peace negotiations. The lengthy talks between the Awami League-led government and the main warring political party of the CHT, the

PCJSS, that ended in the CHT Peace Accord (popularly known as Shanti Chukti) involved no indigenous women. During my interviews with senior indigenous women leaders, some of whom were part of the Shanti Bahini, JSS's armed wing, and later took part in the demobilization and rehabilitation programmes, they stressed that women had 'faith in the leadership of Santu Larma and did not consider it necessary to be present at the negotiations table. Women's interests were looked after by the party.'[11] One senior female activist also commented that while they were not present at the front, they have been involved in a range of diplomatic efforts in the background to ensure that women's issues were not silenced in the accord.

Indigenous women continue to belong to the poorest and most marginalized sectors of society (IWGIA 2001; Nahar and Tripura 2010; ILO 2012). Disproportionately represented in low-income and unreliable forms of employment, many women and their families are unable to afford the prohibitive costs of using the formal justice system and reliable legal representation (Ahmad and Chakma 2011; Chakma 2013). While, as a party to the Convention on the Elimination of all Forms of Discrimination against Women (CEDAW), Bangladesh is obliged to take measures to combat discrimination in all its forms, indigenous women are not particularly targeted in current efforts to promote gender equality.[12]

ARMED CONFLICT, PEACE PROCESS AND DISLOCATION IN THE CHT

The plight of the indigenous peoples in Bangladesh is the result of postcolonial nation building and identity conflict (Mohsin 1997).[13] The CHT region in south-east Bangladesh, consisting of Rangamati, Khagrachari and Bandarban (see Figure 8.1), is the home of eleven diverse groups of indigenous people (Roy 2007).[14] Known as Adivasis, the indigenous people from the hills are easily distinguishable from the people of the plains by their features, socio-cultural practices and economic activities (Shapan 2008). Because of their traditional practice of shifting cultivation, they are also collectively referred as the Jumma people (IDMC 2006: 8). In this chapter, the terms indigenous peoples, Adivasi and Jumma have

FIGURE 8.1: The Chittagong Hill Tracts Region of Bangladesh

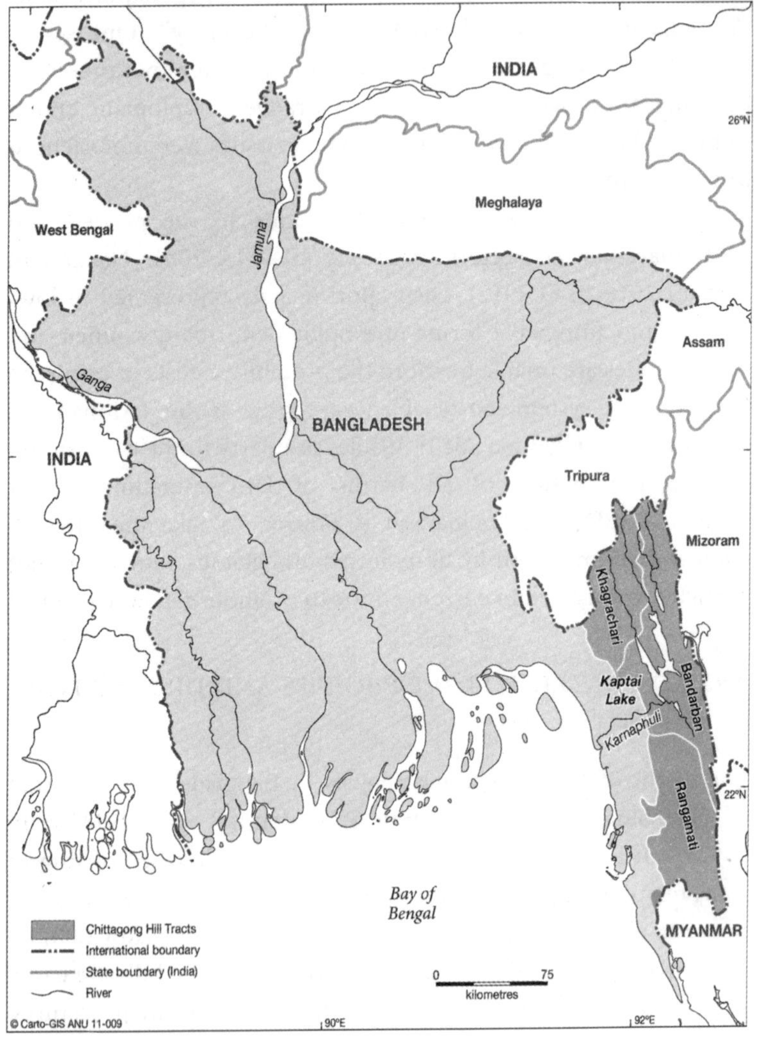

been used interchangeably to refer collectively to all the indigenous groups of the CHT. This region has geopolitical and strategic significance for Bangladeshi and South Asian security due to its location and proximity to India and Burma, and the porosity of the border; its richness in commercial natural resources; and historical, political and social contexts that constitute the communities of the CHT as the 'other' (in times of conflict, also internal enemy) within a Bangladeshi state. A low-intensity conflict that is deeply embedded in the struggle over land and existence in the CHT has contributed to massive internal displacement over the years.[15]

During the colonial period the British annexed the region in 1860 and created an autonomous administrative zone called the Chittagong Hill Tracts within undivided British Bengal. In 1900, the Raj enacted Regulation I of 1900 in order to 'protect' the indigenous communities from economic exploitation by others and to safeguard the traditional socio-cultural and political institutions based on chiefly hierarchies, customary laws and common ownership of land. The CHT was awarded to East Pakistan during partition partly due to its potential for hydroelectric power generation. This was the beginning of the 'resource war' that has led to the present-day violent peace in the CHT. Pakistan amended the 1900 Act several times against the wishes of indigenous communities. The amendments allowed the migration of non-indigenous people from the plains to take advantage of the natural resources of the CHT. Such exploitation continued even after Bangladesh's independence in 1971 following the war of secession from Pakistan. The Constitution of 1972 called for a homogeneous nation-state, with one language. An unsuccessful attempt by a delegation headed by Charu Bikash Chakma endeavoured to ensure separate constitutional safeguards for the indigenous population.[16] Following this, on 15 February 1972, Manabendra Narayan Larma met Sheikh Mujibur Rahman, the first prime minister of Bangladesh, with a charter of four demands.[17] Mujib's advice reportedly was: '*Tora shob bangalee hoiya ja*' (You all should become Bengalis), following which Larma refused to endorse the Constitution. After this, he and other senior political activists of the CHT established the PCJSS in 1972 and in the subsequent years, the Shanti Bahini, its armed wing, was set up as well.[18]

The Intensification of the Conflict: The Construction of the Kaptai Dam

While the long-term benefits from the construction of the Kaptai Dam in order to generate hydroelectricity in 1962 should not be underestimated, the massive dislocation caused by this decision, the seeds of conflict that it sowed, the militarization of the region and its effect on the society, and the huge economic costs of the conflict in the CHT should not be ignored either. It flooded 21,853 hectares of area and displaced 100,000 people, most of whom were Chakmas (IDMC 2006). According to human rights organizations, more than 40,000 Chakmas left for Arunachal Pradesh in India, where the majority still remain stateless (Amnesty International 2000). The construction of the dam led to the initial crisis of internal displacement, loss of control over natural resources, threats of forced assimilation, construction of non-permanent army camps and oppression by the Bangladeshi state, and it resulted in an armed insurgency in the CHT in 1976. As a counter-insurgency strategy, the government relocated over 400,000 poor and landless Bengalis to the region between 1979 and 1983 (AITPN 1998). Many of the Chakmas crossed the border to Mizoram and Tripura. By 1983, nearly 40,000 Chakmas had arrived in Mizoram and by May 1986 another 50,000 had taken shelter in five refugee camps in Tripura (Kharat 2003). There are no accurate statistics on conflict-induced displacement in the CHT and the ethnic composition of the figures often cited. The government task force on internal displacement stated in 2000 that there were 90,208 tribal and 38,156 non-tribal families or 500,000 to 555,000 people. Ironically, the Bangladeshi government also considers the Bengali settlers displaced and pushed for their resettlement in the CHT.

NGOs, Bangladeshi scholars and indigenous leaders argue that this figure is inaccurate (IDMC 2006: 13). Amnesty International (2000: 10) has estimated that 60,000 Adivasis were internally displaced between August 1975 and August 1992.

STATE TERROR AND HUMAN IN(SECURITY): SGBV DURING ARMED CONFLICT

Massive militarization by authoritarian and repressive states is often the response towards indigenous rights movements in various parts of the world.[19] The military is also linked to the highest ranks of the civil administration. The 24th Infantry Division has been in charge of the CHT for the last three decades. Many of the senior officials have also received counter-insurgency training in various parts of the world. The armed conflict in the CHT created extreme vulnerability and poverty.[20] Upendra Lal Chakma, who was interviewed by the CHT Commission (CHTC) in 1991, was at the time a member of the Bangladeshi Parliament.[21] He referred back to the events after liberation as 'genocide', a 'nightmare' (CHTC 1991: 15). While public data is unavailable on exactly how many troops are deployed in the CHT, a rough estimate puts the figure somewhere between 35,000 and 114,500. Military officials state that one-third of the entire Bangladeshi army is deployed in the CHT, an area which accounts for one-tenth of the total territory of the country, making it one of the most heavily militarized zones of a 'peaceful' area. Various NGOs, including Survival International and Anti-Slavery International, gathered first-hand accounts of ill treatment and torture, threats and killings, along with army destruction of houses and temples. Some of the cases are:

1. Mubachari, 15 October 1979: unknown number killed.
2. Kaukhali–Kalampati, 25 March 1980: 300 Jummas killed.
3. Banraibari–Beltali–Belchari, 26 June 1981: hundreds of Jummas murdered.

4. Telafang–Ashalong–Tabalchari, 19 September 1981: hundreds of Jummas murdered.
5. Golakpatimachara–Machyachara–Tarabanchari, June–August 1983: 800 Jummas killed.
6. Bhusanchara, Barkal, 31 May 1984: hundreds of Jummas killed; many women gang-raped and later shot dead.
7. Panchari, 1 May 1986: hundreds of Jummas (actual number not known) killed and injured by the Bangladeshi army; 80,000 (government estimate 50,000 to 70,000) Jummas fled across the border to India.
8. Matiranga, May 1986: at least 70 Jumma civilians gunned down by the Bangladeshi army.
9. Comillatilla, Taindong, 18–19 May 1986: 200 Jummas fired upon by the Bangladesh Rifles while fleeing across the border to India.
10. Langadu, 4 May 1989: 40 Jummas murdered.
11. Hirarchar, Sarbotali, Khagrachari, Pablakhali, 8, 9, 10 August, 1988: hundreds of Jumma civilians killed.
12. Malya, 2 February 1992: 30 Jummas murdered.
13. Logang, 10 April 1992: 138 Jummas killed.
14. Naniachar, 17 November 1993: 29 to 100 Jummas killed; 25 houses burnt.

None of the perpetrators of these massacres were ever brought to justice (Chakma and D'Costa 2012). After the accord was signed, a large faction of the armed resistance groups has surrendered their arms.[22] However, there were no appropriate disarmament, demobilization and reintegration (DDR) responses to their concerns.[23] While the peace accord briefly noted the importance of reconciliation and justice, and also pointed out to the concerns of displacement, more than a decade later, during interviews, senior leaders and CHT rights activists noted that these have not been appropriately addressed. The accord itself is deeply gendered (Dewan 2011, 2012; Guhathakurta 2004; Mohsin 1997) and includes no explicit guarantee to bring the perpetrators of human rights abuses to justice. Sexual and gender-based violence by the security personnel during the conflict was the single most motivating factor for forming the Hill Women's Federation (HWF) in 1988 (Guhathakurta 2004: 11). Yet, to date, none of the alleged perpetrators of SGBV belonging to the security forces have been brought to justice. Many human rights reports and data contain long lists of beatings, of forcible relocation to cluster villages, of detention without trial, torture, rape and unlawful killings by the Bangladeshi security forces over the conflict.[24] They also contain information on arson, destruction of houses and villages, looting of property, curtailment of freedom of expression, reprisal attacks and combing operations by the security forces.[25]

The CHTC conducted one of the most comprehensive studies on violence against women during the armed conflict. In its 1991 *Life Is Not Ours* report, and its three updates, the CHTC provides crucial evidence of SGBV in the region. The first report states that looting, arson, rape, gang-rape, torture to death and murder had been used to evict indigenous people from their land in 1990. One of the women interviewed by the CHTC recalls:

> About 50 army personnel came in the night and rounded up the whole village and gathered us in one place. In the morning all the men were arrested. I was tied up hands and legs, naked. They raped me. There were three women there. They raped me in front of my father-in-law. After that we were tied up together, naked, facing each other. Then they left. Three other girls were raped in front of me. This happened in the month of *Ashar* (June/July) of 1985. (CHTC 1991: 86)

Tripura women who were displaced during the conflict and returned to Khagrachari following the accord recounted stories of rape, gang-rape and assaults committed in front of children by the security personnel during my interviews with them. They told me that while various organizations came to meet them and wrote down their stories, none of the perpetrators had ever been brought to justice. In most cases, the perpetrators had not even bothered to hide their identities. I was quite shaken to hear that none of the women I interviewed expected any justice from either the state or their local communities. They had 'accepted' that violence occurred and that there would be no justice in their lifetime.

The forced marriage of indigenous women to Bengalis was also employed as a strategy to change the demography of the CHT, and created anxieties about religious and ethnic identity (D'Costa 2010). Many women reported that they were forced to convert to Islam. There were also some reports in the 1980s of a secret memo circulating among the army officers encouraging them to marry the indigenous women (CHTC 1991: 88). One respondent told me that young girls in their village and other villages were regularly paraded so the 'good-looking' ones could be selected for marriage to the army personnel.[26] The protracted and intense use of force by the Bangladeshi armed forces also produced a culture of violence in the region, contributing to a range of violence against women and girls in the CHT. One woman told the CHTC:

> I was kidnapped in 1986.... I had two children with this man. One day he sent me to his father's house and at a certain moment when I saw no one around I escaped. I went back to the *jouta khamar* (cluster village) where I had lived before, but when I arrived there, there were no tribals and it was occupied by Muslims. I arrived here in the camps in 1988. (ibid.)

The policy of establishing what were essentially collective farms began in 1964, to encourage Adivasis to settle on permanent land plots rather than continue *jhum* (slash-and-burn) cultivation. However, similar to the Indian army's policies in Mizoram in the late 1960s, they were carried out more ruthlessly. President Ziaur Rahman's counter-insurgency strategy included the forcible movement of the Adivasi population from sensitive, Shanti Bahini-dominated locations in the CHT from late 1977 to *guchchya grams* or cluster villages. The moving of villagers from their ancestral habitats in defensible locations was carried out with total disregard for the indigenous economy, using the forced labour of Adivasis who were issued with identity cards. A food embargo was enforced and army checkpoints were set up to monitor and control the movement of people. Adivasis who were caught violating the restrictions were arrested, tortured, raped and imprisoned.[27]

Sexual torture against children, the most vulnerable and marginalized subjects, had also been used during the conflict to generate terror and manipulate the indigenous population. A former Shanti Bahini rebel soldier recalled that one of his friends, a young girl of 15, was taken to the local army camp by her father to ensure the release of her brother. This respondent, who was 16 at that time, later joined the Shanti Bahini and was captured the following year during an operation and severely tortured.[28] Another respondent told me how he and his peers from a local boarding school in Khagrachari were taken into custody for a few nights when they were 12 years old. They were stripped naked in the middle of the night, beaten with rods and their genitals squeezed. His perpetrator is a well-known figure in current Bangladeshi politics.[29] The CHTC (1991: 43) records that on 28 December 1990, three Chakma girls aged between 12 and 18 were allegedly gang-raped by eight VDP personnel posted at the Number 10 sentry post. They were mutilated and killed along with a 10-year-old boy. The public nature of this kind of torture, killing and mutilation of bodies suggests that these counter-insurgency strategies were employed to create terror in the CHT. No legal action was taken by the state to deal with these crimes. This culture of impunity still continues today.

Kalpana Chakma's enforced disappearance is the most cited case of violence against women during the armed conflict. Just before the Awami League came to power, during the election night of June 1996, Kalpana, the organizing secretary of the CHT Hill

Women's Federation, was forcibly abducted by the army from her home in New Lallyaghona, Rangamati district, along with her two brothers, Khudiram and Kalicharan, in front of their terrified mother, Badhuni Chakma. They were blindfolded and their hands were tied. The ASK Odhikar and Amnesty International, among others, documented that the brothers were shot at, but they managed to escape. The alleged leader of the plainclothes security personnel Lieutenant Ferdous, commander of the Kojoichari army camp, was later promoted to the rank of major and posted at the Karengatoli army camp, close to New Lallyaghona. Kalpana was never found. Several investigations were carried out, including one by the Criminal Investigation Department (CID) and one by a judicial enquiry commission set up by the government, but all have so far failed to identify any named individual involved with the abduction. The three main suspects (as alleged by Kalpana's brothers), in the meantime, have never been questioned as part of any of these investigations. While there is an ongoing enquiry being carried out by the police, there has been little progress. In fact, the court order for this recent investigation specifically asks the investigation officer (I/O) to interrogate all the three suspects and names each of them. Yet, the I/O has failed to follow up on this. It is clear that the state provides impunity to perpetrators of crimes and suspects who are part of the military outfit serving in the CHT (D'Costa 2011b).

Kalpana's disappearance generated the most united response by the CHT advocacy groups for the state to take some action. However, state responses were rather muted. It is feared that she might have been killed if she had not agreed to marry Lieutenant Ferdous, the army officer who led the abduction (CHTC 1991 [1997]). There are also no provisions for monitoring any future incidents of human rights violations or for accountability regarding human rights abuses. In the absence of such attempts at justice, clarification and reconciliation, and as long as the CHT remains militarized, there is no guarantee of any genuine peace.

The Accord of Dissonance

Following the 1997 CHT Accord, signed between the Government of Bangladesh and the PCJSS, the political organization that controlled the insurgents (Shanti Bahini), a large faction of them surrendered their arms.[30] However, there were no appropriate and strategic DDR responses to their specific concerns. The accord calls, among other things, for dismantling all temporary military camps in the CHT and resolving of the land disputes caused by this transmigration programme. Today, both of these commitments are yet to be implemented. Although there have been many democratic and military-backed governments in the meantime, there has not been much change for the case of the CHT in terms of accord implementation. The CHT Accord was expected to bring freedom for the Jummas, withdraw non-permanent army camps from the region, and deal with the repatriation of the Jummas.[31] While at the time of the signing this was internationally considered as a successful case of conflict resolution, it involved no third-party mediation or direct intervention by international actors, nor was civil society involved in the peace process. These factors contributed to the weakness and also failures of the accord. While in 2007 only 35 of the 500 non-permanent army camps were withdrawn from the CHT, by December 2009 there were still around 300 military camps in the region (IDMC 2006). Deeply embedded distrust and vast power inequalities between the state (and the armed forces) and the Adivasis make it difficult to achieve peace and stability in the region (CHTC 2000; Arens and Chakma 2002; Roy 2007; Chakma 2009; Chakma 2014; Ahmed 2011; Kapaeeng Foundation 2012; Maleya Foundation 2013). Following the accord, the Indian government forcefully repatriated 65,000 Chakma refugees from Tripura. Many of the families, upon their return, found their homes occupied by Bengali settlers and their properties appropriated either by the army or the local administration. As a result they became internally displaced.

The accord made no provisions for: (*a*) proper investigation of massacres and other human rights violations of the past; (*b*) the trial and punishment of perpetrators; and (*c*) compensation for those who were affected by these human rights abuses. There were also no provisions for making publicly available the reports of the official enquiries into some of the massacres, human rights violations, disappearances and tortures, such as the official report on the 1993 Naniarchar massacre, and the report concerning the abduction and disappearance of Kalpana Chakma by the members of the Bangladeshi army.

Even after the accord was signed, the situation remains volatile in the CHT. All mainstream political parties in Bangladesh, including the ruling Awami League and the opposition BNP, and the military itself repeatedly advocate that the state has to maintain a strong military presence in the area because of the risk of transnational crime networks operating in some of the impenetrable areas; the illegal movement of people, drugs, arms and other goods on the porous borderland; and the potential armed insurgency. As a consequence, it is not only the military, but the functions of the intelligence, police and border patrol that have significantly increased over the years in the CHT.

Violent Peace: SGBV after the Signing of the Accord

In post-accord CHT, where there is no insurgency, the Bangladeshi government has continued to maintain a heavy military and paramilitary presence. The 'peace' accord stipulates the gradual dismantling and removal of all temporary military and paramilitary camps from the CHT and the retention of six military cantonments. The result of the last thirteen years of sustained campaigning for demilitarization in post-accord CHT is that 42 per cent of the makeshift security camps (235 out of 556) of the military, Bangladesh Defence Rifles and Armed Police Battalion have been withdrawn (Roy and Chakma 2010).[32] Another source claims that less than 7 per cent of the temporary military camps (thirty-five out of five hundred and fifty) have been dismantled, and a single brigade out of five was withdrawn in 2009.[33] The six cantonments in three districts of the CHT, however, are excessive in comparison to the fourteen other cantonments in the rest of the sixty-one districts of Bangladesh. Put another way, the six military cantonments in 9 per cent of the land for less than 1 per cent of the population, compared to fourteen cantonments in the remaining 91 per cent land mass for 99 per cent of the population is highly disproportionate.[34]

State terror against Adivasis in the CHT can be termed as a 'politics of demography' in which the Bangladeshi state at various points envisaged making the indigenous peoples a minority in their own land (Chakma 2010).[35] It secretly planned large-scale transmigration of Bengalis into the CHT, in conjunction with systematic measures to evict and force out the indigenous peoples from their homes and settlements (Adnan 2004: Chapter 4). It has been described as 'the manifestation of a deliberate, ruthless and cynical strategy of deploying state power to change the ethnic composition of the CHT and the distribution of its lands in favour of Bengali settlers with total disregard for the rights and interest of the Hill peoples' (ibid.: 53).[36]

The massive militarization and the transmigration programme that started on a large scale from 1976 onwards have created extreme vulnerability and poverty, and have deeply affected indigenous women and girls' safety and security in the CHT. Further, the Adivasis have long been marginalized from mainstream political and social processes of Bangladeshi society. Numerous background reports and data published by international and national indigenous advocacy and human rights organizations contain long lists of atrocities and human rights abuses committed by the Bangladeshi security forces over the past decades.[37]

The huge military presence has strained the fragile peace and led to violations of the accord. For example, Amnesty International published a report about the Mahalchari incident in 2004 titled

'Chittagong Hill Tracts: A Call for Justice at Mahalchari'. It stated: 'More than six years after the signing of the Chittagong Hill Tracts Peace Accord, the tribal inhabitants of the area continue to live in fear of attacks from Bengali settlers often carried out with the apparent connivance of army personnel.' One of the attacks took place in August 2003 in the Mahalchari area of Khagrachari district. According to the testimonies given to Amnesty International by eyewitnesses, nine women were sexually assaulted, one of whom was subjected to gang-rape; a man was killed in front of his family; a 9-month-old baby was strangled to death and the baby's grandmother was gang-raped by settlers in the presence of soldiers, and her daughter, hiding a few metres away, reportedly saw both the killing of her son and rape of her mother. There were three hundred and twelve houses alleged to have been burnt, sixty-eight houses looted and four temples ransacked. According to witnesses, the police initially refused to accept complaints from the Jummas, but filed complaints on behalf of the Bengali settlers against 4,000 Jummas of attacking the settlers, highlighting longstanding discriminatory practices in the administration of justice.[38]

There were other incidents. For example, on 12 July 2006, the army tortured and brutalized a shopkeeper in Mahalchari. Similarly, there were reports of assaults and rape of indigenous women by settlers or by army men. A woman from Marma tribe was gang-raped on 30 June 2006.[39] Also, illegal settlers from the plains attacked seven indigenous villages of Sajek Union under Baghaichari sub-district in Rangamati on 20 April 2008. During this attack, at least 500 houses were burnt down and an unknown number of women were sexually assaulted.[40] It was clear that sexual violence was used as a way to intimidate people to leave their land. The tension between Bengali settlers in the CHT and the indigenous community is clear. Women are often caught in this vicious cycle of men communicating in the language of violence against other men.

> On 3 April 2006, indigenous Jumma peoples of Saprue Karbari Para village and Noa Para village under Maischari Union of the CHT of Bangladesh were attacked by the illegal plain settlers from Nunchari and Joysen Karbari Para cluster villages who sought to forcibly occupy their lands. About 50 indigenous Jummas, out of which 11 were seriously injured. Two indigenous Jumma women were also raped.[41]

Women themselves are also part of the gendered project of nation building and incite violence against other women. The Asia Centre for Human Rights (ACHR), which monitors human rights abuses in the CHT, documents:

> In the morning of 3 April 2005, a group of Bengali settler women came to the courtyard of Mr R. Marma and began clearing land for the purpose of erecting house structures. Upon being resisted by R. Marma's wife M. Marma (35) and her daughters, the settler women retreated but only to come back shortly with their male members. Initially, about 20 Bengali settler males stood guard while their women numbering 20–25 attacked 6–7 Jumma women. The Bengali settler women beat up R. Marma's wife and his two daughters and later kidnapped both his daughters. When M. Marma tried to rescue her two daughters, the settlers caught and beat her up.[42]

Many Jumma leaders were imprisoned during the state of emergency that was declared in Bangladesh in January 2007 and during the elections in December 2008. CHT political activists alleged that during the caretaker government, the army used the state of emergency as an excuse to increase oppression in the region.[43] In December 2007, Bangladesh issued an official statement saying the allegations of continuing abuse of rights of Adivasis in the CHT were false and baseless, and that they enjoyed more privileges than other citizens (D'Costa 2010b).[44] A senior official of the Ministry of CHT Affairs was quoted in the media as saying: 'The allegation of any violence against the adibashis is totally false. We have found no evidence of it.'[45] In post-accord CHT, the Baghaihat (Sajek) and Khagrachari violence in February 2010 was a prime example that revealed endemic, widespread conflict throughout the region. It resulted in the burning of 500 buildings, most belonging to indigenous peoples and at least three deaths. The conflict broke out as a result of Bengali settlers' ambitions to take over lands that are the villages and homes of the indigenous Jummas in Baghaihat.

On 19 and 20 February 2010, during the Baghaihat (Sajek) incident, Bengali settlers attacked and burnt down over 400 houses and offices, as well as a Buddhist temple and a Baptist church. The massive arson was carried out with active help from the military and civil administration. At least two indigenous villagers, Buddhapudi Chakma, a mother of three, and Lakshmi Bijoy Chakma, a father of seven, were killed in the army firing, and four other indigenous men were reported to be missing.[46] On 23 February, the violence spread to Khagrachari district town where a demonstration against the Baghaihat violence was attacked, resulting in the burning of more houses and businesses owned by Jummas, injuring many and killing a young Bengali settler. In Khagrachari, indigenous people also burnt down Bengali settlers' houses in retaliation. There was serious tension regarding possible further attacks on indigenous peoples in Khagrachari, Rangamati district town, the major town of the CHT, and many other places in the CHT following the Baghaihat and Khagrachari incidents. Many Jummas were reported to have fled their homes.

I travelled to a remote area to interview Purnima, a young woman who was gang-raped by Bengali attackers during this time.[47] Purnima was raped, beaten and choked in a public space, in full view of other men who mocked and encouraged the attackers. She could not recall how many men had raped her. A Buddhist priest later found her and took her to the local health care facility. She was assigned a lawyer by a human rights organization; however, she seldom heard from this lawyer. There was no psychosocial counselling and no discussion of compensation. In her conversation with me, Purnima mentioned that she had recurrent nightmares and experienced severe lower abdomen pain. While human rights activists encouraged her family to file a case, they were not provided with any protection. Intimidation and harassment of the perpetrators has continued after the incident. Similar to the Tripura women who shared about their experiences of rape during armed conflict, Purnima also did not believe that she would ever see any justice.

The protracted and intense use of force by the security forces and everyday violence perpetrated by illegal Bengali settlers who act with impunity have produced a culture of violence in the CHT. The accountability measures introduced through the gender justice mechanisms could improve efforts to realize the rights of communities in the CHT, especially women's rights. As a preliminary step, these could involve considering a commission of enquiry to compile and respond to grievances and also institutional reforms. Land rights is integrated in the justice-seeking agenda of the CHT. Therefore, an open discussion of what it means to achieve economic justice would be key to peace building in the CHT as well.

The violence that ruptures everyday life in the CHT is persistent in producing and reproducing trauma for Adivasis. At least two specific kinds of violent peace in the CHT could be clearly identified. First, for the Adivasis, political and militarized violence has not ended either with the signing of the accord or with regime changes in Dhaka. The deep resentment due to various reasons, such as lack of access to justice, non-implementation of the accord provisions and continual land grabs, has permeated to various levels of Adivasi communities and is the source of periodic political violence. Consequently, not only Bengali settlers, but also Adivasis perpetrate violence in the CHT. One example of this is the curfew imposed in Khagrachari after seven houses in Golabari (an Adivasi neighbourhood) and five houses of Bengali-speaking settlers in Mollah Para and Ganj Para were set on fire in February 2010.[48]

This six-day violence claimed 3 lives and injured 70, while more than 500 houses were set on fire, over 400 of which belonged to the indigenous people. The violence displaced 3,000 Adivasi families and 500 Bengali settlers.[49]

Second, it could be argued that another consequence is the split within the Adivasis and the radicalization of some factions. The United People's Democratic Front's (UPDF) rejection of the accord and its demand for full autonomy of the CHT is well documented. In December 2009, it claimed that seven of its activists were kidnapped, allegedly by supporters of the PCJSS from Manikchhari, some 20 km from Rangamati. Media reported other clashes, for example, the death of the UPDF activist Kalapa Chakma in July and the revenge killing of two PCJSS members, the village chief (*karbari*) Anil Bikash Chakma and activist Kaya Prue Marma, in the same month.[50] The JSS claims that the UPDF intimidated its members and their families, and also harassed Chakma women and girls.

Based on filed cases and interviews, a recent report was published jointly by the CHTC and the Bangladesh Indigenous Women's Network (BIWN) (D'Costa 2014). These case studies include fourteen incidents of sexual assault and rape in Rangamati, sixteen in Khagrachari and ten in Bandarban. Ninety-seven per cent of these cases involved women and girls in extreme poverty. Except for two incidents, in all other cases the alleged perpetrators were either Bengalis—settlers, schoolteachers or staff of the forestry department—or members of the armed forces. In only nine of the total of forty incidents recorded were the perpetrators arrested. Six of the cases were settled through mutual agreements, local *shalish* and involvement of the authorities, including one where the victim's family was forced to settle upon the local army commander's intervention (Case Study 14, 2012, in D'Costa 2014). In another case, which involved army personnel, the commander termed the incident baseless and subsequently no case was filed (Case Study 18, 2012, in D'Costa 2014). In two cases, the police officer responsible for the investigation allegedly demanded bribes, and in one case, the medical staff allegedly refused to provide an accurate report without bribes. Nine of the cases explicitly mention intimidation and harassment either by the perpetrator, released on bail, or the perpetrator's family.[51]

In one case, a failure to reach any settlement resulted in the placement of a girl in a juvenile correction centre, while the perpetrator remained free. In another case, an underage girl was married off to her alleged rapist and was subjected to forced conversion. Societal and cultural interpretations of gender roles have an adverse impact on girls and result in their 'disproportionate suffering'. In yet another case of attempted rape of a 70-year-old woman, the case was not filed by the local police station. The officer-in-charge of the police station was quoted as having said that 'a woman aged 70 years cannot have an active sex drive. Therefore, this case will not be characterised as rape and the victim will be in danger' (Case Study 16, 2011, in D'Costa 2014). While not expressed clearly in all the interviews, 95 per cent of the respondents also highlighted the fear of stigmatization and rejection by the communities. As the case studies articulate, more than 60 per cent of the women and their families reported not pursuing legal avenues to prevent further embarrassment. Many preferred to suffer in silence, in addition to their personal pain and humiliation, rather than going through a formal justice process to avoid a second traumatization. Finally, these cases demonstrate long-term socio-economic implications for the women, girls and indigenous communities. Girls are prevented from going to school and married off early, and women's mobility becomes severely restricted.

GENDER JUSTICE ADVOCACY AND FEMINIST NETWORKS

The first ever National Indigenous Women's Conference of Bangladesh was held in Dhaka in early 2012 and included a total of twenty-three indigenous women's organizations from the country. Organized by the Kapaeeng Foundation and OXFAM, this conference resulted in the formation of an advocacy platform by the indigenous women rights activists and women's organizations named BIWN. A declaration on the concerns of indigenous women was also adopted in the conference, which included the following pledges:

1. Leading a united struggle against all kinds of oppression over the indigenous women in the country.
2. Strengthening networking and solidarity among indigenous women's organizations, activists and organizers.
3. Continuing movements to ensure indigenous women's participation and representation in society and the state.
4. Continuing movements to establish equal dignity and rights of indigenous women in the state, society and family life.
5. Stressing the need for raising public awareness regarding indigenous women's rights.
6. Spreading networks at the international level to communicate successfully with international rights organizations.[52]

International, regional and local/national mobilization in the past three decades, and international legal understanding and tools regarding violence against women have been clarified and sharpened. The engagement of state responsibility in terms of due diligence and/or state-condoned violence against women is an especially crucial normative element that has surfaced.

Following Ershad's resignation, civil society in Bangladesh looked to a more democratic environment and the language of rights became more explicit. Both national and indigenous human rights and women's networks have become the most outspoken and visible of those voicing their grave concerns over these developments. For more than a decade now, cultural, political and religious events have commemorated Kalpana Chakma's disappearance and demanded that the state take action against the perpetrators.

Refer to the appendix for a model of women's and human rights-based networking that reflects my observations of how women's and girls' participatory initiatives develop and grow in the CHT. While not all examples of networks may follow a similar trajectory, this model demonstrates that in the absence of state support to meaningful justice, civil society networks could involve women and girls in developing their own gender justice framework. The model has been developed based on interviews with women's rights advocates and by observing gender justice practices of various institutions in the CHT.

Women's organizations such as the Khagrapur Mahila Kalyan Samity (KMKS) and the YWCA in Khagrachari, the Ananya Kallayan Sangathon (AKS) in Bandarban, and networks such as the BIWN, through their advocacy work, highlight that even after the signing of the 'peace' accord, human rights abuses, in particular SGBV, by the law enforcement personnel and illegal Bengali settlers continue to take place regularly in the CHT with impunity. Both the KMKS and YWCA provide informal and formal advice sessions to young women on various kinds of gender-based violations. Individual women's rights activists are also often approached by families to assist in advising young women in the event of their wish to marry outside their communities, in particular to Bengali Muslims. Because of forced marriages during the armed conflict, even marriages where women have a choice are often met with hostility by indigenous communities. Women and their families rely on the local women's groups and networks to help them cope with the social, cultural and economic pressures that are associated with incidents of SGBV. As the model shows, there are a range of practical ways women help each other during crisis periods, for example, by providing informal counselling or through the provision of informal loans or other resources. Where communities lack choices in other forms of capital, social networks become central in helping individuals and households to recover from and adapt to stresses.

Another example is Moanoghar, a boarding school in Rangamati that provides education to more than 1,500 boys and girls. It also has a health clinic and vocational training facilities. Some of its former students now are well-known lawyers and political, cultural and human rights activists.[53] Moanoghar also assists children who have either been exposed to or have experienced violence, including SGBV. On 16 February 2011, the owner and the manager of the Diamond Hotel in Chittagong raped Puja, a 15-year-old Marma girl from Bandarban.[54] Puja was also forced to take drugs and watch pornography. After her case was filed, another Marma man attempted to broker a deal on behalf of the accused and settle the matter by negotiations.[55] Women's rights leaders in Bandarban intervened and supported the family to pursue the matter in court. Another indigenous women's rights activist informally approached Moanoghar to request that they provide support for Puja and enrol her into their school in Rangamati.[56] During our conversations at various times, it was clear to me that despite all the care she was given in Moanoghar, Puja was still struggling to adapt to the school since all the other students knew about her ordeal. She was also unsuccessful in passing her exams. There was no trauma counselling available to her either. In early 2014, when she went for a visit to her village located in a remote area of Bandarban, she was married off by her family. While we do not know how Puja is coping at present, Moanoghar's support through the indigenous social networks for three years after her rape demonstrates how communities rely on each other in the absence of adequate access to justice for SGBV victims, especially with regard to children. The scale of the problem, combined with the remoteness of the region and security issues means that local women activists often work on protection issues through their own networks, which are not covered by the international and national agencies.

Despite entrenched problems of SGBV in the CHT, there have been some positive developments in the justice sector. First, within the current support framework of the police reform programmes available to victims of SGBV, the government has initiated some collaborative projects between the police and a variety of service provider NGOs. One of the initiatives has included the establishment of Bangladesh's second Victim Support Centre (VSC) in Rangamati under the Bangladesh Police, inaugurated on 1 March 2012. The aim of the VSC was to develop leadership among female police officers and to improve victim support services for the people of Rangamati hill district.[57] The partnership of the police with five of Bangladesh's leading civil society organizations working in Rangamati (BLAST, BMP, Green Hill, Marie Stopes and Family Development Services and Research) has provided legal services, shelter counselling, health care and rehabilitation services.

Second, civil society collaboration, in particular between national human rights and women's rights (for example, ASK, BLAST, Nijera Kori and Naripokkho) and indigenous organizations (like the Kapaeeng Foundation, Bangladesh Indigenous Peoples Forum, BIWN and Adivashi Nari Parishad) have involved indigenous women, who in the past, especially during the armed conflict in the CHT, have found it difficult to engage in national advocacy and decision-making processes. These networks and partnerships include both senior and younger generation of women's rights advocates, those taking the lead in ensuring that the voices of indigenous women, especially of indigenous young women, are heard. The goals of these collaborative efforts bring together both indigenous and Bengali women's rights organizations and individuals from across Bangladesh to share information, identify issues that affect them and identify solutions; and engage actively with the Government of Bangladesh on policy issues as part of a better, more informed and representative dialogue between women and the government.

CONCLUSION

During different political regimes, the state's engagement with Adivasis in terms of confidence-building measures and integration in the broader Bangladeshi society have been somewhat arbitrary. It is the INGOS and NGOs that have provided key development assistance in the CHT through community development activities. However, many of their projects in the areas of health, education and microcredit are framed as 'development' projects and have deliberately left out gender justice as a key component due to government sensitivity. Human rights, especially women's rights, are perceived as an outcome that would automatically be realized if development projects in the area succeed. As such, development projects have not been entirely successful in responding to women's concerns either. Indigenous women and girls remain most vulnerable, with little or no access to employment opportunities. The Bangladeshi state has been relatively uncompromising in recognizing the rights and diversity of its population, and has consistently failed to integrate Adivasi voices in its national security policies. Also, ambiguous and inconsistent management of the CHT's development policies has failed to take account of anxieties faced by women and girls in particular. The first step towards achieving meaningful gender justice needs to be taken by initiating a comprehensive, all-inclusive and sincere dialogue between various interest groups.

APPENDIX: FRAMING INDIGENOUS WOMEN'S AND GIRLS' PARTICIPATORY INITIATIVES

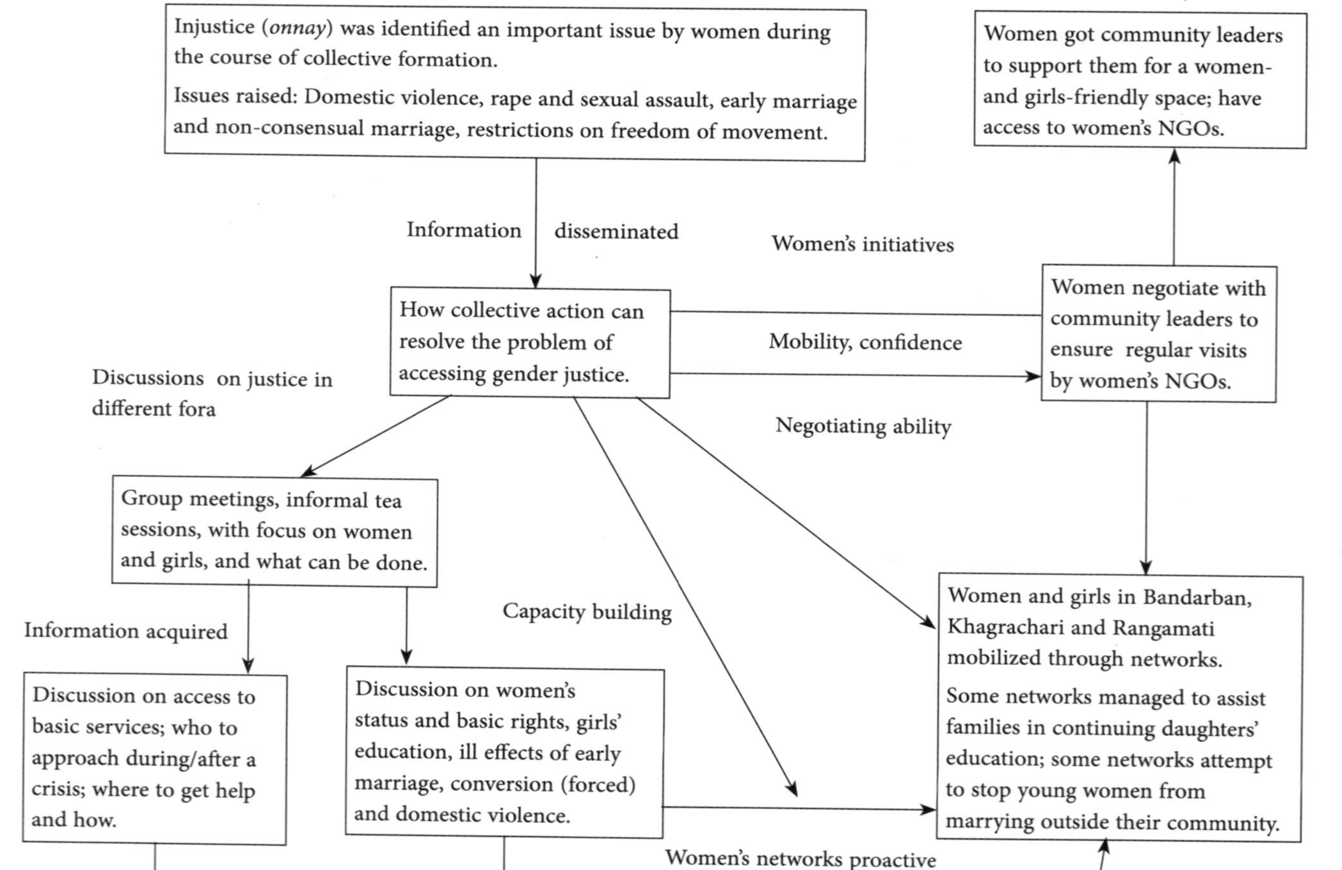

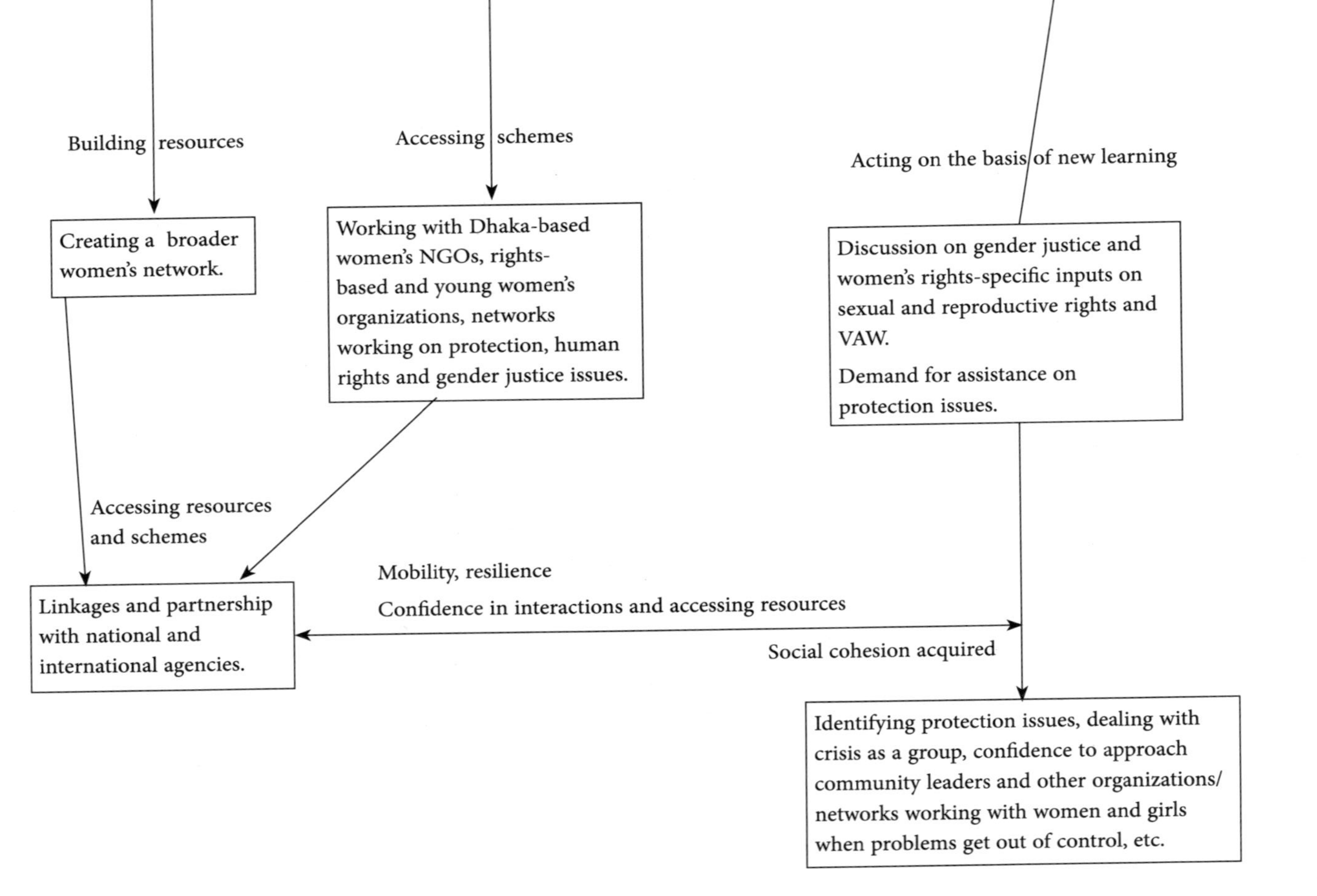
Building resources
Accessing schemes
Acting on the basis of new learning
Creating a broader women's network.
Working with Dhaka-based women's NGOs, rights-based and young women's organizations, networks working on protection, human rights and gender justice issues.
Discussion on gender justice and women's rights-specific inputs on sexual and reproductive rights and VAW.
Demand for assistance on protection issues.
Accessing resources and schemes
Mobility, resilience
Confidence in interactions and accessing resources
Linkages and partnership with national and international agencies.
Social cohesion acquired
Identifying protection issues, dealing with crisis as a group, confidence to approach community leaders and other organizations/networks working with women and girls when problems get out of control, etc.

NOTES

1. For example, in East Timor, faith-based organizations such as Caritas and World Vision, and the Catholic Church played a major role in reconciliation and peace building. However, the role of such organizations in South Asia is riddled with colonial and postcolonial grievances and identity conflicts. Therefore, most Christian organizations are careful to maintain an 'apolitical' position, at least in their rhetoric. Also, these organizations operate within the prevalent patriarchal notion of justice. In the CHT, while the imams do not lead interfaith dialogues, the monks have managed to organize a few of these involving various faith-based actors. In my interviews, however, it was clear that women's issues have never been seriously considered in these dialogues.
2. By peace politics I mean the strategic engagement with the government, especially with the security sector, development agencies and other stakeholders to advocate for peace, human rights and human security. In Sri Lanka, for example, NGOs and human rights activists point to the absence of strong political direction from the government and the recalcitrance of the Tamil Tigers (LTTE) as major obstacles to any reconciliation efforts. While the path of peace in Sri Lanka has been characterized by uncertainty, civil society groups serve as important bridges for building the trust that is essential to continue successful transitional justice negotiations.
3. Conversations with the author.
4. In *Spoiler Problems in Peace Processes*, John Stedman (1997) attempts to develop a typological theory of spoiler management and defines it as 'leaders and parties who believe the emerging peace threatens their power, world view, and interests and who use violence to undermine attempts to achieve it'. He also lists position, number, type and locus as four major problems associated with spoilers.
5. While it is difficult to verify the exact number of troops, 35,000 to 40,000 out of a total of 120,000 army personnel are deployed in the CHT. In addition, 10,000 from the BGB and another 10,000 Ansar and Armed Police Battalions (APBn) personnel are also deployed in the region. For details, see IWGIA (2012: 12).
6. Also see D'Costa (2014).

7. For a comprehensive analysis of land rights, see Roy (2000).
8. Interview with the author.
9. Also see reports on Afghanistan by Kandiyoti (2005) and Moghadam (2005).
10. See D'Costa (2011a), Sooka (2014) and the UN secretary-general's reports (2011, 2012) on Sri Lanka, especially DDR in the Manik Ferm camp.
11. Interviews carried out in Rangamati, CHT, in 2011. Names withheld for confidentiality reasons.
12. On traditional customary laws, see Devasish Roy (2005).
13. Unlike state building or peace building, nation building is usually seen as being an inherently internal process undertaken by local actors. The process of constituting a nation is something that almost by definition describes an endogenous process. For details, see D'Costa and Ford (2009).
14. Some authors have disputed the number and claimed there are thirteen groups. See, for example, Adnan and Dastidar 2011; Panday and Jamil 2009. Note that the 1991 census erroneously listed Mro and Murang as two separate groups.
15. I use the UCDP-PRIO Armed Conflict dataset codebook to classify the CHT as a low-intensity conflict zone. The codebook is available at http://www.pcr.uu.se/research/ucdp/datasets/ucdp_prio_armed_conflict_dataset/ (accessed 10 September 2015).
16. Charu Bikash Chakma was the Awami League leader from Rangamati.
17. In the 1970 elections, M.N. Larma was elected member of the East Pakistan Provincial Assembly as an independent candidate and was the only representative of the indigenous community in the first government of Bangladesh. His four demands were: (*a*) autonomy for the CHT and the establishment of a special legislative body; (*b*) the retention of the Regulation of 1900 in the new Constitution; (*c*) continuation of the offices of the tribal chiefs; and (*d*) a constitutional provision restricting the amendment of the Regulation of 1900 and imposing a ban on Bengali settlement in the CHT.
18. For details, see Chakma and D'Costa (2012).
19. For work on the human security framework, see D'Costa (2008).
20. For an overview of the dynamics of the conflict, see Arens and Chakma (2002).

21. He was the head of the Parbatya Chatoogram Jumma (CHT Jumma) Refugee Welfare Association, which the government speculated to be one of the insurgent front organizations during the armed resistance. Also interviewed by the author in 2011.
22. An estimated 1,947 members of the Shanti Bahini surrendered their weapons (Roy and Chakma 2010).
23. Open-ended interviews with the author.
24. For pre-accord reports, see, for example, Amnesty International (1986); Anti-Slavery Society (1984); CHTC (1991); Survival International (1984). For post-accord reports, see, for example, Amnesty International (2013); Jumma Net (2009); various reports by Survival International, available at http://www.survivalinternational.org/news/countries/Bangladesh (accessed 14 June 2015).
25. See Note 24. Also see CHTC (1991: 13).
26. Interview with author, Geneva, 2013.
27. For details on the CHT counter-insurgency strategies see, Bhaumik (1996); Braithwaite and D'Costa (2012).
28. Interview with author, Geneva, 2013.
29. Interview with author, Khagrachari, 2010.
30. For details on the accord, see Mohsin (2003); Roy (2007). In compliance with the accord, some 1,947 members of the JSS and Shanti Bahini surrendered in some highly publicized arms surrender ceremonies in 1998. With the exception of eleven, others received the promised BDT 50,000 (US$ 700). Sixty-two out of seventy-eight who were eligible were reinstated in their jobs, and 681 have been absorbed into the police. Members of the Shanti Bahini claimed that the money was not enough, and soon poverty and the issue of land became central to their struggle. Also, many refugees who returned from India have not received their old land back, nor received any compensation as promised. The issues relating to land rights remain unresolved and indigenous people continue to face further land-grabbing by the settler population.
31. The BNP, the opposition party, and some of the Pahari political groups such as the UPDF opposed the Accord. See Roy (2007) for details.
32. For details, see Chakma and D'Costa (2012: 142).
33. Ibid.

34. Ibid.
35. For an overview of the dynamics of the conflict, see Arens and Chakma (2002). Also see CHTC 1991 (2000).
36. For details, see Chakma and D'Costa (2012).
37. See Note 24.
38. Also see the film *Terrifying Voices: A Documentary Based on Interviews of the Victims of Attack in Mahalchari, Chittagong Hill Tracts, Bangladesh on 26 August 2003* by the Hill Watch Human Rights Front.
39. See http://www.survivalinternational.org/news/1825 (accessed 15 June 2015).
40. See http://www.achrweb.org/Review/2008/215-08.html (accessed 15 June 2015).
41. From http://www.aitpn.org/UA/BD0206.htm (accessed 2 February 2015).
42. See http://www.achrweb.org/Review/2008/215-08.html (accessed 15 June 2015). Names withheld for confidentiality reasons.
43. Interviews with the author.
44. Originally recorded in a Survival International news brief published in 2007.
45. Stated by Rowshan Ara Begum, courtesy Reuters, Sunday, 2 December 2007, http://africa.reuters.com/world/news/usnDHA31419.html (cited in D'Costa 2010b). However, during my interview with one indigenous local leader he told me how he was tortured following arrest on a false case.
46. The Baghaihat violence has been documented and condemned by national and international human rights bodies and groups, including the European Union, Amnesty International, the CHT Commission, etc. See http://www.consilium.europa.eu/uedocs/cms_Data/docs/pressdata/EN/foraff/113070.pdf; http://www.amnesty.org/en/library/info/ASA13/006/2010/en; http://www.chtcommission.org/wpcontent/uploads/2010/03/MemoToPM_Feb2010SajekAttack-_4.pdf (all accessed 16 June 2015).
47. Name, location and all other details withheld for confidentiality reasons.
48. Reported in the *Daily Star*, 24 February 2010.
49. Reported in the *Daily Star*, 25 February 2010.

50. Reported in the *Daily Star*, 23 July 2006; *Financial Express*, 27 December 2009.
51. For details, refer to D'Costa (2014).
52. For details, see http://kapaeeng.org/1st-national-indigenous-women-conference-held-in-dhaka-indigenous-women-form-a-network-aiming-at-realising-their-rights-through-united-movement/ (accessed 10 September 2015).
53. Because of its potential to act as a powerful political actor, the government has restricted international funding to Moanoghar.
54. Name changed for confidentiality reasons.
55. For details on various cases of SGBV, see D'Costa (2014).
56. I was also approached to assist to cover her education and medical expenses.
57. See the website of the Bangladesh Police Reform Programme, http://www.prp.org.bd (accessed 17 June 2015).

REFERENCES

Ackerly, Brooke and Bina D'Costa. 2008. 'Transnational Feminism and Women's Rights: Successes and Challenges of a Political Strategy', in Anne Marie Goetz (ed.), *Governing Women: Women's Political Effectiveness in Contexts of Democratization and Governance Reform*, pp. 63–86. New York: Taylor & Francis Group.

Ackerly, Brooke and Susan Moller Okin. 1999. 'Feminist Social Criticism and the International Movement for Women's Rights as Human Rights', in Ian Shapiro and Casiano Hacker-Cordòn (eds), *Democracy's Edges*, pp. 134–62. Cambridge: Cambridge University Press.

Adnan, Shapan. 2004. *Migration, Land Alienation and Ethnic Conflict: Causes of Poverty in the Chittagong Hill Tracts of Bangladesh*. Dhaka: Research and Advisory Services.

———. 2008. 'The Political Economy of Border Control and Manipulation in the Context of Ethnic Domination and Capitalist Expansion in the Chittagong Hill Tracts of Bangladesh'. Paper presented at the Social Science Research Council Border Workshop, Dubai.

Adnan, Shapan and Ranajit Dastidar. 2011. *Alienation of the Lands of Indigenous Peoples in the Chittagong Hill Tracts of Bangladesh*. Dhaka:

Chittagong Hill Tracts Commission and Copenhagen: International Work Group for Indigenous Affairs.

Ahmad, Maimuna and Muktasree Sathi Chakma. 2011. *Family Courts in the CHT: At the Intersection of Gender and Ethnic Identity*. Dhaka: Bangladesh Legal Aid and Services Trust.

Ahmed, Hana Shams. 2011. 'Multiple Forms of Discrimination Experienced by Indigenous Women from Chittagong Hill Tracts within Nationalist Framework'. Paper presented at APWLD's Consultation with the Special Rapporteur on Violence against Women, 11–12 January, Kuala Lampur.

Ali, Shaheen Sardar. 2002. 'Women's Rights, CEDAW and International Human Rights Debates Toward Empowerment?', in Jane L. Parpart, Shirin M. Rai and Kathleen Staudt (eds), *Rethinking Empowerment: Gender and Development in a Global/Local World*. New York: Routledge.

Amnesty International. 1986. *Unlawful Killings and Torture in the Chittagong Hill Tracts*. London: Amnesty International.

————. 2000. *Bangladesh: Human Rights in the Chittagong Hill Tracts*. ASA 13/001/2000. http://www.refworld.org/docid/3b83b6db9.html (accessed 17 June 2015).

————. 2004. *Chittagong Hill Tracts: A Call for Justice at Mahalchari*. ASA 13/003/2004. https://www.amnesty.org/download/Documents/.../asa130032004en.pdf (accessed 15 June 2015).

————. 2013. *Pushed to the Edge: Indigenous Rights Denied in Bangladesh's Chittagong Hill Tracts*. London: Amnesty International.

Anti-Slavery Society. 1984. *The Chittagong Hill Tracts: Militarization, Oppression and the Hill Tribes*. London: Anti-Slavery Society.

Arens, Jenneke and Chakma, Kirti Nishan. 2002. 'Bangladesh: Indigenous Struggle in the Chittagong Hill Tracts', in Monique Mekenkamp, Paul van Tongeren and Hans van de Veen (eds), *Searching for Peace in Central and South Asia: An Overview of Conflict Prevention and Peacebuilding Activities*, pp. 304–23. Boulder: Lynne Rienner.

Asian Indigenous and Tribal Peoples Network (AITPN). 1998. 'Disguise Invasion and Ethnic Cleansing'. April, Asian Indigenous and Tribal Peoples Network, New Delhi.

Bhaumik, Shubir. 1996. *Insurgent Crossfire: North-East India*. London: Lancer Publishers (second edition, 2008).

Braithwaite, John and D'Costa, Bina. 2012. 'Cascades of Violence in the

Chittagong Hill Tracts'. http://papers.ssrn.com/sol3/papers.cfm?abstract_id=2249569. Available at http://regnet.anu.edu.au/news/new-working-paper-reviews-violence-bangladesh (accessed 17 June 2015).

Butalia, Urvashi. 1998. *The Other Side of Silence: Voices from the Partition of India*. New Delhi: Penguin Books.

Chakma, Bipasha. 2013. *Justice Delayed, Justice Denied: Hill Tracts and Their Access to Justice*. Dhaka: Kapaeeng Foundation.

Chakma, Bhumitra. 2010. 'The Post-Colonial State and Minorities: Ethnocide in the Chittagong Hill Tracts, Bangladesh', *Commonwealth and Comparative Politics*, 48(3): 281–300.

Chakma, Kabita. 2011. 'The Lands of Kalindi Rani', *Himal Southasian*, July. http://old.himalmag.com/component/content/article/4531-the-lands-of-kalindi-rani.html (accessed 17 September 2015).

Chakma, Kabita and Bina D'Costa. 2012. 'Chittagong Hill Tracts: Diminishing Conflict or Violent Peace?', in Robin Jeffrey Aspinall and Anthony Regan (eds), *Diminished Conflicts in the Asia-Pacific: Why Some Subside and Others Don't*, pp. 137–52. London: Routledge.

Chakma, Mangal Kumar. 2009. *The Status of Adibashi Hill Women in Light of the CHT Accord*. Dhaka: Bangladesh Nari Pragati Sangha.

Chakma, Samari. 2014. Manikchoree Thekey Baghaichoree: Dharshak Jokhon Bangalee, Dhorshon Jokhon Jatigoto Nidhoner Rashtriyo Hatiyar' (translated in English by Irfan Chowdhury, 'When Rapists are Bengali, When Rape is a State Weapon for Ethnic Cleansing). http://alalodulal.org/2014/03/21/when-rapists-are-bengali/ (accessed 17 September 2015).

Charlesworth, Hilary and Christine Chinkin. 2000. *The Boundaries of International Law: A Feminist Analysis*. Manchester: Manchester University Press.

Chittagong Hill Tracts Commission (CHTC). 1991. *Life Is Not Ours: Land and Human Rights in the Chittagong Hill Tracts*. Dhaka: CHTC (updated 1992, 1994, 1997, 2000).

D'Costa, Bina. 2006. 'Marginalized Identity: New Frontiers of Research for IR?' in, Brooke A. Ackerly, Maria Stern and Jacqui True (eds), *Feminist Methodologies for International Relations*, pp. 129–52. New York: Cambridge University Press.

————. 2007. 'Faith based NGOs and the Politics of Secularism in Bangladesh', in Helen James (ed.), *Civil Society, Religion and Global Governance*, pp. 219–38. New York: Routledge.

———. 2008. 'Strangers within Our Borders: Human In(security) in South Asia'. Issues Paper 5, Center for International Governance and Justice, Regulatory Institutions Network.

———. 2010a. *Gender, Displacement and Transitional Justice in South Asia*. New York: International Center for Transitional Justice.

———. 2010b. 'Where the Streets Have No Name', *Daily Star*. http://archive.thedailystar.net/forum/2010/september/where.htm (accessed 10 September 2010).

———. 2011a. *Nationbuilding, Gender and War Crimes in South Asia*. London: Routledge (second edition, 2013).

———. 2011b. 'Protest, Political Terror and Personal Life', *New Age*, 6 November (special issue on the tenth anniversary of Kalpana Chakma).

———. 2014. *Marginalization and Impunity: Violence against Women and Girls in the CHT*. Dhaka: Chittagong Hill Tracts Commission and Copenhagen: International Work Group for Indigenous Affairs.

D'Costa, Bina and Jo Ford. 2009. 'Terminology Matters: Nationbuilding, Peacebuilding and Statebuilding'. Issues paper, Centre for International Governance and Justice, Canberra.

D'Costa, Bina and Katrina Lee Koo. 2013. 'The Politics of Voice: Feminist Security Studies and the Asia Pacific', *International Studies Perspectives*, 14(4): 451–54.

De Mel, Niloufer. 2001. *Women and the Nation's Narratives: Gender and Nationalism in Twentieth Century Sri Lanka*. New Delhi: Kali for Women.

Dewan, Ilira. 2011. *Jum Paharer Odhikar* (Rights of the Jumma Hills). Dhaka: Shudhyoshor.

———. 2012. 'Khomota Chorchai Pahari Narir Obosthan' (Hill Women's Positions in Practising Power), in *Unnoyon Podokhyep*, pp. 77–80. Dhaka: Steps Towards Development.

Flax, J. 1995. 'Race/Gender and the Ethics of Difference: A Reply to Okin's "Gender Inequality and Cultural Differences"', *Political Theory*, 23(3): 500–510.

Goetz, A.M. 2007, 'Gender Justice, Citizenship and Entitlements: Core Concepts, Central Debates and New Directions for Research', M. Mukhopadhyay and N. Singh (eds), *Gender Justice, Citizenship and Development*, pp. 15–57. New Delhi: Zubaan.

Guhathakurta, Meghna. 2001. 'Women's Narratives from the Chittagong

Hill Tracts', in Rita Manchanda (ed.), *Women, War and Peace in South Asia: Beyond Victimhood to Agencies*, New Delhi: Sage.

————. 2004. 'The Chittagong Hill Tracts (CHT) Accord and After: Gendered Dimensions of Peace', in *Gender Equality: Striving for Justice in an Unequal World*, pp. 1–17. Geneva: United Nations Research Institute of Social Development.

————. 2012. *Safe Home, Safe Societies: Preventing Violence against Women in the CHT*. Dhaka: UNDP.

Internal Displacement Monitoring Centre (IDMC). 2006. 'Bangladesh: Minorities Increasingly at Risk of Displacement'. http://www.internal-displacement.org/assets/publications/2006/200603-ap-bangladesh-bangladesh-minorities-increasingly-at-risk-of-displacement-country-en.pdf (accessed 17 June 2015).

International Labour Organization. 2012. 'Indigenous Women Workers: With Case Studies from Bangladesh, Nepal and the Americas'. Working Paper 1/2012. http://www.ilo.org/wcmsp5/groups/public/---dgreports/---gender/documents/publication/wcms_173293.pdf (accessed 10 September 2015).

International Work Group for Indigenous Affairs (IWGIA). 2012. *Militarization in the Chittagong Hill Tracts, Bangladesh: The Slow Demise of the Region's Indigenous Peoples*. Copenhagen: International Work Group for Indigenous Affairs, Organizing Committee CHT Campaign and Shimin Gaikou Centre. http://www.iwgia.org/iwgia_files_publications_files/0577_Igia_report_14_optimized.pdf (accessed 10 September 2015).

Jumma Net. 2009. 'Chittagong Hill Tracts White Paper'. http://www.jummanet.org/webdata/chtdoc/090509CHTWhitepaperE2.pdf (accessed 14 June 2015).

Kandiyoti, Deniz (ed). 1991. *Women, Islam and the State*. London: Macmillan.

————. 2005. 'The Politics of Gender and Reconstruction in Afghanistan'. Occassional Paper, UNRISD, Geneva. http://www.unrisd.org/80256B3C005BCCF9/(httpAuxPages)/3050BE40DA5B871CC125704400534A7A/$file/OPGP4.pdf (accessed 10 September 2015).

Kapaeeng Foundation. 2012. *Human Rights Report 2012: On Indigenous Peoples in Bangladesh*. Dhaka: Kapaeeng Foundation.

Keck, M. and K. Sikkink. 1998. *Activists beyond Borders: Advocacy Networks in International Politics*. Ithaca: Cornell University Press.

Kharat, Rajesh. 2003. 'From Internal Displacement to Refugees: The Trauma of Chakmas in Bangladesh'. Paper presented at the International Conference on IDPs, 7–8 February, Trondheim, Norway.

Khattak, Saba Gul. 2004. 'Adversarial Discourses, Analogous Objectives: Afghan Women's Control', in *Cultural Dynamics*, 6(2): 213–36.

Lutz, Catherine. 2002. 'Making War at Home in the United States: Militarization and the Current Crisis', *American Anthropologist*, 104 (3): 723–35.

Maleya Foundation. 2013. *Development, Environment and Human Rights: Situation Report of Indigenous Peoples of Bangladesh* (March 2012–June 2013). Dhaka: Maleya Foundation and Manusher Jonno Foundation.

Manchanda, Rita. 2001. *Women, War and Peace: Beyond Victimhood to Agency*. New Delhi: Sage.

Mares, David R. 2001. *Violent Peace: Militarized Interstate Bargaining in Latin America*. New York: Columbia University Press.

Menon, Ritu and Kamla Bhasin. 1998. *Borders and Boundaries: Women in India's Partition*. New Delhi: Kali for Women.

Moghadam, Valentine M. (ed). 1994. *Gender and National Identity: Women and Politics in Muslim Societies*. London: Zed Books.

————. 2005. 'Peacebuilding and Reconstruction with Women: Reflections on Afghanistan, Iraq and Palestine', *Development*, 48(3): 63–72.

Mohanty, C.T. 1991. 'Under Western Eyes: Feminist Scholarship and Colonial Discourses', in C.T. Mohanty, A. Russo and L. Lourdes Torres (eds), *Third World Women and the Politics of Feminism*. Bloomington: Indiana University Press.

————. 2003. *Feminism without Borders: Decolonizing Theory, Practicing Solidarity*. Durham, NC: Duke University Press.

Mohsin, Amena. 1997. *The Politics of Nationalism*. Dhaka: University Press Limited (new edition, 2002).

————. 2003. *The Chittagong Hill Tracts, Bangladesh: On the Difficult Road to Peace*. London: Lynne Rienner.

Nahar, Ainoon and Prashanta Tripura. 2010. 'Violence against Indigenous Women', in Naeem Mohaiemen (ed.), *Between Ashes and Hope: Chittagong Hill Tracts in the Blind Spot of Bangladesh Nationalism*. Dhaka: Drishtipat Writers' Collective.

Nussbaum, M.C. 2000. *Women and Human Development: The Capabilities*

Approach (The John Robert Seeley Lectures). Cambridge: Cambridge University Press.

Okin, S.M. 1994. 'Gender Inequality and Cultural Differences', *Political Theory*, 22(1): 5–24.

———. 2004. 'Gender, Justice and Gender: An Unfinished Debate', *Fordham Law Review*, 72(5): 1537–67.

Panday, Pranab Kumar and Ishtiaq Jamil. 2009. 'Conflict in the Chittagong Hill Tracts of Bangladesh: An Unimplemented Accord and Continued Violence', *Asian Survey*, 49(6): 1052–70.

Reilly, N. 2009. *Women's Human Rights*. Cambridge, MA: Polity Press.

Roy, Chandra. 2000. *Land Rights of the Indigenous Peoples of the Chittagong Hill Tracts, Bangladesh*. Copenhagen: International Work Group for Indigenous Affairs.

———. 2004. *Indigenous Women: A Gender Perspective*. Guovdageaidnu/Kautokeino, Norway: Gáldu Resource Center for the Rights of Indigenous Peoples.

Roy, Devasish. 2005. *Traditional Customary Laws and Indigenous Peoples in Asia*. London: Minority Rights Group International.

———. 2007. 'The Discordant Accord: Challenges in the Implementation of the Chittagong Hill Tracts Accord of 1997', in Miek Boltjes (ed.), *Implementing Negotiated Agreements: The Real Challenge to Intrastate Peace*, pp. 115–46. The Hague: T.M.C. Asser Press.

Roy, Pinaki and Shantimoy Chakma. 2010. 'Hurt Not Healed at Hills', *Daily Star*, 2 December. http://archive.thedailystar.net/newDesign/news-details.php?nid=164481 (accessed 14 June 2015).

Sieder, R. and J.A. McNeish. 2013. *Gender Justice and Legal Pluralities: Latin American and African Perspectives*. New York: Routledge.

Sooka, Yasmin. 2014. 'An Unfinished War: Torture and Sexual Violence in Sri Lanka, 2009–2014'. https://www.barhumanrights.org.uk/unfinished-war-torture-and-sexual-violence-sri-lanka-2009-2014 (accessed 10 September 2015).

Spivak, G.C. 1988. 'Can the Subaltern Speak?', in C. Nelson and L. Grossberg (eds), *Marxism and the Interpretation of Culture*. Urbana: University of Illinois Press.

Stedman, John Stephen. 1997. 'Spoiler Problems in Peace Processes', *International Security*, 22(2): 5–53.

Survival International. 1984. 'Genocide in Bangladesh', in *Survival International Annual Review*, 43: 7–28.

United Nations. 2011. *Report of the Secretary-General's Panel of Experts on Accountability in Sri Lanka*. http://www.un.org/News/dh/infocus/Sri_Lanka/POE_Report_Full.pdf (accessed 18 September 2015).

———. 2012. *Report of the Secretary-General's Internal Review Panel on United Nations Action in Sri Lanka*. http://www.un.org/News/dh/infocus/Sri_Lanka/The_Internal_Review_Panel_report_on_Sri_Lanka.pdf (accessed 18 September 2015).

INTERVIEWS, CASE STUDIES AND NARRATIVES

An Interview with Maleka Khan

Experiences of Working for Post-War Rehabilitation of Women*

QURRATUL AIN TAHMINA

(Translated by Mohammad Mahmudul Haque)

In December 1971, under the leadership of Begum Sufia Kamal, a group of women activists took the initiative to rescue and rehabilitate women survivors of violence during the Liberation War. The initiative was instant, spontaneous and private. In 1972, they established the Kendriyo Mohila Punorbashon Shongstha (Central Organization for Women's Rehabilitation, henceforth COWR or Shongstha), which was the first institutional initiative to help the women survivors of violence from the 1971 war. Maleka Khan worked there as a volunteer from the very beginning. She was appointed director from 1973 to 1976. She had also been involved in the Liberation War. Her younger brother, Lieutenant Atique, and a cousin, Lieutenant Colonel Anwar, were both killed by the Pakistani army. Maleka Khan was the secretary of the Girl Guides Association (GGA) in East Pakistan, but after listening to Bangabandhu Sheikh

---

* This interview by Maleka Khan was recorded by the journalist Qurratul Ain Tahmina on 26 November 1997. It was published in the *ASK Bulletin* in December 2009.

Mujibur Rahman's speech on 7 March 1971, she, along with Begum Badrunnesa Ahmed (former Member of Parliament), started training women in civil defence and first aid. In 1972, Maleka Khan played a significant role in Project Sonargaon (Crafts Village) that was established to rehabilitate the women.

Recalling an incident of the Liberation War, Maleka Khan said:

> It was in the middle of 1971 when I was the secretary of the GGA. In those days, we had to move constantly between city and villages. At this point, the Pakistani administration asked the GGA to organize a rally with Girl Guides in Dhaka. As the secretary, I pointed out that since no school or college was open, it would be impossible to organize such a rally. In the meantime, we came to know that a number of women had been held captive in Dhaka Cantonment and a few others in the Nakhalpara M.P. Hostel. Hearing this, we became concerned about our own security, but we got an opportunity to listen directly to the army officers. The head of the GGA was sent for by Brigadier Bashir. Since Tahera Apa [courteous form of address] did not want to go alone, she requested me to accompany her as the secretary of the association. She also took Ms Afifa Haque with her. I went to the Nakhalpara M.P. Hostel with them. My sole concern was to meet the captured women and rescue them. I wanted to know what was going on around us. Interpreting the ongoing conversations there, I got to know that 300 women were held captive inside…
>
> The Nakhalpara M.P. Hostel was almost like a brigade headquarters. There were many people in the room along with Brigadier Bashir. Some of them sat silently while the others were arguing. As we were leaving, we saw blood spattered on the floor and on the wall of one room. It seemed that blood had spurted out on to the wall. The Pakistani army officers present did not admit that there were any detained women.

In fact, Brigadier Bashir asked the GGA leaders to organize a rally with Girl Guides. The GGA leaders replied, 'Both you and

I know how impossible it is to organize a rally in the present conditions in the country.' When Brigadier Bashir repeatedly insisted that the situation of the country was very good, Afifa Haque [deputy commissioner of the GGA] protested saying that 'In a situation in which people in Dhaka can hardly come out of their houses, with everything being very uncertain and many not even knowing if their family members and relatives were alive, how can things be normal?'

Mrs Afifa even said, 'If need be, whip us, but let those women go.' From such conversations, it seems that there must have been female detainees there even if the number was below 300. Later, when I was staying in the village, a girl from Brahmanbaria told me that while she was staying with her in-laws, she peeped through her window and saw that women had been collected together in one place, and some were killed while some others were dragged away as prisoners. The military set fire to a house. My days in 1971 were spent hearing and witnessing such incidents. Where did these women go? Through the GGA, I heard about a lot of incidents of torture on women in 1971 from Khulna, Jessore, Comilla, Narsingdi, Chuwadanga, Rajshahi and Mymensingh. I still remember that a lot of people were waiting when they came out of the M.P. Hostel. Many of them complained that they could not find their relatives. One woman cried, 'Where is my son? Give me back my son.' That was such a heart-wrenching sight. I came to know from these people that many others were still held captive inside the hostel.

The Kendriyo Mohila Punorbashon Shongstha was established on 7 January 1972. But we had started working right after the independence of Bangladesh. I came to Dhaka on 18 December 1971. My younger brother had been killed and many of my relatives were missing. While searching for others, I found out that their situation was even worse. I remembered the women detained in the Nakhalpara M.P. Hostel. I wanted to know what had happened to them. I grew restless.

Then, at the very outbreak of the Liberation War, freedom fighters brought news from different corners of the country about women held captive in bunkers or houses. While searching for their own relatives, a few women came forward to help rescue other women.

Begum Sufia Kamal was one of the women, and Badrunnesa Ahmed was her chief associate. Others were Meher Kabir, Ayesha Noman, Lutfunnesa Haque, Sahera Ahmed, Hasna Hazari, Dr Halima Khatun, Sufia Shahid, Feroza Khatun, Begum Shamsun Nahar and many more. The director of the Social Welfare Department, Bazlur Majid, instructed his office staff to help Begum Sufia Kamal in every way possible. This is how, right after independence, we started the rescue and rehabilitation of women survivors of war violence.

First on the list was to find a house where the rescued women could stay. Initially, they were taken to an abandoned government house opposite Ispahani Colony. Then they came to know about a vacant house on 20 New Eskaton Road. It was the house of the former chief minister of East Pakistan, Nurul Amin. Begum Sufia Kamal, Badrunnesa Ahmed, Meher Kabir and a few others went to that house to make arrangements for the women to stay there. I went with them.

We found that a group of freedom fighters had taken shelter there and were having their meal. Begum Sufia Kamal and Meher Kabir earnestly requested them to vacate the house for the women we had rescued. The next day, we found that the freedom fighters had already left for a different destination. This happened in December.

Badrunnesa Ahmed [Badrun Apa] sent for me. After my office work at the GGA, I went to her house and found two jeeps parked outside. The Indian army was in control of the cantonment at the time. Badrun Apa asked me to carry some clothes to the jeeps, which I did. I got into one of the jeeps and the boys who had brought us information sat in the other. The women were brought

> from a house in the cantonment. This was the first such experience in my life. Four of the women were taken to an abandoned house owned by a non-Bangali close to Mogh Bazar crossing. Badrun Apa, who was waiting there, came and escorted the girls inside. Since it was quite late, she asked me to go home. I still remember that when we went to rescue the women, they appeared to be covered in dust. A few of the women had long hair, but most of them had had their hair cropped short. Most of them barely had any clothes on. It was a terrible sight. We quickly put some clothes on them, or rather draped them, and helped them get into the jeep. We had instructions to take them to a house in New Eskaton Road. I do not know what Badrun Apa did next for their treatment. My job was just to drop them off. We rescued women from five or six different places for the next couple of days. Some of the girls were rescued and kept in the bunker in the Nakhalpara M.P. Hostel. I brought them from there as well. I was asked not to discuss their activities with anyone, be it somebody from my family or any others, lest people panicked.
>
> Afterwards, the government allotted two houses to the COWR at 88 New Eskaton Road and 20 New Eskaton Road. The histories of these girls were recorded upon admission.

I asked Maleka Khan about the women's reactions right after being rescued. She said:

> The girls and I were all speechless. In fact, there was nothing to say. Even when I spoke, I could barely think of an intelligent response. It occurred to me that this could have happened to me, to my sister or someone I knew. This realization scares me even today.
>
> Many people had been involved in giving information or rescuing the women. Local residents, political workers, government and non-governmental personnel voluntarily informed us of the whereabouts of the rape survivors so that we could rescue

> them. Rajshahi's Sultana Zaman, school inspector Umme Ayesha Choudhury, Siria Apa of Moulvi Bazar, Protima Di [older sister/ courteous form of address] of Chandpur [and] Noorjahan of Brahmanbaria helped us in different ways, including by informing us about those women. These women could give us more detailed information.

Maleka Khan also told us of Noorjahan of Brahmanbaria who spoke Urdu:

> During the war, she had provided me with a lot of information. I remember how Noorjahan had planned to save the villagers from the army. Today no one knows where she is.
>
> Many people helped these women of their own accord, they tried to comfort them when they were brought to the organization. Poet Golam Mostafa's daughter Feroza Khatun, Mrs Ayesha Noman [and] Momtaz helped them. Hazera Khatun acted as the first matron in the home. She stayed with the women at night. The rescue mission lasted a year or more. Women from different regions came. Not all the women were pregnant. Some were single mothers, while some were already married and expecting. There were women of different ages. The younger ones faced the greatest challenge. The Pakistani army was least bothered about their ages. Many of them had lost their memory. However, during that time, I experienced some rare instances of humanity. Those who had been unaware of their children's whereabouts and got to know that they were here, came to find them and take them home with them.
>
> These women have sacrificed [a great deal] for the sake of our independence. This is why they are also freedom fighters. But we have to be careful while approaching them. I have noticed that people are now hell-bent on knowing the identities of these unfortunate women and their whereabouts. It is possible that if we ask them to tell us of the incidents of rape of other women in the war, they may refer to their own experiences and

eventually open up. Asking them directly will cause them more pain. Besides, no one has shown a speck of interest about their suffering till now. Such inhuman negligence has been the reason behind their deep, silent grudge. We need to remember this before approaching them. I have myself read the case histories of almost 5,000 women.

Later, the government established the Nari Punorbashon Board (Women's Rehabilitation Board, hereafter WRB) and took on the work of rehabilitation. The duties of the CWR included giving vocational training to women to enable them to become economically self-reliant by providing them with jobs. Their families were given an allowance and their children were enrolled in schools. A training centre was also established on the ground floor of Kormojibi Mohila Hostel (Hostel for Working Women) by the WRB. After two years the government converted this organization into the Nari Kalyan o Punorbashon Foundation (Women Welfare and Rehabilitation Foundation, hereafter WWRF). During General Ershad's military rule, the WWRF was shut down by the government and a Mohila Bishoyok Odhidoptor (Directorate of Women's Affairs, hereafter MWA) was established. It was located in the same building as the WWRF. This is how the initiatives and efforts for the welfare and rehabilitation of women stopped after 1975. Fatema Salam was the last chairperson of the WWRF and I was a board member. The COWR remains a private organization. However, its activities in the districts merged with the WWRF.

Around the end of 1972, we took a decision to set up a crafts village in Sonargaon to rehabilitate the women survivors. The plan was to train them in crafts and to set up a home in the village. Rädda Barnen, a Norwegian agency, expressed its willingness to give financial support; they provided some funds. However, in 1975, with the political change, all these plans ceased. Later on, since there was no hope for the crafts village plan to materialize, I decided to resign from the organization.

We asked Maleka Khan about the steps taken by the Shongstha for the women:

> First they had to be treated as most of them had become emotionally disturbed; some had lost their families. There were women who were in such a helpless state that they didn't even know what they should do from day to day. Some were comparatively normal and they thought about themselves. Schooling facilities were provided according to the age of the women and pregnant mothers were provided with health care facilities. Those who were older were trained in handicrafts. For example, women received training in things like sewing, cooking and grinding spices, so that they could use these skills to earn a living for themselves. The pregnant women and mothers of war babies faced the greatest challenge. People were not willing to adopt children then as they do now. Two ordinances were enacted to resolve their problems. The first was to facilitate adoption and the second to legalize abortion as menstrual regulation. I don't quite remember the exact number of babies who were adopted. There was a separate agency dealing with adoptions. I remember a few foreign doctors who came to assist with abortions. I remember Dr Geoffrey Davis, an Australian surgeon who came to Bangladesh immediately after the war.
>
> We tried to contact their families. Those who had no clue about the whereabouts of their daughters rushed to see them. They cared for nothing else but their children or relatives' well-being. What they wanted was to be reunited with their dear ones. We found this to be true mostly for the educated middle-class families. On the other hand, some of the families could not be traced, while some never took [the girls] back. This was mainly among families who were insolvent or those who lived in villages. Probably their neighbours had heard about their daughters being taken away by the Pakistani army. In such cases, their parents

> thought it wise to leave their daughters in the COWR. They would visit them from time to time.

To a question about how these women reacted when their families visited them, Maleka Khan replied:

> Naturally, they wanted to return home. Seeing their fathers, they would start to cry. The fathers at times would say, 'Not now, we will take you back later.' This would happen due to a difference in perception between the father and his daughter about the problem. Seeing their fathers, many of the women would want to return with them. The fathers, educated or illiterate, considered the social, financial [and] psychological aftermath of taking their children with them, whereas the women did not. All the women naturally wanted to be back in their own homes. Nobody said, 'No we won't leave. We are happy here.' However, when their fathers did not take them even after three or four years, the women realized that their families would not take them back ever. They decided to acquire vocational skills so that they could work…
>
> Most of the women whose parents refused to take them back were from a lower-middle-class background, a few from the middle class. Almost 90 per cent of them returned to their families. Those who were left behind were provided with jobs and married off by the COWR. There were also incidences of families who would not want to take back their daughters immediately to allow them some time to regain their health and learn to work. Some of them never returned. The staff and members of the organization themselves took initiatives to provide such women with jobs. I remember escorting eight women to the Red Cross to apply for the position of attendants. With the help of freedom fighter Gazi Golam Dastagir, they got jobs without much difficulty.

How were they accepted back into society?

> They themselves found a place in society. They befriended the people they used to work for. Eventually, these women got married and started their own families. No one has questioned them about their experiences until now. If they were to be asked today, many may take it positively, but many others may not.

Maleka Khan also told us of instances in which these women had been married to educated men in our society:

> The men or their families might not accept [the women's] past. Therefore, there is no point in raising the past for no good reason. We need to take into account that our questions might be the reason for the woman to lose her shelter/refuge.
>
> Because of my involvement with the Shongstha, I came across different kinds of women. One of the girls' father even filed a case in Kishorgonj. The local administration was also ready to help them, but they lacked witnesses. I remember that one girl agreed to give her child up for adoption, but cried her heart out when everything was finalized. There are instances of husbands taking back their wives as well. Much later, I met a woman who had gone back to her husband from the Shongstha. The woman did not want to meet me again as it would bring back painful memories. She begged me not to tell anyone about her. I heard from the matron that a few women would walk around all night. Even when they slept, they would sob in their sleep. The doctors used to treat them for their insomnia and that helped them gradually ease their painful memories. Many of them started a family life and became busy in their households. However, could they really forget everything?
>
> One woman was acutely traumatized temporarily. But she married a man who truly loved her and this had helped her recover. Instances like this are not rare. The men accepted the women and married them with the help of the Shongstha.
>
> In 1986, I contacted a woman who was married in 1974 with

the help of the Shongstha. I found that she was married with two children. I did not contact her again lest it embarrass her.

There were also incidences of unhappy marriages. I knew a girl whose husband found out after their marriage that she had been raped by the Pakistani army. He asked why she had never told him the truth. She had replied, 'I wanted you to be a part of my sad story, but you didn't want to listen. You said the only thing that mattered to you was that I was your wife.' Later I found out that she had committed suicide.

Some of the women who were rehabilitated by the Shongstha kept in touch with me. Did the past still haunt them? I cited the example of three Korean Comfort women demanding a trial of the Japanese soldiers to two of our women and told them how unfortunate we were to be born in a country where we couldn't even demand a trial. If all of you together demand [it], it would be possible to bring the war criminals to trial. To this, they asked, 'Why did we not fight for a trial on behalf of the victims?' My reply to this was, 'What if after demanding a trial, I find myself all alone?' But the women agreed that it was high time Pakistan apologized and the war criminals were tried for their atrocities.

I remember the story of a woman who was a government official and married with two children. She gave my daughter gold earrings on the day of her wedding. One day, she showed up at my doorstep unannounced. When I asked her about her present situation, she said that she remembered something from her past and was in need of a shoulder to cry on. I could not talk to her that day. However, my daughter attended to her; she cried for a while, self-absorbed. The woman had a low-level government job. She liked one of her colleagues and finally married him. However, she did not tell him anything about her past. She said, 'How do you even talk about these things? How many men are generous?' Most of the rape survivors in the Shongstha were not well educated, but over time they found paid work and settled down.

I wanted to know from Maleka Khan if the women remained in contact with each other.

> The women did keep contact with each other and they updated me about each other. Once the Shongstha decided that we should invite the women to our homes from time to time and make them a part of our family. Our older colleagues said that this would ensure that they would always have a place to come to. For example, one woman brought her husband to my home and introduced me as her aunt. I welcomed them warmly, and made her husband feel that his wife was not alone and helpless.

I asked Maleka Khan if their past affected their position in their workplaces.

> The heads of all the organizations where the women were employed between 1972 and 1976 were told of their background and were requested to be sympathetic. Their colleagues were quite sympathetic towards them learning that they had lost everything during the war. The women were grateful to the Shongstha and to its members as we not only looked after them, but also provided them with jobs. They used to say, 'Well, we were not related to them, yet they were concerned with us.' They used to bring their office colleagues with them so we became friendly with their colleagues as well.

When it comes to a trial of the war criminals, at least one of these women have to step forward, will she?

> I think they will only come forward when they see that they have nothing much left to live for. Until then I don't think anyone will voluntarily ask for justice as the situation is not in their favour. When the situation is such that they will be treated with respect, when they do not have to feel ashamed of presenting themselves as freedom fighters, they will surely come forward. I know it because I have seen them holding a silent grudge against the hostility of

society. If they become aware that these were war crimes, they might come forward to seek justice against war crimes, but till then it is our responsibility to demand justice on their behalf.

Will they feel embarrassed today if their children find out about their past?

Maybe they will. One of them is working really hard to send her child to school. She brought her child to me. I advised the child to always respect his mother. A child who does not respect his mother never stands first. Before leaving, the child's mother said, 'I am helpless, but my child is not. He has his parents.' I felt very pleased. Though I tried to console her, it was she who explained things to me instead.

In 1976, before Maleka Khan left her job, she preserved all the files with the case histories with great care in the office. However, those files are no longer there today.

That same year, 1976, a new working committee was formed. In fact, it was changed without Begum Sufia Kamal being told about it, so she opted out of it. The plan for establishing a craft village in Sonargaon was also forgotten. After she left the Shongstha, Maleka Khan became involved with the production and development of handicrafts and created employment opportunities for women whose lives had been ruined by the war.

In 1986, the Shongstha had to leave the house in 20 New Eskaton Road because it was returned to the relatives of Nurul Amin. I also heard that all the files containing case histories of the women had been destroyed at the time. The next chairperson of the organization, Shamsun Nahar Begum, said that there was no alternative to destroying these documents lest it harm the women. No one realized the importance of preserving those documents. What an irrevocable pain!

An elderly lady lives in the Shongstha's hostel. She gets annoyed

> if anyone asks her anything. Often, she complains, 'You know, apa, many a time, people come and ask me what happened to me during the war. I get very irritated. Young people of my grandchildren's age ask me questions like what happened to me and how long I have been here. I don't like it at all.'

I asked Maleka Khan if the rape survivors have been really rehabilitated after all these years.

> That's difficult to say. The families of the martyrs of 1971 are yet to get due respect from many in society. Many people do not even know about their sacrifices. In a situation like this, it is really difficult to answer how these people, whom once I regularly met and worked with, got their due recognition and established themselves in society. However, I can tell you that many of them were relieved thinking that at least they did not have to commit suicide like others. Since they are still alive, I think there is time to pay homage to them.

If Pakistan gave a general apology, will it make them happy or would they be indifferent?

> The women still cry and say that it is not possible to forget those days. Those who are comparatively more conscious accuse us of not following up with the trial of war criminals. One said that her younger brother had been killed in her own house. As a matter of fact, these women are still traumatized. They are struggling to fight social oppression by raising their children and earning a living. They are neither in a position to revisit their past nor to think anew about anything. I think it is our job, not theirs.

However, if we can accomplish this task, will it be of any comfort to them or will it do any good to society?

> I am not sure about social good since I don't know how we define humanity for ourselves, but yes, there will be a change in their

mental condition. They keep saying that we could not do much about bringing them justice. On a more personal note, I can tell you that in 1971, the people who launched a barbarous attack on the Bangalis and committed genocide, looted their possessions, destroyed their assets will be brought to trial today or tomorrow. But there were other considerations. We want to ensure our daily supply of food first before we think of anything else. At present, our war is against hunger; we are fighting for our survival. I cannot say anything individually on behalf of the people who were tortured in 1971. However, I am sure that they will find mental peace when they hear that Pakistan has apologized to Bangladesh for their barbarity in 1971 and the war criminals are put on trial. This will give them mental peace, it definitely will to my mother.

MALEKA KHAN is an educationist and social worker. In 1971, she was secretary of the Girl Guides Association. She joined the COWR as director and continued there until 1975. She has also been actively engaged in the development of crafts in Bangladesh. She is a member of Banglacraft, a craft marketing and development organization.

An Interview with Nilima Ibrahim

Liberation War in 1971 and the Women Rehabilitation Foundation*

SURAIYA BEGUM

(Translated by Mohammad Mahmudul Haque)

Between 1996 and 1999, the ASK, in its Oral History Project of the Liberation War, documented the experiences of women survivors as evidence of war crimes committed by the Pakistani army and their local accomplices in 1971. The narratives of nineteen women were selected for publication in *Narir Ekattor o Juddhoporoborti Kothhokahini* (Women's '71: Post-War Voices/Stories) in 2001.

In addition to these oral histories, ASK's researchers interviewed several people who had actively helped and supported women survivors of rape, and women in refugee camps and in rehabilitation homes.

Suraiya Begum: Apa, I have heard that you had tried to build a resistance within the country in 1971. Nawshaba Apa [Nawshaba Sharafi] told us that you started to collect clothes for the Mukti Bahini. Could you please tell me more about it?

---

* Nilima Ibrahim's interview taken by Suraiya Begum was first published in the *ASK Bulletin* in September 2009.

Dr Nilima Ibrahim: I was not quite professionally connected with Nawshaba. I left Dhaka and moved to the interior of the country to build resistance. I had direct contact with the *mukti*s (freedom fighters). I used to receive written requests from them [saying], 'We are dying in winter. Please send us fifty cardigans, black in colour.' Then I had to look for the wool to buy and contact the people who would knit cardigans with that wool, and finally I sent those cardigans to the *mukti*s. Many of the *mukti*s were quite daring and would risk coming to Dhaka. They used to meet me.

SB: Was there any resistance by women at that time? By 'resistance', we actually mean different forms of it.

NI: Hm… resistance by women… well, I had a daughter and so did Nawshaba, and our daughters, in fact, connected us and used to work on our behalf. Both of them used to wear shalwar kameez and speak fluent Urdu and English, which is why the Pakistani soldiers never suspected their Bengali identity. They were not only available for delivering messages, but also for myriad other tasks. Both of them were expert drivers even at that age so there was no problem. My husband and I were in a village, while my daughter's husband had left for Kolkata. However, the kids were with me. The first thing that we did in our village was to establish something similar to a recruiting centre. People used to go to the front and the border was not very far from there. Many a time, we heard that people had been killed, and we used to always send clothes for their children. But my key role was in Dhaka University. During those days, I was constantly followed. At night, the *mukti*s used to stay at my place. I had to make arrangements for at least one meal for them. They used to sleep on this carpet, spreading a sheet on it, with a cushion under their heads.

SB: Were you here at this house [the apartment at Shegun Bagicha where the interview was conducted] then?

NI: No, I used to stay at the university area adjacent to Iqbal Hall.

The *muktis* would stay at Professor Rafiqul Islam's and mine; the commoners were scared of them. Eventually, I got deeply involved with them [the *muktis*]. Tikka Khan issued me a written warning, which is on display at the National Museum now. During those days, from time to time, I used to visit Dhaka on business and then leave again. But the problem was, I could not conduct bank transactions lest they trace me. However, at this point, All India Radio announced that I had been killed. This certainly gave me an edge in this situation, so I was safe for quite a few days. Though I had to wear a burqa, I could move around freely. Then somehow they came to know that I was still alive.

SB: Maybe somebody informed them.

NI: Oh yeah, there were plenty who could do so. One day, Dr Ibrahim called on me with some information from somebody from the Pakistani army. The person was from Allahabad who had once been in the British army with Ibrahim. I had no idea about their meeting; if I had had, I would have never allowed him to go meet him. Ibrahim said, 'He is my old friend, a good fellow from Allahabad.' They said to Dr Ibrahim, 'See, we had fifty-one queries about your wife from different foreign countries. You have to at least give them an answer. We have news that she has survived and is alive.' When the situation of the country turned serious, the guy from Allahabad said to Dr Ibrahim, 'Ask her to come to Dhaka. If she is to die, she should die here. We never know how the army would harass her in an unknown place. At least, we have control over here.' I came to Dhaka at the end of August. At that time, it was quite normal to hear sounds of bombs or crackers. They had already arrested Rafique, while Muniruzzaman had fled. I was left with Anwar Pasha, Munir Choudhury and others.[1] We had nothing to do but chit-chat idly all day long.

SB: When you were out of Dhaka, did you see any resistance by women?

NI: I have seen the unthinkable sacrifices made by women in resisting the military. They used to feed anyone passing by who was heading for India, and also nurse the wounded and sick EPR [East Pakistan Rifles] soldiers lying around. They used to swathe them in clothes so that they could not be identified.

SB: In which area did you see this?

NI: I was in a village called Adiyabad in Narsingdi. The village was quite far from Narsingdi town and to be reached by river. The EPRs were there to provide with all kinds of resistance.

SB: Is it possible to reach the Indian border from Narsingdi?

NI: Yes. They had to manage anyhow. With all modes of transport suspended, they had to walk.

SB: When exactly was this? Was it when Dhaka was raging after 25 March?

NI: Many people managed to flee by launch without much trouble. Those returning to our area as *beer muktijoddha* [valiant freedom fighters] were political people. They left and returned without much hardship. On the other hand, an ordinary woman came to me with her fourteen-year-old son saying, 'Enlist him. He will be killed by the Pakistani army anyway. Let him sacrifice his life for his country.' If this is not an act of glory, and this woman not a freedom fighter, then what and who is?

SB: That is exactly what we have been looking for.

NI: I have written before that so many male freedom fighters were given different titles like '*beer bikram*' [valiant hero], '*beer sreshtho*' [most valiant hero], '*beer pratik*' [idol of courage], whereas the female fighters were summarily dubbed as '*birangona*' [brave women], which later people changed into *barangona* [prostitute].[2] So, does that mean that our women, like our mothers, wives and daughters, made no significant contribution to the war of independence in any way?

SB: Of course, they did.

NI: There was no such assessment. I wrote about Begum Fazilatunnesa Mujib [Sheikh Mujibur Rahman's wife]. In my opinion, she is the greatest freedom fighter of Bangladesh.

SB: Her sacrifice lasted her lifetime.

NI: You would not have had Sheikh Mujib without her. When Sheikh Mujib was arrested in 1971, Sheikh Kamal and Sheikh Jamal had already left, and Hasina [Mujib's daughter] was expecting at any moment. Her labour pains started, and she was taken to a hospital. The military did not let [her mother] join her daughter in the hospital, saying, 'You are no doctor. You should not go.' The family had barely any food to eat. They could at best have a meal a day or none at all. While the soldiers on duty used to eat in front of them, five-year-old Russel would stare at them. Mrs Mujib said later, 'The next morning, a pot of tea and some toast, biscuits came from a house across the street; maybe they took pity on us.' This is how she was tortured. Besides, Hasina's paternal grandparents were ill and kept in a room in Dhaka PG Hospital. Their houses back in their home district had been set on fire, which left them in a state of shock. Begum Mujib used to call on her in-laws at PG [Hospital] and exchange slips with the *mukti*s there. She was an iron lady. But none of them even mentions her. They mourn over Bangabandhu's [Sheikh Mujibur Rahman] death on 15 August, but what about her? Didn't she make any contribution?

SB: Let me change the topic. How were you involved with the Nari Punorbashon Kendro [Women's Rehabilitation Foundation, hereafter NPK] that was established either right after 16 December 1971 or at the beginning of 1972?

NI: I was involved formally. The NPK was set up by then PM Sheikh Mujib, and Justice K.M. Sobhan was made the chairman of it. Basanti Guhathakurata, Momtaj Begum, MP and I became members of it. The NPK's contribution was remarkable.

SB: How was it structured?

NI: It was structured simply in response to needs. Bangabandhu himself supervised it. Upon his return, as soon as the women came to know about such a service, they started pouring in.

SB: When did it start?

NI: Upon Bangabandhu's return, if not in January, sometime around the first week of February. Women started flooding the centre at that time. Before that, many committed suicide, while many others fled the country, etcetera.

SB: What do you mean by fleeing the country? Where did they go?

NI: I mean they fell prey to human trafficking. During that time, the traffickers were very active; they sold those poor women to every possible country.

SB: Thirty to forty women left the country with the Pakistani army. Did they leave before the formation of the NPK?

NI: I can't give you the exact date, but yes, it was before the formation of the NPK. On his return, Bangabandhu issued an order to send back the prisoners. As he let the war prisoners leave for India, I came to know that thirty to forty women were accompanying the prisoners.

SB: Did you write about this in detail anywhere?

NI: No, I did not. There was no way I could write the names and still I can't. If I do so, those poor women will be doomed. That is why I did not use any real names in *Ami Birangona Bolchi* [the title of Nilima Ibrahim's book, translated as 'I am a Birangona Speaking', published in 1998].

SB: You are absolutely right. But did those women leave forever or return afterwards?

NI: I know about one person who returned, but don't know about the rest. On the day the women left, I took Nawshaba and Sharifa Khatun from the Department of Education at the University of Dhaka there with me. At first, I went to an officer called Brigadier Asok Vora of the Indian High Commission. I asked him whether our women were really leaving. When he replied in the affirmative, I asked him how I could meet them. He said that it was not in their hands, but in the hands of the Bangladeshi army. I met them and they asked me to meet them the following day at ten. They said that they would arrange the meeting. When I went there to interview those women, I visited the torture chambers. It was nothing but horror. I saw swirled ropes in those small chambers.

SB: Was that in Dhaka Cantonment?

NI: Yes, it was. I enquired what the ropes were for. An Indian sentry shook one of the ropes. It was covered with a whole lot of giant flies. The women who were tortured said that they had been beaten [till they bled] and the blood had soaked into the ropes. Flies sat on those ropes. It was unthinkably gruesome. It was impossible for me to stay normal. When I made an attempt to talk to those women, they started interrogating us instead. I would like to ask the men of this country why they fled leaving those women behind, yet did not spare them from being punished. One day a major brought a sari to the NPK for his wife. I asked him why he had brought the sari instead of taking his wife with him. He replied that it was not possible for him to do so as his sister was getting married. I told him that his wife was also somebody's sister. With a suave reply, he had left, to never return. I saw fathers who came and took their daughters with them, but those who could not cried. The big brothers never came while the young ones did. However, the latter were very much aware of their social status. Except for these, no other relatives came to see these women.

SB: Let us get back to our previous topic, the policy of the NPK. Could you tell me more about it?

NI: The first policy was medical treatment, that is, abortion. A foetus up to four months could be aborted. There were two Polish doctors who performed as many abortions as they could.

SB: Do you remember the names of the Polish doctors?

NI: I do not, but we met every day.

SB: Did you have to visit the foundation regularly?

NI: Basanti Guhothakurata and I used to visit regularly. However, Basanti would stay longer, while I could not because of my job, university, Bangla Academy, etcetera. Still, I used to go every day.

SB: Apart from medical treatment and abortion, what else was in the policy?

NI: Another was to make a decision about what to do with the war children. This was a major problem.

SB: What was the decision made?

NI: The decision was we would put up the war children for adoption if any foreign country showed interest.

SB: Wasn't there anyone within the country interested in adopting these children?

NI: There was no state policy about this. Bangabandhu made this rule that anybody willing to adopt a child could get one.

SB: What if a mother did not want to give up her child?

NI: Comparatively older moms did not want to keep their children as they realized that they had no place to go with them. But the teenage first-timers became very emotional and wanted to keep their babies. I believe most of the children are in Canada and in different Scandinavian countries.

SB: Can you give me a rough idea how many children the NPK gave up for adoption? Is there any documentation about the number?

NI: I don't know. All the documents should be preserved, but we don't have access to those any more. I'm not sure, but the Mohila Odhidoptor [Department of Women's Affairs] may have the documents. There should be a record of nurses from various countries coming to adopt the children. They would see the children and then decide which ones to take.

SB: Who were in charge of making policies about abortion, medical treatment, adoption, etcetera?

NI: It was our PM's decision. We were facing so many problems at the same time that we were not in a position to make decisions. So it was only Bangabandhu who had to make decisions.

SB: What kinds of problems did you face?

NI: The local religious leaders protested against adoption, arguing that the adopting parents would turn those children into Christians. I went to Bangabandhu, and he said that he only believed in humanity—a human child should be raised as nothing but a human and he or she can choose his or her religion later.

SB: Indeed. The right to live should be the principal concern.

NI: Right. Bangabandhu also took other initiatives, but this chapter was closed after 1975. He also wanted these women to become literate so that they could find decent jobs. The foundation used to offer typing and sewing courses. A few women got jobs. One day I went to the Red Cross Building and saw a lot of people standing there. I asked why they were standing there. They said that they came to see the *birangona*s. The result was many of those unfortunate girls never wanted to get back to work. Another decision was made that the illiterate women would be married off. So far as I remember, ten of them were given BDT 10,000 each, and Begum Mujib provided them with sewing machines and other household articles. But some took money that was offered for marriage with a *birangona* but they did not take the wife.

SB: We also heard that there were many who took money and dowry to get married.

NI: Mrs Mujib left no stone unturned. Nobody helped her with this. Even I did not see any women leaders. I saw Nurjahan Murshed once or twice, and also saw Momtaz Begum, an MP. I don't remember anybody else.

SB: I'd like to know more about the NPK. Who ran the organization?

NI: One of the directors was Justice Sobhan. There was a general secretary and a nurse.

SB: We have heard that the foundation wrote down the case history of every woman who went there along with their name and address. But when these women were given the title of '*birangona*', society reacted against it so vehemently that the staff at the foundation decided to destroy them.

NI: Not true. If any such thing had happened, I would have definitely heard about it since I had also been involved with this foundation. These stories were all made up. It is very difficult to write the actual history as people often make up false stories. You always have to dig out the truth. It is, however, true that the title *birangona* was given after Bangabandhu's return. The truth was nobody actually cared for the *birangonas*. Their own relatives refused to accommodate them, let alone society at large. Those who said that these documents were destroyed had managed to get a job at the NPK and were protecting their own interests. Every woman had a case history.

SB: If that is true, where are those documents now?

NI: Only those who say these documents were burnt know where they are. For example many used to say there were no documents on the assassination of Bangabandhu as everything had been destroyed. But now all those documents are available. Similarly, the case histories of those women were not destroyed either. I am sure they are somewhere.

SB: Was there any particular rule for giving appointments at the NPK?

NI: There was no rule per se. Like when I was appointed as the DG of Bangla Academy, only a government letter was issued. And that's it. There was no interview or anything of that sort. Similarly, only a structure was formed for the NPK. As Justice Sobhan agreed, he was made the president. There were also a few members.

SB: When it came to making decisions, were all of you part of the process?

NI: Well, honestly speaking, before making any decision, Justice Sobhan used to inform Bangabandhu. Once Bangabandhu okayed it, the decision would get finalized. As a joint effort, a poultry farm was established in Mirpur and it is still there. The women used to work there. To keep them busy with something, they were also taught shorthand and typing. As a matter of fact, the ultimate motto was to create opportunities for the women to earn money so that they could establish themselves in society.

SB: Did you keep a personal record of how many women came and how many left the centre, or, say, how many had an abortion?

NI: Not quite. However, I wrote down the interesting cases in my diary. But records were there as there was a secretary responsible for official record keeping.

SB: Were there any follow-ups made on the women who had left the centre?

NI: So far as I know, there was no such follow-up. Some died, some moved to brothels, and some settled down in Tan Bazar in Narayanganj.

SB: Is it a fact that they had moved to pros quarters or is it just conjecture?

NI: Well, I cannot produce any document in support of it. But I heard people saying that they had found a place. As I was involved with the overall national policies and politics, I never directly worked with these women and didn't actually have enough time to go over all the details of those women. As I was a woman, the PM really wanted me to work for these unfortunate women. Some of these women fell prey to the traffickers and were sent abroad to countries like India, Pakistan and to the Middle East. Many of them were promised marriages, good jobs, etcetera.

SB: I heard that some of them moved to Tan Bazar while some others to the brothels of the English Road.

NI: Those who are in Tan Bazar must be 60-plus now. They were lost forever, but you may find them if you search really hard. Once, Ayesha [chairperson of the Mohila Porishad] with a few of her colleagues tried to conduct a study on those women. I am not sure if it was ever completed.

SB: Did any of those women keep in touch with you or the organization?

NI: Not with me, but they went to Bangabandhu. He was always available for them, and used to say to them, 'You guys are my ma.' He always helped them in their need, though I am not sure how many of them actually took help from him. In fact, after his death, I withdrew from everything. We used to be obsessed by the thought of being arrested or tortured. This is why I could not update myself on matters of the women's rehabilitation.

SB: Didn't you ever want to contact any of these women? Did you have their contact information?

NI: Even if I had had their contact info, I would not have [contacted them]. In fact, I had the contact information for a few of them, but I was not in a position to go look for them. I was quite busy trying to save my own family.

SB: Later, were you curious about how those women were doing?

NI: Personally, I was very much interested to do a follow-up on their lives. I found out that some of them were living abroad, while some others were here in the country.

SB: Yes, I read about some of them in your book, *Ami Birangona Bolchi*.

NI: The ones I mentioned in my book are well settled abroad. It is not that the women who stayed back here were not settled, but most of them got lost. Those who were literate found jobs and fought back. But most of them were lost forever.

SB: Were you asked for any advice when the NPK and the Mohila Odhidoptor [Department of Women's Affairs] merged?

NI: Not at all. We did not have any say at all. It was completely Ziaur Rahman's decision.

SB: Mohila Odhidoptor is an established organization now. Do you know if they gave priority to these women while recruiting in the early stage?

NI: No, I don't know. But it is clear that there were no questions of giving priority since *birangona*s were hardly even recognized and [even] considered enemies. A few days ago, a delegation of high officials came to Dhaka. The Khateeb of Lahore's Shahi Mosque, one of the delegates, said, 'I strongly condemn the atrocities on the Bangladeshis. Believe it or not, we had no idea about what was happening here.' Another delegate told me that the editor of one of their newspapers called Mr Malek Quraish had been arrested for writing about the massacres in what was then East Pakistan. Tahera Mazhar Ali, a trade unionist and social worker, earnestly apologized to all the Bengalis for the inhumane torture inflicted on them. I thanked the *maulana*, saying that one of their women made an apology, but none of the men did so.

SB: What do you think the present generation should do to contribute towards the betterment of these women?

NI: Nothing, actually.

SB: We would like to know the true history.

NI: Of course you do, but unfortunately none of those women would respond. That was a shameful chapter in their life. The whole thing lost its significance to those who settled abroad and they are no longer bothered by it. If getting married three times is not an issue, why would this be? After all, they were just victims of the situation.

SB: We are actually trying to bring out the truth regarding 1971 in a documentary. If ever there is a trial of the war criminals, this could be helpful. Otherwise, we will not be able to establish our history. In future, if this question is raised, 'What is the proof that 2 million women got raped?', there would not be any answer.

NI: Even the people in power in our own country are saying that these are not true.

SB: We are trying to find the victims so that their cases can be produced in court. We want to understand the pain they had to endure and also their present condition. Like you did not reveal the real identity of those women in your book as it would jeopardize their present, we also don't want to do so.

NI: Listen, I am the daughter and also the granddaughter of a lawyer. Let me tell you that you cannot file a case without revealing the names and addresses of the victims, the people who victimized them and without describing how they were victimized. Otherwise, the case will fall flat.

SB: Who victimized them?

NI: Our countrymen. I have no complaints against the Pakistani soldiers, and I differ with others on this. I did not find a single woman who was not tortured by our very own people. Later, those who tortured them presented them to the armies as gifts.

SB: This is horrific. How come nobody ever mentions this?

NI: I do it. It is not that the Pakistani army just came and molested us. They came here to fight a war and they would do whatever they could. But no, they did not. They searched my house many times. Every time there was an officer accompanied by three to four soldiers, but they never misbehaved with us. The officer never said anything except while leaving. Before leaving, they repeatedly apologized for disturbing us. How would I blame them? They came to fight a war, and kill their opponents. But for the rape of the *birangona*s, we are responsible. It is only possible in Bangladesh that the chairman of the Shanti Committee can serve as the president for five years.[3]

SB: Why don't you expose them? The true identity of the victims must come to light since these are solid documents.

NI: The truth is already exposed. I don't think I have any right to bring ruin to a family by exposing unpleasant truths that will snatch away the happiness of the women who have a content family life now.

SB: We do not have that right either; neither do we wish to do so.

NI: A few young boys phoned me to ask for their addresses. They wanted to visit those women and give them flowers. I told them that they had already paid their tributes by placing flowers on the graves of the dead, why bother the living ones? Their children are all grown up now, studying at colleges and universities. The moment these boys show up at their doorstep, their long-nurtured happiness will be shaken to the core. Their husbands and children would start hating them. Anyway, give it a try, but there isn't much you can do without any help from the government.

SB: What do you actually mean by 'help from the government'?

NI: I mean asking for the files. Even if they don't want to give the files to you, why don't you demand them through a lawyer?

SB: Yes, we must. Do you have plans to write more about them in the future?

NI: Well, I am going to Madras [Chennai, India] for eye treatment. On my return, when I have my eyesight fixed, I will write again.

SB: If you have a problem with your eyesight, you can always dictate to somebody reliable to get the writing done.

NI: I won't do this through dictation.

SB: During 1971, did you actually hear of women being forcibly taken when you were living outside Dhaka? Did such news get reported while the war was going on or were they published later?

NI: No, these incidents happened during the war. As I was in a village then, I heard about them, but no one except the *razakar*s [war criminals] committed these acts.

SB: Why do you think people of our own country committed such atrocities?

NI: To please the army and earn rewards in return. Some of them grabbed people's houses, while others took possession of their cars.

SB: If that is the case, why were these women first tortured by our own people? Why didn't they directly hand the women to the Pakistani army? Why did the war criminals torture them first?

NI: That is because they did not want to miss their chance. They wanted to satisfy their own lust before letting others do the same. Besides, these criminals set innocent civilians' houses on fire and destroyed them, seized mothers and daughters by force and raped them together, and we blame the Pakistani army instead.

SB: Do you know the identity of any of those war criminals?

NI: Who doesn't? Ask anyone on the streets and they will give you their names. You can trace them very specifically in every area. Our president, the chairman of the former Peace Committee, himself can give you plenty of names. Give it a try. My blessings are with you.

SB: Thank you so very much.

NOTES

1. Munir Choudhury, Professor of English at the University of Dhaka, was kidnapped and killed on 14 December 1971.
2. In the 1971 Bangladesh Liberation War, more than 200,000 women and girls were systematically raped and tortured. After Bangladesh gained independence, these women were ignored by a society where rape is seen as a source of shame for the victim.
3. The East Pakistan Central Peace Committee, commonly known as the Peace Committee or Shanti Committee, was one of several committees formed in East Pakistan (present-day Bangladesh) in 1971 by the Pakistani army to aid its efforts in crushing the rebellion for Bangladesh's independence. Ghulam Azam, as a leader of the Jamaat-e-Islami, led the formation of the Shanti Committee to thwart the Mukti Bahini, which fought for the independence of Bangladesh.

NILIMA IBRAHIM was Professor of Bangla at the University of Dhaka. In 1971, she was very active in support of the liberation struggle. After independence she was appointed chairperson of the Bangla Academy and also president of the Bangladesh Mahila Samity.

An Interview with Krishna Banerjee

Experiences at the Refugee Camp in 1971*

QURRATUL AIN TAHMINA
(Translated by Mohammad Shafiqul Islam)

Krishna Banerjee was associated with a volunteer organization named Women's Welfare in Kolkata in 1971. She remembers listening repeatedly to a recording of Sheikh Mujibur Rahman's historic speech of 7 March 1971. The events of that day stirred them intensely—she herself participated in many meetings held in Kolkata around the month of March in support of the Liberation War. They also felt ashamed that though they were Bengalis, inhabitants of West Bengal, they could not do anything for Bangla.

Mrs Protima Roy, the director of the organization, told them on either 30 or 31 March to work with the girls in the refugee camp. They divided the work among themselves. Krishna Banerjee, who had been in charge of the home welfare section of the organization, which helped with income generation, was entrusted with the responsibility of supervising the stitching of thousands of petticoats and blouses of different sizes. Protima Roy collected the cloth. They helped survivors of rape who were in refugee camps by arranging

---

* Krishna Banerjee's interview taken by Qurratul Ain Tahmina was first published in the *ASK Bulletin* of June 2009.

medical care and shelter. Krishna Banerjee, accompanied by two or three others, also maintained a record of the number of girls in the camps and where they would stay.

Salt Lake in Kolkata was a vacant area at that time. Thousands of refugees were kept in tents there. As far as Krishna Banerjee knew, girls who had been raped or subjected to violence were brought to this camp from different places. When she went to the refugee camp for the first time, it seemed like a sea of people. She can also remember how the American volunteers sent by Senator Edward Kennedy helped to repair the camp.

> I used to go there almost every day ... We would talk to the girls kept in a particular place. They had told us not to disturb the girls by asking too many questions because they were emotionally vulnerable. They also told us to accept whatever the girls said. I saw girls of all ages there. There were young girls in the camp for sure. That means from 10 to 12 years old to middle-aged women—they became pregnant.

So many girls came here from different places in Bangladesh during the war. Krishna Banerjee's first task was to collect clothes. The Indian government proposed to donate low-priced saris for them. They also began to sew other types of dresses for them.

> Another task was to take care of the girls who were pregnant. Some of the girls underwent abortions or they were kept in the camp until they gave birth. Then we arranged to have the babies adopted or the babies were kept in a shelter. There were not so many shelters in Kolkata at the time. Mother Teresa took some children into her home.
>
> There were not that many charitable organizations during that time. Members of a few such organizations or of the Congress [Party] came to help. I used to inform a woman named Pannadi, a member of an organization based at Taliganj on Ashok Avenue, about the number of girls expected to arrive, so that the

organization could arrange everything they needed. Some other organizations were also active, but I cannot remember them properly. The charitable organizations working with refugees from Bangladesh formed a Coordinating Committee; there were a large number of women's organizations. The Coordinating Committee used to communicate regularly with the Mujibnagar government. But the Mujibnagar government was very busy with the war effort and the problems faced by the girls were not taken up separately. They were considered as part of the overall refugee crisis.

The rape survivors were taken in groups from the refugee camp to other places where they were treated with care and their condition remained confidential. After their abortions, they were brought back to the camp again. Those who gave birth to children were kept in a number of homes. Between April and December, I must have worked with a few hundred women at least.

The girls sometimes came with their families and sometimes alone. There were many girls who had come with their families and were taken away by their family members [later]—so far as I know, they returned to their families after abortions. Many, on the other hand, did not want to go back. They were so traumatized that they would neither want to talk to their family members nor go with them. These girls were from both Hindu and Muslim communities.

The Coordinating Committee arranged counselling for the girls who wanted to return to their families. I was not involved with the counselling, but I thought that it was not done properly. It was just to convince the girls to go home—[asking] why they did not want to go. But now I feel, if I had had the experience, I could have helped them more.

Many girls were also given jobs. They were asked to come back to Bangladesh after December. The Government of Bangladesh was also interested to take them back. Though the Indian government too advised them to go back, many of them, especially Hindu girls, wanted to stay in Kolkata. But many others gradually went back to Bangladesh.

About the girls who stayed or wanted to stay, Krishna Banerjee said:

> [They] were either poor or from the lower middle class. Those who were from a well-off class somehow found safe havens among their relatives or with acquaintances. They did not come to the refugee camp. The girls who were left to our care were from lower or lower middle classes.
>
> We arranged trainings for these girls as nurses or as domestic help. We found jobs for some of them, but subsequently many of them went back to Bangladesh. Most of the babies were adopted by foreigners. Indeed, I arranged the adoption of seventy, seventy-five children. The foreign families travelled from abroad to adopt the babies. We knew the adopted babies would be looked after. I can still remember that both government and non-government organizations that helped with the adoptions were very good in checking their backgrounds.
>
> Many girls, at least 40 per cent of them, were in a traumatized state. That was not unusual considering their experience. Some of them wanted to talk. Many of them felt that they were stigmatized because they had been raped. Some of them bore marks of injuries and they showed us the marks … Many of them would talk too much as though they wanted to tell us everything … they tried to tell us in detail what had happened to them. Many others were, on the other hand, utterly silent. They did not want to say anything.
>
> I remember an incident that happened in the refugee camp. Many men would come to distribute relief and some of them, some well known, some ordinary, considered that the girls were 'spoilt' because they had been raped. I saw some men trying to touch the girls. I also observed that they tried to use the girls for sex work. However, we remained alert for all such behaviour. But I thought that some of the men might take away some girls from the home. The girls were indeed extremely poor and angst-ridden.
>
> Some of the girls were from cities but most were from villages.

They used to tell us that the men who tortured them or raped them were 'Khan army personnel'. I remember an older woman who did not know where her children were. She was raped and became pregnant. She aborted her pregnancy. She could not put the experience behind her—she kept saying: 'Drive away this demon—when shall I get back my real children?' She was unable to forget what had happened and was only thinking of how she would find her own children.

I don't know if the woman got back her children through the enquiry centre in the refugee camp. It was not possible to make enquiries in such a large area because we worked separately in small areas and the matter was very serious. Later, when it was all over, I tried to find out, but everyone had scattered by then.

The rape survivors bore several marks of torture, cuts and other wounds on their bodies; we had to treat those as well. They would tell us about other kinds of torture. They said, 'Many people held us down—some of them beat us.' The rapes seemed to be a part of the torture. They suffered not only because they were raped, but they were extremely traumatized by the violence. We could see from their eyes and faces. They would say, 'Why did this happen?' And they would curse the torturers with all the abuses they knew. They were furious ... They would call them demons, monsters and so forth.

These girls were not well educated. Besides, we had been told earlier not to ask them too many questions. But they talked a lot on their own. They uncovered themselves and showed us their wounds. They bore terrible marks of beating—blue marks on the back and cuts on the rest of their bodies. And I have told you about the branding—I don't know what it was—but the girls told us that 'the torturers had marked us so everyone would know that we had been raped'. They had been branded, and I saw the marks in many other women.

We asked Krishna Banerjee if all the girls recovered.

> There were some girls who became mentally imbalanced. I do not think they became well again. The vaginas of many of the girls had been slashed viciously. Some of them also died … Unable to bear the beating, starvation and psychological trauma, many of them became severely mentally ill. The critically injured were treated the best we could. They were also subsequently sent back to Bangladesh. We were very impressed by the support given by the Indian government. International support was also there, but the treatment was not according to the standards available for refugees at present.
>
> I listened to many young women who told us of their experiences. Many girls would say that they were happy to come to the camp, at the same grief-stricken that their sisters had been killed. In some cases both the mother and daughter were raped, but maybe only one of them was rescued and brought to the camp. I used to listen to all their experiences.

Did these girls who came to the refugee camp know why they had to go through this horrible ordeal? Why did the war happen?

> From what I understood, they did not know what was going on… They even said, 'The war was their own matter, but they made the girls their victims!' ... No one helped them understand what the Liberation War was about … Those who were uneducated or who had no political exposure were completely ignorant of this. It is very surprising that the boys in their families had gone to fight, but the girls did not know anything. It is incomprehensible. I think those who were a bit educated could understand. But we took it for granted that the girls were ignorant.

Krishna Banerjee was asked about the medical treatment available to these girls and women, about abortions and the adoption of the babies. What was the mental state of the girls? Did they feel emotionally able to start again or try to understand?

> Some of them were strong-minded … most of them were. They wanted to get back to their previous life, to their families with whom they had lived. Some of them, very few, were terribly frustrated, as though their lives were crushed. And the kind of counselling that was necessary for them to reassure them that 'it is not your fault', was not provided.
>
> I can remember a young girl who was raped. There were a lot of torture marks on her body. She had not become pregnant. This girl, along with others, also worked in the camp. They were given sewing machines. This girl would help many other girls in the camp. Later, the girl found her father and went home with him.

We asked Krishna Banerjee what the girls felt about beginning a new life or living in a free country.

> I do not think that they had any clear idea about this. But they were told that when they returned to their country, they would not experience the same again. But they were afraid, and felt insecure. Their lives had taken an incomprehensible turn, which had no doubt shaken the foundation of their faith. They were reassured many times that the same thing would not happen again—you go to the enquiry centre and find out about your people—but it was in vain … They did not understand, they did not know why the war happened. They could not believe that their condition could change after returning to their country.

Communication with their families was disrupted for some girls, and they were unsure if they would be accepted again. Krishna Banerjee heard about a girl who was not taken back by her family. She was given a job in an organization. Mrs Protima Roy had told them about many incidents of when the families took back girls. She maintained communication with Bangladesh and she would frequently visit the country. She would ask about the whereabouts of the girls she knew. She found some others—they had returned to the family and were working well. On the other hand, she was unable to trace many others. She was often told that girls from Hindu families were not accepted.

The rape survivors in the refugee camp were very sympathetic to each other, but they would also quarrel among themselves. When they fought, they would accuse the other girl, saying, 'I was raped forcibly, but she gave herself willingly', Krishna Banerjee told us. She also told us about when the survivors told them of the oppression and torture:

> The rape—that is what they would feel so bad about. They would say that it would have been better if they had been killed. I always felt angry about this—it seemed to me death is a very bad thing. The fact that I had been raped was not my fault. Why is a particular part of my body more important than other parts? ... I tried to make them understand this time and again. But it is a matter of great sorrow that there were some women in our group who would say, 'That is indeed right. They are raped—what could be worse?' ... In my view apart from a very few, most of the women considered rape as the worst form of violence. I said, 'Your sister was killed before your own eyes. Do you [still] think rape is worse than death?' But they insisted, 'No, nothing remains after rape.'
>
> Their highest expectation was that their family members would forgive them when they returned to the family since they had not committed any crime.

KRISHNA BANERJEE was a social worker in Kolkata. In 1971, she worked in the refugee camps set up by the Government of India.

The *Birangonas* are Brave Freedom Fighters

KEYA CHOWDHURY

(Translated by Mohammad Mahmudul Haque)

Every incident has a background. The history of contemporary Bangladesh centres predominantly around the Liberation War. The experience of the war has been profound. It is a history of self-sacrifice, courage and gallantry. The war continued for nine months. The Father of the Nation, Bangabandhu Sheikh Mujibur Rahman, called on the entire Bangali nation to free the country, and both men and women nationwide responded to his call by spontaneously joining the war. However, the reality is that the direct and indirect participation of women in the Liberation War and their unthinkable sacrifices were never recognized with fairness, equal to that of men. Therefore, history failed to portray the real story. Collection and examination of local history and relevant statistics reveal that the history of the Liberation War is replete with sacrifices of millions of people, both known and unknown.

As a daughter of a freedom fighter, when I found that knowledge about the Liberation War was very limited, I decided to update myself on its history, which, in fact, is a living record of unparalleled bravery and sacrifice of our people. It is comparatively easier to learn about the national history of our war, but very difficult to know our local histories. Scarcity of necessary documents is the principal reason. In 2006, when I was studying law, I got an opportunity to interact with villagers in Habiganj and became excited to unearth the accounts of the Liberation War in their local areas. I got to know many hitherto unknown stories of the war through informal conversations with them. This is how I started my search for female freedom fighters, especially the *birangonas*.[1] I began to understand their angst of loss and self-sacrifice, of what it meant to be a *birangona*. Mantu Baidya, the son of a freedom fighter, was a client of Mr Abdul Hye, a senior lawyer. It was through him that I came to know about the barbarous attack on the village Gochhapara in Chunarughat on 12 Baishakh 1971 and the killing of the family members of Dhopa Bari (literally, washerman's house).[2] Hearing about this, I became curious about the details of the incident. The other reason that fuelled my interest was that my respected father Manik Chowdhury, who has always been my inspiration, said: 'The history of the liberation war of Sylhet has a special place in the overall history of the war. In order to provide an authentic picture of the war, it is necessary to preserve the local history of the war' (*Daily Jubok League*, 24 March 1971).

If the history of the war in Sylhet is portrayed properly, micro or local history will find its due place within the macro or broader one. I lost my father in my childhood. So far as I remember, I first heard the term Bangabandhu from him. Pointing at a photograph hanging in the drawing room, my father had said, 'This is Bangabandhu Sheikh Mujibur Rahman.' This is how I was introduced to Bangabandhu Sheikh Mujibur Rahman. I was shocked beyond words when I learnt that the war stories and self-sacrifice of Habiganj and its people did not find any place in the national history of the war. Even the new generation in Habiganj had heard of neither Mantu Baidya nor of the great sacrifice made by his family. I decided to spend my entire time, beyond my professional engagement, updating myself about the local stories of war. I heard from Mantu Baidya that not only the male members of his family were killed by the Pakistani army with the help of the Razakars, but two of the women were taken by force, and kept in the Pakistani camp for two months.[3] They were tortured both physically and mentally. These two women, namely, Maloti Rani Shukla Baidya and Pushpa Rani Shukla Baidya, heightened my concern. I went to their village and tried to visit them several times to win their trust. Every time I went to visit their house, I was insulted and abused by the male members of the family. I believe that there was a deep silent grudge that resulted in a lack of trust on their part since they had had a really difficult time during the war. They could neither trust nor rely on anyone. It was very difficult for me to win their trust and faith. I was shocked to find that the family in question wanted to erase all their memories of the inhuman torture inflicted upon them in 1971. A persisting sense of insecurity engulfed them. I became very curious to know why they would want to hide the fact that four male members of their family had been killed.

I observed this family for two and a half years. At the same time, I started enquiring if the Gochhapara incident had ever found a place in history as a chapter in a book or in anyone's personal memoir. I was disappointed to see that even many of the local inhabitants, including the freedom fighters, wanted to evade the topic. I decided to have a go at breaking the long-fossilized fear and sense of insecurity of Maloti Rani and Pushpa Rani. I had to turn their sorrows into strength. While talking to them, instead of asking questions related to painful wartime memories, I tried to highlight their contributions to the creation of Bangladesh. I tried to convince them by saying that they were highly respectable for each and every individual of Bangladesh. I told them that I wanted Bangladeshis to know about them and their sacrifice, and that whatever had happened to them was not their fault. Placing my hands on theirs, I tried to communicate my empathy and concern to them, and encouraged them to consider whatever happened to them in wartime as their valuable sacrifice for the independence of Bangladesh. Finally, Maloti Rani and Pushpa Rani both agreed to describe what happened to them in 1971.

After I had come to know about Maloti Rani and Pushpa Rani, I started searching for other women survivors of violence in different parts of Habiganj. While interviewing one freedom fighter after another, I came to know about *birangona* freedom fighters like Sabeda, Hiramoni and Sabitree. It was difficult for me to trace these women as I did not have their exact names and addresses. Many a time I had to go to the same place again and again. Many people confused me with misleading information. Some said that Sabitree Nayek had died, while others said that she had left for India with her family after independence. I kept struggling with this contradictory information to make my way through to them. At first, I put more emphasis on collecting the names of the *birangona*s and was quite successful in this endeavour. When I went to Sabeda's house, she helped me with relevant information. However, her family never allowed me to use that information. In a bus stand adjacent to a tea garden in Chandpur, I came to know from an elderly tea labourer that Sabitree was alive, but this brave soul was now not known as Sabitree but as Julekha Begum. After the war, Keramot Ali paid Sabitree her due respect and married her. They started a new family together. The history of Sabitree Nayek is that of boldness and courage. She saved hundreds of women from being raped by offering her own life in exchange. Having been confined in different tea garden bungalows, she succumbed to torture. Even after the independence of Bangladesh on 16 December 1971, Sabitree was not set free. On 17 December, before fleeing, the Pakistani army left her unconscious in the middle of a room in Chandpur tea garden.

I got to know about Hiramoni Shaontal from Sabitree. Together, we went to see Hiramoni. When we reached Hiramoni's shabby and impoverished hut, it was difficult for me to control my tears. I saw a woman, emaciated and weak, barely hanging on to life. Hiramoni was a very sensitive woman who was also very quiet. I couldn't find out much about this unfortunate woman. I quickly made up my mind about taking the necessary measures to help her recover before I went ahead with the interview. I contacted Dr

Sarwar Ali, the trustee of the Dhaka LWM, and Dr Fouzia, and brought Hiramoni to Dhaka. She was treated for seventeen days in Dhaka's BIRDEM Hospital. Suffering from malnutrition and respiratory problems for long, she was fighting death every day. After seventeen days of treatment, Hiramoni recovered to a large extent. Due to our regular meetings in those days, we became close. Now, when Hiramoni Shaontal sees me, she smiles and draws me close with fondness. With her weak hands, she ushers me to a seat next to her. [Back then,] in response to my questions, she related those nightmarish tales to me quite frankly.

In 1971, she was the wife of Lakkhan Shaontal living in a slum in Loharpur in Chandpur tea garden in the *upazilla* Chunarughat. The Pakistani soldiers used to grab various poultry and cattle, for example, chickens, ducks, cows and goats from the poor and helpless tea workers; they also launched frequent attacks on their wives. This was how Hiramoni Shaontal fell prey to their attack.

When I was busy with Maloti Rani, Pushpa Rani, Sabitree and Hiramoni, almost all the freedom fighters of Habiganj came to know that Keya Chowdhury, the daughter of Manik Chowdhury, was trying to trace the *birangona*s through an organization called Chetona '71, Habiganj. Many of the freedom fighters did not accept this and many others made jeering comments. However, a few others offered help by providing relevant information, but not always the names and addresses of the rape survivors. Maybe it made the freedom fighters think about the unthinkable ordeal that these women had to go through during the war.

Such a freedom fighter was Gauraprasad Roy. He told me about a *birangona* freedom fighter called Razia Khatun. She begged for help from a lot of the social elite, but nobody helped her. Even the freedom fighters whom she had met in the battlefield on a regular basis did not help her. The moment I came to know about Razia Khatun from Gaura Kaka [Uncle Gaura], I contacted her instantly. Razia lived in Puran Bazar, Shaistaganj. Talking to her, I came to know that she was not only a *birangona*, but also fought in the front in Sector 3. Ravished by the Pakistani army, this brave lady crossed the border and went to India. She started working as a cook in the Khowai Training Centre for freedom fighters and was sent to the battlefield to keep a watch on the Pakistani army. Coming back, she used to report to the freedom fighters and based on her reports, they used to take decisions about their next plan of attack. Razia performed this highly risky task with her fellow fighter Angura. She helped me with a lot of rare information. The courage and determination I saw in her helped me overcome the problems I faced while working with the *birangona* freedom fighters.

Dear readers, at the beginning of my write-up, I mentioned Sabeda Khatun. At the age of 12, she was raped by the Pakistani army in front of her parents. Though she told me about it frankly, I did not get consent from her family to write about it. That is why, even if I applied on her behalf to the Liberation War Ministry to register her as a freedom fighter so she could obtain benefits, I had to withhold the process. There is another lady called Fariza Khatun whose situation was a little different. In 1971, she was hit by a shell and became crippled. She could not enlist her name in the official gazette even after trying for a long time. Getting herself enlisted was a daily endeavour. Though the Father of the Nation gave her BDT 2,000 and a letter, she has never been recognized for her sacrifice in all these years since 1971.

At the time I started working with the aforementioned six *birangonas*, the organization called Chetona '71, Habiganj had not been not formed. As I worked to ensure rights and facilities for the *birangonas*, I realized that personal initiatives were never enough and organizational initiatives were needed. Through Chetona '71, in March 2009, I applied on behalf of the six aforementioned *birangonas* to the Ministry of Liberation War Affairs. The subject of my application was a prayer to officially recognize these women as *birangonas* and ensure facilities similar to those of a freedom fighter.

In 2009, when I applied, the government had no such policy. That is why I had to wait from 2009 until 2013. In the meantime, as a part of the application process, the *birangonas* were brought to Dhaka and were questioned by different officials in the Ministry of Liberation War Affairs. Previously, these six *birangonas* were subject to negligence and indifference, and had become weak and vulnerable. Chetona '71 facilitated their necessary treatment and helped them out of poverty. I am indebted to the LWM and other organizations that inspired and encouraged me throughout. The official procedure started in 2009 and ended in 2013.

NOTES

1. *Birangona* literally means 'brave woman'. In the 1971 Bangladesh Liberation War, innumerable women and girls were systematically raped and tortured. After Bangladesh gained independence these women were ignored by a society where rape is seen as a source of shame for the victim.
2. Baishakh is the first month of the Bengali calendar, extending from the middle of April to the middle of May.
3. The Razakars were an East Pakistani militia formed by the Pakistani army to assist the latter against the Mukti Bahini during the Bangladesh Liberation War.

KEYA CHOWDHURY is currently a member of the Bangladesh Parliament. She has done field investigations in Sylhet to trace women survivors of violence.

Five Case Studies of Sexual Violence on Indigenous Women in the Chittagong Hill Tracts

ILIRA DEWAN

BACKGROUND

The CHT is the region situated in the south-east of Bangladesh. There are diversities in the history of the administration, social systems, rituals, language, culture and lifestyle in this region. The peaceful life of the indigenous people in the CHT was disrupted first by the construction of a dam on the Karnaphuli river in the 1960s and later by the forced settlement of Bengalis from the plains in the 1970s. The embankment caused 40 per cent of agricultural land in the CHT to go under water. Many became homeless and had to leave. Those who had built houses recently in the region were neither compensated nor rehabilitated. As they turned homeless, their social ties broke down and their economic condition deteriorated. The 1971 Liberation War led to further impoverishment. Later, to protect their own identity, they began the movement for autonomy of the CHT and established the PCJSS. The Government of Bangladesh did not try to understand the grievances of the indigenous people and the roots of the problem, which resulted in the CHT crisis becoming increasingly complicated.

M.N. Larma, the undisputed leader of the CHT, acutely felt the need for the participation of women in their movement from the very beginning. As a result, an organization of women called the Parbatya Chattagram Mahila Samiti (Chittagong Hill Tracts Women's Organization) came into being on 21 February 1975. Its main objective was to unite the women for supporting the movement. The organization arranged programmes to bring political awareness among indigenous women. When the military took power in 1975, a large number of army personnel were posted in the CHT. As the activities of the PCJSS were banned by the Bangladesh government, the activities of the women's organization became restricted as well.

Violence against indigenous people in the area rose in the 1980s. Women were harassed in two ways: as indigenous and as women. Rape and torture were used as tools against the indigenous people during clashes. Violence against indigenous women did not decrease after the signing of the CHT Peace Accord in 1997. The Hill Women's Federation was formed on 8 March 1988. Its main goal was to stop all kinds of violence against women in the CHT, eradicate discrimination between men and women, hand down exemplary punishment to the criminals who violated the law, ensure justice for women victims of violence in the Chittagong Hill Tracts, and demand withdrawal of the military from the region.

The vulnerability and insecurity of the women was exemplified by Kalpana Chakma's abduction. On 12 June 1996, Kalpana Chakma, the central organizing secretary of the Hill Women's Federation, was allegedly abducted in the dead of the night from her village home at Lallyghona, Baghaichari, in Rangamati by some members of the security forces in civil dress; Kalpana's brother recognized them. In the eighteen years since her abduction, no government has taken proper steps to trace her, although several investigations have been carried out. Kalpana Chakma's family and members of her organization have for the past two decades demanded a fair and neutral enquiry. During the eighteen years of the trial, her abduction has been the focus of international concern. As in this case, other incidents of violence on indigenous women in the CHT have been neglected by the legal system.

The Kapaeeng Foundation, an indigenous human rights organization, has reported that violence against women has not lessened even after the CHT Peace Accord (Kapaeeng Foundation 2014). In 2012, 2013 and 2014, there were reported to be fifty-five, fifty-three and fifty-one incidents of violence against women respectively (IVA 2015)' which included rape, attempted rape, killing after rape and physical torture. Mainly settler Bengalis were involved in these incidents, but in some cases so were members of the security forces. The statistics show that indigenous women were not safe to move freely even after the peace accord, and that they may have become more insecure because the settler Bengalis can move unrestrictedly in their villages. Under the accord, all temporary camps of the security forces, except the Border Guard Bangladesh (BGB) and six permanent cantonments, were to be withdrawn. As per the Kapaeeng Foundation, only some out of more than 500 military camps have been withdrawn, whereas according to the government report, more than 200 camps were withdrawn at different times. The PCJSS was not given a list of those camps. On the other hand, Operation Uttaran has established a sort of military rule since September 2001. It is alleged that the land of the indigenous people in Khagrachari and Bandarban was occupied in order to establish camps and expand them. Indigenous people have been threatened with eviction as a result of the occupation of their land to establish a military garrison and the BGB headquarters at Ruma *upazila* and sector headquarters of the BGB in the Kraikshang-Hansama area in Bandarban. In the meantime, twenty-one indigenous families of two villages have been evicted from their land for the establishment of the BGB's headquarters at Babuchara in Khagrachari.

Statistics show an increase in sectarian violence. More than fifteen incidents of sectarian attacks occurred after the peace accord, including at Babuchara in Khagrachari in 1999, Ramgarh in 2001, Mahalchhari in 2003, Maicchari in 2006, Sajek of Baghaichari in 2008, Baghaihat of Khagrachari in 2010, Ramgarh of Manikchari in 2011, the city of Rangamati in 2012, Taindang of Matiranga in 2013, and Bogaichari of Naniarchar on 16 December in 2014.

District and divisional officials have been entrusted with civil and criminal trials as well as enforcing traditional laws in the CHT. To enforce the Prevention of Women and Child Repression Act in three districts, the high court established three different courts on 24 February 2008. Yet indigenous women do not get justice due to delays in trials, non-cooperation from administration personnel, lack of adequate legal aid, financial incapability of indigenous women and so forth. A tendency for non-cooperation by the administration is evident in destroying evidence of rape, delays in medical tests, or procrastinating or giving negative medical reports so as to avoid legal complexities. These impede the path of justice for women.

Five case studies of sexual violence on women that occurred in the CHT at different times have been cited here. Among victims, two were children, one was a college student and two were housewives. One was killed after rape, three were raped, and the fifth suffered an attempt at rape. Members of the security forces were accused in two and settler Bengalis in three incidents. A study of the cases shows that although law-enforcement agencies may arrest the criminals, they are often acquitted due to the filing of weak charges. The police take years to submit the charge sheet. In a case where the accused was a member of the security forces, he was taken into military custody and it was assured that he would be tried under military law. But two years later, there was no progress reported on the case. In many cases, the families of the victims of sexual violence are offered money as compromise, and if this is not accepted, they face threats. In these five cases, the families could not follow legal processes because they were ignorant of the judicial system and lacked financial resources. Disappointing experiences with laws and trials in the past have made the indigenous people apprehensive of legal procedures.

So far, no exemplary punishment has been given to the criminals accused of killing, raping and abducting women in the CHT. The criminals are often acquitted because of the biased role of the administration and delays in the trial process. Thus, in most of the cases of violence against women, indigenous women are being deprived of justice. This acts as an encouragement for criminals and has led to an increase in violence on women,

To ensure a rule of law in the CHT, it is very important to implement the peace accord effectively. Since land grabbing is a major reason for violence on indigenous women, it is imperative to resolve land disputes by activating the Parbatya Chattagram Bhumi Birodh Nishpatti Commission (CHT Land Disputes Settlement Commission). It is also necessary to withdraw the army from the region and to maintain the demilitarization process.

CASE STUDY 1: SABITA CHAKMA

The Incident

Losing his parents at an early age, Debratna Chakma, 32, grew up in a relative's house in village Kamalchari in Sadar *upazila*, Khagrachari. He had little education, so he chose masonry as his profession. Sabita Chakma is Debratna Chakma's wife. They had one daughter, Tripti Chakma, who was in class three at the local government primary school at the time of the incident. They were hard-working and led a good life. But their happiness was destroyed when Sabita Chakma was tortured and choked to death at noon on 15 February 2014. Debratna's family fell apart that day.

On Saturday,15 February 2014, Debratna was in a hurry to leave for work in the morning. As usual, Sabita finished her cooking, fed her daughter and sent her to school. Then she went to the nearby Chengi river to collect grass for the cows. It was after 10 AM. It was while she was there that she was raped and tortured to death.

On his return home after work at 5 PM, Debratna began to look for his wife and daughter, who were not home. He found his daughter playing with other girls in another house, but did not find his wife. So he, along with his brother-in-law Shantibikash Chakma, started looking for Sabita. They found her body after 6 PM, under a bush, almost naked and covered with blood. The body bore marks of torture on the eyes, face and throat, along with an oily black paste. Sabita's sandal, a sickle for cutting grass and a sack were found nearby. Debratna and his brother-in-law informed the village leaders. Subsequently, the Khagrachari thana police came and retrieved the body.

Birbahu Chakma, a village elder, said that most of the people of Kamalchari village go to that area in the vegetable fields to work in the early morning. They return home at about 11 AM for lunch, a little after the time Sabita used to go there to cut grass. Thus, the area remains isolated at that time, which was when Birbahu thought this brutal act must have taken place.

The Suspects

People had been collecting sand from the Chengi river for many days. The tractor for sand collection went out of order at about 11 AM on the day of the incident. The tractor driver, with the other workers, worked for a long time to try to mend it and they were there till 4 PM. The villagers thought the workers and tractor drivers (four Bengalis and one indigenous) might have committed the crime.

Corruption of the Police

Debratna Chakma, accompanied by elders and village representatives, went to the police station to lodge a case. As the thana police started to draft the complaint on the computer, there was a power cut. The officer-in-charge (OC) suggested that the report be lodged the next day. So Debratna and others went back home that night. The next day, they found that the police had already printed a copy of the complaint. Since there was an urgency to take the body home after the autopsy for the burial ceremony and Debratna was extremely traumatized, he signed the complaint without reading it. He said that when he went to the police station to file the case on the first day, he described the incident in detail to the policeman who was typing on the computer. He also told the policeman what should be written in the statement. But the names of the driver of the tractor, Md Mizan, and the four workers, Md Ziaul Haque, Md Anwar, Md Razzak and Lasu Marma, were not included in the statement. This case was filed with the Khagrachari police station as case number 04, dated 16 February 2014, under Section 302 and 34.

After the case was filed, the police arrested Lasu Marma and sent him to jail through court proceedings. Even after a year, the police had not arrested the other suspects. It is worth mentioning again that all the suspects except one are Bengalis. The OC of the Khagrachari police station, Mizanur Rahman, said that the police had started an enquiry into the case. Only one suspect was arrested and he was in jail.

Dissatisfaction of Villagers over Medical Report

The medical report mentioned that Sabita Chakma was choked to death. There were no marks of rape. The people of Kamalchari village expressed their disappointment and anger over the medical report. Apoyna Chakma, 35, a housewife in the village, said:

> I saw the retrieval of the body and was present during the burial too. During the recovery, I saw black oily smudges [oil like the kind used on machines] on different parts of the body. There were black spots in the throat, marks of bites on the face and chest, and the body was found almost naked. After autopsy and before burial, black marks were also found on the body when it was washed. Besides, there were marks of torture on the throat and eyes of the dead body. Her sexual organs were swollen.

Threat of Violence

A day after the incident, the villagers of Kamalchari and the HWF together organized protests in Khagrachari town. They demanded the immediate arrest of the killers of Sabita Chakma and exemplary punishment. Since the Bengalis were accused as suspects in the murder, the Hill Tracts Bengali Student Parishad arranged a human chain to protest the allegations in Khagrachari city on 25 February 2014. Most of the participants of this human chain came from the adjacent Bengali *guchchagram* (cluster village) of Bhuyochari. They went to Khagrachari city through a village called Headmanpara, avoiding Kamalchari. But after their programme, they returned to their own village through Kamalchari, purposefully riding on a *chander gari* (an open-hood jeep, a common vehicle in the CHT) and shouting slogans to incite the people of the village. That day (25 February) was Sabita Chakma's *shraddha* (a religious ceremony) and this agitated the people participating in the ceremony, which led to a confrontation. As they came face to face, at least six people from both sides were injured. The administration enforced Section 144 in Kamalchari union to control the situation.

Present Condition of Debratna Chakma

Debratna Chakma's life turned upside down with his wife's death. He filed a case, but has had to manage funds to cover costs of the case. He sent his daughter Tripti to stay with her grandmother and to study there. Debratna was also living in a relative's house. He now thinks about his daughter and is worried about her future. He demands that the killers of Sabita be arrested immediately and punished so that such incidents do not happen again.

Civil Society Demands for Justice

Many human rights organizations and people's representatives demanded exemplary punishment to the criminals who had killed

Sabita Chakma. Ushaton Talukder, member of Parliament from Rangamati, raised this demand in Parliament. Moreover, many organizations, including the Chittagong Hill Tracts International Commission, Manusher Jonno Foundation, Women's Resource Network, HWF and Pahari Chattra Parishad, demanded that the killers be arrested immediately and brought to justice.

CASE STUDY 2: ASHA TRIPURA

The Case

Kananbala Tripura (pseudonym) is a housewife in a village. She is not educated, but is a strong-minded woman. Ignoring all hurdles and allurements, she filed a complaint in the police station against a policeman named Rashedul Alam (pseudonym) for raping her daughter. The case was transferred to the court, but as the witnesses could not be brought in at the scheduled time, the case became weak. The court acquitted the defendant and dismissed the case. At the time of writing, even though fourteen months had passed since the dismissal, the plaintiff did not know that and was still waiting for justice for her daughter's rape. She still hopes the criminal will get his due punishment some day.

The Incident

At about 10 AM, on 21 August 2012, Kananbala Tripura's daughters, Asha and Drishti, from the Tapan Karbari area of Noymail ward (ward number 1) in 1 Merung union, went to the jungle as usual to tend cattle. On their way, the sisters became panic-stricken upon seeing two policemen from the nearby Ataltila police camp and ran away to a safe place. When they thought that the policemen had left, the older sister, Asha, returned to collect some wild vegetables, leaving the other girl behind. After some time, when she couldn't find Asha, Drishti returned home. When her mother, Kananbala, asked her about Asha, Drishti said that she must have returned home much earlier. Since Asha had not returned, Kananbala and Drishti went to the place of the incident. When Kananbala called out Asha's name, she came out from the jungle, weeping. It was about 2.30 PM. Kananbala found Asha critically injured and smeared with blood. The girl told her mother that one of the policemen had pounced on her from behind on her way home. She had tried to struggle to save herself, but the man hit her and intimidated her. He beat her with a tree branch and then raped her. After listening to Asha's account, the mother and two daughters went to the Ataltila police camp near the village. When Md Shah Alam, the camp-in-charge, was informed of the incident, he told them to identify the rapist. He told all the camp residents to come together in one place. Asha identified the rapist, who was then wearing a red singlet: Md Rashedul Alam (pseudonym), 21, originally from Bashbari, Panchagarh district, staying at the Ataltila police camp, Dighinala, Khagrachari, during the incident. The camp-in-charge proposed that the incident of the rape be settled with the policeman paying BDT 1,000; he made the plea in the name of religion. He also told Md Rashedul Alam to seek forgiveness from Kananbala Tripura. But Kananbala Tripura rejected this proposal and returned home.

Kananbala informed the village elders about the incident. When this news spread, the villagers, including leaders of the Tripura community, leaders of the Tripura Student Forum, women's rights activists and local activists of development organizations, began to crowd in the Noymail area. On the other hand, hearing the news of the incident, extra police forces from the Dighinala Sadar *upazila*, as well as armed forces were sent to the area. The police and members of the armed forces again proposed a settlement. But Kananbala Tripura rejected the proposal a second time. A case was filed with the Dighinala police station on the same day, after 9 PM, under Section 9(1) of the Prevention of Women and Child Repression Act 2000, Amendment 2003.

Medical Report

Asha was admitted to the Dighinala Upazila Health Complex at 10 PM on the day of the incident. She had vaginal bleeding. After primary treatment there, she was sent to Sadar Hospital, where her medical test was done. The next day (22 August), Asha's statement was supposed to be recorded in court, but since her physical condition was critical, the court ordered that she should be given treatment instead. She was released from the hospital on 25 August and her statement was to be recorded on 26 August in court. To record her statement, the police kept Asha in their custody (Khagrachari District Jail) for one night. The plaintiff of the case did not know anything about her medical report. When the hospital authorities were asked about it, they said that it had been submitted to the police station. The relevant police officer informed Kananbala that she would need to get an order from the court to obtain the report. The results of the report were not made available because of complex official procedures, but unofficially it was learned that the medical test was negative.

Producing Witnesses in Court

Kananbala Tripura owns a small paddy field in which seasonal crops are cultivated. Living in extreme poverty, she struggles to manage two meals a day for her family. She did not have the funds to cover the costs of the case. Even so, she filed a report in the hope of justice for her daughter. With the help of a few activists of a local development organization, she testified in court three or four times. She did not have the financial capability to keep the case going, nor did she have any experience or awareness about the judicial system. As a result of this, the family was not able to produce witnesses in court regularly.

The Verdict

The case was filed on 21 August 2012. The police submitted the probe report to the court on 25 October 2012. The Prevention of Women and Child Repression Tribunal of the Khagrachari District Judge Court declared its verdict (number 42/12) on 13 November 2013. The court acquitted the only defendant of the case, Md Rashedul Alam, of all charges against him and disposed of the case.

Reactions

Lalosha Chakma, an activist of the Khagrachari Women's Rights Movement, who had followed the case and the girl's admission in the hospital, expressed her disappointment at the court's verdict acquitting the single defendant. She talked about the limitations of indigenous people in using the complex judicial system, particularly their lack of awareness and their financial incapability. She also said that the plaintiff had neglected the case. Many people thought that the case became weak because of the absence of the plaintiff in court and an inability to produce witnesses in the proper time. The defendant was acquitted quickly although he had been identified.

She also said that there were many reasons why indigenous people are deprived of justice.

> They do not have funds to pursue the legal case. They are not able to produce witnesses in court in proper time. It has been alleged that negative reports on the victims' medical tests are often given by the hospital [especially Khagrachari District Sadar Hospital]. Even though the victims are taken to the hospital in proper time, there is a tendency amongst hospital authority to delay the report. In some cases the evidence is destroyed. The doctors in government hospitals tend to give negative reports in order to remain aloof and uninvolved.

What Asha's Guardians Say

We talked to the victim's parents in the Noymail area of Dighinala on 2 February 2015. The plaintiff of the case, Kananbala Tripura, hoped for justice some day. She felt that the person who committed such an atrocity on her daughter should be punished. She said, 'There were hurdles, allurements, pressure and threats for negotiation after the incident, but ignoring everything, I filed the case at the police station. I filed the case only for justice. I want that my daughter's rapist be given exemplary punishment.' The victim's father said, 'We are poor and live hand to mouth. In this financial crisis, it is not possible for us to bear the expenses of a court case. Even so, we went to the court when the human rights activists told us to go. Now we do not know the status of the case.'

CASE STUDY 3: SANTWANA CHAKMA

Background

One of the eight *upazila*s in Khagrachari, Dighinala borders the Indian state of Tripura towards the north. Like many other areas of the CHT, it was a site of sectarian violence in 1986. Village after village of indigenous people was burnt down. Even Buddhist temples were looted and burnt. The indigenous people of numerous villages left their houses for security in unknown places. Some of them crossed the border and took shelter in neighbouring India. Sumon Chakma's family is one of those who lost their homes. Evicted from their own land, they remained homeless for a long time. After the peace accord, they got back their land, but their financial situation deteriorated. Despite this, they tried to lead a normal life.

The Incident

Santwana Chakma (pseudonym) is an ordinary village housewife. Her family members include her husband and two children. Her husband Sumon Chakma (pseudonym) is a farmer. They are poor, but both of them work together to look after the family.

On the day of the incident (18 September 2012), Sumon left his work to join a burial ceremony in Nalkata village. Before leaving, he asked his wife to take their four cows to graze. It had been drizzling since morning, but ignoring the rain, Santwana went to the top of a hill to bring back the cows at about 2 PM, leaving her two small children at home. When she reached the hill, a settler Bengali grabbed her from behind and pushed her on to the ground before she could understand what was happening. He smothered her with one hand and tried to take her clothes off with the other. Santwana struggled to save herself but she was overpowered, and the man raped her. At this moment, she bit his hand. This infuriated him and he began to hit her. He beat her brutally. While protecting herself from him, Santwana's thumb was pushed into his mouth and she was bitten.

During this time, Mohendra Chakma (Santwana Chakma's father-in-law) called Santwana as their cows were in the paddy fields. He was also heading towards the place where the incident took place. Hearing Mohendra's voice, the attacker left Santwana and ran. Freed from his grip, Santwana called out to Mohendra and returned home with his help. Santwana broke down both mentally and physically after this incident.

Santwana was able to identify the criminal. His name was Md Azhar Uddin, 30, of Uttar Milonpur, Khagrachari. He was in the logging business and would come to this area frequently for business. He was known to everyone in the village.

Speaking to us, Mohendra Chakma said:

> I went to the location of the incident after hearing Santwana's shout. At that time, I saw someone running away fast, but could not recognize him from behind. Later, I learnt the name of the criminal from Santwana. I found Santwana lying on the ground after he had run away, and took her home. As her physical

condition began to deteriorate fast after she was brought home, she was taken to the Dighinala Upazila Health Complex with the help of the villagers. She was given primary treatment there, and her injured finger was bandaged. Then Santwana Chakma was transferred to Khagrachari District Sadar Hospital for medical tests as well as for better treatment.

Santwana Chakma's husband Sumon Chakma filed a report with Dighinala police station (case number 4, dated 18 September 2012, under Section 9[1] of the Prevention of Women and Child Repression Act 2000, Amendment 2003). The report named Md Azhar Uddin as the single accused. Santwana had to undergo treatment at Khagrachari District Sadar Hospital for about two weeks. Her finger was so critically wounded that it began to decompose. With better treatment later, the finger was saved from amputation. The police recorded her statement while she was in the hospital.

The Accused

The police could not arrest the accused though his name was clearly mentioned in the report. Sumon Chakma complained that they did not try to arrest him. To show to the villagers that they were carrying out an enquiry, the Dighinala thana police came to Nalkata village only once. Sumon said:

> Though my wife was sick at the time, they forced her to go to the place where the incident had occurred and describe the incident in detail. The police said that the defendant had gone into hiding, though he was seen in public a few days after the incident. The defendant put pressure on us to withdraw the case and threatened us. Later, along with my family, I was forced to take shelter in another village, leaving my own village due to lack of security.

Threats

The defendant began to threaten the family to withdraw the report filed with the police. Santwana's family left the village three or four months after the incident. At the time of writing, they had taken shelter in Pulin Headman area of the same union. As Sumon does not have any landed property there, he is working as a day labourer for his family's survival.

Prabin Bikash Chakma, the *karbari* (village chief) of Nalkata village, confirmed that the family of Santwana Chakma received frequent threats from the defendant a few months after the incident and had to leave their home for their security. He says, 'Though I am the *karbari* of this village, I cannot ensure security for these people. The present situation is so critical that our own lives are not safe.'

Current Status of the Case

Santwana Chakma's husband filed a report immediately after the incident, but he did not have the funds to carry on with the case or to appoint a lawyer. He had little awareness of legal procedures and was unable to follow the progress of the case. He said,

> It was important to file the report after the incident, and so I filed it. Now the state will take the responsibility. I live hand to mouth. I do not have the ability to run the case. But I demand exemplary punishment of the criminal, because a poor man like me cannot run a case properly though it was filed in due time. Moreover, who will give us the assurance if we go to the court that we will get justice in time? Criminals are acquitted as usual. As a result, they commit the same crimes over again. So I demand that the criminals, whoever they are, be brought to justice and be given due punishment.

Though Santwana Chakma, along with her family, lives in

another village at present, she still feels insecure. Even though she has overcome her mental distress, she still has pain around her neck. She cannot move her thumb properly any more.

CASE STUDY 4: KRAJAI MARMA

Krajai Marma (pseudonym), a 17-year-old girl, lives in a remote village named Toktanala, which is quite a distance from Bilaichari Sadar *upazila* of Rangamati. After passing her Secondary School Certificate exam, she took admission in a degree college in the next *upazila* for higher studies. When she came to the city to attend college, she fell prey to harassment by a law enforcement officer and her educational future became uncertain.

Krajai along with her two friends lived in a rented house beside the college. When she was in the twelfth class, at about 1.30 AM on 9 September 2012, the law enforcement officer in question broke down the door of their house and attempted to rape Krajai. She and her friends had been asleep at the time.

Krajai says that she woke up as soon as he clamped her mouth shut. She tried to shout, but could not do so. The light switch was near the bed and she managed to switch on the light in the room. As soon as the light came on, he ran away. Then Krajai cried out. Her roommates woke up and the neighbours also came out. Krajai could identify the man as she had switched on the light. He lived in the same area and was frequently seen around. But she had never spoken to him. Later his full identity was known. His name was Md Abul Hossen (pseudonym), 20, of Boroichari, Rangamati. Krajai informed us that she learnt later that Md Abul Hossen served in the army.

Krajai's two roommates, Sanai Marma and Mekrau Marma, said that they woke up on hearing her cries and also saw the man run away. They too recognized the miscreant. Mekrau said that the main door of the house was very weak and could be easily broken. They told what had happened to the neighbours who had come out immediately.

Krajai Marma filed a report with the local police station that same day. The case number was 1, dated 9 September 2012 (later General Register number 236/012). The single defendant named was Md Abul Hossen. The police arrested him and took him to the police station. When the police were preparing to hand over the defendant to the court, a group of soldiers came to take him in their custody. The soldiers informed the police that Md Abul Hossen had served in the army so he would be tried as per army rules. A few days later, the police started to deny that they had arrested him. As a result, there was no progress on the case. There was no news of military departmental action either.

After the incident, the Bangladesh Marma Students' Council (BMSC) waged a huge protest, and launched a demonstration in the city of Rangamati. Sathoai Marma, the leader of the Rangamati District Committee of the BMSC, said he was familiar with Abul Hossen. They lived in the same area and had studied in the same school. He informed us that Abul Hossen had done this sort of thing earlier.

Local representatives and indigenous leaders involved in national politics put pressure to settle the case. Krajai's parents were threatened over the phone and asked to withdraw the case. Those who helped Krajai were also given death threats.

After the incident, Krajai had to go into hiding because of the lack of security. She had to stop going to college as well. She sat for her Higher Secondary Certificate (HSC) examination that year facing insecurity and fear, but she could not succeed in the final examination because of extreme mental pressure. She did not have the courage to retake the examination for the next two years.

Later Krajai began to work in a beauty parlour in Chittagong to help her parents, who were poor. But they were so worried after the incident that they feared for her safety away from them. So they brought their daughter back to the village. In spite of so many hurdles, Krajai is preparing to sit for the HSC examination again.

When we asked about the status of the case, Krajai told us that they did not have the latest updates. She had to stay in hiding for her own security and because of the death threats to those who had supported her. She has lost interest in the case as she has had to think about the safety of others.

She told us that it was the responsibility of the state to bring the criminal, whoever he might be, to justice and hand punishment if found guilty. As these criminals go unpunished, they are encouraged to repeat their crimes. If there had been a single instance of exemplary punishment to a criminal, culprits would think twice about the consequences of committing a crime. She further said, 'I demand that all criminals, including the miscreant in my case, involved in each and every incident of sexual violence against women in the CHT, be brought to justice and handed down exemplary punishment.'[1]

CASE STUDY 5: SWAPNA TRIPURA

The Incident

Swapna Tripura (pseudonym) was raped at Ranyabari village in ward number 4 of Bhaibonchora union, Sadar *upazila*, Khagrachari, on 2 October 2014. The incident took place on the day of Sharodiya Durgapuja, the main festival of Hindus. That day, like all other days, Swapna's father, Purnodhor Tripura (pseudonym), the only earning member of the family, left the house early in the morning and went to the forest to cut down trees. Her mother, Pushpobala Tripura, along, with her two children, Sumon, 10, and Poheli, 8, went to Bhaibonchora bazaar to celebrate Durgapuja after finishing her household chores. She asked her elder daughter Swapna, 13, to stay home to look after 1-year-old Mayarani (all pseudonyms). Swapna was to go to the puja after her mother returned from the temple.

In the words of the victim's mother, when she came home at 11 AM, she found Swapna trembling and unable to move properly. When Pushpobala asked what had happened, Swapna told her that a Bengali had come to their house at 10 AM and asked for a glass of water. Finding Swapna alone in the house, the man clutched her throat tight, hit her on the head and face, and raped her. Swapna told her mother that she would recognize the man—he carried passengers on his motorbike. Her rapist also threatened that he would kill her if she disclosed the incident to anyone.

The miscreant alleged to have raped Swapna Tripura is Md Ziaur Rahman (pseudonym), 32, of Bhaibonchora, Sadar *upazila*, Khagrachari. He is a motorbike driver by profession and ferries passengers. Ranyabari village is 4 km away from Bhaibonchora bazaar. Swapna Tripura's house is situated by Tobolchori Road at Bhaibonchora. No vehicles commute regularly, but motorbikes often carry passengers on this road.

Some time after the rape, Ziaur Rahman came to Ranyabari village with a passenger, Sotrong Tripura (pseudonym) of Ranyabari, on the motorbike. Pushpobala stopped them on the way and Swapna identified Ziaur Rahman as her rapist. When Pushpobala and Sotrong confronted him, he admitted that he had raped the girl. He proposed that he would bear the expenses of Swapna's treatment. Because Pushpobala did not agree to his proposal, Ziaur Rahman tried to flee, but the locals were able to catch him and hand him over to the police.

At 8 PM the same day, the victim's father, Purnodhor Tripura, filed a report against Ziaur Rahman under Section 9(1) of the Prevention of Women and Child Repression Act 2000, Amendment 2003, with the Khagrachari Sadar police station. The police submitted the enquiry report to the court. In the report, the case was shown filed under Section 9(4) of the Prevention of Women and Child Repression Act 2000, Amendment 2003. The charge sheet of the case was to be framed in the Khagrachari Cognizance Court on 17 February 2015.

Consequences

Pushpobala said that since their house is situated in an isolated place and there are no other houses in the surrounding area, they have felt very unsafe since the incident. Purnodhor said he came back home at about 4 PM on the day of the incident after hearing the news over his mobile phone. He found his daughter in a critical condition, so without much delay he took her to Khagrachari District Sadar Hospital.

Swapna Tripura had to undergo treatment in hospital for four days. The treatment continued after she returned home from the hospital. Swapna had not fully recovered even after four months (31 January 2015). She sometimes felt pain around her neck and her head was unsteady. Purnodhor Tripura could not afford to take his daughter to a good doctor. She was receiving homoeopathic treatment.

Purnodhor's family cultivate crops in the hills. They work hard for their survival. Though very poor, he has educated his children. Thirteen-year-old Swapna Tripura is in class two in Chotobari Para Government Primary School, while her younger brother Sumon is in class four. Swapna was admitted late to school because as the eldest child she had to help her parents on the farm.

Swapna Tripura's family has been living in uncertainty since the incident. Pushpobala said that Ziaur Rahman has threatened to kill her daughter:

> We cultivate our crops on the hills and need to go to different places at different times while our children stay home. But motorbike drivers also carry passengers along the road beside our home which is worrying. We filed a case, and the defendant is still in jail so we are afraid in case his cohorts attack us in revenge. My daughter will have to bear the stigma her whole life. It is an irreparable loss for her. We demand that the criminal be given exemplary punishment. But we do not know where we shall get justice for the crime that Ziaur committed. We neither

understand nor know laws, courts, etcetera. We only demand that the criminal be punished. We are now extremely worried about the future of our daughter.

NOTES

1. This interview was taken over the phone.

REFERENCES

Kapaeeng Foundation. 2014. *Human Rights Report 2013 on Indigenous Peoples in Bangladesh*. http://kapaeeng.org/wpcontent/uploads/2014/03/HR-Report-2013-for-website02.pdf (accessed 23 October 2015).

Indigenous Voices in Asia (IVA). 2015. 'Bangladesh: BIWN Organizes a Press Conference in Dhaka and Shares the Situation of Violence against Indigenous Women Reported in 2014', 2 February. http://iva.aippnet.org/biwn-organizes-a-press-conference-in-dhaka-and-shares-the-situation-of-violence-against-indigenous-women-reported-in-2014/ (accessed 23 October 2015).

ILIRA DEWAN is a member of the CHTC and secretary of the HWF. These case studies were translated by Mohammad Shafiqul Islam, Assistant Professor, Department of English, Shahjalal University of Science and Technology, Sylhet.

Stories of Two Women Survivors of Rape in 1971

MALEKA KHAN

(Translated by Mohammad Mahmudul Haque)

There is a world of difference between 1971 and 2015—a lot of water has passed under the bridge. It is now time to speak out. During the Liberation War, innumerable women sacrificed their lives for independence. In 2014, the state recognized them as freedom fighters. We are obliged by our conscience to listen to their stories, acknowledge their sacrifice, and honour them as war heroes.

I recount here the stories told to me by two women who were raped and tortured during the war. They are, of course, freedom fighters, bearing the marks of the atrocities committed against women by the Pakistani army and their local allies. As a student of social welfare, I had studied different methodologies of case work, group work, community development and social research to understand human psychology and behaviour, as well as sociology, political science, anthropology and economics, and to some extent we studied the human body too. I tried to work with them as a professional without allowing my personal emotions to guide me.

NARRATIVE ONE: CHAMELI

Chameli (pseudonym) was about 17 years old in 1971. Her ancestral home was in northern Mymensingh. Her father ran a shop in a nearby bazaar. As there was no son in the family, Chameli had to do all the work, for example, attend to her father, help her mother in the kitchen, look after her younger sisters. Since she had to help her mother with household chores, she could no longer go to school. After giving birth to her youngest child, Chameli's mother fell seriously ill and died in 1967. Chameli was in class five in 1971. Though she could not finish primary school, she knew how to read and write both in Bangla and English to some extent.

During the political movements and protests in March, Chameli went to a distant aunt's house. The aunt, out of affection, also took Chameli's younger sister with her since she was now an orphan. Though a distant relative, the aunt was very close to them and regularly looked after their welfare. She lived in a sub-divisional town and with a family business selling wholesale garments, they were well-off. Chameli's family lived off the income generated from a small piece of agricultural land and from her father's shop. Though not as affluent as the aunt, they were not poor either; they were financially stable.

The entire village broke into celebrations during (in her words) the 'Joy Bangla Vote' (the election of 1970 in which the Awami League won 167 out of 169 seats from East Pakistan). There were processions on the streets to celebrate the election victory. Children of Chameli's age had learned from adults about the political protests in East Pakistan (now Bangladesh) against the injustices of West Pakistan. They heard that the Pakistani army had killed and massacred a large number of people on 25 March in Dhaka and caused massive destruction. They heard rampant gunshots. The grown-ups were very worried about the situation in Dhaka. People were saying that they could not utter slogans such as 'Joy Bangla' (Victory to Bangladesh) any more. They also heard that from Dhaka a large number of people were going off to villages to save their lives, and saw countless dead bodies on the streets while they were fleeing.

Chameli was terrified by such news. Her father told her that she should not go out. He came to know that the Pakistani soldiers had set up temporary camps near the local railway station and villagers were fleeing northwards. In mid-May, the Pakistani army set fire to the local bazaar and burnt it to ashes. They arrested all the men. One day, when Chameli's father was in his shop, Pakistani soldiers broke into their house. Urging Chameli to hide at the back of their house, the terrified neighbours started running away. Chameli, dumbfounded, failed to escape, and shut the door instead. The soldiers kicked the door open, and dragged Chameli out of the room. She saw many people loudly urging the soldiers to spare their lives as they hit them with the hafts of their guns. One of the soldiers grabbed Chameli by her hair and another by her hand. In the process, her right hand was badly injured. She was continuously kicked in her back and shoulders with heavy boots. She was dragged into the back of a jeep like a sandsack. A number of women, in dishevelled clothes lay with their faces down in the jeep. Scared out of wits, and bereft of speech at the shouting by the soldiers, Chameli covered her head and face with the loose end of her sari and sat there curled up. The jeep drove them to a long tin-shed building. She heard men speaking in Urdu. Snippets of conversation in Bangla also came wafting through the air. The captured women were quiet as they were hauled out of the jeep. She could see other men there. Nudging her with a baton, one of the soldiers jibed at her, 'Why are you so shy?' A deep shudder racked through her. Someone said in Bangla, 'Hey, be careful! Any attempt to run away will be disastrous.' All the women were shoved into a room. Chameli could no longer hold herself together and passed out. As she regained consciousness and tried to move, she felt someone move next to her. It was a woman offering her a mug of water, saying, 'Here, drink.'

The captured women, including Chameli, were dragged out

of the room into another. She heard a woman's repeated clamour of 'Let me go, let me go.' Chameli was in a panic and felt an unbearable pain in her injured hand. What followed, in Chameli's words, was 'horrendous torture'. She said, 'I could not save myself.' A lot of women, she said, were mauled, molested and gang-raped throughout the night. Chameli's suffering was two-fold: not only was she raped, she had to witness the abuse of other women. Many of the women in the room were gang-raped and some of then were shot dead, while many others were thrown out as the soldiers left. Given the unbearable pain, Chameli fainted a number of times.

When she revived finally, she discovered that she was lying on marshy land under the open sky, being watched by a few people. They were Bengalis wanting to help, but Chameli did not have even the slightest strength to move. They said that the army camp was quite far away and she was out of danger. Even so, she could not gather the courage to speak. Two of the men put her on a makeshift stretcher and carried her to their house, where there was not a single female member in the family. However, the rescuers gave her a bath with warm water and helped her change into old but clean clothes. They massaged her injured hand and shoulder with mustard oil. At night they offered her watery soft boiled rice only and apologized for not having anything better. They very affectionately addressed her as 'mother'. As she was in a severely injured state, a few of them decided to take her to Mymensingh Hospital as that was the only option to save her life. Finally, they left with Chameli for Mymensingh on a boat. These rescuers, risking their own lives, informed the employees of Mymensingh Hospital that she had been raped by Pakistani soldiers and admitted her in the hospital, where she stayed safely for a few months. The doctors and nurses slowly nursed her back to health. But she had no information about her father or sisters. The doctors who examined her told her that she was pregnant and gave her the necessary treatment. However, Chameli was scared of the social stigma and pleaded with the doctors to abort her pregnancy. But the doctors did not agree on health grounds. In December, as the country became independent, a kind hospital nurse sent somebody to the address that Chameli had given them earlier to contact her parents. But the house seemed deserted. The neighbours did not have any clue about Chameli's family's whereabouts. In January, the same nurse came to know about the COWR in Dhaka, and contacted them to enquire whether Chameli could stay there. The COWR agreed to take her in. There, Chameli met other women who were in distress like her and felt somewhat reassured.

Due to her poor physical condition she was admitted to Dhaka Medical College Hospital, where she gave birth to a baby girl. Chameli breastfed the child and tended to her for twelve days. Torn between her fears of social rejection and affection for the infant, she finally decided against keeping the child. Grief-stricken, she came back to the COWR with the hope of starting a new life. With the help of the organization, she was ultimately able to track her father down. He was seriously ill at that time, in his house. Chameli decided to visit him, but, unfortunately, some members of the community considered her disgraced because she had been raped in a Pakistani camp. She was not accepted by the community. She could not face the social stigma nor take the blame, since she hadn't gone to the Pakistani camp of her own accord. What sort of justice was that? Nobody even raised such a just question, but said instead that it would not be fair to punish Chameli's father for his daughter's 'disgrace'. Therefore, she had to leave her own home. As for her other sisters, they also went through a very difficult time; however, they were never tortured by the Pakistani soldiers. Starved, and always on the run from one village to another, they managed to survive without being caught. They remained in Mymensingh town. Society gave its verdict: if Chameli lived there, it would bring disgrace to her other sisters too. Shocked and in tears, Chameli returned to the COWR after two days. The employees there consoled her and managed to calm her down a little. This was the end of the first chapter of Chameli's life.

Soon, Chameli became busy attending various training courses offered by the COWR. She was given *Aesop's Fables* (in Bangla) to read. She not only read it herself, but read it out to others too. The rest of her time was spent on making bags from jute fibre and cloth. She concentrated fully on producing them and her trainer was impressed by her skill and innovativeness, and inspired her to improve her designs. At one point, she realized that she could lead an independent life with her earnings. Her life found a new rhythm in the COWR. She heard that her child had been given away for adoption, along with many other children, who were sent to different foreign countries.

The next stage of Chameli's life had a different start. Her sisters were 15 and 5. One day they came to the COWR to visit Chameli. She was overjoyed because they were allowed to stay with her for a few days. It was agreed that her sisters would visit often henceforth and spend a few days with her. They used to write to her from their home district and regularly asked after her. In other words, it was a struggle for a normal life. Chameli never went home because she did not want to listen to the slander about her. She was not at fault; why should society punish her? She considered 20 Eskaton the location of the COWR, her real address and prayed that her perpetrators would be brought to trial.

Chameli was determined to earn enough to become self-reliant. Then, if possible, she would bring her father and sisters to stay with her. She hoped that society's attitude would change by then. Out of concern for the survivors' future, the COWR would pay them whatever money they had earned from the sale of their products when they left the home. Encouraged by such support, Chameli became confident of her own potential to start a new life in independent Bangladesh.

NARRATIVE TWO: MOYNA

Moyna (pseudonym) was approximately 44 years old in March 1971. Her husband was a schoolteacher by profession. Moyna had studied up to the eighth standard. She had five children. The eldest one was a 15-year-old girl, who was married, then an 11-year-old son, followed by three daughters, who were 9, 6 and 3. The family was solvent; they owned a piece of agricultural land, a pond, a cowshed and fruit trees. They were self-sufficient in food and enough paddy had been stored in the family granary. Both Moyna's and her husband's ancestral homes were in Bikrampur.

During the non-cooperation movement in March 1971, Moyna's whole family came from Bikrampur to visit her married elder daughter's in-laws in Kushtia town. The residence of Moyna's husband's elder sister was adjacent to her daughter's in-laws' house in Kushtia. Moyna's family planned to visit both the houses and stay there for some days before returning to Bikrampur. Moyna's husband left his family in his elder sister's house and went to Jessore for some work. He planned to come to Kushtia after finishing his work and all of them were to return to Bikrampur. In Jessore, Moyna's husband stayed at his friend's house, who was also a teacher. But while raiding the area, the Pakistani army entered his friend's house forcibly, and tortured and shot all the inmates of the house, including Moyna's husband.

Moyna, in Kushtia, learned about the crackdown, large-scale killings and destruction in Dhaka by the Pakistani army on March 25. Her family cancelled the plan to return to Bikrampur, which was near Dhaka, because the journey would be hazardous. By the middle of April, even Kushtia was not safe and people were running away from there towards India by whatever means they could muster. Moyna's sister-in-law's family had already set out for India. Moyna too, with her four children, a few relatives and her daughter-in-law, started her journey to India. It was the last week of April. On their way to the Indian border, a violent storm broke out, which made their journey even more difficult. In the rough, inclement weather, drenched, they tried to cross the border, at times on foot, and at times on bullock carts. However, during this backbreaking journey, Moyna lost contact with her only son.

She hoped that he had crossed the border with another group or—who knew—maybe he had joined the freedom fighters. What added to her tension was that her third daughter developed a fever. It became almost impossible for Moyna to move on, so she stopped. Unfortunately, Moyna's ten-member group, consisting of women and children, could not cross the border and were caught by the Pakistani soldiers. There were gunshots everywhere. Cries for help and loud clamour hung heavy in the air. They were herded into a police outpost. After a while, the soldiers separated the children from the rest of the group. Hitting the women with their rifle butts, they shoved them into a room.

In that room, Moyna, like many others, had to succumb to the atrocities and gang-rape by the Pakistani soldiers. It was a harrowing sight. They did not even spare the underage girls they had captured. The savagery continued almost till dawn. Moyna heard the cries of the captured children who had been separated from their mothers earlier. The soldiers hit Moyna and a few other women with rifle butts and kicked them out of the room. Once outside, Moyna, with great difficulty, crawled into the room in which the children had been kept. Two other women followed Moyna. Each of them grabbed their children and ran for their lives. None of them knew exactly where they were going. Back with their mothers, the children fell quiet. Moyna dragged her sick daughter along on her way to the border. Before dawn, they approached the Indian border. Seeing women and children running for their lives, a middle-aged man came forward to help. He showed them the way to the Indian border police camp. The man lifted Moyna's daughter onto his shoulder. Holding the youngest in her lap and the other by her hand, Moyna continued her journey. Having reached the border safely, the man laid Moyna's ill child on the grass and cried out, 'Oh God! She is no more!' Moyna pressed her ear on her daughter's chest, checked for a sign of breath, and shook her by her cheeks. One of the Indian border policemen threw a blanket to them. Moyna froze into inaction, while others were saying, 'It looks as if the girl is dead.' Moyna, grief-stricken and exhausted, fainted.

Regaining consciousness, she realized that she was lying in a tent in a refugee camp in India. Children were playing in front of the tent, laughing and frisking around. Moyna was exhausted from her long strenuous walk, and weakened by the stress of her mental and physical pain. Her fellow refugees informed her that her daughter had been buried within the border of Bangladesh since she had died there. The kind stranger who had lifted Moyna's child over his shoulder had arranged everything. Consumed by grief for her child, Moyna fainted again. When she opened her eyes, she saw that her 3-year-old daughter was lying next to her. While gently stroking her child, she felt that the child was running a high fever. Worn out, she drew her daughter close to her.

She saw that thousands of people were pouring in from Bangladesh. She tried to stand up and somebody gave her a bowl of liquid rice. Moyna ate and felt better. In the refugee camp, everyone was helping everyone else. Somebody brought a pot of food for the children, and they ate and played. One day, a doctor came to the refugee camp to examine both children and women. When a female doctor examined Moyna she was quite open and told the doctor what had happened to her. The doctor gave her medicine. She felt safer and reassured that no one would torture her here. But she was fearful that she would lose all her children one by one. Her anxiety made her feel even more ill. Her youngest daughter Tia (pseudonym) was diagnosed with pneumonia, and within a few days of that, with tuberculosis. Her treatment continued, but it was a real challenge as medicines were scarce. It was difficult to get the proper diet for patients, but not quite impossible. The hardship continued for a few months.

One day, the news came that Bangladesh had become independent. The Pakistani soldiers had surrendered and the freedom fighters were going back to their homes. When she heard this news, Moyna joined a group going home. The Indian government handed them over to representatives of the Bangladeshi government at the border. Eventually, with the help of Bangladeshi government officials and a group of freedom fighters, Moyna and her two daughters were given shelter at the COWR home at 20 Eskaton Road in Dhaka.

Moyna arrived at the COWR in March 1972. She was provided with a special room in the office compound and her daughter Tia received medical treatment in a tuberculosis hospital. But in the meantime, suffering from unbearable grief for her husband, lost and suffering children, and the haunting memory of rape, Moyna's mental health deteriorated. The employees of the COWR tried to nurse her back to health. Special arrangements were made to help Moyna recover and also her child. Unfortunately, Moyna's mental condition worsened. The COWR tried to contact Moyna's family in Bikrampur and found out that her son's whereabouts were not known to them though they confirmed her husband's death. An unconfirmed news about her eldest daughter and son-in-law came in October 1973 that they might have stayed back in India. As per advice of Professor Nazimuddowla, Moyna was admitted into Pabna Mental Hospital for treatment, while Tia remained in the tuberculosis hospital till she was cured. Moyna's youngest daughter was taken care of at the COWR's Baby Care Unit.

MALEKA KHAN is an educationist and social worker. In 1971, she was secretary of the Girl Guides Association. She joined the COWR as director and continued there until 1975. She has also been actively engaged in the development of crafts in Bangladesh. She is a member of Banglacraft, a craft marketing and development organization.

About the Editors and Contributors

THE EDITORS

Hameeda Hossain started her career in publishing as an editor with the Oxford University Press in Karachi and later with University Press Limited in Dhaka. She was editor of *Forum*, a political weekly, which was banned by the Pakistani military government in 1971. Her professional interests have spanned across human rights, women's rights and craft development. As founder member and research director at Ain o Salish Kendra, she has edited its annual reports on Human Rights in Bangladesh between 1996 and 2006. She co-authored Bangladesh's *Shadow Report* for CEDAW in 2004 and the *Alternative Report* in 2010. She has written extensively on women's rights, workers' rights and human rights. Her publications include: *No Better Options? Industrial Women Workers in Bangladesh* (co-authored), *Violence against Women and the Legal System* (co-authored), 'Gender in the Development Discourse' in *The Decade of Stagnation*. After the war in 1971, she worked actively with women survivors and subsequently published several articles on women's experiences of the war. Between 1996 and 1999 ASK undertook an Oral History Project of the Liberation War that documented the experiences of women survivors as evidence of war crimes committed by the Pakistani army and their local accomplices in 1971. Narratives of 19 women were selected for publication in Narir Ekattor: Juddhoporoborti Kothhokahini (Women's '71: Post-War Voices/Stories) in 2001.

Amena Mohsin teaches in the Department of International Relations, University of Dhaka. She graduated from the same department and later received her MA and Ph.D. degrees from the University of Hawaii, USA, and Cambridge University, UK. She has received several national and international fellowships, which include the East-West Center Graduate Fellowship, CIDA International Fellowship, Commonwealth Staff Fellowship, SSRC Fellowship and Freedom Foundation Fellowship. She has written extensively on rights issues, state, democracy, civil–military relations and human security. She is the author of *The Politics of Nationalism: The Case of Chittagong Hill Tracts, Bangladesh*, *The Chittagong Hill Tracts, Bangladesh: On the Difficult Road to Peace* and *Ethnic Minorities of Bangladesh: Some Reflections the Saontals and Rakhaines*; and co-editor of *Women and Militancy: South Asian Complexities* (with Imtiaz Ahmed) and *Conflict and Partition, CHT, Bangladesh* (with Delwar Hossain).

THE CONTRIBUTORS

Shahidul Alam is a photographer, writer, curator and activist. He obtained a Ph.D. in chemistry at London University before switching to photography. A former president of the Bangladesh Photographic Society, Alam set up the award-winning Drik Agency, Bangladesh Photographic Institute, Chobi Mela Festival, Majority World Agency and Pathshala, the South Asian Media Institute. He has exhibited in MOMA, New York, Centre Georges Pompidou, Paris, Royal Albert Hall and Tate Modern, London, and the Museum of Contemporary Arts. Tehran. He has been a guest curator of Whitechapel Gallery, Winterthur Gallery, National Art Gallery, Malaysia, Musee de Quai Branly and Brussels Biennale. His awards include Mother Jones, Howard Chapnick Grant, Open Society Institute Audience Engagement Grant and the Shilpakala Award, the highest honour given to Bangladeshi artists. He has been a speaker at Harvard, Stanford and UCLA universities in the USA, Oxford and Cambridge universities in the UK, and Powerhouse

Museum in Brisbane, as well as TEDx, POPTech and National Geographic. Alam has also served on the juries of prestigious international contests, including World Press Photo, which he chaired, and Prix Pictet, chaired by Kofi Anan. An Honorary Fellow of the Royal Photographic Society, Alam is a visiting professor at Sunderland University in the UK and advisory board member of the National Geographic Society and Eugene Smith Fund. He has written one book, *My Journey as a Witness*. His edited work *Birth Pangs of a Nation* was voted the best book of 2012 at the Asian Publishing Convention. His recent show 'Kalpana's Warriors' was voted 'Best Exhibition' at the Dali Festival in China in 2015.

Kabita Chakma is a trilingual poet who writes in Bangla, English and her native language, Chakma. Her book of poems *Jali Na'Udhim Kittei/Rukhe Darab Na Kena* in Chakma and Bangla was published in 1992 by Narigrantha Prabartana, Dhaka. The book was also published under the title *Why Mustn't I Flare Up?* which was translated by Sajed Kamal in 2002. Educated both in Bangladesh and Australia, Kabita Chakma, formally trained as an architect, is also a writer and researcher.

Bina D'Costa is a peace and conflict specialist at the Department of International Relations, Coral Bell School of Asia-Pacific Affairs, Australian National University, Canberra. She has worked in South and South-East Asia, South Africa and East Africa; and contributed to policy research as well. Bina is also on the UNDP Gender, Crisis Prevention and Recovery expert panel and is a member of the Advisory Council of its International Center for Gender, Peace and Security. She is the author of *Nationbuilding, Gender and War Crimes in South Asia* and *Children and Global Conflict* (co-authored); editor of *Children and Violence: Politics of Conflict in South Asia*; and co-editor of *Gender and the Global Politics of the Asia-Pacific*. D'Costa is currently finishing a manuscript with John Braithwaite titled *Cascades of Violence in South Asia*.

Ishita Dutta is a legal researcher with the Bangladesh Legal Aid & Services Trust in Dhaka. Her work focuses mainly on issues of women's rights—including on violence against women and sexual and reproductive health and rights, equality and non-discrimination and workers' rights. She obtained her BBA LL.B from Symbiosis International University, Pune, India, and an LL.M from NYU School of Law, New York, United States.

Meghna Guhathakurta taught international relations at the University of Dhaka, Bangladesh, from 1984 to 2007. She is currently Executive Director of Research Initiatives, Bangladesh (RIB), a research support organization based in Dhaka, which specializes in action research with marginalized communities. Dr Guhathakurta graduated from the University of Dhaka and received her Ph.D. from the University of York, UK, in politics. Her field of specialization has broadly been international development, gender relations and South Asian politics. She has published on migration trends in partition histories, peace building in post-conflict societies and minority rights in South Asia. She is also associate editor of the *Journal of Social Studies* published from the Centre for Social Studies in Dhaka. She is adviser to the International Chittagong Hill Tracts Commission, an advocacy watchdog, and has been coordinator of RIB's project in the official Rohingya camps as implementing partner of UNHCR since 2011.

Faustina Pereira is a lawyer, a human rights activist, and a law and development specialist. She is Director for the Human Rights and Legal Aid Services programme at BRAC. As of October 2015, she is on leave from BRAC to join the International Development Law Organization (ILDO) as its Director, Global Justice Initiatives. She obtained her doctorate in international human rights law from the University of Notre Dame, USA, in 1998 and completed her post-doctorate at the National University of Ireland, Galway, as a Bank of Ireland Fellow in 2001–2. In 2006, she was named Young

Global Leader by the World Economic Forum. She is the author of *Fractured Scales: The Search for a Uniform Personal Code.*

Dina M. Siddiqi divides her time between New York and Dhaka, where she is Professor of Anthropology in the Department of Economics and Social Sciences at BRAC University. Dr Siddiqi's research engages with issues relating to gender, labour, human rights, Islam and transnational feminisms across South Asia. With a particular focus on Bangladesh, her numerous publications have addressed topics including women in the garments industry, minority rights, and the relationship between religion, politics and the state. Dr Siddiqi has previously taught at the University of Pennsylvania, Bryn Mawr, the New School and Columbia University. She serves on the editorial board of Routledge's Women in Asia Publication Series, is on the Advisory Committee of the Gender Initiative at Lahore University of Management Sciences (LUMS), and is a member of the Advisory Council for SANGAT, South Asia. She has a Ph.D. in anthropology from the University of Michigan, Ann Arbor.

People Involved in the Project

Advisors

Amena Mohsin
Hameeda Hossain
Kishali Pinto Jayawardena
Kumari Jayawardena
Mandira Sharma
Nighat Said Khan
Saba Gul Khattak
Sahba Husain
Sharmila Rege
Uma Chakravarti

Country Groups and Coordinators

Bangladesh: Ain o Salish Kendra
Amena Mohsin
Hameeda Hossain

India: Zubaan
Ishani Butalia
Laxmi Murthy
Meghna Singh
Satish Sharma
Shweta Vachani
Urvashi Butalia

Nepal: Advocacy Forum
Mandira Sharma

Pakistan: Simorgh
Hira Azmat
Neelam Hussain
Zahaid Rehman

Sri Lanka
Priya Thangarajah
S. Sumathy

Researchers and Writers

Abira Ashfaq
Afiya Zia
Amena Mohsin
Bani Gill
Bina D'Costa
Bishnu Maya Bhusal
Chulani Kodikara
Dhiraj Pokhrel
Dina Siddiqi
Divya Arya
Dolly Kikon
Essar Batool
Farzana Haniffa
Faustina Pereira
Gazala Peer
Hameeda Hossain
Hooria Khan
Huma Qurban Fouladi
Iftikhar Firdous
Ishita Dutta

Ifrah Butt
Jagdalpur Legal Aid Group
Jayshree P. Mangubhai
Jeannine Guthrie
Kabita Chakma
Kamala Visweswaran
Kavita Panjabi
Kishali Pinto Jayawardena
Laxmi Murthy
Maliha Zia
Mallika Aryal
Mandira Sharma
Meena Saraswathi Seshu
Meghna Guhathakurta
Munaza Rashid
Natasha Rather
Neelam Hussain
Neha Dixit
Noreen Naseer
Pranika Koyu
Pratiksha Baxi
Priya Thangarajah
Rajashri Dasgupta
Reshma Thapa
Rohini Mohan
Roshmi Goswami
Rubina Saigol
S. Sumathy
Sahar Bandial
Sahba Husain
Samreen Mushtaq
Sanjay Barbora
Sarah Zaman
Sarala Emmanuel

Seira Tamang
Shahidul Alam
Shobna Sonpar
Surabhi Pudasaini
Tanya Matthen
Uma Chakravarti
V. Geetha
Zainab Qureshi

Zubaan Team

Ishani Butalia
Laxmi Murthy
Meghna Singh
Satish Sharma
Shweta Vachani
Urvashi Butalia

IDRC

Navsharan Singh